Through Words and Deeds

Polish and Polish American Women in History

Edited by

John J. Bukowczyk

COMMON THREADS

An anthology from the University of Illinois Press

Library of Congress Control Number: 2021939969
ISBN 978-0-252-08623-6 (paperback)
ISBN 978-0-252-05314-6 (e-book)

Contents

Introduction

John J. Bukowczyk

In another era, when history was made by heroes and villains, Queen Jadwiga—whose marriage to Lithuanian Grand Duke Jogaila (later Jagiełło) in 1386 birthed the Polish-Lithuanian Commonwealth—may have been the sole image of a Polish heroine for young Polish girls. In more recent times, when historians now recognize structural causes and great social forces as the engines powering historical movements, heroes (and heroines) have receded from the foreground of historical narratives, save for the occasional person of at best minor distinction whom painstaking research, often in novel sources, has rescued from obscurity. While some of these individuals have ably performed the office of role model and exemplar of virtue, more often their lives have been lived in shades of gray, and they are merely representative of the otherwise nondescript persons who have collectively made history. In this rendering, the extraordinary—the leader, the hero or heroine—merely becomes the one astute enough to recognize where the people wanted to go, or where anonymous historical (social, economic, discursive) currents were taking them, and then to "lead" them there.

But the "faceless masses" were always composed of individuals who made unique choices and endured their own personal, often considerable, sacrifices to become part of this machine of historical change. It was individual women and men who toiled, marched, wrote, shouted, protested, prayed, voted, fought, taught, learned, lived, and died—and organized. Their stories touch upon many of history's large themes—gender, class, ethnicity, race, nationality, and the like—which may lead us to ruminate about their identity.

Who were the women who made the history of Poland and of the Polish diaspora? How did others see them? How did they see themselves? How did they see and experience family, community, society, and nation? How were their world and consciousness different from those of Polish and Polish American men?

By assembling articles drawn from the pages of *The Polish Review* and *Polish American Studies*, this book provides a sampling of research about women in Polish and Polish American history. It is necessarily a small cross-section of what Polish and Polish American women were thinking and doing as they sometimes singly, sometimes in collaboration with others, shaped this nationality group's history. Taken together, their histories are Poland's and the Polish diaspora's history—from the much celebrated Queen Jadwiga to the million everyday Polish heroines.

Through Words and Deeds: Polish and Polish American Women in History follows a roughly chronological organizational structure. The first part, The Polish Female Ideal and Real, explores womanhood in the distant Polish past. The contributions by Thaddeus V. Gromada and Anna Brzezińska examine the mythic and real Jadwiga of Anjou vis-à-vis the Polish feminine ideal, the importance of historiography, and the relationship between historical sources and the writing of history. Lynn Lubamersky's piece steps beyond the medieval Polish queen to examine the place and role of aristocratic women in the Polish-Lithuanian Commonwealth's political and social life during the late Middle Ages. Władysław Roczniak's contribution looks at the notable life of a woman known as Poland's first female doctor, a life that took her from a remote corner of eastern Poland to the courts of the Ottoman Empire, where she practiced her craft.

At its peak, the multiethnic and multireligious Polish-Lithuanian Commonwealth was the largest state in Europe, stretching from the Black Sea to the Ottoman Empire and from Prussia to Muscovy. Nonetheless, during the eighteenth century, internal weaknesses, external pressures, and domestic and foreign intrigues resulted in the Commonwealth's dismemberment. The era of the Polish partitions saw the country divided among Prussia, the Austro-Hungarian Empire, and the Russian Empire; the Commonwealth disappeared from the map of independent and sovereign European states. Partition also fostered a Polish diaspora that included political émigrés, adventurers, settlers, and labor migrants. The second section of the book, Bridging Polish and Polish Diasporic Lives, samples the experiences of women in the Polish diaspora. James S. Pula reviews the life of Ernestine Potowska Rose, a Jewish expatriate who struck off on her own and settled in the United States. There, in the mid-nineteenth century, she campaigned for women's rights—specifically, for legislation to permit married women to own property. Contributions by Jan Molenda and Laura Anker examine the role of Polish female labor migrants in the late nineteenth- and early twentieth-century industrial economies of, respectively, the Rhein-Westphalia region of Germany and the industrial region of Connecticut. Next, Polish immigrant women as political and social actors receive treatment in pieces by William J. Galush and Robert Szymczak. The latter gives an example of immigrant women taking an intense interest in the Polish nationalist struggle and in the welfare of their ancestral homeland, reconstituted as an independent state after World War I under the terms of the Treaty of Versailles. The last three chapters in the section examine Polish women in relation to social transformation, cultural preservation, and national regeneration in Poland and Polish America. Karen Majewski and Lori A. Matten illuminate the role of Polish immigrant women in what some observers construed as the "crisis of the immigrant and ethnic family" under immigration conditions. Finally, Nameeta Mathur's contribution reveals the role envisioned for Polish women in their country's rebirth.

The third section of the collection, Image, Identities, and Consciousness: Gender, Class, and Ethnicity Entwined, considers the subjective dimensions of Polish women's lives. John J. Bukowczyk discusses the stereotyping—and "othering"—of Polish American women and their relationship to Polish American feminism. Grazyna J. Kozaczka, Rita Gladsky, and Bożena Karwowska present rich, varied expressions of Polish female identities as developed in Polish ethnic and émigré fiction writing. The concluding chapter, by Halina Filipowicz, provides a sophisticated theoretical context and perspective on the subject and themes of the volume. At the end of the collection is a select list of additional readings for readers who wish to explore these subjects and themes further.

A short collection of articles cannot tell the full story of these women—their victories and losses, their triumphs and sorrows, and the ways in which they lived their lives. It can, however, beckon readers newly interested in their fascinating history further to explore their moral and material world(s). Along the way, they may meet not just one, but many of these heroines, albeit women who might not have thought of themselves (and whom historians might not have described) in this way. In this journey of discovery, essays such as those assembled in this collection may also lead us to ask questions about our own relationships to family, community, society, and nation. Most fundamentally, they may lead us to ask questions about ourselves, even as they show the many roles that Polish and Polish American women could inhabit.

• • •

A few words of appreciation are in order. Thanks go firstly to Alexa Colella of the University of Illinois Press, who developed the Common Threads series and supported a volume on this theme. Much appreciation is extended to past editors of *The Polish Review* and *Polish American Studies*—James S. Pula, Charles Kraszewski, and Joseph W. Wieczerzak—during whose editorial tenure the articles included in this volume originally appeared. Finally, a warm thank you to Anna D. Jaroszyńska-Kirchmann, Neal Pease, and Halina Filipowicz, who are recent or current editors of these two journals, and to the officers and boards of the Polish American Historical Association and the Polish Institute of Arts and Sciences of America, whose acquiescence to, cooperation with, or active support of this project is gratefully acknowledged.

Part One

The Polish Female Ideal and Real

Oscar Halecki's Vision of Saint Jadwiga of Anjou

Thaddeus V. Gromada

On the face of it, it seems incredible or impossible that a young princess who lived toward the end of the fourteenth century, who happened to be made "king" of Poland at the age of ten, and died fifteen years later at the tender age of 25, could have decisively influenced not only the development of Poland but the whole region of the European continent called East Central Europe. Yet this is the thesis of one of Poland's greatest historians, Oskar Halecki, my mentor, who died in 1973. Halecki believed that Queen Jadwiga's greatness was comparable to the greatness of Bolesław Chrobry and Casimir the Great. Thus, according to Halecki, Jadwiga is not only Poland's greatest queen but one of Poland's greatest rulers. This historical judgment was shared by one of America's greatest specialists in Slavic and Eastern European history, S. Harrison Thomson of the University of Colorado, who in his splendid work *Europe in Renaissance and Reformation* wrote in 1963, "the queen on her part showed statesmanlike qualities perhaps superior to those of her brilliant husband (Władysław Jagiełło)." Noting her great contribution in the cultural, religious, and social fields, he added "She was, simply put, one of Poland's greatest rulers" (pp. 193–194).

Who was this Jadwiga of Anjou? She was the daughter of Louis the Great (King of Hungary, Ruler of Croatia, Slavonia, Dalmatia, who also claimed the crown of Naples, and from 1370, was also King of Poland), and of Elizabeth of Bosnia. She

---

This article is based on a paper drawn entirely from Oscar Halecki's posthumous publication *Jadwiga of Anjou and the Rise of East Central Europe* (New York: Columbia University Press, 1991) and delivered on June 19, 1999, at a session "Jadwiga of Anjou, 1399–1999, Contributions, Images and Heritage" during the 57th Annual Meeting of the Polish Institute of Arts and Sciences of America, held at Fordham University, Lincoln Center Campus, New York.

From *The Polish Review*, vol. 44, no. 4 (1999), pp. 433–437.

was born on February 18, 1374, in Buda, more than 600 years ago. Both of Jadwiga's parents were half Polish. On her father's side, her grandmother was Elizabeth of the Piast family, Queen Mother, sister of Casimir the Great (d. 1380), and the daughter of Władysław Łokietek, who knew Jadwiga well, leaving her an inspiring Polish heritage. Her other grandmother was Elizabeth, Princess of Gniewków, also of the Piast family. At least three of her great grandmothers were also Polish. Halecki shows in his posthumous monograph that Jadwiga had more Polish blood than any other. Her genealogical tree clearly shows that no less than seven of its branches directly lead to the earliest members of the Piast family. Despite this, Jadwiga does not belong exclusively to Poland, but rather to all the nations of East Central Europe who contributed to her Western, later Catholic, heritage in the field of ideas. Jadwiga was reared in a religious atmosphere above and beyond that which was required. She was always present at daily Mass at which the king and his entire court were in attendance. She was named after St. Jadwiga of Silesia, one of her direct ancestors, who was the wife of the Silesian Duke, Henry the Bearded, and mother of Henry the Pious. She was famous for her ascetic piety and was canonized in 1267. The devotion to the cult of St. Jadwiga was strong in Buda and must have been a strong example to the young Jadwiga.

Before coming to Poland at the age of ten, Jadwiga lived at the highly sophisticated courts of Buda and Vienna (1378–1380) where Italian and French influences were great, and where she was being trained to be a queen. She was in Vienna for some time because the future Queen of Poland was originally to have married a Habsburg, Prince William, and rule Austria.

When her father, Louis of Anjou died in 1382, Jadwiga inherited the Polish crown. She was considered by the Poles as the natural, legitimate successor of the last Piast king rather than the successor of her unpopular father, Louis of Anjou. Jadwiga, however, did not arrive in Poland until 1384, probably in the month of May. Then, a few months later, she was joyfully crowned King of Poland (*Hedvigis coronatur, in regem Poloniae*), thus ending the growing disorder and confusion in Poland during the interregnum.

It is a rather interesting coincidence that only a few weeks before Jadwiga's coronation Vladislaus II of Opole, Duke of Silesia, close collaborator of Louis of Anjou, brought the miraculous icon of the Virgin Mary (the famous Black Madonna) to the Monastery of Częstochowa, founded in 1382. The young Jadwiga, under the impression of this event, offered a gift to Bishop Jan Radlica, in whose diocese Częstochowa was located, a chalice on which she had engraved an inscription asking "Blessed Virgin Mary to take Poland under her protection." Many historians, including some Polish specialists, continue to emphasize that Jadwiga, in the first crucial period of her reign—that is, 1384–1388—was simply a child, a mere passive tool of her advisors. Professor Halecki disputed this interpretation. He pointed out that Jadwiga was an exceptional teenager who matured rapidly, and that she was recognized as such by her contemporaries. Her stimulating experiences and painful trials and challenges only encouraged Jadwiga's rapid emotional and intellectual development.

One of the greatest trials that Jadwiga had to face very early was the necessity to give up any chances for personal happiness for the good of Poland and Christianity, that is, to give up her beloved William of Habsburg for the 36-year-old Jogaila, Grand Duke of Lithuania.

Halecki insisted that Jadwiga ultimately made a free decision to give up William of Habsburg. It was not an easy decision to make because Jadwiga really loved William. But this only underscores the greatness of her sacrifice. No wonder that Jadwiga's sacrifice had become a symbol of the noblest ideals in Polish national life. It does seem that she was finally moved to a decision to renounce William and accept Jogaila from religious motives.

Jogaila had made an offer to the Poles that they hardly could afford to refuse. He promised in the Treaty of Krewo (August 14, 1385) to unite the Lithuanian and Ruthenian lands with Poland to help recover the *terras suas Lithuaniae et Russiae coronae Regni Poloniae perpetuo applicare*. One should never forget that Jadwiga was a co-king and was much more active in governing and making decisions than many historians care to admit.

What would have happened if Jadwiga had not married Jogaila? One can only speculate. Jogaila certainly would have had to follow an appeasement policy toward the growing Grand Duchy of Moscow and perhaps even toward the German State of the Teutonic Order. Tensions between East and West would have developed creating a dangerous situation for Poland and the rest of Europe. The marriage of Jadwiga and Jogaila is sometimes compared to the marriage of Ferdinand and Isabella in the fifteenth century which permitted the Union of the Crowns of Castile and Aragon, facilitated the expulsion of the Moors and launched Spain into a period of great power status and cultural greatness.

The establishment of a loose union of Poland and Lithuania created a state with potentially great power, a state that reached the frontiers of the Grand Duchy of Moscow and close to the sphere of influence of the Tatar Mongols around the Black Sea. It was immediately challenged from the outside by the Teutonic Knights, who lost their reason for existence with the peaceful Christianization of Lithuania, and by Sigismund of Luxembourg, co-king of Hungary (with Jadwiga's sister Mary). There was also an internal challenge, coming from Lithuania from Jogaila's (Jagiełło's) jealous cousin Vytautas (Witold). Indeed, there was a plan for partitioning Poland among Hungary, Brandenburg and the Teutonic Order, to whom the whole of Lithuania was to be abandoned, whereas it seems that ambitious and brilliant Vytautas was planning to separate Lithuania from Poland and set up a separate kingdom with himself as king.

If the new, precarious Polish-Lithuanian Union survived the very critical period, roughly from 1389 to 1396, it was due largely to the wisdom, to the diplomatic skills of the Anjou princess, Jadwiga. Very often, the role of Jadwiga is underestimated in this protracted crisis. She was a very skillful negotiator, noted for her wisdom and fairness. It was this skill which she used in negotiating with her brother-in-law, Sigismund, in 1392, that caused the abandonment of the partition plan. The same year, Jadwiga was chiefly responsible for arranging a compromise between Jogaila and Vytautas, thus ending a dangerous situation, and inaugurating an era of close collaboration between the two cousins which lasted until their deaths. Vytautas, after that compromise agreement, paid Jadwiga an unusual solemn act of homage on August 4, 1392.

It was Jadwiga who facilitated the peaceful transfer of the Halicz region to Poland in 1387, from Hungarian administration, by personally leading Polish forces into the area as far as Lwów. This almost automatically expanded Polish influence into Moldavia and the Black Sea region. The Hospodar of Moldavia immediately paid her homage and became a vassal of Poland and Lithuania. Yet, when her sister Mary died in Hungary in 1395, she did not enforce her hereditary rights to the crown of Hungary. Hungary was threatened by the Ottoman Moslem Turks and she did not wish to involve Poland in a needless war.

Poland used Jadwiga's diplomatic talents in dealing with its most dangerous enemies, the German Teutonic Knights, especially in 1397–1398. In personal discussions with their Grand Master Konrad von Jungingen, Jadwiga tried to bring the Teutonic Order to reason and justice. She argued with patience for Polish rights, and, at one point, warned prophetically that if the Teutonic Knights did not make concessions, they would be punished for all the harm they had done to Poland after the death of the peace-loving queen.

Sometimes Jadwiga is criticized for following a peaceful, appeasement policy in regard to the German order. Yet, she wisely postponed a war which was unavoidable, but for which Poland and Lithuania at that time were not ready. Jogaila (Jagiełło) later recognized this when he faced the Teutonic Knights in 1410 at the Battle of Grunwald. He was grateful that Jadwiga had given him more time, delaying a premature action which would have led to a fatal defeat. Charlotte Kellogg, Jadwiga's biographer, has written that "Jadwiga's diplomatic struggle to bring the Teutonic Order to reason and justice was to stand as one of the extraordinary episodes of European history" (*Poland's Great Queen*, New York: 1931).

I believe that Queen Jadwiga would have preferred to concentrate her attention on cultural and religious matters rather than on diplomatic matters and international policies. Her accomplishments in the cultural, social and religious fields are perhaps even greater from the long-range point of view than in the political-diplomatic areas, and therefore we must examine them here briefly.

Jadwiga was known for her charitable activities. She was continuously involved in establishing new hospitals, schools, monasteries, and churches, and enlarging older ones. She visited the sick and unfortunate, and listened to appeals for justice and mercy.

Very importantly, Jadwiga seems to be one of the first to appreciate the beauty and importance of the Polish language. It was through her insistence that Polish was used in church services (in hymn singing and prayers). Also, it was Jadwiga who ordered the translation of the Scriptures into the Polish language. In this way, and in many other ways, she prepared the way for the Polish Renaissance by introducing the vernacular language.

Jadwiga realized that in order to strengthen the Polish-Lithuanian Union, mere legalistic arrangements would not suffice. It would be necessary to create a cultural community between the two nations. This is what motivated her and her husband to revive and enlarge the university that had been founded by King Casimir the Great in 1364 but which was in bad order and in need of complete reorganization, in particular the need to add to its various schools a faculty of theology modeled after that of the University of Paris. In a document, Jadwiga speaks of many sleepless nights, concerned about this problem and what to do about it.

It was in January 1397 that Pope Boniface IX granted Jadwiga's request to enlarge Cracow University and, at the same time, praised her and Jagiełło for their devotion. Since Jadwiga considered it urgent that Lithuanians and their neighbors (meaning Ruthenians) should have a well-trained, mature clergy, she did not wait for the reorganization of Cracow University, which she knew would take several years. She decided to immediately endow a college for Lithuanians at the University of Prague on July 20, 1397.

As far as the reorganization of Cracow University is concerned, Jadwiga drew on the experience and help of such academicians as Matthew, the learned Cracovian doctor from the University of Prague, who left Heidelberg as rector and came to Cracow; also Peter Wysz, doctor of Padua University, who in 1372 had become Bishop of Cracow thanks to Jadwiga. Mention should be made at this point that Jadwiga had the support of women in her court, for example, Constance of Koniecpolska, wife of the Governor of Sieradź; Jagiełło's sister, Duchess Alexandra of Mazovia, and Katherine Meżykowa. Gradually Jadwiga began buying houses along St. Anne's Street, running out from Cracow's marketplace, for the university.

The reformed and reorganized university, later to produce Copernicus, was inaugurated on July 26, 1400, after the death of Jadwiga in July 1399. But the university was still on her mind even a few days before her tragic death, and also before the tragic death of her infant child, Elizabeth Bonifacia. Queen Jadwiga told her two friends, Bishop Peter and Knight Jasko, "My will is simple: one half of the proceeds of the sale of all that I have, jewels, clothes, ornaments, possessions of every kind, I leave to the University of Cracow, and the other half to be divided among the poor. Let my body be placed beside that of my baby on the gospel side of the altar with a plain inscription on the facing marble to mark the place."

Jadwiga died on July 17, 1399, after giving birth to Elizabeth Bonifacia, who had died a few days before. The announcement of her death stated: "Today, at noon died Jadwiga, Queen of Poland, unwearied creator of divine culture, protectoress of the Church, administrator of justice, servant of all virtues, humble and beneficent, mother of orphans who in her time has had no equal or royal blood in the eyes of men in the whole world." The story of Jadwiga did not really end with the terrible tragedy which occurred on July 17, 1399. Not only was the planned consolidation of the Polish-Lithuanian Union carried out according to her intentions in the famous charters of the following years, but it can be shown that she had prepared also most of the other achievements of the opening century. Two hundred years later, a more perfect union was concluded in Lublin in 1569, and in 1596 the Union of Brest united Latin and Eastern Christians in the Jagiellonian Commonwealth.

Why return to Jadwiga's traditions and heritage? Most certainly, it can never be forgotten that she was a great queen, a queen of Western Christian origin who brought to the eastern borderlands of Christian Europe a message of peace and increased the chances of a federal system which could be extended to the whole region, even today.

Jadwiga of Anjou as the Image of a Good Queen in Late Medieval and Early Modern Poland

Anna Brzezińska

In this article I propose to reconstruct the portrayal of Queen Jadwiga on the basis of writings from the fifteenth and sixteenth centuries. I have defined my chosen authors as belonging to three groups: those for whom Queen Jadwiga is a part of the immediate past; Jan Długosz, who calls for individual treatment, along with the subsequent historiographical tradition that was based on his annals, and, finally, the writings of the late sixteenth century, largely originating during the Interregnum. Thus, I have concentrated on three periods: first, when the authors could rely on their own memory of Queen Jadwiga and their testimonies could be verified by the persons from her surroundings, including her husband, Władysław II Jagiełło; second, when her picture as a good queen was codified in historical writings; third, when this portrayal was established well enough to be modified and utilized for current political purposes. I do not plan to probe the validity of the picture of Queen Jadwiga in some particular testimonies. Instead, the wide selection of sources makes it possible to explore the positive image of a royal woman both as a portrayal of a real person and as a didactic program for royal consorts. It also demonstrates that, despite the failure at establishing Queen Jadwiga as a dynastic saint, her image deeply influenced ideas concerning queenship at the time of the Jagiellonian dynasty, entered the common imagery and was further employed to guide individual queens.

This article is based on a paper delivered on June 19, 1999, at a session, "Jadwiga of Anjou 1399–1999, Contributions, Images and Heritage," during the 57th Annual Meeting of the Polish Institute of Arts and Sciences of America held at Fordham University, Lincoln Center Campus, New York.

From *The Polish Review*, vol. 44, no. 4 (1999), pp. 407–418.

I would like to start my analysis with *Soloqium de transitu Hedvigis Reginae Poloniae* written by Stanislas of Skarbimierz during Jadwiga's fatal illness.[1] Stanislas describes Queen Jadwiga as a mother broken by the pains of delivery, illnesses and the death of her baby, a daughter, eventually being responsible for Jadwiga's own death. In his deeply emotional plea for Jadwiga's recovery, he makes a parallel between carnal and symbolic motherhood. For Stanislas of Skarbimierz, Jadwiga constitutes the mother who, despite the death of her first-born child, could still bear the so much needed heir to the kingdom and was as well the spiritual mother of the kingdom, the mother of all its poor, weak and ill.[2] Rather than employing the traditional and favored image of the ecclesiastical patroness beside her royal husband, Stanislas focuses his attention on the personal qualities of the dying queen, on her religious and moral virtues. The non-institutional tone of this portrayal suggests already the main trait of the development of the sermonic tradition about Queen Jadwiga.

Fortunately, we know the series of sermons written soon after her death, such as, the sermon of Stanislas of Skarbimierz written for her funeral in 1399; the sermon of John Isner written in 1399 or 1400; the sermon of Stanislas of Skarbimierz written in 1401 or 1409; two sermons of Francis of Brzeg, from 1420 and 1426; an anonymous sermon composed between 1422 and 1426; the sermon of John Elgot from 1428; the sermon of Paul of Zator from 1430; and an anonymous sermon dated approximately at 1433. All preachers shared a deep conviction about the exceptional qualities of the dead queen whom Stanislas of Skarbimierz proclaimed "the most Christian queen"[3] clearly with the purpose of promoting her canonization process, and whose posthumous cult—the wax figures hung at her grave—was implied by Paul of Zator.[4] Since all the sermons were concerned mostly with her personal piety, the question of the role she played in the public affairs of the Polish-Lithuanian Commonwealth is not crucial to it. Stanislas of Skarbimierz and Francis of Brzeg attribute to Queen Jadwiga the virtues that traditionally distinguished a royal wife:

1. About Stanislas of Skarbimierz, consult Mirosław Korolko, "Wprowadzenie" [Introduction] in Stanisław ze Skarbimierza, *Mowy wybrane o mądrości* [Selected Orations on Wisdom], edited by Mirosław Korolko (Cracow: Arcana, 1997), pp. 9–22.

2. *Dimitte tamen, Domine, matrem, dimitte ut generet, dimitte matrem pauperum, dimitte ipsam etsi non propter pauperes, debiles et claudos, caecos et surdos.* Stanislas of Skarbimierz, "Soloqium de transitu Hedvigis Reginae Poloniae," in *Mowy wybrane . . .*, p. 212.

3. . . . *christianissima principe domina HEDVIGI* . . . , Stanislas of Skarbimierz, "Sermo latinus in exequiis Dominae Hedvigis Reginae Poloniae" in Jerzy Wolny and Roman Maria Zawadzki, "Królowa Jadwiga w tradycji kaznodziejskiej XV wieku" [Queen Jadwiga in the Sermon Tradition of the Fifteenth Century], *Analecta Cracoviensia*, vol. 7 (1975), p. 78.

4. *Hoc ipsum et figurae cereae, supra tumulum eius dependentes liquide demonstrant et velut signa effectuum vitae eius pristinae indicant sanctitatem.* Paul of Zator, "Sermonis *Eadem Quippe Mensura* Fragmentum" in Wolny and Zawadzki, p. 82.

she was of high birth, beautiful but chaste, and her beauty stands principally for her moral perfection; she interceded between the petitioners and her husband, pleading for mercy and providing him with good advice.[5] Nonetheless, the sermons stress that the glory of her noble birth was even exceeded by the glory of her good deeds, her humility and mercy.[6] She is commonly called the mother of the poor, the protector of the orphans, the shelter of the persecuted and the solace of the troubled.[7] The preachers deployed here the largely traditional language of female sanctity, and, in the pattern of *Soloqium*, they perceived Queen Jadwiga as a benefactor of her people. Furthermore, they clearly adopted some elements of Marian vocabulary, which additionally strengthens the image of Queen Jadwiga as a patron and a spiritual mother of her country. In their eyes, she was not merely a divine instrument for turning her husband and his country from paganism; neither did they limit Jadwiga's religious perfection to her attitude to the institutional Church; even so they emphasized her devotion in funding new churches and her respect toward Church authority.[8] They underlined her role in the restoration of the University of Cracow, which is not particularly surprising since all the sermons emerge from the milieu of the university. However, this foundation is perceived mostly through its religious and moral significance since, as claimed by the author of an anonymous sermon, the university promotes virtue that is derived from knowledge.[9] Thus, in the early sermonic tradition Queen Jadwiga represents the female virtues of mercy, benevolence and kindness, which were traditionally attributed to holy women since

---

5. *Vidimus enim quod fuit mater spiritualium, benefactrix viduarum, consolatio orphanorum, clipeus pauperum, refugium opressorum, interventrix a facie domini nostri regis expulsorum. Quod enim quandoque formido domini nostri regis et sua iustitia exterruit, has ipsa suo interventu laetificavit. Vidimus et cognovimus quam decora vultu, quam affabilis affatu, quam nobilis genere, sed nobilior moribus, quam profunde humilis, licet multum fuisset sublimis.* Stanislas of Skarbimierz, "Sermo ad regem et proceres eius de obitu Hedvigis Reginae et vita eius" in Wolny and Zawadzki, p. 24. . . . *similiter quod exstitit speculum castitatis, humilitatis et simplicitatis in victu quam amictu iuxta decentiam sui status quod erat examplat morum et virtutum et regula vivendi respectu aliarum dominarum.* Francis of Brzeg, "Sermo in exequiis Dominae Hedvigis, Reginae Poloniae" in Wolny and Zawadzki, p. 68. See also "Sermonis pro defunctis fragmentum" in Wolny and Zawadzki, p. 84.

6. . . . *nobilis genere sed fide nobilior*, Wolny and Zawadzki, p. 84.

7. Jan Elgot, "Sermonis in recommendatione Hedvigis Reginae Fragmentum" in Wolny and Zawadzki, p. 80; Francis of Brzeg, p. 68; Stanislas of Skarbimierz, "Sermo ad regem et proceres," p. 24.

8. Paul of Zator, p. 82; Francis of Brzeg, p. 68, Stanislas of Skarbimierz, "Sermo ad regem et proceres," pp. 24 and 26.

9. *Ipsa fuit causa erectioinis et fundationis huius sanctae Universatis Cracoviensis nee maius bonum facere potuit. Lumen enim erexit, quo totum regnum, immo tota christianitas illustratur, docetur et ad virtutes inducitur.* "Sermo in anniversario venerandae Hedvigis, Reginae Poloniae, ipsa die beati Alexii Confessoris" in Wolny and Zawadzki, p. 42.

the times of the early Church. We see her also as a benefactress of the churches and a patroness of the learned. On the one hand, she displays the long-established image of sanctity, on the other, she also symbolizes the benevolent aspect of rulership, its responsibility for the old, sick and unprivileged.

Nicholas Lasocki's oration interestingly demonstrates the extent to which opinion about the holiness of Queen Jadwiga could have been utilized by the Polish court in the days of the first attempts at her canonization. Written thirty-five years after Queen Jadwiga's death and presented during the Council of Basle, it should be interpreted in the context of the perpetuated conflict between Poland and the Teutonic Order. In one attempt to discharge the indictment against Władysław Jagiełło, who was accused of devious conversion to Catholicism and an alliance with the Hussites, Nicholas Lasocki skillfully utilized the memory of his consort, Queen Jadwiga. In his relation, she plays the time-honored role of pious royal counselor, occupied with the salvation of the soul of her freshly converted husband and thus promoting him in Christian faith and customs. Consequently, Lasocki associates her with the nature of queenship in its symbolic dimension and the image of the ideal royal spouse who was not only faithful to her husband but also taking care of his religious conduct and salvation.[10] To strengthen her picture as a pious influence on Władysław Jagiełło, Lasocki dwells on Jadwiga's presumed sanctity and refers to the numerous miracles that would happen at her shrine; furthermore, he resorts to the authority of the Holy See, mentioning Polish attempts at her canonization.[11]

The annals of Jan Długosz provide us with another trait of literary tradition concerning Queen Jadwiga. The full analysis of her image in the late medieval and early modem historiography goes beyond the scope of this article, particularly because in the chronicles Queen Jadwiga is characterized not only directly, in her posthumous portrayals, but also through her actions. In accord with the previous tradition, Jan Długosz describes her as an exceptionally beautiful woman;[12] it seems, however, that

---

10. John Carmi Parsons, "Ritual and Symbol in the English Medieval Queenship to 1500," in *Women and Sovereignty*, edited by Louise O. Fradenburg (Edinburgh: Edinburgh University Press, 1992), pp. 60–77.

11. *Profuit non mediocriter in hiis omnibus praefatae reginae sanctissimae conversatio. Cum enim mulier ipsa devotissima at mirae sanctitatis esset, nihil aliud sibi tantae curae fuit, quam et ea, quae ad animae viri et aliorum salutem atque ad ipsorum in bonis moribus eruditionem pertinerent, procuraret. . . . Nam et mortuos susitatos et infirmos plerosque sanitati restitutos ad ipsius tumulum certissimum est.* For the full text of the oration, consult: Karolina Grodziska, "Mikołaja Lasockiego pochwała Władyslawa Jagiełły i królowej Jadwigi na soborze bazylejskim" [Nicholas Lasocki's Praise of Ladislas Jagiełło and Queen Jadwiga at the Council of Basle], *Analecta Cracoviensia*, vol. 20 (1988), pp. 381–399.

12. When he mentions Jadwiga for the first time, the chronicler states that she was more beautiful than her sister: *natu quidem minorem sed prestanciorem forma*, Jan Długosz, *Annales seu Cronicae incliti Regni Poloniae. Liber X. 1370–1405*, edited by Stanisław Gawęda et al.

her physical beauty represents essentially her moral perfection.[13] He lays emphasis on her wisdom and feminine virtues—such as nobility, chastity, modesty, moderation, kindness, and female decency, which he attributes to her already in infancy, utilizing the topos of *puer/puella senex.*[14] It was her great merits, claims Długosz, that earned for Queen Jadwiga the common love of her subjects who, despite her fragile, female condition, crowned her Queen of Poland.[15] Furthermore, Długosz undeniably implies that Queen Jadwiga prevailed over the innate weakness of female nature since during her marriage to Władysław Jagiełło she acts as a good counselor, and he does not hesitate to juxtapose her wisdom with the evident imprudence of Jagiełło. This picture is not only consistent with his opinion about Władysław and his general attitude toward the Jagiellonian dynasty, but it also demonstrates the manly qualities of Queen Jadwiga and the divine gift of wisdom.[16]

The description of the religious and moral virtues of Queen Jadwiga keeps up the elements that have already appeared in the sermonic tradition. Thus, Jan Długosz dwells on her upright manners, her chastity,[17] her gentleness, and generosity for widows, pilgrims and all unfortunate people, her pious influence on the king.[18] This traditional phraseology is, however, tinged with allusions to new forms of female piety. Particularly her posthumous portrayal, the description of her ascetic practices and spiritual readings let us trace mystical and penitential aspects of the spirituality of Queen Jadwiga.[19] She could have been partly inspired by Henry Bitterfeld of Brzeg,

---

(Warsaw: PWN, 1985), p. 42 [1375]. See also Gawęda, p. 142 (*pro illa tempestate in orbe universo parem in forma non habere credita sit*) and Gawęda, p. 152 (*Cuius speciem et decorem et contemplans et admirans (neque enim pro ea tempestate in orbe universo parem in pulchritudine estimata est habuisse)*).

13. This becomes obvious from Długosz' remark that her physical beauty was far exceeded by her moral purity: *Facie venustissima, sed moribus et virtutibus venustior,* Gawęda, pp. 141–142.

14. . . . *in qua omnis virtutis numerus ab incunabulis usque instillatus cum lactis nutrimento putabatur. Que infancie annos egressa ita mature et graviter sapere cepit, ut quicquide dicere/, qicquid faceret, ex anni gravitate manare videretur,* Gawęda, p. 142.

15. *Tanta autem erat erga illiam prelatum et baronum Polonie affecio et tam caritam immensa, ut viros se esse obliti, parere tam insigni et virtuose femine putarent non inglorium. Ea insuper caritate et affectione devicti, nono dato, non procurato illi sponso, quasi ipsa sola ad gybernandum Regnum Polonie sine marito sufficet . . . procurarunt in Polonie reginam diademate reginali et consecrari . . .*, Gawęda, p. 141. See also Jadwiga's excursion to Red Rus: *Cuius tanta etar apud milites affectio et caritas, ut omnes illi exta ac viro parerent et singula que iubebat, obedienter exequerentur,* Gawęda, p. 182.

16. Długosz, p. 217. See also p. 226.

17. Długosz, pp. 141–142.

18. In her posthumous portrayal, Długosz, pp. 231–232.

19. Długosz, p. 232.

whose *De vita contemplativa et vita activa* was—not without reason—dedicated to Queen Jadwiga.[20]

Additional information concerning Queen Jadwiga's religiosity emerges from the story of her government in Poland, and Długosz commonly stresses the religious inspiration of her actions. First of all, in a few passages he states that she conceded to the marriage to Władysław Jagiełło not for the sake of carnal pleasures but with the purpose of having his country baptised.[21] Her attitude toward the poor finds its illustration in the story of the peasants being robbed of their property by men of her husband.[22] Furthermore, Długosz states that Queen Jadwiga had a prophetic gift, a power that was traditionally attributed to saintly women. As claimed by Długosz, *by some divine inspiration* Queen Jadwiga predicted that after her death the Teutonic Order would face grave disasters;[23] she also foresaw the defeat of Witold's excursion against the Tatars,[24] and, anticipating her own death, she advised her husband to marry Anne of Cilli.[25] Finally, Długosz explicitly confirms these allusions to Queen Jadwiga's holiness in her posthumous portrayal, in which he asserts that the dead are resurrected and the ill are healed at her shrine.[26]

Yet, Długosz' picture of her is hardly consistent. First of all, he apparently has doubts concerning the legal nature of Jadwiga's betrothal/marriage to Wilhelm of Habsburg. The chronicler claims that in 1375 Louis the Great gave his daughter

20. Jerzy Wolny and Roman Maria Zawadzki, "Królowa Jadwiga w tradycji kaznodziejskiej XV wieku" [Queen Jadwiga in the Preaching Tradition of the Fifteenth Century], *Analecta Cracoviensia*, vol. 7 (1975), pp. 88–89.

21. *Verum maior et anior pars Christiane fidei favore et dilatacione principaliter et quiete Regni Polonie aliisque condicionibus, que a Lithwano offerebantur, permota Iagellonem pro rege assumendum, aversas sentencias et regine Hedvigis fastidium magnarum gencium atque populorum ad fidei katholice accessione confutans, decernbat amplissimum meritum, amplissimamque commendacionem et laudem omni memorandam eva Regnum Polonie consequturum astruens, si per illius operam katholice fidei splendor et puritas aput Lithwanicac Samagitticasque et ceteras barbaras naciones proluxerit. Hec sentancia cum Hadvigis regine, femine iam tunc devote et religiosissime, fastdium solo fidei Christiane respectu temperasset, facile quoque ab aliis excepta est.* Długosz, p. 145. . . . *non voluptatis aut libidinis explende causa, sed fidei orthodoxe amplitudinem et Christianorum quietem procuratura, consentiret.* Długosz, p. 153.

22. Długosz, p. 158.

23. *Etiam id femina benedicta celesti quodam inspirata sensu adiecit se quidem vivente bellicum, ob presentes et preteritas iniurias Polonie Regno illatas, suppressuram furorem; fatis vera absumpta, scirent maximas sibi clades eventuras.* Długosz, p. 220.

24. . . . *nisi Hedvigis Polonie regina, Spiritu revelante, Alexandri magni ducis Lithwanie et katholici exercitus ruinam, barbarorum vera victoriam previcens.* Długosz, p. 226.

25. Długosz, p. 237.

26. Długosz, p. 234.

Jadwiga in marriage to the Austrian prince.[27] Besides, in 1383 he states that there were doubts concerning Jadwiga's marriage: some claimed that she had been married to Wilhelm, while some others maintained that she had been only betrothed.[28] Długosz does not feel it necessary to reconcile these contradictions. Moreover, in 1386 he explains that Queen Jadwiga's resistance against the marriage with Władysław Jagiełło stemmed from the fact that she had already consummated her union with Wilhelm. According to the annals of Jan Długosz, Queen Jadwiga was compelled by the Polish lords to concede to an adulterous marriage with a pagan.[29] However, the emphasis put on Jadwiga's struggle against the second, bigamous, marriage makes it possible for Długosz to free her of guilt, which is passed onto the lords who concocted the marriage. Since in the relation of Długosz Queen Jadwiga is presented as a victim, the doubts concerning the legal status of her marriage to Jagiełło do not contradict her virtues and piety. Similarly, when in 1389 we see Jadwiga suspected of adultery, a charge from which she finally had to clear herself by a solemn oath, Długosz decisively rejects the accusation and claims that from then on the marital life of the royal couple was entirely harmonious.[30] To a certain extent, this statement is challenged by the remark attributed to the pregnant Queen, who allegedly stated that God had finally relieved her from the shame of infertility.[31] As the main duty of a queen was to provide an heir to the kingdom, Jadwiga's words not only imply that her prolonged sterility caused some tension within the royal court, but also they suggest that eventually she fulfilled her duty and conceived a child.

On the average, Długosz's portrayal of Queen Jadwiga passed down to sixteenth century historiography. However, the symbolic connotations of some of her features become uncertain. For example, Joachim Bielski depicts her adorning herself for the meeting with Jagiełło—a situation virtually unknown in the previous tradition—and states that she was as beautiful as Helena [Helen of Troy], while he obviously does not recognize the symbolic meaning of her physical perfection.[32]

---

27. *Alteram filiarum suarum Hedwigim . . . Ludovigus . . . Wilhelma duci Austrie, filio Lupoldi desponsat.* Długosz, p. 42.

28. . . . *alteramfiliam natu minorem Hedwigim (Vilhelmo) Austrie duci a Lodowogo rege in coniugium repromissam (et iuxta nonnullorum assercionem desponsatam)* . . . Długosz, pp. 115–116.

29. *Neque enim a plurimorum noticia sciebat ignoratum, quod cum prefato Vilhelmo Austrie duce post contracta de presenti sponsalia quindecim diebus in thoro, carnali copula eciam subsequta, manserat* . . . , Długosz, p. 154.

30. Długosz, pp. 176–177.

31. . . . *qui sterilitas opprobio ablato fecunditatem prestitit,* Długosz, p. 231.

32. Joachim Bielski, *Kronika polska* [Polish Chronicle], edited by Kazimierz Józef Turowski (Sanok: Karol Pollak, 1856), p. 473. See also Martin Kromer, *Kronika polska* [edited and translated by Marcin Błażowski, (Sanok: Karol Pollak, 1868), vol. I, pp. 706–707.

Likewise, in sixteenth century chronicles we do not hear much either about Queen Jadwiga as a royal counselor or about her exceptional wisdom; moreover, Marcin Kromer maintains that from the outset of her rule in Poland the lords insisted on marrying her off since they did not find enough authority and defense in the young lady.[33] Generally, sixteenth century historiography does not stress the intellectual inconsistency between her and her husband. Still, the general scheme of Długosz's story prevailed almost without modifications, and the sixteenth century tradition does not contribute much more to our knowledge concerning Queen Jadwiga.

Adopted from the chronicles, the story of Queen Jadwiga was widely known in the sixteenth century, and, with clearly political undercurrents, it appears again during the electoral debate of the Interregnum.[34] As the main line of the Jagiellons became extinct, the senators opted to elect Anna, daughter of Sigismund I, *Infans Regni Poloniae.* The political situation within the realm obviously implied some similarities to that of the late fourteenth century, when the minor Jadwiga was placed in custody of Polish lords and crowned King of Poland. Princess Anna was rigorously guarded to prevent the potential influence her choice of husband could have on the election of the king.[35] Under these circumstances, the story of Jadwiga set a good example of patriotism and sacrifice rather than as a figure of speech. However, we would look in vain in these polemical pieces for the precise characteristics of Jadwiga: she is presented almost entirely in her relation to the nobility and their claim to choose her a husband who would become King of Poland. Her significance is defined by her position as heir to the kingdom, and the literature of the Interregnum emphasized that her objections concerning the person of the prospective groom were overcome by the wisdom of the Poles who promoted her marriage to Władysław Jagiełło, and, accordingly, concluded the union between Poland and Lithuania and thus the Christianizing of the vast pagan lands of Lithuania. Here we can observe a significant shift in the Polish electoral tradition: the early literary allusions to the story of Jadwiga imply the role of the lords rather than the wide masses of the nobility. However, during the Interregnum the factual

33. Kromer, vol. 1, pp. 706–707.

34. Świętosław Orzelski, *Bezkrólewia ksiąg osmioro* [Interregnum, Eight Volumes], edited by Włodzimierz Spasowicz (Petersburg & Mohilew: B. M. Wolff, 1856), vol. 1, pp. 62–63; vol. 2, p. 248; "Sententia de eligendo novo rege ex duce Moschorum," in *Pisma polityczne z czasów pierwszego bezkrólewia* [Political Writings from the Times of the First Interregnum], edited by Jan Czubek (Cracow: Akademia Umiejcętności, 1906), p. 355; "Gdyby panowie Polacy cesarza albo Niemca obrali, toby na nie przyść musiało" [If the Polish Lords Elected the Emperor or a German, it would be obligatory upon them] in Czubek, p. 360.

35. Jan Dymitr Solikowski, *Krótki pamiętnik rzeczy polskich od zgonu Zygmunta August* [A Brief Memoir of Polish Matters from the Demise of Sigmund Augustus], edited by Władysław Syrokomla (Petersburg & Mohilew: B. M. Wolff, 1854), p. 13. See also Maria Bogucka, *Anna Jagiellonka* [Anna Jagiellon] (Wrocław: Ossolineum, 1994), pp. 77–97.

political status quo was much more diverse. In the eyes of the nobility, who after the death of Sigismund Augustus took command of the government in Poland, it was not only the senators but the lower gentry as well who were entitled to choose the husband for the princess.[36] This tendency is conspicuous in *De electione novi regis* whose author states explicitly that both the lords and *szlachta* were entitled to participate in royal elections and that they, together, selected a groom for Jadwiga,[37] while other pieces use more ambiguous terms, "the Poles"[38] or "our ancestors."[39]

Furthermore, the allusions to Queen Jadwiga were employed in favor—or more frequently in defiance—of certain particular candidates to the Polish throne and, consequently, to the hand of Anna Jagiellon. Interestingly enough, these references show once again how much the interpretation of historical examples depended on literary context as well as the political opinion of a particular author. Most often, Jadwiga's story served as an example of Polish resistance against the German ruler. As stated by an anonymous author: "rather than to be ruled by a German our ancestors preferred to vote for a pagan, whom they married to the princess and made him Polish sovereign."[40] A similar attitude was shared by Świętosław Orzelski, who quotes his own oration in which he praised the Poles for not letting Wilhelm of Habsburg consummate his union with Queen Jadwiga.[41] Yet, the same image was used in favor of the German candidate as well. Another circular of the Interregnum argues that, since Jadwiga's betrothal to Wilhelm of Habsburg was denied, it would be appropriate to correct this mistake and marry Anna Jagiellon to a member of the Habsburg dynasty.[42] Evidently, the interpretation of the same fact led to a completely opposite conclusion, but the frequency of Queen Jadwiga's story quoted in the polemical writings suggests both that it was commonly known to the nobility

---

36. On this controversy between the nobility and the senators, to whom Anna was entrusted by the last will of Sigismund Augustus, consult Orzelski, vol. 2, pp. 277, 328–329, 331.

37. "De electione novi regis," pp. 399–401.

38. "Gdyby panowie Polacy . . . ," p. 360; "Rozmowa Lecha z Piastem, napominająca swych obywatelów, jakiego pana mają sobie i królewstwu temu obrać" [Conversation of a Lech with a Piast, Reminding their Citizens What Kind of Lord They are to Elect for Themselves and the Kingdom] in Czubek, p. 40.

39. "Sententia de eligendo novo rege ex duce Moschorum," p. 355; Andrzej Lubieniecki, *Poloneutychia*, edited by Alina Linda et al. (Warsaw & Łódź: PWN, 1982), p. 66. (The author cites the oration of John Zamoyski.)

40. "Sententia de eligendo novo rege . . . ," p. 355; see also "Gdyby panowie Polacy cesarza albo Niemca obrali . . . ," p. 360; "De electione novi regis . . . ," p. 401.

41. Orzelski, vol. 2, p. 248.

42. "Rationes et cautelae in novi regis electione observandae," in *Pisma polityczne z czasów pierwszego bezkrólewia* [Political Writings from the Times of the First Interregnum], edited by Jan Czubek (Cracow: Akademia Umiejętności, 1906), p. 441.

and that, owing to its popularity and complexity, it created many opportunities for an author to utilize different threads and aspects.

This attractiveness of the story of Queen Jadwiga becomes evident also in a small book *Oeconomia albo gospodarstwo. To jest nauka jako wszelki krześcijański człowiek w gospodarstwie sprawować się ma,* published in 1546 in Königsburg by John Seklucjan.[43] *Oeconomia* contains very interesting passages about Queen Jadwiga in its parts related to the ideal consort of a Christian prince. In accordance with the Polish historiographical tradition, the author stresses that the exceptional virtues of Jadwiga made Jagiełło want to marry her, embrace Christianity, release Polish captives, and link his land forever with the Polish Kingdom. He also mentions the story of the robbed peasants, which was the most commonly quoted illustration of Jadwiga's charity and the benevolent influence she had on her husband.[44] Since the book was dedicated to Duchess Dorothea of Prussia, the author makes parallels between her and Queen Jadwiga as alms-giver, supporter of poor students and founder of a university.[45] Apparently, in stressing these elements the author of *Oeconomia* does not contradict the previous relations about Queen Jadwiga. However, he shows surprising ignorance, claiming that God praised the Polish royal family for the holy deeds of Queen Jadwiga, since he made her son Wladislas King of Poland and Hungary, and furthermore, the author of *Oeconomia* enumerates among her descendants the Duke of Prussia, King of Poland and numerous German princes.[46] Certainly, the author confuses here two wives of Władysław II Jagiełło: Queen Jadwiga who did not leave any heir and Queen Sophia (Sonka) of Holszany

43. About John Seklucjan and a discussion concerning the authorship of the work, see Stanisław Rospond, "Wstęp" [Introduction] in Jan Seklucjan, *Wybór pism* [Selected Writings], edited by Stanisław Rospond (Olsztyn: Pojezierze, 1979), pp. xxvi–xxvii.

44. John Seklucyan, *Oeconomia alba gospodarstwo,* edited by Zygmunt Celichowski (Cracow: Uniwersytet Jagielloński, 1890), pp. 39–41.

45. "Niemniejszy przykład po sobie zostawiła szlachetna Jadwiga królowa Polska wyżej namieniona; ta cnotliwie żywiąc, wiele dobrego niedostatecznym a ubogim ludziom czyniła, ubogie studenty zakładala i żywiła, na ostatek wszystko swe kosztowne odzienie i klejnoty dała, aby Collegium w Grakchowie zbudowano, które był Kazimierz wtóry, król Polski, począł budować i zakładał," Seklucyan, pp. 71–72.

46. "Szczęścią pan Bóg dla tej szlachetnej małżonki natenczas dom królewski i wszystka korona Polski i Węgierski, iże jej syn Władysław, gdy był wybran królem węgierskim, wielekroć nad okrutnym nieprzyjacielem Turkiem zwycięstwo otrzymał i tak go był potłumić, że też u niego ten okrutny nieprzyjaciel przemierze zabrać musiał. Szczęści jeszcze i dziś pan Bóg tej ślachetnej a krześcijańskiej malżonki swem blogosławieństwem potomki i szeroko je rozmnożył jako są dzisiejsi najjaśniejsi królowie Polscy, najoświecećsze książe Pruskie, i ine książęta w ziemiech niemieckich. A wierzą, że ten ślachetny dom albo potomek nigdy nie zginie," Seklucyan, pp. 39–41.

(Alsenai), Władysław's mother, subsequently elected King of Poland and Hungary. Unfortunately, we lack any information about the intellectual background of the author—he mentions only that he spent many years at the court of the Duke of Prussia—and we cannot guess how profound his knowledge of Polish history was. His mistake, however, demonstrates that even in this false context Queen Jadwiga still served as a paragon of a good queen and that as such, she was endowed by the author of *Oeconomia* with the royal progeny she, in fact, lacked. This might be a reflection of both the long-lasting conviction that women are redeemed through bearing children and the author's urge to relate his protector, Duchess Dorothy, with Queen Jadwiga, who in his interpretation became a saintly ancestor of the Prussian ruling house.

To sum up, I believe that the few texts presented in this study demonstrate that the image of Queen Jadwiga was far more complicated than that of an ecclesiastic benefactress and the intercessor beside her husband, and that her image stands apart from typical royal consorts who are virtually invisible in the narrative sources. Obviously, her position as a successor to a kingdom and her role in the conversion of Lithuania predisposed her to attract the attention of both contemporary and posthumous writers. However, she was conspicuous not only because of her royal heritage and her political activities in the Polish Kingdom and the Grand Duchy of Lithuania; even so the precedence of the heiress to the kingdom being wedded by the members of the Polish lords deeply inspired the Polish nobility during the subsequent Interregnum. Without doubt, the ambiguous story of her betrothal/marriage to Wilhelm of Austria and the allegedly discordant marriage with Władysław Jagiełło made her story more complex. Still, her personal virtues, deep religiosity that earned her the opinion of sanctity, and, last but not least, her role in the restoration of the Cracovian University made her the image of the good queen. And, as demonstrated by the parallel made between Queen Jadwiga and Duchess Dorothea of Prussia, this common desideratum concerning royal consorts also remained virtually untouched in the sixteenth century.

Typus Fundationis Academiae Cracoviensis

A woodcut prepared in the XVIIth century from a painting which used to be in the Cathedral Church in Cracow.

On the left side is King Ladislas Jagello, protecting his Lithuanians who are being baptized by a bishop.

Behind the King is the Bishop of Cracow, Zbigniew Oleśnicki, Chancellor of the University of Cracow.

On the right side is Queen Jadwiga with the Orthodox Ruthenians.

Behind the Queen is King Casimir the Great, founder of the University of Cracow.

Both monarchs are holding a model of the University of Cracow, as can be seen from the insignia of the university placed high on the building.

From: *University of Cracow, Documents Concerning Its Origins* (Dundee and Tayport: Polish Committee in Scotland for the Commemoration of Poland's Millennium of Christianity, 1966), facing p. 4.

Women and Political Patronage in the Politics of the Polish-Lithuanian Commonwealth

Lynn Lubamersky

Natalie Zemon Davis first put forth the thesis that women were increasingly subjugated over the course of the early modem period, from the sixteenth to the eighteenth century.[1] This subjugation resulted from the processes of state-building and capitalism. Within the patriarchal family itself, subjugation resulted from family centralization, necessary for "more efficient property acquisition, social mobility, and preservation of the line." Subjugation proceeded at such a pace that by the eighteenth century, "married women in France and England had largely lost what independent legal personality they had formerly had, they had less legal right to make decisions on their own about their dowries than at an earlier period, [and] propertied women were involved less and less in local and regional political assemblies.[2]

Zemon Davis' judgment that women's legal, economic and political status declined in the early modern period only applied to states that were becoming centralized. But now, over twenty years after she first enunciated her thesis, historians view the link between the centralization of the state and the centralization of the patriarchal family as a more complex process. Scholars have begun to view family formation, landholding and office-holding as systems in which women were not merely spectators but prime participants in early modern state-building.[3] Because

1. Natalie Zemon Davis, "Women on Top," *Society and Culture in Early Modern France* (Stanford, California: Stanford University Press, 1975).

2. Zemon Davis, p. 126.

3. Sarah Hanley, "Engendering the State: Family Formation and State Building in Early Modern France," *French Historical Studies,* vol. 16, no. 1 (1989), p. 27.

From *The Polish Review,* vol. 44, no. 3 (1999), pp. 259–275.

they were so important in building social relationships and kinship networks, women were not excluded from political power after all.[4] Scholars of early modern Europe have also stressed that in both centralizing and decentralized states political power was exercised through patronage, which brought with it the ability to skirt the law and to manipulate institutions to one's own advantage. Far from being a rigid, inflexible system which limited women's power, the Old Regime now seems to have been a period in which some noblewomen managed to achieve a remarkable degree of political, social and economic influence through their role as patrons.[5] Gary Kates, an historian of gender in eighteenth century France, summed up this paradox of modernity for women's status:

> Ironically, the history of European women shows that upper-class women fared better in a hierarchically structured society like the Old Regime than in the more democratic systems that followed in the nineteenth century. Eighteenth-century societies were all characterized to one degree or another by privilege rather than by public laws . . . [and] winning exceptions to the law was what being an aristocrat was all about. During the eighteenth century, anyone with enough power, status, or wealth tried to raise himself above the law. In this context where legal and social institutions were unusually flexible, aristocratic women often benefited.[6]

The fluid character of the Old Regime and the nature of privilege allowed opportunities for noblewomen, and especially for noblewomen in the Polish-Lithuanian Commonwealth, because of the extent of aristocratic privilege there.

In the eighteenth century, foreign observers took disparaging note of the tremendous aristocratic privilege they saw in the Polish-Lithuanian Commonwealth. In 1778, William Coxe characterized this system of noble privilege as "a turbulent system of aristocratic licentiousness, where a few members of the community are above the control of the law, and the majority are excluded from its protection."[7] By the mid-eighteenth century, a group of families dominated all aspects of life in the Commonwealth, and in some of these families women played a significant role.

While there was a tradition of equality among the nobility in the Crown of Poland, there was a tradition of "*de facto* oligarchy in the Grand Duchy [of Lithuania], (which) was, from time to time, replaced by *de facto* tyranny of one clan over

4. Carolyn C. Lougee, *Le Paradis de Femmes: Women, Salons and Social Stratification in Seventeenth-Century France* (Princeton: Princeton University Press, 1976).

5. Sharon Kettering, "Patronage and Kinship in Early Modern France," *French Historical Studies*, vol. 16, no. 2 (1989), p. 421.

6. Gary Kates, *Monsieur d'Eon is a Woman* (New York: Basic Books, 1995), p. xix.

7. William Coxe, *Travels in Poland and Russia* (London: 1802; reprint, New York: Arno, 1970), p. 13.

the rest of the country. These were the Radziwiłł, Chodkiewicz, Sapieha, and Pac clans."[8]

This article will examine the role of women in the Radziwiłł family during the eighteenth century. At the beginning of the century, the Radziwiłł family's position among the Lithuanian magnates was relatively weaker than it had been a century before. They found themselves in the shadow of the growing power of the Sapieha family, led by Kazimierz Jan Sapieha, Hetman of the Grand Duchy of Lithuania. The Radziwiłł family also found rivals among the Ogiński and Wiśniowiecki families, who were gaining economic and political power.[9] So, by examining the Radziwiłł family of the eighteenth century, one can observe the waxing and waning of noble fortunes and evaluate the elements that went into constituting and preserving family wealth. In the case of the Radziwiłł family, that fortune was improved by the contribution of able women, and during the eighteenth century, the political significance and wealth of the Radziwiłłs grew. Not until recently have reliable estimates of their wealth been calculated. One study showed that the number of peasants on Radziwiłł lands in 1709 was about 11,600, but that number had increased to approximately 502,700 by 1750:

> . . . the possessions of all lines of this house made up 23 fortified castles, 426 smaller and larger cities . . . 2,032 manors and 10,053 villages in which 502,658 people lived. Their estimated income was 27 million Polish złoty annually.[10]

This estimate is exaggerated, but there is no doubt that the Radziwiłłs were a tremendously wealthy family who were lords to over half a million people, commanded a relatively large share of the national wealth, and accumulated much of this wealth over the course of the eighteenth century.

This article focuses on one branch of the Radziwiłł family, consisting of Barbara z Zawiszów Radziwiłłowa (1690–1770), her husband Mikołaj Faustyn Radziwiłł (1688–1746), the voivode, or provincial governor, of Nowogródek in the Grand Duchy of Lithuania, and their children. Mikołaj Faustyn Radziwiłł was descended from Dominik Mikołaj Radziwiłł, heir to the Kleck entail. Because Mikołaj Faustyn

---

8. Andrzej Kamiński, *Republic vs. Autocracy: Poland-Lithuania and Russia 1686–1697* (Cambridge: Harvard University Press, 1993), p. 34.

9. Zbigniew Anusik and Andrzej Stroynowski, "Problemy majątkowe Radziwiłłów w XVIII w." [Problems Relating to the Property of the Radziwiłłs in the Eighteenth Century], *Roczniki dziejów społecznych i gospodarczych* [Annals of Social and Economic History], vol. 68 (1987), p. 80. Cited from K. F. Eichhorn's *Stosunek xiążęcego domu Radziwiłłów do innych domów xiążęcych w Niemczech* [Relations Between the Princely House of Radziwiłł and Other Princely Houses in Germany], p. 27.

10. Anusik and Stroynowski, "Problemy," pp. 83–84. All translations from the Polish in this article are by its author.

was the third son, he did not inherit this entail. His branch of the family has been dubbed the "berdyczowska line," because the most substantial piece of property they brought into the family was the Berdyczów estate located in Ukraine, the property of Barbara Radziwiłłowa.[11] Instead of calling the "the berdyczowska Radziwiłłs," it is more fitting to call them the Radziwiłłs of Zdzięcioł, because this was the estate where Mikolaj Faustyn was born and where he and his family lived, although they never referred to themselves in that way. The Radziwiłłs of Zdzięcioł were therefore a weaker branch of the Radziwiłł family, because much of their land was encumbered with debt.[12] During the eighteenth century, the most wealthy branch of the Radziwiłł family was that branch which had inherited the Nieśwież entail; so this branch could be called the Nieśwież branch of the Radziwiłł family.

Women accumulated much of the Radziwiłł family fortune of the eighteenth century. Anna z Sanguszków Radziwiłłowa and Barbara z Zawiszów Radziwiłłowa were the most significant contributors adding to the family fortune and improving their position in society:

> In the modern history of all the contemporary magnate houses of the eighteenth century, there were members who played the most energetic roles in accumulating property, and in establishing the position of the family. . . . In the case of the Radziwiłłs, this role was played by women—Anna z Sanguszków and Barbara z Zawiszów.[13]

Whereas Anna Radziwiłłowa concentrated her efforts on economic matters, Barbara Radziwiłłowa directed her energies and ambitions toward political affairs.[14] Despite the fact that they could not hold political office, these noblewomen brought wealth in the form of income-producing property, which was one of the bases of political power in the Commonwealth.

Antoni Mączak outlined the main characteristics of the of the eighteenth century Polish-Lithuanian political system in his book *Klientela* [Clientage or Clientele].[15] "Patronage was a routine way of exercising power and authority at

---

11. Zbigniew Anusik and Andrzej Stroynowski, "Radziwiłłowie w epoce Saskiej: Zarys dziejów politycznych i majątkowych" [The Radziwiłłs in the Saxon Era: Sketch of Political and Estate History], in *Acta Universitatis Lodziensis Folia Historica*, vol. 33 (1989), p. 40.

12. Teresa Zielińska, "Radziwiłłowie herbu Trąby—dzieje rodu" [The Radziwiłłs of the Horn Coat-of-Arms—History of the Family], in *Radziwiłłowie herbu Trąby* (Warsaw: Archiwum Glówne Akt Dawnych, 1996), p. 24.

13. Anusik and Stroynowski, "Radziwiłłowie w epoce Saskiej," p. 57.

14. Zielińska, p. 24.

15. Antoni Mączak, *Klientela: nieformalne systemy władzy w Polsce i Europie XVI–XVIII w.* [Clientage: Informal Systems of Authority in Poland and Europe in the Sixteenth to Eighteenth Centuries] (Warsaw: Semper, 1994).

a time when the public and the private were not yet clearly separated."[16] In this article, Mączak's model of patron-client relationships will be used to discuss how the Radziwiłł family used its political clientele to further their own interests in the provincial *Sejmiki* [Dietines] and in the *Sejm* [Diet]. It will also evaluate how women fit into the system of patronage by focusing on the example of Barbara z Zawiszów Radziwiłłowa, and, finally, it will examine how a woman could exercise power within this political system and show that women could act both as patrons and as clients, influencing family politics and therefore the political system as a whole.

In discussing the system of clientage, we must ask whether people thought of themselves as clients and patrons. Neither of the Latin terms, *cliens* or *patronus*, were commonly used to describe relationships in the Commonwealth. The terms that were used most often were *dobrodziej* [patron] for a person bestowing largesse, and *przyjaciel* [friend] for the receiver of the benefits. The political system of the Commonwealth was a "political clientage," in that the main evidence of clientage came when the client voted according to the wishes of the patron.[17] In this system, noble landholder-voters were organized to vote in *Sejmiki* according to the political interest of the magnate.

The Commonwealth developed the institution of magnate patronage instead of the royal patronage (which had been such an essential part of the centralizing process in France) because the Commonwealth was an elective monarchy, and not a dynastic state.[18] The elective monarchy destabilized relationships with the royal court. It meant that noble families could create dynasties but the monarchy could not.[19] Magnate influence was a result of the fact that the unpopular King August III, who ruled from 1733 to 1763, depended upon those magnates popular among the nobility in order to rule peacefully. The magnates were aware that these long-standing relationships worked in their favor and against the king. In 1619, Krzysztof Radziwiłł noted that the length and longevity of service to the house of Radziwiłł was of great importance among political *przyjaciele*. Long-standing family alliances

16. Antoni Mączak, "From Aristocratic Household to Princely Court: Restructuring patronage in the Sixteenth and Seventeenth Centuries," in *Princes, Patronage, and the Nobility: The Court at the Beginning of the Modern Age c. 1450–1650*, edited by Ronald G. Asch and Adolf M. Birke, (London: Oxford University Press, 1991), p. 316.

17. Mączak, *Klientela . . .*, p. 28.

18. Zofia Zielińska, "Mechanizm sejmikowy i klientela radziwiłłowska za Sasów" [The Dietine Mechanism and the Radziwiłł Clientele in Saxon Times], in *Przegląd Historyczny* [Historical Review], vol. 62, no. 3 (1971), p. 412, citing Szymon Askenazy, "Przedostatnie bezkrólewie" [The Penultimate Interregnum], in *Dwa stulecia* [Two Centuries] (Warsaw: 1903), vol. I, p. 59.

19. Zielińska, "Mechanizm . . . ," p. 413.

united not just individuals, but were seen as the union of one family with a generation of another.[20]

Another way in which patron-client relationships in the Commonwealth differed from the European trend toward absolutism was in the institution of the court. Where between the sixteenth and the eighteenth centuries service at an absolute monarch's court became one condition of European noble "citizenship," in the Commonwealth service at a magnate's court served a parallel function.[21] Where the royal patron-as-educator served a centralizing function in the absolute monarchy, the magnate patron-as-educator created many centers of regional cultural and political authority in the Commonwealth. The practice of raising children at another magnate's court was a school of upbringing and socialization which linked families and solidified ties within the family.

The fact that a noble boy or girl had been educated at a magnate's court did not mean that he or she was now that magnate's client. Only a grown-up had the right to a certain degree of independence. The child's authority was limited by that of his father and family. Only "receiving property, undertaking a profession, or marrying gave any real freedom, or freedom to enter into a patron/client relationship."[22]

The Radziwiłł clientage fits Mączak's model of "an informal federation of patrons."[23] The Radziwiłł family as a house of magnate patrons also had within it an internal set of patron-client relationships, in which weaker members of the family depended upon stronger members to act as their patrons.

One of the best witnesses to the Radziwiłł clientage system is Marcin Matuszewicz (1714–1773), a client of the Radziwiłłs for part of his political life.[24] Matuszewicz viewed himself, and was viewed by others, as the Radziwiłłs' political agent in the Brest *Sejmik*. The Radziwiłłs had a long tradition of relying upon agents to further their interests in both the *Sejmiki* and in the *Sejm*. As the Radziwiłłs' agent, Matuszewicz would await the instructions of his patrons before the Brest *Sejmik*. Magnates would meet in council before an important *Sejmik* to decide on their choice of candidates for election, to formulate election strategy, and to write instructions for the agents.

Concrete evidence of the activity of the magnate council's composition and inner workings is rare, but sometimes appears in financial records and correspondence. In 1756, the Radziwiłł family council and their allies convened at the estate of the Marshal of Lithuania, Ignacy Ogiński at Iwie. The first order of business was

20. Mączak, *Klientela* . . . , p. 257.
21. Mączak, *Klientela* . . . , p. 287.
22. Mączak, *Klientela* . . . , p. 287.
23. Mączak, *Klientela* . . . , p. 304.
24. Marcin Matuszewicz, *Diariusz życia mego* [A Diary of My Life], edited by Bohdan Królikowski and Zofia Zielińska (Warsaw: PIW, 1986), two volumes.

for each of the allies to dedicate a sum of money to the election to assure that plans would be fulfilled. A fragment of the protocol has been preserved; it states that each of Ogiński's allies pledged mutual fidelity as well as the following sums to fund the election:

Voivode of Wilno (Michał Kazimierz Radziwiłł):	53,000 złotys
Marshal of Lithuania (Ignacy Ogiński):	25,000 złotys
Ensign of Lithuania (Hieronim Florian Radziwiłł):	50,000 złotys
Grand Seneschal of Lithuania (Ludwik Pociej):	10,000 złotys
General of Artillery (Antoni Dowojna Sołłohub):	8,000 złotys
	146,000 total[25]

It appears at first glance that this is an agreement between two Radziwiłłs and three other unrelated people, but this was not the case. All had ties of kinship to the Radziwiłł family. Two of the men in the group had married into the Radziwiłł family of Zdzięcioł: Pociej's daughter was married to Stanisław Radziwiłł, and Sołłohub was married to Brygida Radziwiłłówna. Even Ignacy Ogiński had a blood relationship with the Radziwiłł family: he was Barbara Radziwiłłowa's first cousin once removed.[26] So although this might seem to have been a council of magnates belonging to a political bloc, it was rather a council of magnates linked by family connections. Family connections cemented magnate alliances, and can be viewed as one of the main bases for such alliances, even above and beyond political programs.

After declaring the 146,000 złotys, the magnates divided the districts among themselves. Next, they would call in the most active noblemen, who were well-known in the given district, to act on their behalf. They would also call in a public leader, the director of the *Sejmik,* who served the magnate council and was their leader on the ground.[27] Matuszewicz would serve this function for the Radziwiłł family at the Brest *Sejmik.* However, even in the Grand Duchy of Lithuania, the director was not always a magnate's agent.[28] The director should generally be a friend of the magnate and have numerous friends among the nobility. The choice of director depended on several factors: there were family ties, called *parentela* (descent from a common ancestor), which carried great weight in the *Sejmik,* as well as in society. Second, loyalty was inspired by the patronage of the magnate's court. Matuszewicz instructed his men to ply the nobles with food, drink, and

25. Zielińska, "Mechanizm . . . ," p. 399.

26. Ignacy Ogiński was the son of Marcjan Michał Ogiński. Barbara Radziwiłł's father was the son of Alexandra Ogińska. Marcjan and Alexandra were brother and sister. From Krzysztof Zawisza, *Pamiętniki Wojewody Mińskiego (1666–1721)* [Memoirs of the Minsk Voivode (1666–1721)] (Warsaw: Nakładem Jana Zawiszy, 1862), p. v.

27. Zielińska, "Mechanizm . . . ," p. 400.

28. Zielińska, "Mechanizm . . . ," p. 404.

to distribute money to them. This was the expected perquisite for attending the *Sejmik*, but it was not necessarily the only basis for such "friendship." Third, the magnate engendered loyalty through the practice of leasing out estates or housing the landless, or small-farm-holding nobility. Fourth, many state functionaries in the court system, like Castle Court Judges, owed their positions to the influence of their patron. This elevated their prestige and gave their actions more weight and influence at the *Sejmik*. Finally, there were transitory allies whose support could be purchased with the magnate's money. They would abandon this director should the magnate's financial support be somehow disrupted.[29] The final stage of the *Sejmik* was the act of writing instructions to the *Sejm*. Instructions were often written before and sometimes after the *Sejmik*, in the magnate's residence. Each director received commands from the magnate underscoring which elements were essential and could not be changed.[30]

Given this system of patron-client relations, could women play any role within it as clients or patrons? Obviously, noblewomen did not play exactly the same role as noblemen did, given the fact that they could not hold public office. Women could not act as directors of the *Sejmik*, or as Castle Court or Tribunal Judges. But these were not necessarily limits for women, as such public functions were not the most important elements of political life. As shown above, the most important part of the *Sejmik* took place privately, behind closed doors, in a magnate residence when magnates met to arrange their strategy. And *parentela* was the most important element in determining *Sejmik* alliances. Women played an important role in most of the activities connected with forming, maintaining and exploiting patronage networks. In this discussion of patron-client relations, the focus will be limited to those elements of the clientage system delineated by Mączak's model.

The patronage networks that were used to get ahead were of paramount importance in the political system of the Commonwealth, and women used those networks to promote their own clients. Barbara z Zawiszów Radziwiłłowa was instrumental in helping the Radziwiłł family to advance during the eighteenth century in several ways. Władysław Konopczyński wrote that Barbara Radziwiłłowa was:

> The mover and shaker of her husband's fortune and clientage. She often led him and his rich relatives.... She was the most robust, intelligent person in the family, conducting foreign and domestic politics. She nurtured the growth of the family fortune.... She publicly managed family affairs so that the house was held in honor, [and] her sons had a fortune of millions settled on them.[31]

29. Zielińska, "Mechanizm . . . ," p. 401.

30. Zielińska, "Mechanizm . . . ," p. 407.

31. Władysław Konopczyński, "Książe Udalryk Radziwiłł z dziejów naszej bezpartyjności" [Prince Udalryk Radziwiłł from the History of Our Non-Party Affiliation], *Mrok i świt* [The Darkness and the Dawn] (Warsaw: Gebethner and Wolff, 1911), pp. 140 and 148.

As Konopczyński notes, one of Barbara Radziwiłłowa's primary contributions was financial: she brought wealth into the family because ultimately she inherited most of her father's property and brought it into the Radziwiłł family.

> In 1736 after her brother Ignacy, Lithuanian Court Marshal, died without issue Barbara Radziwiłłowa inherited the large property of Berdyczów, including the city, [and] more than 20 villages valued at some tens of millions of Polish zloty.[32]

But her inheritance was only one of many means that Barbara Radziwiłłowa used to advance her family's fortunes. Another way in which she improved her family's financial position was by acting as a client of the Russian government.

After the death of August II in 1733, there was a disputed election in which two candidates, Stanislaw Leszczyński and August III, were elected to the throne of the Commonwealth. Russia and Austria backed August III, the Saxon candidate, and so did the Radziwiłłs. They were financially rewarded for their support during the course of the interregnum. The Radziwiłłs of Zdzięcioł had a relationship with the Russian court that was based on both direct and indirect contact. Mikołaj Faustyn Radziwiłł took his first bribe during the disputed election from the Russian ambassador, who gave it as an incentive for Radziwiłł to support August III.[33] This relationship continued through correspondence over the course of years.[34] Barbara Radziwiłłowa was eventually sent to St. Petersburg in April 1736 to make direct contact, by meeting with Empress Anna,[35] and the result of the meeting was that from the interregnum on, her family enjoyed an annual pension of 5,000 rubles from the Russian court.[36] Barbara Radziwiłłowa did not view this as unethical, feeling herself to be "walking in the path of right." She believed that her actions were in tune with the spirit of the time:

> It has been a politicized world for some time now, and Rome does not recognize saints as quickly as it did in the primitive church. . . . We must consider the times we are in, and always be an ethical and good patriot. . . . [But] ethical people are not accustomed to the diabolical school. But now [the diabolical school] is very fashionable and one must understand it, but not imitate it.[37]

In other words, she believed that one should not try to be a political saint while all around are sinning, especially when the system of elective monarchy encouraged

32. Anusik and Stroynowski, "Radziwiłłowie," p. 40.

33. Konopczyński, p. 138.

34. *Archiwum Główne Akt Dawnych w Warszawie - Archiwum Radziwiłłów* [Central Archives of Historical Records in Warsaw - Radziwiłł Archive, hereafter AR], dział [section, hereafter dz.] IV, teka [folder, hereafter t.] 47, koperty [envelopes, hereafter k.] 637, 638, 639.

35. AR, dz. IV, t. 47, k. 637, p. 53.

36. Konopczyński, p. 140.

37. Konopczyński, p. 140.

corruption. In this case, Barbara Radziwiłłowa was acting, like Marcin Matuszewicz, as a political agent for her family when she acted as an emissary to the Russian court. Such direct and indirect efforts as a client of the Russian court cultivated the family's patronage network, and they paid off in financial and political advancement.

Barbara Radziwiłłowa worked on behalf of the Radziwiłł family as its agent, distributing patronage money. The disputed election of 1735 offered clear proof of this phenomenon. The distribution of patronage money was an essential part of the political system, and in this case, one can see that the distribution of these monies was directed by one woman, Anna z Sanguszków Radziwiłłowa, and distributed by another, Barbara z Zawiszów Radziwiłłowa. In May 1735, Barbara Radziwiłłowa was sent to Wilno to lobby the bishop and to distribute Radziwiłł family monies. In a letter written to Anna Radziwiłłowa attesting to the fact that she had carried out her assignment, Barbara Radziwiłłowa wrote:

> It is a great pleasure to serve you with diligence. I have written to the Prince Bishop of Wilno [Michał Jan Zienkowicz], and was surprised that I had no difficulties with the Prince Canon. My Patroness' property—provisions and money—were given out. The distribution was registered in the notebook. Let these small services of mine be the proof that I am with great respect at your service. . . .[38]

Another way in which Barbara Radziwiłłowa worked for the political advancement of the Radziwiłłs of Zdzięcioł was by lobbying the Nieśwież branch of the family on behalf of her son's promotion to high office and to make the best marriages for her daughters. This sort of lobbying often bore fruit. The most fruitful period came during the interregnum of 1734–1735: the eldest Radziwiłł son, Udalryk, was appointed to two offices. He first received the office of Master of the Horse (July 1734), and then a colonel's post in the infantry (November 1735). Barbara Radziwiłłowa's father Krzysztof Zawisza, had been *starosta* [district supervisor] and mayor of Minsk, and when he died in 1738, her son Udalryk was granted these offices. The fact that he was granted the offices argues for the presence of a type of succession along the female line—her status as daughter of Krzysztof Zawisza was political collateral that could be passed on to her son.[39]

Barbara Radziwiłłowa acted both as a patroness and a client in this case: as a client working on her children's behalf, and as her children's patroness. She had the same dual role for her birth family, the Zawiszas.[40] She acted as a client for the Zawisza family, asking the Radziwiłłs to intercede on behalf of family members involved in court cases, pleading that they be "protected" or looked after. In writing

38. May 19, 1735, from Wilno, AR, dz. IV, t. 47, k. 637, p. 34.
39. Konopczyński, p. 139.
40. AR, dz. IV, t., 47, k. 637 and 638, pp. 31, 94 and 105.

to one of her nephews, probably Leon Michał Radziwiłł, she asked that "you might help my sister [Brygida Święcicka], true orphan, with a letter of recommendation."[41] She also acted again as a client by interceding to secure a leaseholding for her on Radziwiłł lands. Writing on behalf of her sister, she pleaded to continue the lease her sister held on Radziwiłł property:

> I am so bold as to ask your grace in great respect on behalf of my sister . . . for continued tenure at Samuełowa. That you would deign to do this for our House, would make us especially anxious to serve you.[42]

This plea was answered. Her sister did retain the lease to this Radziwiłł estate at Samuełowa, which was 8,650 square meters, with fertile land and broad meadows. It was an income-producing estate, since there was a watermill located on it, and she also benefited from the pub or taproom tax (*propinacja*) to be paid to the leaseholder. Throughout the mid-eighteenth century, the lease was held by the Święcicki Radziwiłł family, presumably after the death of Barbara Radziwiłłowa's relatives.[43] In this lease agreement, as in other cases, it is clear that Barbara Radziwiłłowa was the Zawisza family's patroness in the Radziwiłł family, helping to defend them against an arbitrary legal system.

There were some aspects of patron-client relations which demanded direct, personal contact that were central to the culture of the eighteenth century; lavish entertainment was one of them. Hospitality was an essential political skill. Weddings, funerals and other family gatherings, which to a modern observer might appear to be private functions, were large, splendid and public events with a political, not just a social, function. Having a good time in someone's house could bring the hostess lasting "friendship" and monetary benefits. After the death of her husband, Barbara Radziwiłłowa lost the income from his offices, and she might have lost the family's annual pension from Russia if not for the "intervention of Colonel Lieven, who together with Prince M. Wołkoński, had enjoyed themselves so much at (her home in) Zdzięcioł that it was decided to pay a pension to the widow."[44] When her eldest son Udalryk's performance in the *Sejm* was evaluated by the Russian court at the end of 1748, Count Aleksei Bestuzhev-Riumin, Grand Chancellor of Russia, recommended that Udalryk be given a raise in light of his mother's good reputation

---

41. October 16, 1734, AR, dz. IV, t. 47, k. 637, p. 31.

42. March 12, 1754, AR, dz. IV, t. 47, k. 640, p. 349.

43. *Słownik geograficzny Królestwa Polskiego i innych krajów słowiańskich* [Geographic Dictionary of the Kingdom of Poland and Other Slavic Countries], (Warsaw: Nakładem Filipa Sulimirskiego i Władysława Walewskiego, druk. "Wieku," 1880), vol. 10, p. 259.

44. Ewa Szklarska, "Mikołaj Faustyn Radziwiłł," *Polski Slownik Biograficzny* [Polish Biographical Dictionary, hereafter PSB], Emanuel Rostworoski, editor, (Wrocław: Ossolineum, 1987), vol. 32, no. 125, p. 363.

and influence in the Voivodeship of Nowogródek[45] This is a case where the fact that Barbara Radziwiłłowa made a good impression and was known for her largesse, a private attribute to the modern observer, had public repercussions in political practice. Seemingly private attributes like hospitality were essential in the public sphere and in the political life of the Commonwealth.

Another case of mixing the public and the private was the *Sejmik* itself. The *Sejmik* was an opportunity to take part not only in the public life, but in the social life of the nobility. *Sejmiki* in the Grand Duchy of Lithuania were often held in churches, and diary accounts and paintings show crowds of noblemen and women socializing and conferring at them.[46] In the conduct of the political process, there was no separation between secular and religious space and no separation by gender or wealth.

The system of patronage also created alternate sources of political and cultural power in the eighteenth-century Commonwealth. The placement of children in magnate residences was an important element in creating regional courts that served as centers of cultural and political authority outside of Warsaw or Dresden. Elite parents placed their children in the homes of wealthy or better-connected friends and relatives. This was not unlike the practice in other states of early modern Europe. Barbara Harris discussed this practice in Tudor England, pointing out that noble girls customarily entered the service of high-ranking noblewomen or paid them extended visits.[47] In this way women became patrons, helping girls to find husbands and introducing them at court. The situation was similar in the Commonwealth, except that there was one important difference: while English noblewomen might be educated at a friend's court, in the Commonwealth one would generally be educated or serve in the home of a powerful relative.

Among the Radziwiłłs of Zdzięcioł, several of the children of the family served in the homes of the wealthier and more powerful Nieśwież branch. Of the eight sons, four of whom survived, the eldest, Udalryk, studied at the Piarist school in Warsaw and spent a great deal of time at the home of Michał Kazimierz "Rybeńko" Radziwiłł.[48] The career of the second son, Jerzy, began when he followed exactly the same course: attending the Piarist school in Warsaw and living at Nieśwież with Michał Kazimierz "Rybeńko" Radziwiłł.[49] Albrycht, the third son, also studied at

45. Konopczyński, p. 145.

46. Wojciech Kriegseisen, *Sejmiki Rzeczypospolitej szlacheckiej w XVII i XVIII wieku* [Dietines of the Noble Republic in the Seventeenth and Eighteenth Centuries] (Warsaw: Wydawnictwo Sejmowe, 1991), pp. 173 and 223.

47. Barbara J. Harris, "Women and Politics in Early Tudor England," *The Historical Journal*, vol. 33, no. 2 (1990), p. 262.

48. Maciej Mycielski, "Udalryk Krzysztof Radziwiłł," PSB, vol. 32, no. 125, p. 373.

49. Hanna Dymnicka-Wołoszyńska, "Jerzy Radziwiłł," PSB, vol. 32, no. 125, p. 237.

the Piarist school in Warsaw and was named Voivode of Rzeczyca. He held this post throughout his life. In it he was occupied with the affairs of Hieronim Florian Radziwiłł, Rybeńko's brother.[50] Stanisław, the fourth and youngest son, studied at the Jesuit college in Nieśwież, and later entered the army.[51] Thus all or the surviving sons in this branch of the family served at the court of the more powerful Nieśwież branch.

Of seven daughters, four of whom survived, two married and two entered the convent at age 17 and 18. Teresa Barbara left home to live at the Nieśwież branch's court in Biała. The circumstances of her stay there are unknown, except for the fact that she was abruptly and unexpectedly dismissed from service, and her mother had to arrange for her travel home.[52] The other children's upbringing was accomplished uneventfully. The family correspondence is full of requests that a son or daughter be released from service and allowed to return home. These contacts underline the fact that service at a relative's court was an initiation into noble life and a chance to make contacts at the residence of the wealthier and more influential branch of the family.

One of the prerequisites of Mączak's model of patron-client relations is that both parties had to be adults. Women in many parts of early modem Europe, especially English women living under the common law, were not legal adults. Under the common law, women were legally incapacitated, having the same status as minor children, their legal personality "covered" by their fathers as children and their husbands as wives. It is difficult to make blanket statements regarding women's legal position in the Commonwealth, as there were a number of legal systems operating at once, but one can state that there was no such "covering" in Polish Land Law, in the Magdeburg Law for some cities, or in the three Lithuanian statutes which applied in the Grand Duchy of Lithuania. There are features in the Lithuanian Statute which show us that women were regarded as legal adults. The clause addressing people who were regarded as incapable of drawing up a will delineates those who were legally incapacitated:

> First, minor children; monks in a monastic order who have taken vows; sons dependent upon their father, . . . ; violent madmen, heretics, slaves, [and] those who have gone out of their minds. However, when they become themselves [again, they] have the right to draw up their wills.[53]

---

50. Edward Kotłubaj, *Galerja Nieświeżska: Portretów Radziwiłłowskich* [The Nieśwież Gallery of Radziwiłł Portraits] (Wilno: 1857), p. 47.

51. Wacław Szczygielski, "Stanisław Radziwiłł," PSB, vol. 32, no. 125, p. 370.

52. July 14, 1739, AR, dz. IV, k. 638, pp. 114–115.

53. Karl von Loewe, editor and translator, *The Lithuanian Statute of 1529* (Leiden: E. J. Brill, 1976), p. 54.

One could argue that just because women are not mentioned, this does not necessarily mean that they are not included. But in an adjoining article it defines those people who are not allowed to witness wills as "those who themselves are not fit to compile wills, and also women, executors, or guardians of that will."[54] Women were fit to compile wills, and therefore considered legal adults, capable of entering into a patron-client relationship.

Not only were women considered legally capable, but evidence preserved in correspondence shows that a married couple presented itself as a unit headed jointly by husband and wife. In Mikołaj Faustyn Radziwiłł's existing correspondence of 560 letters preserved at the Central Archive of Historical Documents in Warsaw [*Archiwum Główne Akt Dawnych* - AGAD], 36 were letters sent jointly with his wife. Such joint letters appear throughout the course of their marriage, and they are, for the most part, not letters of greeting but reports on the course of the *Sejmiki*, and general news of a political nature.[55] This is not an exceptional case. Similar joint letters can be found in the correspondence of Anna z Sanguszków Radziwiłłowa and Karol Stanisław Radziwiłł. The sending of joint letters shows that a couple presented itself as a unit in formal correspondence, so it indicates that they presented themselves as a unit in society.

By examining one significant event in the history of the Radziwiłłs of Zdzięcioł, one can draw conclusions about the character of family alliances. In 1755 the Voivode of Nowogródek's office was vacant, since Jerzy Radziwiłł had died. This office had been in the Radziwiłł family for 45 years, and one would have expected it to go to the eldest son among the Radziwiłłs of Zdzięcioł. But it did not go to him. The office was bought by Józef Jabłonowski for the price of 350,000 złotys.[56] At first this appears to be proof of the waning influence of Barbara Radziwiłłowa, since she apparently could not secure the office for her son, and also as a setback for the Radziwiłłs. But by 1755, Barbara Radziwiłłowa was no longer her son's patroness. She judged Udalryk unworthy of her backing because he was disobedient, and had strayed too far from the family line. In 1769, she was moved to present a public manifesto, denouncing him and his actions.[57] It was not a setback for the Radziwiłłs either, because Jabłonowski was married to Karolina Teresa Radziwiłłowa of the Nieśwież branch, so the office was connected to the family through this in-law relationship. Thanks to *koligacja*, or in-law connections, the office remained in the family. In 1762, when speaking about Udalryk and his ostracism from the family,

54. Von Loewe, p. 55.

55. AR, dz. IV, t. 37, k. 529–537.

56. Konopczyński, p. 153.

57. Biblioteka Narodowa [National Library] (Warsaw), Biblioteka Ordynacji Zamojskiej [Zamojski Entail Library], sygn. 32918, pp. 197–198.

Karol Radziwiłł, "Panie Kochanku," said that Udalryk had "released himself to the fate of justice [by] wandering so far from the family. . . ."[58] This is an example of how the strains of an individual's independence or unorthodox thinking could put him out of the family fold when it came to protection and promotion. Blood was not thicker than water. Udalryk had made life too difficult for his mother and the rest of the family, so he was left to the harsh justice of the political system toward those who had no protection.

In the case of the Radziwiłł family, the most important factor in constructing clientage networks was family ties, and kinship was the most significant tie linking individuals in society. Kinship ties could also have about them the character of patron-client relationships, with the less wealthy, less powerful branches of a family acting as the clients of the stronger branch. A more appropriate way in which to understand the structure of the elite of the Commonwealth is the way in which they understood themselves: not as individuals but as family members linked by bonds of blood as well as self-interest or monetary gain. If the "informal system of authority" was not clientage based upon financial interest but authority based upon traditional family ties, with the family as the central structure of society, then the role of women becomes more central than it would be within a system in which society was linked mainly by an "informal federation of patrons."

The final question that must be answered in this context is whether Barbara Radziwiłłowa's direct and indirect contacts were effective. Did this woman's political activity change her family's political course or the political course of the Commonwealth? Were her letters of promotion and intercession influential or did they fall upon deaf ears? The first point arguing for the significance of her letters of petition, supplication, and demand is their very existence. The archivists at Nieśwież must have kept them for a reason. The almost 600 letters kept in the main family archive would not have been preserved if they were not felt to be of importance.

There are a few situations in which it can be proven decisively that a woman's actions or influence decisively affected political history, but one example can be taken from the pages of Marcin Matuszewicz's memoirs. Matuszewicz writes that the Radziwiłł princesses, Anna z Sanguszków Radziwiłłowa and Barbara z Zawiszów Radziwiłłowa, were influential in inspiring discontent against the royal election of Stanisław Leszczyński of 1733 and turning the tide against him. They were motivated by ties of family loyalty, and worked in the interest of *protekcja:* protecting the honor of the family and the interests of a son. Matuszewicz described how the discontent against Leszczyński began at the Radziwiłł stronghold of Nowogródek when debate

58. Konopczyński, p. 183.

began to tum against Michał Kazimierz "Rybeńko" Radziwiłł. His mother, Anna z Sanguszków Radziwiłłowa,

> . . . as a lady of proud humor, as a mother loving her son, was incensed. So much so that through her great wealth, she had numerous friends to build up significant animosity toward the pro-Stanisław party. She had her own brother Prince Sanguszko, later Marshal of the Grand Duchy of Lithuania, her son-in-law Prince [Michał Serwacy] Korybut Wiśniowiecki, Chancellor and Deputy Hetman of the Lithuanian army. Besides this, there was Mikołaj Radziwiłł, Voivode of Nowogródek, with his wife Barbara Zawiszanka, daughter of the Voivode of Minsk, a lady of great intelligence and resourcefulness, equally disconcerted with this Sejm. . . .[59]

Matuszewicz interpreted that these were the conditions which created the opposition to King Stanisław Leszczyński's election, and caused the union of the pro-Saxon party to come about. So, to Matuszewicz, the Radziwiłł women's political activity was one of the causes of the disputed election of 1733. He attributed the success of Anna Radziwiłłowa and Barbara Radziwiłłowa in influencing the course of events to their wealth and to their connections with powerful men, both their numerous friends and their brothers and husbands, who could work directly as political officeholders. Ultimately, though, Matuszewicz writes that the disputed election would not have taken place without the bribes given by foreign patrons and their agents in the Commonwealth and the pressure of potential foreign occupation.

> The aversion or disgust toward King Stanisław began to grow at the *sejmik* of Nowogródek through the fomenting of the Princess [Anna Radziwiłłowa] herself, (and the) sister of the Prince Master of the Hunt [Tekla Radziwiłłówna, wife of Michał Korybut Wiśniowiecki]. Prince Wiśniowiecki won on the election field. . . . It was said that Saxon and Muscovite money was flying about Warsaw, and what's more, that they were rushing in from Moscow. . . .[60]

Another example proving that women could exercise influence as political patrons has to do not with national politics but with the day-to-day politics of appointments to the Tribunal. It shows that Barbara Radziwiłłowa could exercise her political influence to get her chosen candidate a judicial appointment. In December of 1747, judicial appointments were being made by the Hetman of Lithuania, Michał Kazimierz "Rybeńko" Radziwiłł. At the last moment, "Rybeńko" changed his mind regarding the appointment of the Scribe of the Castle Court in the district of Rus. Instead of appointing Wiktor Chełchowski, as he had planned, he appointed the Vice-Viovode of Nowogródek, Antoni Rdułtowski, who was Barbara Radziwiłłowa's candidate for the position.[61]

---

59. Matuszewicz, *Pamiętniki,* vol. 1, p. 54.

60. Matuszewicz, *Pamiętniki* . . . , p. 56.

61. Zofia Zielińska, *Walka "Familii" o reformę Rzeczypospolitej 1743–1752* [Struggle of The Family for Reform of the Commonwealth 1743–1752] (Warsaw: PWN, 1983), p. 229.

Barbara Radziwiłłowa fit most if not all of the criteria that Mączak outlined for participating in patron-client relationships: she acted as a political agent and emissary, she acted as a lobbyist and protector on behalf of her family and others, and the decentralization of the Commonwealth allowed her to play a central role in the magnate court providing the hospitality and education so significant in sustaining the status of magnate families. Barbara Radziwiłłowa and other women of the Commonwealth played a role in the activities connected with forming, maintaining and exploiting patronage networks.

As many European nations moved toward absolutism and centralization, the Commonwealth of Poland-Lithuania grew more decentralized. Noble families, with their private armies and wealth, influenced the politics of the state through a system based on family alliances. Scholars have identified and studied political factions, but they have not considered the role that women played in family politics, thereby influencing society as a whole. This article has examined the Radziwiłł family of Zdzięcioł, and the matriarch of that family, Barbara z Zawiszów Radziwiłłowa. By studying the relationship of the less powerful Zdzięcioł branch with the more powerful Nieśwież branch of the Radziwiłł family, one can trace the inner workings of family politics. Only by understanding the dynamics of family politics, and the place of women within them, can one come to a full understanding of the social and political history of the Polish-Lithuanian Commonwealth during the eighteenth century.

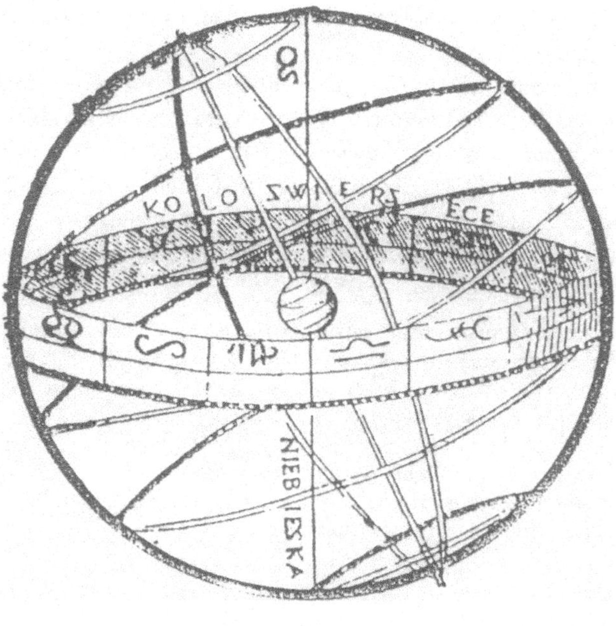

Power in Powerlessness

The Strange Journey and Career of Regina Salomea Pilsztynowa

Władysław Roczniak

"My parents married me at a young age to doctor Jacob Halpir, who took me that very year from the Nowogródek Voivodeship in Lithuania to Istanbul, where we moved among fine people, and because my husband was a very capable medical doctor, and by God's grace, we attained some money."[1] So begins the richly detailed and so far virtually unknown memoir of Regina Salomea Pilsztynowa, a Polish female physician whose life spans eighteenth century Eastern and Southern Europe from the Ottoman Empire and the Balkans to Poland and Russia.[2] The account of her travels and adventures offers us an intimate and exciting glimpse of a period and a society that is at once distant, and yet still resonates to our contemporary experiences.

A stranger in a foreign land, a female Catholic Pole in a Muslim male-dominated society, Salomea managed to successfully carve out for herself a viable niche, an early "room of her own." Contrary to every modern expectation, she became a highly sought-after and well-respected practitioner of the medical arts, especially ophthalmology and, as a result, became the official court physician to Turkish pashas and Hungarian princes, and indeed, even to the Sultan Mustafa III (1757–1773) himself.

---

1. Regina Salomea z Rusieckich Pilsztynowa, *Proceder podróży i życia mego Awantur [An Account of My Journeys and Life s Adventures]*, ed. Roman Pollak (Krakow: Wydawnictwo Literackie, 1957), p. 37. *W młodym wieku moim wydali mnie rodzice moje . . . za mąż z Litwy, województwa nowogrodzkiego, za doktora Jakuba Halpira, z którym to doktorem tegoi roku pojechalam do Stambułu a zaraz wzięci my byli pomiędzy godnymi ludźmi, ponieważ że był ekstra dobrym medycyny doktorem i Pan Bóg nam pobłogosławił.*

2. Regina Salomea was born in 1718. Her death date, which (obviously) occurred after she wrote her memoirs in 1760, is still a matter of speculation.

From *The Polish Review*, vol. 53, no. 1 (2008), pp. 25–51.

Called "Poland's first female doctor" by the very few historians who know of her, her story offers us a window on eighteenth-century social, professional, and gender interaction between Christians, Jews, and Muslims. It is also a richly woven tapestry of everyday life, in which are recorded fascinating vignettes of love, travel, romance, popular superstitions, war, black magic, serial killers, and bandits—and that's only in the very first chapter alone. Her memoir forms an invaluable repository of personal accounts, as well as historical, ethnographic, religious, and geographical anecdotes about Southern- and Eastern-European affairs—areas that are poorly documented in Anglophone memoir literature.[3]

As a Christian woman in a male-dominated Muslim society, and as a female doctor in a male-dominated medical profession, by all standards Pilsztynowa should have remained entirely marginalized, powerless, and helpless, at the mercy of her environment. That she refused such victimization, but rather turned her apparent disadvantages to her advantage—a power in powerlessness so to speak—forms the core of her account. How she managed to use the curious novelty of her status as a Christian female physician to become socially and professionally successful in what one assumes was an inhospitable environment reflects her indefatigable resourcefulness. Her excuses that "since I was a Pole and a Christian," and "that I was Polish, and a visitor in his country," apparently allowed her to go and do what was impossible for Turkish ladies of even much higher standing. Indeed, her ability to successfully overcome and subvert the gender and social bonds of her age allowed this supremely self-confident and complicated woman to interact with some of the great historical actors of the time period, such as Frederick the Great and the Empresses Anna and Elizabeth of Russia.

The original manuscript of 388 pen-and-pencil written pages of Pilsztynowa's memoir is held in the Czartoryski Museum archives in Kraków, Poland, as manuscript no. 1482. It is well-preserved, with Turkish-style ornamentations.[4] The manuscript itself is written in an unschooled fashion (perhaps "self-taught" would be a better way of expressing it); in eighteenth-century Cosmopolitan Polish, a regionally-flavored dialect (in this case that of the Eastern Polish frontier) replete with phrases borrowed from a multitude of other tongues, a few from Latin and German, but especially Russian and Turkish.

---

3. The correspondence of Lady Montague might be the most famous female-written English language account of events in the Ottoman Empire in the first half of the eighteenth century. See: *Letters of Lady Mary Wortley Montague, written during her travels in Europe, Asia, and Africa, to which are added poems by the same author* (Bourdeaux: J. Pinard, 1805).

4. The edition cited throughout is Regina Salomea z Rusieckich Pilsztynowa, *Proceder podróży i życia mego Awantur* [*An Account of My Journeys and Life's Adventures*], ed. Roman Pollak (Kraków: Wydawnictwo Literackie, 1957). Cf. p. 25.

Pilsztynowa, as her memoir clearly suggests, did not come close to being a great writer, or even a good writer. From the perspective of sentence structure and grammar, her writings are a veritable nightmare for her editors and now for her translators as well. Very often her sentences stretch into near-infinity, a single one canvassing an entire paragraph, or lapse into arduous repetitions, as when she begins all her sentences in a given paragraph with the Polish phrase *i tak* [and so . . .]. It should be remembered, however, that she was writing her memoirs while living for many years in the Ottoman Empire, in a language she probably no longer spoke every day. Also, her style is generally comparable to that of other memoirs written during the same time period; moreover, any of her failings as a writer do not in any way detract from the importance of her writing. As such, her work can stand proudly among the voluminous production of Old Polish memoir literature, among such female luminaries as, for instance, Anna Stanisławska.[5]

It is therefore unfortunate that a manuscript of such great significance to, for instance, gender or East- and Southeast-European studies, has so far seen very little interest and analysis in English-language academic circles. Some conference papers by Prof. Lynn Lubamersky of Boise State University, and a specialist article in the history of ophthalmology by Dr. Janina Konczacki of the Mount Saint Vincent University of Halifax, are seemingly all that exist on the current English-language scene.[6] Doubtless the difficulties presented by eighteenth-century Cosmopolitan Polish explain the dearth of present day scholarship. An English translation of the manuscript would therefore allow scholars access to this rich and fascinating source of ethnographic, gender study, and interfaith issues.

Polish historians, linguistically better equipped than their English-speaking counterparts, could also be faulted for ignoring such a rich source of historic material. Although her work was "discovered" in the last decade of the nineteenth century by L. Glatman, and later brought to light by Roman Pollak in the 1957 edited version of her entire manuscript (which so far remains the only full version of her work in any language), unfortunately, interest in her fascinating story has remained spotty at best. A mention of her name in a French compilation on female physicians hardly comprises a corpus of work which is obviously due this fascinating and resourceful figure.[7]

5. In 1685, Anna Stanisławska wrote one of the first Polish female memoirs: a six thousand-verse manuscript entitled *Transakcyja albo opisanie całego życia jednej sieroty* [*Transaction or the Description of the Life of One Poor Orphan*].

6. Janina Konczacki, "Regina Salomea Pilsztynowa, Ophthalmologist in 18th-Century Poland," *Survey of Ophthalmology* 47:2 (2002): 189–95; Lynn Lubamersky, "The Life of Regina Salomea Pilsztynowa: a Feminist Analysis," a paper presented at The International Conference on Polish Literary and Cultural Studies, 2006, Toronto, Canada.

7. Such works as, for instance, Mélina Lipinska, *Les femmes et le progrès des sciences médicales* [*Women and the Progress of Medical Science*] (Paris: Masson, 1930).

Pilsztynowa's writings were meant to serve the dual purpose of entertainment and personal *apologia*. As she stated numerous times, her book was meant *Dla rozrywki ludzkiej, Dla dobrych ludzi rozrywki* [for /good/ people's entertainment],[8] as well as, and more importantly, to answer the charge *że ja, będąc urodzoną, Polką, mając męża i dzieci w Polsce i wszystkie te moje doczesne pociechy opuściłam, a sama jedna w cudzy kraj bez wszelkiej pomocy i pociechy puścilam się żyć i w Bogu umrzeć w tym kraju* [that I, having been born Polish, with my husband and children and all my earthly joys in Poland, would leave them all, and go to live and die in God all alone in a foreign country without any help or hope].[9] She explained her final decision to emigrate permanently in a particularly moving paragraph towards the end of her work:

> Teraz podaję to zebranie moich awantur do uwagi ludzkiej. Kto je czytać będzie, niech uważa, ze w wielu już byłam niebezpieczeństwach życia i wiele razy fortuna mnie bogaciła i nazbyt zubożywala. Niech zrozumie, czy miałam ja co dobrego od mężów i od utrapionego kawalera, od dzieci i sług. I czy mam się po co do Polski wracać w moim teraźniejszym wieku rachując w tym roku 1760 lat z łaski Bożej czterdzieści i dwa? Chyba na to, żeby mnie znowu z ostatniego, uchowaj Boże, obdarli.[10]

> [Now I bring this collection of my adventures to people's attention. Whoever will read them, let them know that I have already passed through many of life's dangers and many times did fortune enrich me, only to take everything away shortly thereafter. Let them think about whether I received anything good from my husbands and from that troublesome suitor, from my children or my servants. And is there anything that I should return to Poland for, in this year of 1760, at my current God-given age of forty-two? If I did, maybe they would only take everything away from me once again, which God forbid].

Pilsztynowa's memoir, if substantially true, takes us on an unprecedented odyssey stretching through a vast quadrilateral of lands bordered by, beginning in the North, St. Petersburg, then Kiev in the East, Istanbul and Sofia in the South, and Wrocław in the West. Within this geographical setting, her life, both professional and personal, underwent a succession of triumphs and defeats, dreams realized and hopes broken—a veritable tapestry of events and drama that comprise what is, in effect, a very unusual career for a young woman from a minor noble family. Her story began in Lithuania when, at the age fourteen, she was given in marriage by her parents to a Lutheran physician, Jacob Halpir. He immediately took her to Istanbul where he established a lucrative medical practice in which, apparently, his young wife took a more than casual interest. This first part of her story paints Istanbul as a

8. Pilsztynowa, pp. 40, 243.
9. Pilsztynowa, p. 35.
10. Pilsztynowa, p. 239.

fascinating, lively, and cosmopolitan city where, however, business and professional opportunities come attached with their corresponding inherent dangers, especially for the practitioners of medicine. In this case, her nemesis revealed himself as a certain Dr. Fonseca, a Jewish physician; jealous (she claimed) of her success, and someone who poisoned one of her husband's patients.[11] Other doctors, both Muslim and Jewish, stood in her way as well—some forbade her to practice, on account of her gender—others used what she perceived as dark magic to physically attack her. It is during one such supposedly occult-induced sickness that her husband abandoned her and moved out, leaving her all alone in her newly-adopted city. What is interesting in this part of her account is that behind the veneer of her naiveté, her superstitions, and her ramblings about "godless" Jews, there hides a description of a cut-throat, dog-eat-dog, take-no-prisoners competition fought over patients by a virtual army of Istanbul's doctors. Her own more and more successful entry into the male-dominated medical scene, marked by a constant increase in the number of patients, especially female patients, whom she treated, must have affected the already existing precarious balance of doctor supply and demand.

In the matter of faith and vocation, therefore, her manuscript often describes the thick webs of identity that bound the professional interactions of Istanbul's leading medical practitioners. As a Christian, she professionally interacted with the dominant players in the mid-eighteenth century Istanbul medical establishment—Muslim and Jewish doctors.[12] Although she often betrayed a marked preference for Muslims over Jews, her memoirs also reveal amicable cooperation and professional respect as well as vocational jealousy, avarice, and competition over clients. On the one hand, accusations of malpractice, directed at her and her husband, threatened both their lives, while she was more than willing to show her satisfaction that "the Jew almost went mad!" when she caused her enemy, Doctor Fonseca, whom she outwitted, to lose to her his house and pharmacy. On the other hand, stories of cooperation among doctors give strong hints as to the ways medicinal knowledge spread and proliferated. Pilsztynowa herself learned all she knew about medicine from friendly physicians, like a certain Turk from Babylon, or a Maltese Italian, and also from her very husband, Jacob Halpir.

Following her husband's departure, Pilsztynowa took their infant daughter and traveled throughout the Balkans, encountering new friends and foes, but always surviving through the medical knowledge at her disposal. It is at this time that she

11. Daniel de Fonseca (1672–c. 1740) was a well-known Jewish physician, writer, and philosopher. Of Portuguese extraction, he became first the physician to the French Embassy in Istanbul, then, till 1730, to the Sultan himself. Fred Skolnik and Michael Berenbaum eds., *Encyclopedia Judaica,* Second Edition, Volume 7 (New York: Thompson/Gale, 2007), p. 115.

12. Jewish doctors were a staple in Istanbul. Many, like Dr. Fonseca at one point, bore the title of Court Physicians.

fell into the hands of bandits, had to escape the untoward advances of a powerful Hungarian prince, and eventually participated in the burgeoning slave trade by purchasing Austrian prisoners of war, one of them, a certain ensign Pilsztyn (Pilstein in German) who shortly thereafter became her second husband (Dr. Halpir having previously passed away).

Pilsztynowa soon left the Ottoman Empire, however, and traveled to St. Petersburg by way of Poland to recover some Turkish prisoners-of-war in Russian hands. The road was dangerous, and near Revel she had to fight off another attack on her person. Once in St. Petersburg she moved among the high echelons of society, met Tsaritsa Anna, as well as the future Empress Elizabeth, and remained at the Imperial Court for several months. Very interested in court rumors, she reported on the goings-on of the high Russian aristocracy, including an account of the famous "Ice Wedding" of Prince Golitsin and his chosen bride, a common cleaning woman.[13] Back in Poland, her marriage to Ensign Pilsztyn, whom she managed to place in the service of Prince Radziwiłł, came painfully undone. Although she bore him two sons, not only did her husband cheat on her, but he also tried to poison her, and although she survived, she tells us that *mnie zęby powypadały, włosy oblazły, paznokcie schropowaciały, nawet wszystka skóra ze mnie się złupiła* [my teeth fell out, I lost my hair, my fingernails roughened, and even my entire skin became flayed].[14]

Though surely the damage must not have been as severe as she described, the shock of her loved one turning on her in such a fashion was considerable indeed, especially when, after a short reconciliation, Mr. Pilsztyn suggested that, in order for her to leave the troubles of this world behind, next time *she* should poison *herself.* After this unhappy event she separated from her husband, though she refused to divorce him, and traveled again, stopping in Wrocław to meet King Frederick II the Great.

When she returned to Poland she became a victim of what she termed "Golden Polish Liberty" as certain noblemen, seeing her wealth, and untouchable by law or justice, turned on her and deprived her of her hard earned gains.[15] Her bad experiences in Poland did much to affect her later decision to leave her homeland for good and settle permanently in the Ottoman Empire. She was particularly disappointed

---

13. Pilsztynowa, pp. 113–114. When Empress Anna heard that Prince Golitsin was set on marrying a commoner she consented to the wedding provided that the new couple spend their wedding night in an intricately carved Ice Palace where all the furniture, even the wedding bed, was made of ice.

14. Pilsztynowa, p. 172.

15. Pilsztynowa, pp. 186, 193. *Ach mój Boże, jak mnie ten świat ucisnął był i złota wolność polska!* [Oh Dear God, how this world and this Golden Polish Liberty weighs heavily upon me]. General Bekierski, the commander of the fortress of Kamieniec Podolski deprived her of her fortune and plotted to deprive her of her liberty and even life.

in the way she was treated there, a topic that she returns to again and again in the pages of her memoirs:

> Ale ja nic nigdy nie mogłam wskórać u naszych panów polskich, z czegom miała wielki smutek przypominając sobie, że miałam w cudzych krajach estymację korzyść, i pomoc od cesarzów i innych godnych osób, a tu jestem w swoim kraju i mówię Panem Jezusem, że „przyszedłem do swoich, a swoi mnie nie poznali," i tak wcale zostałam opuszczona i wiele ekspensu podjęłam, bom w Polsce zawsze straciła to, co w cudzych krajach profitowałam.[16]
>
> [But I could never manage anything with our Polish lords, which disappointed me greatly when I remembered that, in foreign lands, I was held in esteem and had every advantage and support from emperors and other worthy individuals, while here, in my own country I could exclaim with Jesus, "I came among my own people, and they did not recognize me," and I was totally abandoned and suffered great expense, because in Poland I always lost that which I had earned in foreign nations].

It was also in Poland that she encountered a certain *amorat, kawaler,* or lover, a very false and irresolute nobleman, seven years her junior, who proceeded to take absolute advantage of her good will and interest towards him. Her involvement with this man, whom she discreetly identifies only by the acronym J.M.C.Z., led to many unfortunate incidents that eventually included the death of one of her sons and her estrangement from the other.[17] It is interesting to note that the passages dealing with this drunkard[18] and dissolute "suitor" show Pilsztynowa in a very different light from her previous escapades. Here her intelligence, energy, and cunning are nowhere to be seen, as she describes herself totally smitten and lost in his presence, naively open to all sorts of lies and deceits.

Finally despairing, Pilsztynowa left again for Istanbul, to gain fame and fortune as the court physician to the Sultan's harem. What happened to her after 1760, after she wrote her memoir, remains at this moment unclear. Further work in the archives, especially Turkish ones, will, for certain, shed more light on the life and role of this fascinating eighteenth century woman.

Salomea's personality and character is as involved as the account of her life and travels. Even her own name becomes problematic in light of her often unclear

---

16. Pilsztynowa, pp. 215–216.

17. Pilsztynowa, p. 240. She blames her *kawaler,* for taking the life of one of her sons and the fortune of the other. *Jednemu synowi wziął życie przez jego złe sumienie i niedoglądanie tegoż, drugiemu fortunę, albowiem co tylko zostawiłam z depozytu, to wszystko do wielowładnych rąk swoich przez szalbierstwo jak magnes przyciągnął. . .* [Through his unconscionable behavior and lack of care he took the life of one son, and the fortune of the other, because whatever I left on deposit, through deceit like a magnet he attracted into his manipulative hands].

18. Pilsztynowa, p. 166. Salomea hated drunkenness. *Nad wszystkie złe uczynki pijaństwo najgorsze* [Of all evil deeds drunkenness is the worst].

writing; after all, what should this woman be called? In her work she persistently called herself Salomea rather than Regina.[19] That is also how her name appears on the title page of her manuscript, though under her dedication to Countess Potocka, she signs her name in reverse, with Regina taking precedence. Her surname creates an even greater difficulty. The title page bears the inscription de Pilsztyn (Pilstein), the name of her second husband, but once again the dedication introduces a wholly different name, that of Makowska. Possibly, Salomea got married for a third time to a certain (as yet unknown) Mr. Makowski. Pollak's suggestions that this "Makowski" might have been her *amoral* is a distinctive possibility, if we bear in mind that the acronym she used for him—J.M.C.Z.—does contain the letter "M," although such a supposition must be researched further before anything more certain might be alleged. Again, Pollak's proposal that, in view of Salomea's confusing multiple marriages and her functional and financial independence she should be known to posterity by her maiden name of Rusiecka, should bear some consideration. However, her constant use of Pilsztyn (a possible reason for which appears below), and the opinion of Prof. Lynn Lubamersky, that Polish-Lithuanian Commonwealth women of noble upbringing would never identify themselves by their maiden name, alone stands against it.[20]

A particular and disturbing factor of her character involves her persistent anti-Semitism, an aspect of her persona evident throughout her memoirs. Except for a few instances of amicable dealings that included her relationship with one of her servants and a Jewish patient of hers who might have (so she hoped) expressed an interest in converting, all her other professional and social relations with members of the Jewish faith seemed to have been of an extremely negative nature. Her brand of anti-Semitism appears to be of two types: the religiously-based intolerance so prevalent in Christians of her time (here the Jews are seen as God-killers and stubborn in their religious convictions); and a brand of distaste born out of professional interaction and jealousy. All the named Jewish members of her profession who appear in her writings, especially in chapter one, such as Drs. Ebeulu, Samson, and especially Dr. Fonseca, are treated as personal banes and enemies. It is Dr. Fonseca, for instance, whom she accuses of poisoning her husband's patient, while it is Dr. Samson who, *nie wiedząc, co mnie miał czynić z złości zdrowiu memu i fortunie mojej . . .* [not knowing in his anger what to do about my health and my fortune], used black magic to take away her reason.[21] Here professional competition and jealousy stroke already developed religious prejudices and superstitions.

19. Pilsztynowa, p. 94. When asked her name by the Russian Empress Anna, she unequivocally answered "Salomea."

20. Pilsztynowa, p. 24. The present author discussed this issue with Professor Lubamersky at the 2007 Annual PIASA Conference in Washington, DC.

21. Pilsztynowa, p. 50.

Again, her interaction with Muslims seems much more amicable than her relations with Jews. Although the Turkish system of government, and especially its legal code, bore heavily on her at times—she was once accused of being a spy and was sentenced to die, and there were many Turks (especially the families of some of her or her husband's patients) who tried to take advantage of her—her writings in general betray no deep-seated animosity towards them. How could there be if she eventually decided to settle in the Ottoman Empire for good, finding it the most amiable and pleasant of all the places she visited? It was only twice that she morally censured a Turkish official in her writing. The first one was the Grand Vizier Ismail who had her husband arrested, and the second was a certain Basha whom she worked for, who, on the Sultan's orders, conducted a massacre of Christians. Her professional relations with Turkish doctors also appear better than those with the Jewish physicians, though here too there was competition and jealousy. Hakim Basha, the Sultan's chief physician, went from an enemy to a friend, and an ally in her struggle against Dr. Fonseca, while other Muslim doctors and practitioners shared their medical knowledge with her.

Salomea described her final confrontation with Hakim Basha in a dramatic paragraph. Called in front of the Sultan's chief physician she came to answer the charges that, though forbidden to do so, she still practiced medicine on male patients:

> I tak imć pan Hekim Basha (byl to człek stary, ale urodziwy, Francuz, z jakiejś okazji Turczynem został i zaraz wielkim doktorem cesarskim) i ten do mnie tak mówił: "Widzę, żeś młoda białogłowa, a doktorstwa i mężczyźnie trzeba się długo uczyć. A kiedyś się tego doskonałego doktorstwa nauczyła?" Dałam rację: "Z pomocy P. Boga i tego się tylko podejmuję, co umiem." Mówił mnie: "A coś osobliwego umiesz?" Mówiłam: "Za pomocą P. Boga choćby kto dwadzieścia lat nie widział na oczy, to go doskonale wykuruję." Mówił starszy doktor: "Bardzo dobrze. Jest tu w moim domu stara białogłowa, mamka syna mego, ślepa od siedmiu lat. Jeśli ją wykurujesz to już będę wierzył i sam cię będę rekomendował największym panom stambulskim." I tak mnie zaprowadził do tego pokoju, gdzie była ta ślepa białogłowa i podjęłam się wykurować, i tak mnie P. Bóg dopomógł, żem ją wykurowała doskonale i dobrze we dni czterdzieści.[22]

> [And Hakim Basha (who was an old, but a good-looking Frenchman who somehow became a Turk and a great doctor to the Sultan) addressed me in such a way: "It takes a long time for a man to learn how to be a doctor. You, I see, are a young woman. When had you time to learn your excellent craft?" "With God's help I only do that which I know," I explained. "And what is it that you know?" he asked. "With God's help," I said, "even if someone lost their sight for twenty years, I can cure them perfectly." "Very good," said the senior doctor, "there is in my house an old woman, my son's wet nurse, who is blind now for seven years. If you can cure

22. Pilsztynowa, pp. 46–47.

her, I will believe you, and myself will recommend you to the greatest lords of Istanbul." He led me to the room with the blind woman, and I undertook to cure her, and with God's help I did so perfectly well in forty days.]

After this success Hakim Basha became her friend and colleague, and even helped her in setting up her own pharmacy (first taking it away from Dr. Fonseca), after which she never experienced any more difficulties regarding her medical practice in Istanbul.

She even became interested in Islam, not so much to convert (she had several opportunities to do so), for she always retained her strong, one might say almost fanatical conviction in Roman Catholicism, but enough to dedicate one of her later chapters to a popular explanation of the Muslim system of beliefs. She had a Turk read passages from the Koran to her, and she was also apparently acquainted with Islamic folk tradition, such as why, for instance, Muslim women cover their faces, why Muslims pray five times each day, and the belief that the Prophet Muhammad will take the Virgin Mary as his tenth wife in heaven.[23] She actually took great interest in religious and spiritual stories, especially ones dealing with the deeds of saints or the miraculous legends associated with the foundation of churches and monasteries. She also participated in religious discussions, defending her Catholic beliefs against the charges of her Turkish neighbors and colleagues,[24] and even in extended disputations with the Jews, whom she again found stubborn and obdurate. She also expressed a wish that Christians would be as fervent about their faith as the Turks were about theirs, or that there would be more Polish pilgrims going to Jerusalem.[25] An account of these religious dialogues that include ideas stemming

---

23. Pilsztynowa, pp. 243–244, 255. *I to Turcy mówią, że Mehmet będzie prosił u Pana Boga o Maryję, żeby mu pozwolił wziąć, bo jemu było naznaczone mieć na świecie dziesięć żonek, a on tylko dziewięć żonek miał. I na tym weselu wielka radość będzie* [The Turks say that Muhammad will ask God for the hand of the Virgin Mary, because he was appointed to have ten wives in this world, and only had nine. And there will be great merriment at that wedding].

24. Pilsztynowa, p. 276. Her defense of Catholicism against Islam shows Salomea's favored method in religious discussion—she used passages from her rivals' religious books to support her own positions. She was therefore a woman not satisfied in merely being aware of her own dogmas of faith but also hungry for knowledge of other people's beliefs. In this case she claimed that, according to the Koran, the Muslims themselves believed that Jesus was taken up alive into the Sixth Heaven, while Muhammad, though a prophet, still a simple man, lived and died normally. How much better was it then to dedicate one's life, she concluded, to the one so admittedly revered by God as to remain permanently at His side, than to one who remained, in essence, a mortal.

25. Pilsztynowa, pp. 258, 268. *Czemuż tam na odpust Francuzi, Niemcy, Czesi, Moskale etc. ludzie przyjeżdżają na to święte miejsce, tylko nik [sic] się pochwalić nie może, że Polaka lub Polkę widzial?* [Why is it that the French, the Germans, the Czechs, the Russians and others come to that holy place to receive indulgences, but no one can boast of seeing a Polish man or woman?]

from the Bible, the Koran, and the Talmud (Salomea tried to convince a Jewish interlocutor of the existence of the Holy Trinity by citing supposedly Talmudic examples of God appearing to Moses as a spirit in the Burning Bush [the Holy Spirit], as a young man bearing a standard at the moment of Exodus [the Son], and as an old man with a beard at the giving of the Ten Commandments [the Father]), and other holy and obscure books, permeates the last two chapters of her memoir.[26]

But how did this complex woman who was, after all, with all her faults, all her dogmas—"all her warts," as it were—a product of her times, manage to achieve the pinnacle of professional success in a society that catered neither to her faith nor to her gender? The answer to this question forms the most fascinating part of her account. It seemed that she well understood that her perceived weakness, being a foreign woman, could actually be transformed into a source of strength and advantage. That awareness comprised many of her actions, and became a veritable strategy utilized to accomplish her goals. It is she, for instance, who helped out her husband by accusing other doctors of poisoning his patient in front of the Turkish vizier, an action her husband wanted nothing to do with:

> I tak ja kryjomo od męża mego i w niebytność jego kazałam sobie suplikę dobrą napisać z wyrażeniem okazji cazusa śmierci . . . a to z okazji trucizny danej doktora Żyda Fonseki i aptekarza Johana. I tak mając gotową suplikę kazałam się ponieść w sekrecie na Dywan, przed sąd wezyrski. Już to pierwszego wezyra Smaila zrzucili z funkcji, już drugi łaskawszy był, Ali Pasza, i tak dałam mu moją suplikę i ustnie dana mnie była audiencja mówić, co chcę. I takem ja wyraziła, że jestem Polka i przychodnia w ich kraju i tam wiele innych słów należących do dyskursu, i prosiłam, żeby ten aptekarz Johan i doktor Żyd Fonseka był zaraz postawiony w oczach moich przed sąd, ale obligowałam, żeby im nie mówić przyczyny, za co ich wołają do wezyra, a to dlatego, aby się oni nie gotowali z racjami naprzeciwko mnie.[27]

> [So without telling him [her husband], I secretly had a petition prepared describing the circumstances of the official's death . . . all on account of Doctor Fonseca's poison, and Johann the apothecary's collusion. With the petition in hand I had myself carried to the vizier's law court. Ismail had already fallen, replaced by the more benign Ali-pasha, to whom I presented my petition and was allowed to talk freely. I told him that I was Polish, and a visitor in his country, and requested him in many words that Johann the apothecary and Doctor Fonseca be brought immediately in front of me to the vizier's court, but without informing them of the reasons for their summons, so that they would not have the occasion to prepare their defenses against me].

26. Pilsztynowa, 272–282.
27. Pilsztynowa, pp. 39–40.

When her husband learned of her actions, and without even waiting for the account of the proceedings, he ran away in fear and came back only when she assured him of her success.[28]

On another occasion, while having a banquet in the city gardens with the family of one of her patients, a guard patrol came across a bottle of wine that she carried in her coach. Since it was forbidden to drink, or even possess alcoholic beverages in Muslim Istanbul, a member of her party was arrested, but Salomea was untouched. *A mnie Bóg salwował łaską swoją i strój mój polski, żem się ekskuzowała, żem jest chrześcijanka i nie turecka poddanka, profesji mojej doktorka, i tak mnie przecie nie brali, tylko wolno puścili.*[29] [Thanks to my Polish garments and to God's grace I was able to excuse myself as a Christian, and not a Turkish subject, and a doctor by profession, so they let me go]. Still, feeling guilty about the incident, she decided to confront the officials and secure the release of her imprisoned friend. The image of a lone woman arguing with male Turkish officers must have been an unusual sight, but it was not in the least off-putting to this resolute Polish lady. *Ja też chrześcijanka, Polka. Wolno mnie z białogłowami, i z mężczyznami gadać* . . . [Since I was a Pole and a Christian, it was permissible for me to talk to both men and women].[30]

Her status as a female physician profited her in another way as well: women patients often preferred female doctors, and felt more comfortable discussing their ills with them than with male practitioners. Likewise, husbands and fathers, especially in the Muslim lands that prized the concepts of female "honor," however limiting and ill-defined, also preferred to give access to their daughters' and wives' private spaces only to women physicians.[31]

This awareness of her "special" status and, one might say, unique circumstances, finds constant expression throughout Pilsztynowa's writings. She was very proud, for instance, that . . . *to było na podziw ludzki, że tu w Stambule białogłowom nie godzi się za próg wyjść, a mnie wolno w aptece siedzieć, między tak wielkim tumultem ludzi* . . . [it made people marvel that here, in Istanbul, where it is not proper for women

28. Pilsztynowa, p. 40.

29. Pilsztynowa, p. 42.

30. Pilsztynowa, p. 42.

31. Pilsztynowa, pp. 47, 95. Pilsztynowa was very aware of this psychological effect on her practice and took great advantage of it. During her stay in St. Petersburg she noticed that *ponieważ żem białogłowa i każda dama rna większą poufałość opowiedzieć swoje defekta białogłowie* [because I am a woman, and every lady feels freer to discuss her defects with another woman]. In the Turkish lands she easily noticed that *Turcy nieradzi do żon swoich i do córek swoich mężczyzn doktorów* [Turks do not like to allow male doctors to visit their wives and daughters].

to cross the threshold of the house, I was allowed to stay in a pharmacy among a great throng of people . . .].[32]

Turning to her other characteristics one immediately notices a strange infusion of medical professionalism sprinkled with the most outlandish superstition. Although by the beginning of the eighteenth century scientific knowledge has not yet separated itself fully from the shackles of the occult (note here that Sir Isaac Newton, for instance, wrote more about demonology than he did about physics, and Mesmer was practicing his brand of *animal magnetism* well into the 1780s), the delineating of the two was well on its way.[33] Pilsztynowa's beliefs, however, encompassed not only the Aristotelian approach to medicine, but all aspects of popular and religious superstitions that sometimes aided in her work, and sometimes didn't. She felt she was a witness to miracles on more than one occasion, and was a subject to miraculous visions:

> Tej nocy widzialam we śnie, że moja jedna bardzo dobra znajoma i za żywota wielka przyjaciółka, która przy pierwszym dziecięciu umarła i przyniosła mi słoik maści, i radziła mnie z wesołą miną twierdząc, że ta maść pomoże mnie na moją nogę. Ja odebrałam i obiecałam w łaźni się nasmarować. Potem powiadam: "Powiedz mnie, co to za maść? Ja sto razy lepsze zażywałam do mojej nogi." I tak ona mnie powiedziała prosta maść cyrulicka i miałam to za nic. Ocknąwszy się upominam się u sługi mego o tę zieloną maść, co mnie w nocy dali. Dziwował się, skąd ta maść i także ja pomiarkowałam się, że to we śnie było, ale że ponieważ dobrzem pamiętała, jak się ta maść robi i zrobiłam zupełnie tę maść, i była podobna w kolorze do tej, com widziała we śnie.[34]
>
> [That night I had a vision in my sleep, that a very good acquaintance of mine—and while she was alive a very good friend—who died while giving birth to her first child, brought me a jar of cream, and with a happy expression on her face advised me that the cream would help my leg. I took it from her and promised to use it in the sauna. Then I asked her, "Tell me, what is this cream? I already used creams a

---

32. Pilsztynowa, p. 47.

33. For a more complete treatment of medicine in the eighteenth century please consult W.F. Bynum and Roy Porter, eds., *Medical Fringe and Medical Orthodoxy 1750–1850* [Wellcome Institute Series in the History of Medicine] (London: Croom Helm, Ltd., 1987); Andrew Cunningham and Roger French, eds., *The Medical Enlightenment of the Eighteenth Century* [History of Medicine] (Cambridge: Cambridge University Press, 1990); Ludmilla Jordanova, *The Sense of a Past in Eighteenth-Century Medicine* (Reading: University of Reading Press, 1999); Mary Lindemann, *Health and Healing in Eighteenth-Century Germany* (Baltimore: Johns Hopkins University Press, 1996); Vivian Nutton, ed., *Medicine at the Courts of Europe, 1500–1837* (London and New York: Routledge, 1990); Roy Porter, ed., *The Popularization of Medicine, 1650–1800* (London and New York: Routledge, 1992); Marie Mulvey Roberts and Roy Porter, eds., *Literature and Medicine During the Eighteenth Century* (London and New York: Routledge, 1993).

34. Pilsztynowa, p. 54.

hundred times better for my leg." She told me that it was a simple surgeon's cream, to which I paid no attention. Having awoken I asked my servant to bring me the green cream that was given to me in the night. He wondered what cream I meant and I too realized that it all happened in a dream, but because I well remembered how to prepare such a cream, I made one exactly like it, so that even the color was similar to the one I saw in the dream].

She also shared with her readers stories she heard about purported saints and wizards, including an account of one young man near Wrocław who could turn invisible with the use of an enchanted chalice.[35]

She constantly attributed her own health problems to curses and harmful magic. *A ja pod ten czas bardzo ciężko chorowałam na powietrze i na czary. Jedną nogę miałam uschłą i krótszą od drugiej na pół łokcia, i wszędzie po ciele ból nieznośny* [At that time I was very sick, suffering from bad air and spells. One of my legs was withered and shorter than the other by half an ell, and my body was wracked with unbearable pain].[36] Another time she was able to identify the source of her affliction:

> Drugi Żyd doktor, sąsiad mój, co się zwał Samson, i ten był mój wielki nieprzyjaciel. Nie wiedząc, co mnie miał czynić z złości zdrowiu memu i fortunie mojej, zażył na mnie sposobu tego. Kazał ode mnie odkraść patynek jeden haftowany, w którym ja co dzień chodziła i tym patynkiem jakieś czary, gusła czynił, że ja i bez tego ciężko chorowała na powietrze, a ten niezbożny Żyd jeszcze przyczynił, że mnie ręce i nogi odjęło, i rozum ludzki, bo mnie się zdawało, że ja jestem dziecię, że ja powinnam w kołysce leżeć i musieli mnie kołyskę sporządzić, posłać, i kołysać. Kiedym znienacka obaczyła rękę lub nogę swoją, tom gwałtu wołała: "odejmcie ode mnie te cudze ręce i nogi!" ja rozumiałam, że ja powinna mieć ręce i nogi jak dziecię w roku. Męża i sług moich najwierniejszych w takiej nienawiści miałam, żem na żyw Boga wołała, żeby ode mnie precz odeszli, bo mnie się zdawało, że mają gołe pałasze w ręku i chcą mnie rozsiekać, i wszystko, co jest w domu, pozabierać. Kiedym chciała w okno, które zajrzeć, tom widywała jakieś straszydło w postaci starego człeka, który miał brodę ekstra długą, a włosy grube jak gruba nić.[37]
>
> [My other Jewish neighbor, Doctor Samson by name, was also a great enemy of mine. In his anger he didn't know what to do about my health and my fortune, and so he used the following method: He ordered the robbery of one of my embroidered slippers that I walked in every day, and used the slipper for some sorcery and magic, and though I was already very sick with the pestilence without that, the godless Jew now caused me to lose the use of my arms and legs, as well as of my mind, because it seemed to me that I was a child, and should be put and rocked in a crib, which was made and prepared for me. When I suddenly saw my arm or leg, I screamed out in panic: "Take away these foreign arms and legs!" because I thought that my arms and legs should be those of a year-old child. I so hated my

35. Pilsztynowa, pp. 166–167.
36. Pilsztynowa, p. 38.
37. Pilsztynowa, p. 50.

> own husband and my most loyal servants that I loudly prayed to God they would leave me alone, because I imagined that they held naked swords in their hands and wanted to chop me into little bits and steal everything in the house. When I wanted to look through a window, I saw there some terror in the form of an old man with a very long beard and coarse hair as thick as thread].

She even upbraided her first husband, Dr. Halpir, a practicing Protestant who, "belonging to the Lutheran sect, was difficult to convince that a person might die because of black magic."[38]

That last comment informs us not only of Regina's contradictory nature as an avowed "scientific" healer and a strong believer in superstitious cures and curses (she clearly believed she was afflicted by supernatural ailments on more than one occasion), but also points us towards a more general question of attempting to define what the term "medical doctor" meant in Salomea's time. She was obviously very proud of her identification with the medical profession and often called herself a "doctor," although obviously as a woman all formal higher academic training was closed to her. Her conception of medical practice was thus very different from modem standards, and closely approached the idea of artisanship, where hands-on practical experience provided the necessary credentials. Her medical education was informal and alienated from higher learning. She was first under the tutelage of her husband, and later studied with other physicians and herbalists. Despite the fact that she did not acquire an academic degree, it is clear that those who sought her help considered her to be fully capable and operating within the prescribed context of a "professional." A "doctor," apparently was a doer, a practicing physician recognized as such by the professional environment (here other medical "doers" as well as patients) as opposed to someone "created" by an academic institution. Her vocational story thus serves as an example of a woman who utilized alternative strategies to accomplish her professional goals.[39]

It is also interesting to note that for all her religiosity and spirituality, she liked to live a very worldly life, and was very materialistic and opportunistic, keenly aware of her improving social status, and on a constant lookout for fame and fortune. Her medical practice netted her more and more resources, something she was very happy to state in the pages of her memoir:

> Ponieważ byłam wzięta u ludzi, żem życie moje i com mogła, po ludzku się obchodziła i bardzom się brała, abym doskonale doktorstwo i okulistwo umiała i poczęli

38. Pilsztynowa, pp. 52–53. ". . . *mąż mój był religii luterskiej, czyli sekty, trudno mu to wmówić, ze przez czary może człek i umrzeć.*"

39. See Rebecca Tannenbaum, *The Healer's Calling: Women and Medicine in New England* (Ithaca, NY: Cornell University Press, 2002), pp. x, 5–7, for a fuller discussion of the seventeenth and eighteenth-century meaning of the term "doctor."

mię ludzie wielce zażywać w doktorstwie . . . Tu zaś co dzień tak wiele tureckich karet pąsowym suknem z nadworku obite i innego koloru suknami, ale natenczas byłam w bardzo młodym wieku, w leciech siedemnaście, tu zaś miewałam manele złote na ręku ze sto czerwonych złotych, na szyi na sznurkach trzysta czerwonych złotych, na głowie klejnoty, pierścienie diamentowe, kulce diamentowe etc. z opatrzności P. Boga, suknie suto bogate.[40]

[I behaved and lived humanely, and was very attentive to being the best doctor and oculist that I could be, and because of that I became popular with people, who began to come to me for cures . . . So many Turkish carriages, studded with ponceau- and multi-colored cloth came to me every day, and there I was, very young, in my seventeenth year, by the Grace of God with golden bracelets worth a hundred red złoty on my arms, necklaces worth three hundred red złoty on my neck, and on my head gems, diamond rings, diamond earrings, very rich vestments, etc.].

It is also realistic to surmise that her refusal to divorce her second husband, the ensign de Pilsztyn (Pilstein), and her retention of his name, even after his attempted poisoning and their separation, might have been motivated by the material need on her part to provide a noble-sounding name to her children.

Besides constantly noting her own possessions she also describes the wealth of others and always takes the time to catalogue the things she saw. She uses the following account to describe the wealth of the Hungarian Prince Rákóczi, the same one she eventually had to run away from:

Wiele kolorów w świecie widziałam aksamitów, to jest karmazynowy, zielony, złoty, czarny, niebieski, pąsowy, fioletowy, wiśniowy, granatowy, amarantowy, takie suknie miał królewicz Rakoczy, złotymi galonami i diamentowymi haftkami spodnie każde, kapelusze, czapki węgierskie, sobole futra pod płaszcze i suknie, sobole czapki węgierskie diamentami nasadzone, taborety, także różnego koloru aksamity, złotymi galonami i frędzlami, i obicie także z aksamitu różnych kolorów, pokoje obite także galonami złotymi i srebrnymi, karety, cugi, konie ekstra śliczne, szory srebrne pozłacane i półsrebrne na jedwabnych taśmach, wierzchowe konie, kulbaki, rzędy złote z klejnotami, ludzie ze strusimi piórami ekstra urodziwi, a pióra diamentami nasadzone. Takich miał ludzi dwudziestu czterech i wiele a wiele galanterii, zegarków, tabakierek, ksiąg i księdza kapłana.[41]

[I have seen in the world velvets of many colors—crimson, green, yellow, black, blue, poppy red, violet, cherry, pomegranate, amaranthine—Prince Rákóczi had such garb, all his trousers, hats, Hungarian caps, sable furs for overcoats and gowns studded with gold galloons and diamond embroidery, diamond studded sable Hungarian caps, stools, also velvets of different colors with gold galloons and fringe knots, and also velvet padding of various colors; the rooms were also studded with

40. Pilsztynowa, p. 48.
41. Pilsztynowa, p. 72.

gold and silver galloons; there were carriages, coach horses, very beautiful riding horses, gold plated silver and half-silver velvet-band horse harnesses, chargers, saddles, bejeweled gold horse harnesses with collars, also very handsome people with diamond studded ostrich feathers. He had twenty-four such people, as well as great numbers of haberdashery, clocks, snuffboxes, books, and a chaplain].

Like many others of her time and place she was also very obsequious and sycophantic when need be. When the bandit that captured her on the road to Sofia arrived at the place she was held, she wanted to personally take off his boots as a sign of total submission—an understandable action in the circumstances she found herself.[42]

Upon closer analysis her writings tend to betray a strong inclination towards the maintenance of rigid class structures and social hierarchies, which is an interesting concept, considering how much she herself challenged the established gender roles of her day. She adamantly believed that masters were owed fealty by their subjects and servants. Good service was rewarded by God, while bad service was punished. To illustrate this point she used an example of a Christian rebellion against the Turks that occurred in 1739 in Serbia and Bulgaria upon the entry of an Imperial Austrian army under General Seckendorff:

> Te wszystkie klucze włości zrebelizowały się na Turków, bo im ten generał Sekendorff dał tę radę, mówić do tych niewinnych ludzi: "nie bójcie się Turkow, bądzcie mnie na pomocy. Już ja Nysę wziąłem, wezmę i ja Sofię i Widyń Turecki, nawet Stambuł." I tak ci biedni chrześcijanie uwierzyli temu generałowi Sekendorffowi i podniesli rebelię na Turkow . . . I takem widziała karę P. Boga nad biednymi chrześcijanami, że taka była góra głów chrześcijańskich, jakby jaka wielka obszerna karczma.[43]
>
> [All of these lands rebelled against the Turks on the advice of this General Sekendorff, who told these innocent people "Do not fear the Turks and help me. I have already captured Nis, I will now take Sofia and Turkish Viddin, and maybe even Istanbul." And so these poor Christians believed this General Sekendorff and started a revolt against the Turks . . . And so I saw the poor Christians punished by God, the mountain of their severed heads being as large as a spacious tavern].

Takie to złe nagrody odbierają złe sługi, she moralized later on, *i każdemu przewrotnemu żeby Bóg tak zaplacił* [Such are the evil rewards received by bad servants, and may God reward all those unfaithful in such a way].[44]

In the matter of war, she did not believe that women and children should follow the army, and condemns such practices in her writing: *Jak też zwyczaj niedobry w*

42. Pilsztynowa, pp. 60–61. *I tak ja sama chciałam mu buty z nóg ściągnąć, ale on żadną miarą na to nie pozwolił* [I myself wanted to take off his boots, but he in no way allowed that].
43. Pilsztynowa, pp. 65–67.
44. Pilsztynowa, p. 130.

niektórych nacjach, że i żony i dzieci biorą na wojnę i tak wszystkie hurmem żony i dzieci w niewolę wpadły, i widziałam niemal w każdym domu niewolnika lub niewolnicę, lub dziecię w niewoli tureckiej [There is a bad custom in some countries that wives and children are taken on campaigns, and so they are altogether captured as well, and I saw a male or a female or a child slave in almost every house].[45]

For all her peripatetic experiences and travels, however, she was not very well versed geographically, as was made clear from her attempt to explain the presence of hot springs in the Bulgarian city of Karlov: *Ja na świecie tak wielu wód krynicznych nie widziałam, jak w Karłowie. Które wody z gór do miasta się zlewają strumieniami, bo w każdym dworze jest tam młynek i łaźnia, a te wody, co do łaźni idą, tak same przez się gorące, tak rozumiem, czyli nie z góry Etny, co z niej zawsze ogień wybucha* [I have never seen so many mineral waters as I did in Karlov. The waters flow in streams down into the city from the mountains, and every estate has a mill and a sauna. The waters that go into the sauna are themselves naturally hot, as I understand it, that is, not from Mount Etna, which always spits fire].[46]

Perhaps the most difficult aspect of her character to untangle deals with her identity as a "mother." Here the reader is faced with two contradictory prospects. On one hand it is easy to dismiss her, as Glatman once did, as a "bad mother."[47] She faced basically all the troubles that single mothers of today face in rearing up their children alone. She was also a professional woman, and it is clear from her writing that material considerations and her own career seemed paramount. Her children often had to bear the burden of that decision—being left in the care of others while their mother was away, traveling throughout South-Eastern Europe in search of well-to-do patients. Often the children were not left in the proper hands. This became especially obvious when their guardian, the certain J.M.C.Z. locked her younger son in a cold cellar, forgot about him, and thus caused the child's death through exposure:

> Widząc ja, że źle, odjechałam z Przemyśla do Lwowa i zostawiłam kawalera mego w Przemyślu z dziewką moją służebną i dwoje dziatek moich, Franciszka i Stanisława, i wina kilka antałów i różne mobilia. Kawaler mój rad był podpijać i z dziewką żartować, dlategoż syna mego Franciszka, który miał lat dziewięć, zostawiłam go, żeby do szkół chodził, a kawaler bał się, żeby dziecię to nie powiadalo przede mną, co widział i dlatego to dziecię zamykał do ciemnego sklepu przez trzy miesiące i

45. Pilsztynowa, p. 68.

46. Pilsztynowa, p. 60.

47. L. Glatman "Doktorka medycyny i okulistka polska w XVIII wieku w Stambule" [A Polish Female Doctor and Oculist in XVIIIth Century Istanbul], *Przewodnik Naukowy i Literacki,* 24 (1896), pp. 85–86.

zapomniał o nim, że mu czasem we trzy dni ledwie chleba dawał i tak to dziecię na gołej ziemi leżało, przestraszyło się, spuchło i z tego umarło.[48]

[Seeing that it isn't going well /between her and her *amorat*/ I left Przemyśl for Lwów and left my suitor in Przemyśl with my serving girl and my two children, Franciszek and Stanisław, and a few casks of wine and various movables. My suitor enjoyed getting drunk and flirting with the serving girl and was afraid that my son Franciszek, who was nine years old, and whom I left so he could go to school, would tell me what he saw, and that's why he locked the child in a dark vault and went on forgetting about him, so that sometimes for three days he would only feed him bread, and the child lay on the cold ground, became scared, swollen, and died because of it].

It is very difficult to read the passage in which Salomea chooses to describe that heart-wrenching event. She treats the death of her son in an almost dispassionate voice, very matter-of-factly and appears, as the very next paragraph shows, far more concerned with the financial damages her *amorat* caused her:[49]

Piszę do niego ze Lwowa do Przemyśla, żeby mnie dzieci przywiózł, wino i ruchomości. Tedy sam przyjechał i nie zajechał do mnie, tylko na przedmieście i najął piwnicę, i złożył wina, kulbaki etc. u Żyda. Pytam się, czemu to w karczmie, czemu nie u mnie w kamienicy, aleć ja pójdę, obaczę wina, odpieczętuję lewarem, każę ciągnąć, aż tu tylko cokolwiek lagru na spodzie. Narzekam na niego: "Miły amancie, a na cóż było za podwody płacić i próżne antały wozić?" Mówił, że Żyd pokradł wina i narobił mnie z Żydem kłótni, pozywania i kosztu. Pytam się, gdzie obicia moje, chusty etc. Mówi: "Nie wiem." A służący człek mówi, ze Mariance dał. Pytam się, gdzie krowy moje, mówi, że są na wsi. Ja proszę: "jedź, czyli idź ode mnie na miłość boską," bo mnie syn umarł we Lwowie, co go zamykał, aleć mówi kawaler: "daj mnie waćpani wózek i parę koni, i człeka, pojadę po krowy." Ja uwierzyłam, dałam konie; pojechał kawaler po krowy i sprzedał wraz z cielętami, i pieniądze przehulal, a człeka, chwała Bogu, z końmi i z wózkiem nazad przysłał.

[I wrote to him in Przemyśl to bring the children, the wine, and the movables to Lwów. He arrived alone and did not come to me, but from a Jew he rented a cellar in the suburbs where he put the wine, the saddles, and the other things. I asked him why he stayed at an inn and not with me in the apartment house, and so I went over, I saw the wine, I unsealed it with a lever, ordered it carried back with me, but there was only a little bit at the bottom. I complained to him, "My dear *amant*, why pay for the rented wagons and carry empty casks?" He told me that the Jew stole the wine and so caused an argument between me and the Jew, which led to court summons and expenses. I asked him, where are my tapestries, my cloth, and other things? He said, "I don't know." Meanwhile a servant told me that he gave them all to Marianka /apparently the name of her serving girl whom she left with her suitor in Przemyśl/. I asked him where is my cattle, and he answered that it's in the

48. Pilsztynowa, p. 200.
49. Pilsztynowa, p. 200.

> countryside. I asked him, "For God's sake, run, or walk away from me," because my son, whom he locked up, died in Lwów /actually the child died in Przemyśl/, but my suitor told me, "Give me a cart and a couple of horses, and a man, and I will fetch the cattle." I believed him and gave him the horses; so my suitor went to fetch the cattle and sold it, together with the calves, and squandered all the money on revels, but the man with the horses and the cart, thank God, he sent back].

The death of her son seems here to have been just one of the considerations in the long litany of material losses suffered on account of Mr. J.M.C.Z.

On the other hand there is no question that she loved her children very much and was greatly concerned about providing them with a good future (which she understood as service to a distinguished and powerful noble family). Her retention of the noble-sounding name de Pilsztyn might have been for that very reason. One can only imagine the picture of Salomea with her little baby girl bundled in her arms making her way through the treacherous Balkan mountains in search of employment in Adrianopole after her first husband, Dr. Halpir, left them to their own devices. At the end of her memoir, her true maternal concerns shine through when she bemoans the fact that her former *amator* once again interfered in her life, this time turning her surviving son against her. Personally hurt by her son's refusal to speak to her, Salomea ended her account by announcing plans to travel to Egypt and to Jerusalem.

Finally, and this is probably one of the most important questions that can be asked about her: was Salomea a feminist ahead of her time, providing such an appellation can even be suggested for someone living in the middle of the eighteenth century?[50] She definitely satisfies the requirement placed on female emancipation by Mary Wollstonecraft and possessed material and vocational independence, a room of her own, which allowed her to lead her life according to her own wishes. Throughout her journeys she showed a marked interest in powerful women. She wanted to see Empress Anna because *Tu zaś słyszałam, że dama panuje w Moskwie i życzyłam sobie tego szczęścia od P. Boga, aby mnie uczynił godną to oczyma oglądać . . .* [I heard that there was a lady ruling Muscovy and I wished from God such happiness to be worthy of seeing that with my own eyes . . .].[51] There was, therefore, an awareness of the unusual nature of such a state of affairs, and an unconcealed pride in it. But Pilsztynowa's heartfelt excitement about the role of women seems to stop where the lower stratum of society was concerned; whereas highborn women are given their due respect, are named, and are highly praised in her pages, the ordinary women

50. For a fine discussion of the role and meaning of "woman," both in theory and practice in the Old Polish society see Maria Bogucka, *Women in Early Modern Polish Society, Against the European Background* (Aldershot, England: Ashgate, 2004); also see Lubamersky, "The Life of Regina Salomea Pilsztynowa: a Feminist Analysis."

51. Pilsztynowa, p. 93.

Pilsztynowa interacted with on a daily basis are not afforded such mention and are pretty much ignored. Salomea often does not even state the names of the women she interacted with—only that of their husbands. These women are usually defined as "wives" of the named or mentioned individual. Examples of this are frequent in her writing: *W Tatar Pazardziuku kurowałam żonę jednego Ibrahim Efendiego* [In Pazardzik I took care of the wife of one Ibrahim Efendi];[52] *Ale ta sąsiada doktorka, Ebeulu żona, odezwala się wrzeszcząc, że ona jest umiejętna, a na mnie wołała, że ja nic nie umiem mniej* [But the wife of the Doctor Ebeulu, my neighbor, started to shout that she is more capable, and screamed at me that I knew nothing];[53] *Ale miałam jedną pacjentkę, kafedzia żonę, która kilka lat nie widziała na oczy i tę ja z łaski P. Boga wykurowała* [But at that time I had a patient, the wife of a certain coffee merchant, who for a few years went entirely blind, and whom, through the Grace of God, I cured].[54] When speaking of her parents, she didn't even give the name of her mother: *W młodym wieku moim wydali mnie rodzice moje (Joachim Rusiecki) za mąż . . . za doktora Jakuba Halpira . . .* [My parents (Joachim Rusiecki) married me at a young age to doctor Jacob Halpir . . .].[55] Such treatment of women with no high social station or status, is, however, routine in memoir literature of the age, and thus betrays no special negative predisposition. Besides, she is quick to mention the names of her female servants and acquaintances who mistreated her or whom she accused of stealing from her.[56]

Interesting in their own light are several instances of gender bending. Once she wore, *Amazońskie suknie* [Amazon garb].[57] She also had no problems dressing up as a man when the situation, and especially her safety, warranted it. Several times on difficult journeys she wore the garb of a man, and once even the uniform of a janissary: *Przyjechawszy szczęśliwie do Widynia tureckiego konno, przebrana po męsku, po turecku jak janczar . . .* [After successfully arriving in Viddin by horse, dressed in male clothing of a Turkish janissary . . .].[58] Such precautions were often demanded by the inhospitable nature of the environment she traveled through, and the constant presence of bandits. As she tells us, on one occasion, *I tak sobie kupiłam konia za 400 tynfów i sprawiłam sobie tureckie męskie suknie* [I bought for myself a horse for four hundred *tynf* and arranged for male Turkish garments . . .]. But the disguise did not work, and she was captured by a bandit who promptly asked

52. Pilsztynowa, p. 57.

53. Pilsztynowa, p. 48.

54. Pilsztynowa, p. 41.

55. Pilsztynowa, p. 37.

56. Pilsztynowa, p. 190. Like Zofia Berezdecka, a serving girl, who stole from Salomea a hundred and three red złoty while she stayed in Kamieniec in 1743.

57. Pilsztynowa, p. 223.

58. Pilsztynowa, p. 68.

her, *Klaniam, p. doktorko, gdzie się ważysz jechać z małą córeczką i z fortuną swoją?* [My regards, lady doctor, where are you daring to go with your little daughter and your fortune?] To which she answered, obviously in order to protect herself, *Ja nie doktorka, ja jestem mężczyzną, i jadę za pańskim interesem* [I am not a lady doctor, I am a man, and I'm traveling on my master's business].[59]

She was definitely a woman of action, carrying and using pistols on several occasions. Once she was besieged in an inn near Revel by bandits; another time by the Tatars in the town of Fuksany. When threatened by a Turk who refused to compensate her for buying him out of Russian prisoner-of-war camp, she had no trouble confronting him on equal ground:

> I tak wyszliśmy z domu sędziego, a Husein Aga z wielką furią na mnie i przysięgą, potwierdza, że mnie zabije. A ja śmiechem do niego mówię: "Panie Husein, rozumiesz, że nasze Polki zajęcze serca mają, jak wasze Bułgarki albo Wołoszki?" I wyjęłam parę krócic z kieszeni nabitych i mówię do niego; "I mnie stanie na proch dla przysługi waćpana. Oddaj waćpan mnie co należy, a potem niech to będzie, co P. Bóg da."[60]
>
> [After we left the judge's house Husein Aga turned on me with great fury and made an oath to kill me. I told him, laughing, "Mr. Husein, do you believe that Polish women have hearts of rabbits, like your Bulgarian or Wallachian women?" I took out from my pockets a loaded pair of small pistols and told him, "I have enough black powder to serve your needs. Give me back what belongs to me, and later may it happen what God wills"].

Extraordinary. But was she a feminist? Well, both Glatman and Pollak, that is, her earliest interpreter and her modern editor, definitely thought that she was. For Pollak she formed a noble link, a continuation, between the semi-mythical Nawojka, or the heroic Anna Chrzanowska of Trembowla's fame, and later heroines and activists like Konopnicka, Orzeszkowa, Modrzejewska, and Curie-Skłodowska,[61] who, through their struggles, "against the point of heaviest resistance, subjecting themselves to scoffing, to the bad words of their closest environment"[62] defined

59. Pilsztynowa, pp. 58–59.

60. Pilsztynowa, p. 181.

61. Nawojka was a legendary woman who attended Krakow's academy in male garb until discovered and made an abbess of a monastery; Anna Chrzanowska was the wife of the commander of the fortress of Trembowla who motivated her husband to defend his post against an army of twenty thousand Turks in 1675; Maria Konopnicka was a Polish poet and Eliza Orzeszkowa a writer and novelist of the Partition period; Helena Modrzejewska (Modjeska in English) was a successful Polish-American stage star at the end of the nineteenth century, while Marie Curie-Skłodowska was one of the most famous scientists in the world.

62. Pilsztynowa, p. 5. "*Po linii największego oporu, narażając się na szyderstwa, na złe języki najbliższego otoczenia . . .*"

the role and worth of women in Polish history and society, so that "when Polish [gender] relations are compared to others it can be said without exaggeration, that as far as that is concerned we stand at least in the front rank of other societies."[63]

For the earlier Glatman, Salomea represented feminism as well, but his pronouncement sounds so very different from Pollak's. In 1896, Glatman wrote that she was

> the prototype of all our current "emancipated" women [and that] by shunning the responsibilities of a mother and a wife through adventurism, she chased after fortune, professional fame and success throughout the entire world, and only at the end, after many tens of years of such pursuits, coming to the conclusion that neither riches, nor far-spread fame can replace familial love and warmth which only, and exclusively, for all time, can bring happiness to a woman.[64]

---

63. Pilsztynowa, p. 5. "Porównując stosunki polskie z obcymi można powiedzieć bez przesady, że na tym odcinku stanęlismy co najmniej w pierwszym szeregu wśród innych społeczeństw."

64. L. Glatman "Doktorka medycyny i okulistka polska w XVIII wieku w Stambule," *Przewodnik Naukowy i Literacki*, 24 (1896), pp. 856, 861. *Prototypem wszystkich naszych dzisiejszych emancypantek; Z zaniedbaniem obowiązków matki i żony uganiała się w awanturniczy sposób za fortuną, sławą lekarską, i szczęściem po calym świecie i w końcu po kilkudziesięciu latach takiej gonitwy do tej konkluzji przyszła, że ani majątek, ani rozgłośna sława nie zastąpią miłości i ciepła rodzinnego, które jedynie i wyłącznie po wszystkie czasy kobietę uszczęśliwić mogą.* Dr. Glatman, a man of his times, obviously did not approve of Pilsztynowa's independence. *Wiadomo,* he wrote, *że z takimi kobietami po wieczne czasy była, jest i będzie wierlka bieda i kłopot dla otoczenia* [It is well known that throughout eternity such women were, are, and will be a great problem and misfortune for society]. In fact, borrowing an analogy from medical science, he treated Pilsztynowa's quest for independence and career as a symptom of a more prevalent disease of "emancipation." *Przeczytawszy ten pamiętnik, nasuwa się mimo woli myśl, że ubieganie się kobiet o rozgłos i o zajmowanie stanowisk dzierżonych przez mężczyzn, to rzecz nie nowa, że emancypacyjne dążenia płci pięknej istniały po wszystkie wieki i istnieć będą jak długo egzystować będą kobiety chore, nerwowe, w pożyciu małżeńskim nieszczęśliwe, niehigienicznie chowane, szczytnych swych zadań nie pojmujące lub żadne sławy i niezwyklych przygód. Różnica między ubiegłymi wiekami a obecnym jest tylko ta, że choroba owa w minionych wiekach sporadyczna, dziś grasuje modnie i epidemicznie w calym niemal cywilizowanym świecie* [Having read this memoir, an involuntary thought enters the mind that this female quest for publicity and to take over the positions now held by men is not entirely new, that this drive towards emancipation of the fair sex existed in every century and will exist as long as there will exist women who are sick, nervous, in marriage unhappy, not hygienically brought up, without an understanding of their top priorities, or ones wanting fame and unusual adventures. The difference between previous centuries and this one is only such, that this disease, only sporadic in past centuries, today seems in fashion and prowls like an epidemic throughout nearly the entire civilized world].

To sum up his observations about her, Dr. Glatman wrote that "Pilsztynowa is the type of a shrew found in operettas, experiencing in her life almost incredible adventures, but when we look deeper into her pained heart and soul we behold the heroine of a shocking drama and the picture of a wasted life lived in foreign lands by a Polish woman. She did not experience happiness, because she searched for it where no woman may find it."[65]

65. Glatman, p. 946. *Pilsztynowa to typ awanturnicy operetkowej, doznającej w życiu niemal nieprawdopodobnych przygód, gdy zaś w głąb jej zbolałego serca i duszy spojrzymy, to mamy przed sobą bohaterkę wstrząsającego dramatu i obraz zmarnowanego na obczyżnie życia polskiej niewiasty. Nie zaznala ona szczęścia, szukała go bowiem tam, gdzie go kobieta nigdy nie znajdzie.*

Part Two

Bridging Polish and Polish Diasporic Lives

"Not as a Gift of Charity"

Ernestine Potowska Rose and the Married Woman's Property Laws

James S. Pula

Born in Piotrków, in the Russian-occupied section of partitioned Poland, on January 13, 1810, Ernestine Potowska was the first child of a respected local Orthodox rabbi. Though a cause for congratulations, the celebrations were muted for the community, in keeping with its religious and social beliefs, which valued the birth of a son more than that of a daughter. In fact, the rabbi had hoped for the birth of a son to carry on his own interest in religious scholarship.[1] Regardless of any disappointment the rabbi may have felt, it appears that he allowed his daughter to gain sufficient education to stimulate her active mind and inquiring sense of curiosity.

According to the daughter's later testimony, she established a reputation as "a rebel at the age of five."[2] Although Torah scholarship was a privileged occupation reserved for males, Rabbi Potowski's daughter insisted not only upon studying the sacred document, but learning Hebrew to read it without recourse to a secondary translation. What she found was at once intellectually stimulating and personally irritating. Although her curiosity and thirst for knowledge were further excited, what she learned did not always conform with her growing social awareness. Particularly distasteful to her was the daily prayer in which the supplicant recited, "I thank thee, Lord, that Thou hast not created me a woman."[3] Possessed of a disposition as stubborn as her mind was inquisitive, the young woman refused to recite prayers

1. Yuri Suhl, *Ernestine L. Rose and the Battle for Human Rights* (New York: Reynal & Company, 1959), 1, 3, 8; Miriam Gurko, *The Ladies of Seneca Falls: The Birth of the Woman's Rights Movement* (New York: Schocken Books, 1976), 88.

2. Suhl, 1, quoting an autobiographical article by Rose.

3. Gurko, 88.

From *Polish American Studies,* vol. 58, no. 2 (Autumn 2001), pp. 33–73.

she regarded as demeaning to her gender and completely rejected both sacred and secular rules that promoted the inferiority of women.[4]

By the time her mother passed away when Ernestine was sixteen, her father found his teenage daughter's growing rebelliousness difficult to manage. To solve the problem, and rid himself of responsibility for the troublesome girl, Rabbi Potowski, in keeping with established tradition, selected a groom for his daughter, offering the man as a dowry the inheritance Ernestine received from her mother.[5] Much to the consternation of both the rabbi and the groom, the young woman refused to marry someone she did not love, whereupon the rejected fiancé announced that if she would not honor the contract of marriage he would nevertheless retain the dowry. Under normal circumstances, a dispute over a marriage contract would be taken to the local rabbi for adjudication. In this case, however, since the rabbi was the plaintiff's father, Ernestine took the unusual step of filing a legal action in the Polish secular court in Kalisz. Even more unusual was the court verdict that awarded Ernestine full and complete title to the inheritance.[6]

Her finances secure, the young rebel soon determined to seek her future abroad. Although exchanging her homeland for the uncertainty of life abroad, Potowska took with her the formative experiences of her childhood that shaped her future interests and activities in Germany, France, England, and the United States. From her Jewish heritage she came to deplore the second-class treatment of women and to question the religious precepts that supported the negative treatment of females as subservient to men. Her Polish background reinforced her revulsion at gender and class inequities, while also providing her with a positive experience in the use of the legal system to seek redress. From both experiences—the persecution of Jews and the suffering of Poles under the oppressive rule of foreign nations—she also gained an affinity for the cause of the downtrodden. In the future, although she would renounce organized religion to become a "freethinker," she would consistently speak out on behalf of what she referred to as "and the downtrodden and persecuted people called the Jews" and "poor, crushed Poland." She would be a firm

---

4. Suhl, 9–10; Carol A. Kolmerten, *The American Life of Ernestine L. Rose* (Syracuse: Syracuse University Press, 1999), 7.

5. Suhl, 11. There is considerable disagreement about how old Ernestine was when her mother passed away. While Suhl cites the age of sixteen, information in his research papers also indicates the age as six. A contemporary, L. E. Barnard ("Mrs. Ernestine L. Rose," *The Liberator*, May 15, 1856), cites sixteen and Jenny D'Héricourt ("Madame Rose," *La Revue Philosophique et Religieuse* [1856]), who interviewed Rose, says it happened when she was a "teenager," thus I have used the age of sixteen.

6. Suhl, 12–13, 15; Daniel L. Rabishaw, "Ernestine L. Rose: A brief Biography," a research paper presented to Hebrew Union College and Jewish Institute of Religion, Cincinnati, Ohio; Yuri Suhl Papers, Boston University.

supporter of social and legal equality for all classes and races of people, and would make her most significant contribution in the pursuit of legal remedies to achieve equality of rights for women.

In 1827, at the age of seventeen, she left Piotrków for Berlin, a very unusual course for a young woman in the early nineteenth century. In Berlin, however, her search for a conducive living environment was unsuccessful because Prussian law limited the time foreign Jews could reside in the country without special permission.[7] Although she was successful in her petition to remain in the Prussian city, she soon continued her journey in search of a place where she could experience the freedom she sought.

In June, 1829, Potowska left Germany for Holland, then quickly moved on to Belgium and France. In the French capital she met Adam Mickiewicz who was endeavoring to rally support for the Polish cause. Considering herself a loyal Pole, she actively joined his effort. When Mickiewicz attempted to return to Poland, only to be stopped by Prussian authorities in Poznan, Potowska also attempted to reach her homeland but was stopped in Coblenz on the Rhine River. Thus frustrated in their attempts to return to Poland's aid, Mickiewicz returned to Paris while Potowska chose to move on to London.[8]

In England, Potowska supported herself by teaching Hebrew and German while learning English. After a brief transition period, she engaged in selling an air-freshening product of her own invention that she promoted as "aromatherapy." With her daily needs thus provided for, she was free to engage in the passionate reform movements then sweeping the island nation.[9] Drawn equally to the intellectual aspects of social reform and the excitement of activism, Potowska soon met Robert Owen, a British industrialist and philanthropist generally regarded as the

---

7. Suhl, 15, 17, 21; Gurko, 88. Rabishaw maintains that while Ernestine fought in the Polish Court for control of her inheritance, her father married a 16-year-old and the two women did not get along. The new step-mother wanted to control the household and Ernestine wanted to control her own life. So, Rabishaw states, Ernestine gave up her inheritance as the price of leaving Piotrków. Thus, she arrived in Berlin without significant funds (see Rabishaw, 4). Morris U. Schappes gives still another version of the story in a letter to Fanny Goldstein, December 30, 1936 (in the American Jewish Archives). In it he states that a woman in whose home Rose once resided as a guest for "some days" told him that Rose conveyed the following account: When Ernestine refused to marry, her father "locked her up in her room, and kept her on but bread and water—a slim allowance of bread, I judge, as she became very weak and emaciated." Ernestine apparently pretended to submit, but secretly had most of her inheritance transferred to precious stones and sewed them into the linings of her clothing. When the wedding day arrived, she, with aid of some English friends, went instead by a carriage they had waiting for her, and escaped, leaving the guests waiting at the synagogue.

8. Suhl, 24–26.

9. Suhl, 21.

originator of utopian socialism. In his *New View of Society*, published in 1813, he advocated cooperative production and believed that people were exclusively the products of their environments. Owen believed reform could best be instituted through the organization of new social units and spent his life attempting to develop ideal environments through labor reform, "rational" education, and the establishment of Utopian colonies.[10]

Herself already an enthusiastic advocate of universal suffrage and social reform, Potowska eagerly joined Owen's group and soon began to speak to public audiences in support of Owen's theories and her own favorite reform topic, women's rights. Her first effort, in somewhat halting, heavily accented English, was nevertheless reported a success because of her obvious passion for her subject.[11]

In 1835 she participated with Owen in the establishment of the "Association of All Classes of All Nations," an organization devoted to "protecting the human rights of all people." In an article written for the *Albany Morning Express* years later, Potowska reflected proudly on her Owenite experience in the following words: "I stood on the woman's rights platform before that name was known, and twenty years ago I presided over an association for the protection of human rights which embraced all colors, and nations, and sects, and I stand on the same platform still."[12]

While working for the Owenite movement, Potowska met William E. Rose, a London jeweler and silversmith who was a prominent Protestant member of Owen's Utopian socialist community. The couple opted for a civil ceremony of marriage. Soon thereafter they decided to move to the United States.[13]

Ernestine Rose arrived in New York in May, 1836, at the age of 26. The couple settled on the Lower East Side in Manhattan where William set up shop as a silversmith. It was not long before Ernestine found herself drawn to the major social reforms of the day—education, temperance, abolitionism, and women's rights.[14] In particular, she took a serious interest in the plight of women, adopting the legal status of women as her particular *cause celebre*. In the years to come, the pillars of the nineteenth century women's rights movement would be noted for varied contributions: Elizabeth Cady Stanton vigorously argued in favor of women's rights within marriage and easing of the divorce laws. Lucretia Mott used her detailed study of the Bible to denounce clergy who used scripture to sanction belief in women's inferiority. Harriet Hunt fought against prevailing medical opinion ascribing physical inferiority to women. And, for her part, Ernestine Rose became known for her

10. Gurko, 88; Suhl, 28; Kolmerten, 10–13.

11. Gurko, 88; Suhl, 29, 32.

12. Suzanne Griffel, "Ernestine L. Rose, as Jew and Social Activist," unpublished paper submitted to Hebrew Union College, American Jewish Archives, 2; *Albany Morning Express*, 1854.

13. Gurko, 88; Suhl, 33.

14. Suhl, 37, 48; Kolmerten, 2.

emphasis on obtaining legal rights for women. In this, historian Eleanor Flexner credits Rose with being "one of the first women to try to improve the position of her sex through legislative action."[15]

Rose's choice reflects no fear of confrontation, for the legal status of women in New York was at that time restrictive in the extreme, relegating married women to little more than possessions of the husband. Married women enjoyed no claim to their own property, or even their own wages, yet their tax obligations were equal to those of men who enjoyed full legal and civil rights. In fact, she found New York law in some respects more restrictive than the English Common Law on which it was based. "By marriage," explained Sir William Blackstone, "the husband and the wife are one person in law; that is, the very being or legal existence of the woman is suspended during her marriage, or at least, is consolidated into that of her husband under whose wing, protection and cover, she performs everything."[16] New York law provided the same condition. The act of marriage created one legal entity before the law, and that entity was controlled exclusively by the husband. A married woman had no legal status aside from that of her husband. She could not hold property in her own name, she could not make contracts without her husband's permission, she could not sue in court unless her husband instituted the suit, and she could not even claim an inheritance if her husband died intestate. Additionally, local laws, policies, and procedures virtually excluded women from professions such as medicine, law, and engineering, forcing most into the three generally approved women's careers as domestic workers, seamstresses, or school teachers.[17]

In the very month the Roses arrived in New York from London, Judge Thomas Herttell, a reformer already known for his public stands on social issues, attempted to introduce the plight of married women into the state political dialogue. As a sixty-five-year-old member of New York State Assembly, the lower house of the state legislature, he offered the following resolution:

> Resolved, That a select committee be appointed to inquire and report to this house, at the present or succeeding session of the legislature, what provisions, if any, will be proper and necessary to be made by law, the better to protect the rights and property of married women from injury and waste by means of improvident, prodigal, intemperate and dissolute habits and practices of their husbands.[18]

---

15. Carol Hymowitz and Michaele Weissman, *A History of Women in America* (New York: Bantam Books, 1978), 100; quote from Eleanor Flexner, *Century of Struggle: The Woman's Rights Movement in the United States* (Cambridge, MA: The Belknap Press of Harvard University Press, 1970), 65.

16. Sarah Grimke, *Letters on the Equality of the Sexes and the Condition of Woman* (Boston: Knapp, 1838), 75, citing Sir William Blackstone's *Commentaries on the Law.*

17. Suhl, 49–51.

18. Suhl, 53.

Ernestine Potowska Rose
Photo courtesy of the Jacob Rader Marcus Center of the American Jewish Archives.

Opponents of the resolution immediately branded Judge Herttell an "infidel," asking him rhetorically if he were trying to "Undermine the marital structure" or "[d]isturb the harmonious balance of the husband-wife relationship." The judge replied that "One of the evils which these bad laws were breeding was the mercenary marriage." Yet, Herttell was willing to go only so far. He was not, he explained, suggesting a new law, only attempting to place the subject in the public forum. In the end, this was a very modest goal indeed. Clearly, there was a need for a champion to move the discussion forward.[19]

19. Suhl, 53.

When Rose began speaking out in public, her vision of a new society based upon human equality and community of property reflected her philosophical indoctrination into the Owenite movement that by then had spread its influences across the Atlantic to North America. Chief among her concerns was the legal plight of married women in her adopted state. To address this issue, she developed a petition to the state legislature calling for the enactment of a law to protect a woman's right to own property. This was introduced into the New York State Assembly in its fall, 1840, session by Judge Herttell as "An Act For The Protection And Preservation Of The Rights And Property Of Married Women."[20]

In introducing the new legislation, Herttell embarked on an oration that stretched eighty printed pages. The crux of his argument was that "The common law of England, by which the property of married women is taken from them and given to their respective husbands, is not and never was constitutional law in this state." To support his position he cited the New York State Constitution that said, in part, "all such parts of the 'common law' and such of the said acts and parts thereof as are repugnant to the Constitution are hereby abrogated." "Did anyone doubt," Herrttell asked, "that this 'common law' as applied to the rights of married women was repugnant to the constitution?" Pursuing the issue, he quoted further from the New York State Constitution, noting that "no member of the state shall be disenfranchised or deprived of any of the rights and privileges secured to any citizen thereof, unless by the law of the land or the judgement of his peers," and "no person shall be deprived of life, liberty or property without due process of law." To further illustrate his point, Herttell noted that societies such as the Quakers were peaceable and well-ordered, but allowed women to own property.[21]

To support this legislative effort, Rose determined to circulate petitions for forwarding to the state legislature in support of the proposed law. Women, she reasoned, would surely sign, and some might convince their husbands to do so as well. Fired with enthusiasm, Rose went door-to-door for five months, meeting much more rejection than she ever imagined. Women generally believed the effort doomed to failure at best, or at worst openly hostile to efforts that might upset the marital home. Men similarly rejected the appeal, and in the end five months of effort yielded only five signatures. "After a good deal of trouble I obtained five signatures," she lamented. "Some of the ladies said the gentlemen would laugh at them; others, that they had rights enough; and the men said the women had too many rights already."[22]

---

20. Keith E. Melder, *Beginnings of Sisterhood: The American Woman's Rights Movement, 1800–1850* (New York: Schocken Books, 1977).

21. Suhl, 56–57.

22. Melder, 143; quote from letter, Rose to Susan B. Anthony, January 8, 1877, reproduced in Morris U. Schappes, "To Be Included," *Morning Freiheit,* March 13, 1948.

Rose was greatly discouraged by the lack of response to her appeal. The reaction of women was particularly discouraging, for, as she explained, "the most hopeless condition is that when a patient loses all sensation of pain and suffering." Nevertheless, she felt the effort worth the time and trouble despite the discouraging result because "by depicting their condition to themselves, by holding before them the mirror of faces, it had the wholesome effect of an irritant, and roused to some extent, as at least, their dormant energies."[23] Rose sent the five signatures on to Albany, then began a new effort to arouse public support.

During the first months of the petition campaign, Paulina Wright—later Paulina Wright Davis—collected some signatures in the western part of New York State. Since she and Rose were interested in the same issues and tactics, they joined forces to maximize their petition efforts. Some time shortly thereafter, Elizabeth Cady Stanton joined the movement. Thus was born a lifetime collaboration of the initial leaders of the woman's rights movement.[24]

Between 1837 and 1840 Rose pursued a vigorous schedule of speaking engagements to promote her beliefs in social reform. Speaking to an audience at an Owenite community in Skaneateles, New York, she argued that man must resolve the contradictions between his selfish, social, and universal natures to achieve a harmonious society. "Thou shalt not be happy short of the universal happiness of every human being," she warned. "The declaration that 'man is born free and equal' is a dead letter until now. He is born free and equal, he dies free and equal, but he does not live free and equal." Reporting on the meeting the *Herald of Freedom,* published in Concord, New Hampshire, pronounced Rose's speech "truly astonishing; it was the breaking forth of humanity in a concentrated form. . . . It was a most effective appeal and met its response in the tears of the whole audience."[25]

During the summer of 1837 she took part in a thirteen-week debate on the subject "To What Extent May A Community of Property Be Applied To The Happiness Of Mankind?" Challenged by some of the ablest debaters of the era, Rose quickly gained a reputation for her use of wit, sarcasm, and impeccable logic while becoming known as one of the foremost extemporaneous speakers for women's rights. After one of her first speeches, the editor of the *New York Beacon* advised his readers that:

> A Polish lady, of great literary attainments and warmly attached to Robert Owen's system, attended, and delivered her opinions, especially in opposition to Mr. Offen: her views were enlightened, and sentiments liberal; her opinions on religion are

23. Letter, Ernestine L. Rose to Susan B. Anthony, January 8, 1877, in Morris U. Schappes, "To Be Included," *Morning Freiheit,* March 13, 1948.

24. Melder, 143; Gurko, 89.

25. Suhl, 78–80; Kolmerten, 47; *Herald of Freedom,* November 3, 1843.

> those benevolent and liberal opinions of Robert Owen's; those of ours, and of every person who has thought on the subject.[26]

As the debates progressed, the press kept its readers informed of the events. "Last week," the *New York Beacon* reported, "the Polish lady found a new and able opponent, logical and systematic in his reasoning and deficient only in energy; he, however, could only make a beginning, and thereafter we yet expect a continued and interesting debate." Since the debates were held in Tammany Hall, long a sinecure of New York City's corrupt political machine, the reformers were "mocked, derided, and denounced by the clergy and the reactionary press as a band of infidels whose avowed aim it was to undermine religion and shake the pillars of orderly society." The pro-slavery editor of the *New York Herald*, James Gordon Bennett, seemed to make it his personal crusade to assault the motivations and goals of any popular reform movement. When he visited Tammany Hall for one of the lectures, he editorialized "What trash! what blockheads! what genuine asses!"[27] Such denunciations stirred public sentiment against the women's rights movement and its leaders, but did not deter them from further action.

Beginning in 1840, Rose and her associates Wright and Stanton determined to concentrate their efforts directly on the legislature in Albany. "Agitate! Agitate! ought to be the motto of every reformer," Rose once wrote. "Agitation is the opposite of stagnation—the one is life, the other death."[28] That same year she was allowed to address committees of the Senate and Assembly in the New York State Legislature on behalf of the proposed woman's property law. Over the succeeding months, she gave five addresses before various legislative committees. Described by contemporaries as "a master of pointed logic, unsparing wit and telling humor," her speeches led to great excitement in the capital district both from reformers and from conservative forces who hoped to preserve the *status quo*.[29]

While continuing their work with the legislature in Albany, Rose and her associates also pursued their petition drive. "I continued sending petitions with increased numbers of signatures," Rose wrote, but none was sufficient to stir the legislature to action. Nevertheless, the increasing pressure from Rose's speeches, combined with the lengthening lists of signatures, created by 1842 an atmosphere in which the legislature could not simply ignore the growing call for action on the women's demands.[30]

---

26. *New York Beacon*, June 3, 1827. Benjamin Offen was a freethinker who opposed Owen's socialistic ideas.

27. Suhl, 67; *New York Herald*, November 3, 1843.

28. Suhl, 65.

29. "Ernestine Rose—Early Women's Libber," *The Jewish Advocate*, March 25, 1976.

30. Flexner, 65; Suhl, 60.

Called upon to make some comment or take some action on the proposal for a married woman's property law, the Committee on the Judiciary of the New York State Assembly reported

> That the constant pressure of other duties upon the time and attention of this committee, together with their knowledge of the hopelessness of any legislation on this subject, at the present session, under the heavy accumulation of business piled up for action on the tables of the House, has prevented their bestowing upon these petitions the consideration necessary to enable them to mature any measures to carry into practical effect the prayer they urge. They deem it, however, due to the subject not to return them to the House without an expression of their unanimous opinion in favor of a more liberal extension of the rights of married women, in accordance with the general object proposed by these petitioners, though how far it might be proper to go in securing to them the separate possession and control of property, must of course be a subject of much diversity of individual opinion. The present state of the statute and common law in force amongst us unquestionably operates in many cases to the great wrong and oppression of women, and in many respects their condition would be much improved and elevated, and the happiness and well-being of the marriage relation probably benefited, by some considerable extension and protection of their rights of property. In a change so important and delicate, in what may be regarded as the very fundamental institution of society, as it is certainly the most sacred and precious, no degree of caution can be too great, to guard against rash derangement of whatever may be good in the existing settled order of things. Consistently with this principle of prudence they yet think that something of a safe and salutary character could be done and ought to be done, to engraft at least partially upon the hard and stubborn trunk of the common law the more liberal principle in relation to this subject of which a successful precedent has long been held out to as in most of the codes of other countries founded on the civil law. The task of digesting and framing such a measure they are constrained, however, to leave to future legislation, and for the present to content themselves with asking to be discharged from the further consideration of these petitions, and that this report be printed.[31]

Although not the victory Rose had hoped for, the response of the Assembly's Committee on the Judiciary marked the first official response to the petition drives and Rose's addresses to the various legislative committees. Further, the response marked the first time a legislative committee went on record recommending some accommodation, no matter how minimal, to the concerns expressed by Rose and her colleagues.

Buoyed by the response, Rose heightened her efforts on behalf of the property rights bill only to see it defeated in committee during the next legislative session. The arguments raised against the bill were essentially that its passage would be harmful

---

31. *Journal of the Assembly of the State of New York* (Albany: 1836–1848), Assembly No. 189, April 12, 1842.

to the marital bonds causing the institution of marriage to decay to a point where it would "rival France and some of the other continental nations in the laxity of our morals."[32] Her response was to advise that

> [A] new sign has appeared in our social zodiac, prophetic of the most important changes, pregnant with the most beneficial results that have ever taken place in the annals of human history. And to him who can trace the various epochs in human life, it is as cheering as it is interesting to mark the onward movement of the race towards a higher state of human progression—that while nations strive against nations, people against people, to attain the same amount of freedom already possessed in this country, WOMAN is rising in the full dignity of her being to claim the recognition of *her* rights. . . .
>
> But how can we wonder that France, governed as she is by Russian and Austrian despotism, does not recognize the higher laws of humanity in the recognition of the rights of women, when even here, in this far-famed land of freedom and of knowledge, under a republic that has inscribed on its banner the great truth that all men are created free and equal, and are endowed with inalienable rights to life, liberty, and the pursuit of happiness,—a Declaration wafted like the voice of Hope on the breezes of heaven to the remotest parts of earth, to whisper freedom and equality to the oppressed and down trodden children of men,—a Declaration that lies at the very foundation of human freedom and happiness, yet in the very face of that eternal truth, woman, the mockingly so called "better half of man," has yet to plead for her rights, nay, for her life. For what is life without liberty? and what is liberty without equality of rights; and as for the pursuit of happiness, she is not allowed to pursue any line of life that might promote it; she has only thankfully to accept what man, in the plentitude of his wisdom and generosity, decides as proper for her to do, and that is, what he does not choose to do himself.[33]

By 1845 Rose and her associates were successful in spreading agitation for a woman's property law to the smaller towns throughout Upstate New York. One petition signed by forty women from Genesee and Wyoming Counties in Western New York lamented that "Our numerous and yearly petitions for this most desirable object having been disregarded, we now ask your august body to abolish all laws which hold married women more accountable for their acts than infants, idiots and lunatics."[34] Pressure from these petitions, now numbering thousands for signatures, and Rose's continuing public addresses increased to such a degree that between 1846 and 1847 four separate bills regarding married women's property rights were introduced into the Assembly.[35]

In March, 1846, Rose journeyed to Michigan for a speaking tour that included an appearance before the state House of Representatives that passed a resolution

32. Suhl, 62 (quote), 65.
33. Ernestine L. Rose, *Lecture on Woman's Rights* (Boston: J. P. Mendum, 1886), 2–4.
34. Gurko, 89; quote from Suhl, 63.
35. Suhl, 63; Gurko, 89.

praising her oratorical skills and grace. In later years it would be claimed that women's rights agitation in Michigan began with her tour. From there she returned to New York where she continued a robust speaking schedule. On one of these occasions a reporter for the *New York Herald,* an anti-reform publication, informed his readers that "the highly accomplished, talented and intellectually beautiful Mrs. Rose" had taken part in an unsettling meeting.[36]

> It was a lovely Sabbath morning yesterday—the sun shone in all its splendor, and the whole earth seemed to rejoice with great, unbounded gladness, and send forth a hymn of thanksgiving and praise in token of its joy.
>
> There was one spot, however, in this vast metropolis, where an assemblage was congregated for far different purposes with the avowed object of upsetting all earth's theological systems—all sanguine of success—all eager to proceed to the business of demolition.[37]

Critical of the meeting throughout his article, the reporter quoted Rose's speech in exaggerated dialect, but nevertheless concluded that "Mrs. Rose concluded and sat down amid thunders of applause."[38]

In 1847 Rose traveled to Charleston, South Carolina, to undertake the physically dangerous mission of speaking out against slavery. Only recently had Senator William C. Preston warned: "Let an Abolitionist come within the boundaries of South Carolina; if we catch him, we will try him, and notwithstanding all the influence of all the governments on earth, including the Federal government, we will hang him." Undeterred, Rose spoke out in public, regretting that she was "sorry to say" that South Carolina was "a century, at least, behind in the means of civilization."[39]

In early 1848 a new version of the married woman's property bill was presented to the state legislature. Titled "An Act for the More Effectual Protection of the Property of Married Women," the bill passed both houses of the legislature on April 7, 1848. It read as follows:

> The People of the State of New York, represented in Senate and Assembly, do enact as follows:
>
> I. The real and personal property of any female who may hereafter marry, and which she shall own at the time of her marriage, and the rents, issues and profits thereof, shall not be subject to the disposal of her husband nor be liable for his debts and shall continue her sole and separate property as if she were a single female.

---

36. Suhl, 82, 84; Inez Haynes Irwin, *Angels and Amazons: A Hundred Years of American Women* (New York: Doubleday, Doran & Company, 1934), 88. Irwin erroneously dates the speaking tour to 1836.

37. Suhl, 84–85.

38. Suhl, 85; Kolmerten, 56–57.

39. Suhl, 90–91; Kolmerten, 57–58; *The Liberator,* August 19, 1853.

> II. The real personal property and the rents, issues and profits thereof of any female now married shall not be subject to the disposal of her husband; but shall be her sole and separate property as if she were a single female except so far as the same may be liable for the debts of her husband heretofore contracted.
>
> III. It shall be lawful for any married female to receive by gift, grant device or bequest, from any person other than her husband and to hold to her sole and separate use, as if she were a single female, real and personal property and the rents, issues and profits thereof, and the same shall not be subject to the disposal of her husband, nor be liable for his debts.
>
> IV. All contracts made between persons in contemplation of marriage shall remain in full force after such marriage takes place.[40]

After all of the hard work over so many years, Rose could take pride in the fact that her efforts were rewarded with passage of the very first state law protecting married woman's property rights in the United States. Yet in victory she could not help but reflect on two essential disappointments. The first was the almost instantaneous change in many people's attitudes. For more than a decade she scoured New York State seeking signatures on her petitions, more often than not meeting with rebuff even from women. "I continued sending petitions with increased numbers of signatures until 1848 and '49, when the Legislature enacted the law which granted woman the right to keep what was her own," she wrote. "But no sooner did it become legal than all the women said: 'Oh! that is right! We ought always to have had that!'"[41]

Her second disappointment lay in the legislation itself. While the act gave married women control of their own real estate, personal property, and rents and profits derived therefrom, it did not eliminate the right of the husband to control any money a woman earned during the marriage. As such, the legislation protected women from more affluent families likely to inherit property or money, but afforded no protection to women from working families who were more likely to have to rely on earned wages for the support of themselves and their families.[42] While she considered passage of the act "a significant victory in the emerging struggle for women's rights," she also recognized its limitations. "This was not much, to be sure," she wrote, understating her accomplishment, "for at best it was only for the favored few and not for the suffering many. But it was a beginning and an important step for it proved that a law had to be altered and some others might need it just as much. It is a curious fact that as soon as that law passed every one considered it not only perfectly right, but wondered how it ever could have been otherwise."[43]

---

40. Suhl, 63–64.
41. Flexner, 65.
42. Gurko, 90; Hymowitz and Weissman, 118.
43. Suhl, p. 64.

In January, 1850, the Roses attended the 25th Anniversary Thomas Paine celebration in New York City. At the dinner, event president William Allen offered a toast to the celebrated women's rights orator:

> When I think of the once happy but now fallen country of Kosciusco, Pulaski and their dauntless associates a strong sympathy and respect is produced in me for all who can trace their origin to that land of sorrow, and more especially to those who inherit the spirit of Kosciusco, whether they be male or female. I will therefore propose as a sentiment the name of Mrs. Rose—she was the morning glory of Poland; the lily of England; and she is the rose of America.[44]

The First National Women's Rights Convention was held in Worcester, Massachusetts, in 1850. Linking the issues of race and gender equality, the Worcester meeting was considered by contemporaries to be the beginning of the organized women's rights movement. More than 1,000 men and women, both black and white, from eleven different states crammed into Brinley Hall on Main Street to hear a stellar roster of speakers that included such oratorical luminaries of the day as Lucretia Mott, Paulina Wright Davis, Frederick Douglass, Sojourner Truth, William Lloyd Garrison, Wendell Phillips, Ann Phillips, Lucy Stone, and Ernestine Potowska Rose.[45] When it came her opportunity to speak, Rose said, in part,

> We have heard a great deal of our Pilgrim Fathers, but who has heard of the Pilgrim Mothers? Did they not endure as many perils, encounter as many hardships, and do as much to form and fashion the institutions of New England as the Pilgrim Fathers? And were not their trials, and is not their glory equally great? Yet they are hardly remembered. . . . I shall not use the language of censor and blame. So far as there is blame both sexes are entitled to their share of it. Man is as much the victim of his despotism as is woman. . . . I trust that if ever woman touched the sword it would be to sheath it in its scabbard forever. . . . We are not contending here for the rights of women of New England, or of old England, but of the world.[46]

Although well received by those in attendance at the convention, the remarks of Rose and her colleagues did not meet with universal approbation. The correspondent for the *New York Herald* provided an insight into the mentality of the opposition when he reported on what he labeled the "Hen Convention." Characterizing the

---

44. Suhl, 106.

45. Suhl, 109; Kolmerten, 76; Melder, 152–153; Worcester Women's History Project, Worcester, MA; Alma Lutz, *Crusade for Freedom: Women of the Antislavery Movement* (Boston: Beacon Press, 1968), 237.

46. Suhl, 112; *Proceedings of the Woman's Rights Convention, Held at Worcester, October 23rd & 24th, 1850* (Boston: 1851).

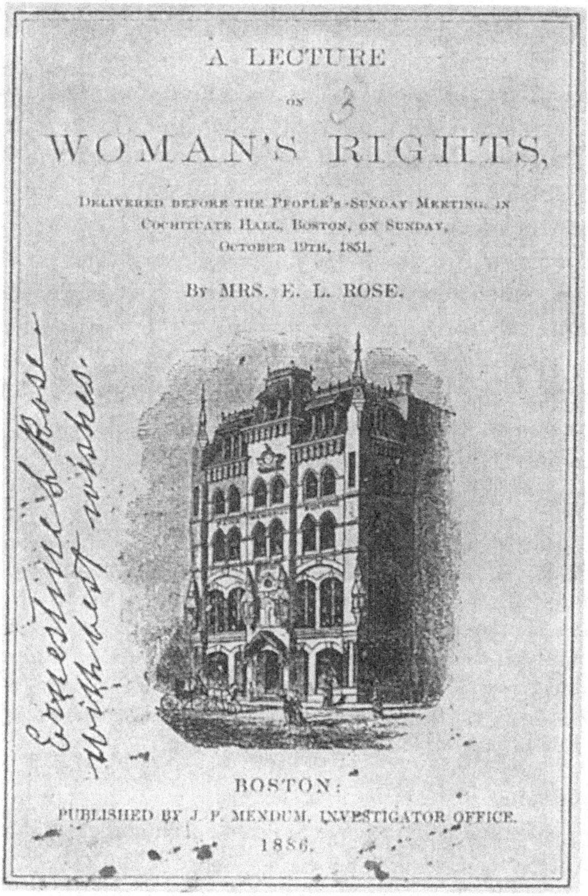
A LECTURE

ON

WOMAN'S RIGHTS,

DELIVERED BEFORE THE PEOPLE'S SUNDAY MEETING IN COCHITUATE HALL, BOSTON, ON SUNDAY, OCTOBER 19TH, 1851.

BY MRS. E. L. ROSE.

BOSTON:

PUBLISHED BY J. P. MENDUM, INVESTIGATOR OFFICE.

1886.

Ernestine L Rose
with best wishes.

Autographed copy an Ernestine L. Rose speech given to Susan B. Anthony.
Courtesy of the Library of Congress.

meeting in a sub-headline as an "Awful Combination of Socialism, Abolitionism, and Infidelity,"[47] he went on to inform the newspaper's readers that

> There is not a lunatic asylum in the country wherein, if the inmates were called together to sit in convention, they would not exhibit more sense, reason, decency and delicacy, and less lunacy, blasphemy and horrible sentiment, than this hybrid, mongrel, piebald, crackerbrained, pitiful, disgusting and ridiculous assemblage.

47. Lutz, 237; *New York Herald,* October 25, 1850.

> And there we drop them, and may God have mercy on their miserable souls. Amen.[48]

The Convention nominated Rose to the Central Committee, and to serve as Chair of the Committee on Civil and Political Functions, the latter including in its membership Lucy Stone, Wendell Phillips, Abby Kelly Foster, William Lloyd Garrison, and Elizabeth Cady Stanton. The organizational work of the meeting was important for, in the words of historian Keith E. Melder, "The Worcester convention climaxed the organizing process of the woman's rights movement. Following this occasion, the movement took on the characteristics of an independent, organized reform crusade, much like the antislavery agitation."[49] In this transformation, Rose played a leading part.

Upon her return to New York City from Worcester, Rose renewed her agitation for legal reform by authoring a petition to the New York State Legislature arguing on behalf of extending to women their right to vote and hold elective office. In defense of her position she argued:

> [I]t will be said that the husband provides for the wife, or in other words, he feeds, clothes, and shelters her! I wish I had the power to make every one before me fully realize the degradation contained in that idea. Yes! he keeps her, and so [he] does a favorite horse; by law they are both considered his property. Again, I shall be told that the law presumes the husband to be kind, affectionate, and ready to provide for and protect his wife. But what right, I ask, has the law to presume at all on the subject? What right has the law to intrust the interest and happiness of one being into the hands of another?[50]

During the summer she went on an extensive speaking tour in Western New York including stops at Rush, Honeoye, Smithtown, and other small village venues. Traveling east at the conclusion of her engagements, she again spoke at Dover and Washington Hollow in Dutchess County before attending the Second National Women's Rights Convention in Worcester on October 15–16.[51]

The second Worcester convention attracted so many people the former Brinley Hall location could not accommodate the crowd. A highlight was a speech best described by participant Paulina Wright Davis, who commented that "In this convention Mrs. Ernestine L. Rose made an address of an hour in length, which has never been surpassed."[52] In her address, Rose replied to criticism leveled at the first

48. *New York Herald,* October 25, 1850

49. Suhl, 113; Kolmerten, 76–82; quote from Melder, 153.

50. Rose's address in 1851 is quoted in Suhl, 82 and 281–284.

51. Suhl, 118–119.

52. Suhl, 122; Paulina Wright Davis, *A History of the National Woman's Rights movement, for Twenty Years* (New York: Journeymen Printers' Co-operative, 1871), 19.

Worcester convention by Rev. Henry Bellows, editor of the Unitarian newspaper *New York Christian Inquirer,* who posed the question "Place woman unbonneted and unshawled before the public gaze, and what becomes of her modesty and virtue?" Rose replied:

> In his benighted mind the modesty and virtue of woman is of so fragile a nature that when it is in contact with the atmosphere it evaporates like chloroform. But I refrain to comment on such a sentiment. It carries with it its own deep condemnation. When I read the article I earnestly wished I had the ladies of the writer's congregation before me, to see whether they could realize the estimation their pastor held them in. Yet I hardly know which sentiment was strongest for me, contempt for such foolish opinions, or pity for a man that has so degrading an opinion of women—of the being that gave him life, that sustained his helpless infancy with her ever-watchful care, and laid the very foundation for the little mind he may possess—of the being he took to his bosom as the partner of his joys and sorrows—the one whom, when he strove to win her affection, he courted, as all such men court women, like some divinity. Such a man deserves our pity; for I cannot realize that a man purposely and willfully degrades his mother, sister, wife, and daughter. No! my better nature, my best knowledge and conviction, forbid me to believe it.[53]

The *New York Herald,* previously quite negative in its portrayal of the first women's gathering in Worcester, reported on this occasion only that "Mrs. Rose spun a very long yarn composed of wit, philosophy and satire."[54] Englishman Joseph Baker characterized Rose as "the most perfect specimen of intellectual and moral excellence I have had the happiness to know. Her powers of mind, her powers of speech, her purse, her health, her life, are one continual sacrifice to humanity. Her eloquence is irresistible. It shakes, it awes, it thrills. To hear her reason you might fancy she was all intelligence; to hear her plead you would think her an incarnation of benevolence."[55]

Following Worcester, Rose spoke before several other Bay State groups, stressing a theme that linked the women's rights movement with the growing abolitionist movement, arguing that a "race is elevated in excellence and power, or kept back in progression, in accordance with the scale of women's position in society."[56]

In Rose's next public debate she took on the venerable liberal educator Horace Mann. Thought to be a friend of the women's rights movement, Mann went on tour in 1852 giving two lectures on the reasons why women should not demand the right to vote. Rose attended his lectures in New York City on February 17 and

53. *Proceedings of the Woman's Rights Convention, Held at Worcester, October 15th and 16th, 1851* (New York: 1852), 45–47.

54. Suhl, 123.

55. Quoted in Suhl, 138; *The Liberator,* November 25, 1854.

56. *A Lecture on Women's Rights, Delivered Before the People's Sunday Meeting, in Cochituate Hall, Boston, on Sunday, October 19, 1851, by Mrs. E. L. Rose* (Boston: J. P. Mendum, 1886), 17.

29, but was denied an opportunity to speak when she requested time to offer an extemporaneous rebuttal. Instead, she wrote to Mann offering the following comment: "[W]hile listening to your lecture I was almost forced to exclaim with one of old, 'Can any good come out of Nazareth?' can a politician be true to any subject that is not popular, when the Honorable gentleman before me can so easily stoop to pamper the vitiated taste of an already prejudiced public opinion, by giving the unthinking multitude the slang and ridicule they admire, instead of the arguments, truth and common sense they so much need?"[57] When no response was forthcoming, she published a formal rejoinder under the title "Review of Horace Mann's Two Lectures."

At the Third National Women's Rights Convention held in Syracuse, New York, in September, 1852, Rev. Antoinette Brown, the first female ordained minister in the United States, felt compelled to offer a rebuttal to the popular argument that the Bible supported man's superiority over women. In response, Susan B. Anthony moved that the meeting adopt a resolution to the effect that the Bible supported women's rights. Rose opposed the motion, arguing that the introduction of Biblical arguments into the debate would shift the focal point away from the primary issue of women's rights. Rather than take a position on Biblical interpretation, Rose reasoned, the convention should concern itself solely with "human rights and freedom, based upon the laws of humanity."[58] "For my part," she reasoned,

> I see no need to appeal to any written authority, particularly when it is so obscure and indefinite as to admit of different interpretations. When the inhabitants of Boston converted their harbor into a teapot rather than submit to unjust taxes, they did not go to the Bible for their authority; for if they had, they would have been told from the same authority to "give unto Caesar what belonged to Caesar." Had the people, when they rose in the might of their right to throw off the British yoke, appealed to the Bible for authority, it would have answered them, "Submit to the powers that be, for they are from God." No! on human rights and freedom, on a subject that is as self-evident as two and two make four, there is no need of any written authority. . . .
>
> I can not object to any one's interpreting the Bible as he or she thinks best; but I do object that such interpretations go forth as the doctrine of this convention, because it is a mere interpretation and not even the authority of the Book. It is the view of Miss Brown only which is as good as that of any other minister, but that is all. For my part I reject both interpretations. Here we claim human rights and freedom based upon the laws of humanity, and we require no written authority

57. Suhl, 126; *Boston Investigator*, April 21, 1852.

58. Suhl, 127; quote from Gurko, 159; *Proceedings of the Woman's Rights Convention, Held at Syracuse, September 8th, 9th, & 10th, 1852* (Syracuse: 1852) in the New York Public Library.

> from Moses or Paul, because the laws of our claim are prior even to these two great men.[59]

With the strong support of Lucretia Mott, Rose was able to mobilize enough support to defeat Anthony's motion and eliminate Biblical interpretation as a major factor in the women's rights debate.

In the same convention, Rose had an opportunity to call upon her unique personal history to plead the case of women's rights from the standpoint of one who was familiar with the lack of civil and human rights and how they could effect a person.

> It is of little importance in what geographical position a person is born, but it is important whether his ideas are based upon facts that can stand the test of reason, and his acts are conducive to the happiness of society. Yet, being a foreigner, I hope you will have some charity on account of speaking in a foreign language. Yes. I am an example of the universality of our claims; for not American women only, but a daughter of poor, crushed Poland, and the downtrodden and persecuted people called the Jews, "a child of Israel," pleads for the equal rights of her sex.
>
> . . . any difference in political, civil and social rights on account of sex, is in direct violation of the principles of justice and humanity, and as such ought to be held up to the contempt and derision of every lover of human freedom. [Women demand rights] not as a gift of charity but as an act of justice.[60]

The 1853 Women's Rights Convention met in New York City in September featuring the usual slate of luminaries on the speaker's docket. When her tum came, Rose explained at length how New York's laws discriminated against women. Although a married woman's property law had been passed, she explained, if a woman sold her property during marriage the money was legally her husband's property. Only the husband had a right to make a will, and if the wife had a will that predated the marriage the husband had the legal right to void that document.[61] A master of sarcasm, she pointed out that

> wills may be made out by all persons, except idiots, persons of unsound mind, married women and infants. Male infants ought to consider it quite an insult to be placed in the same category with married women. No, a married woman has no right to bequeath a dollar of the property, no matter how much she may have brought into marriage, or accumulated in it. Not a dollar to a friend, a relative, or

59. *Proceedings of the Woman's Rights Convention Held at Syracuse, September 8th, 9th, & 10th, 1852* (Syracuse, 1852).

60. Quoted in Henry Lewis, "Ernestine Rose—First Jewish Advocate of Women's Rights," *Forward,* June 19, 1927; excerpted in Marcus, 165.

61. Suhl, 141; *Proceedings of the Woman's Rights Convention Held at the Broadway Tabernacle in the City of New York, on Tuesday and Wednesday, Sept. 6th and 7th, 1853* (New York: 1853).

> even to her own child to keep him from starving. And this is the law in the nineteenth century, in the enlightened United States, under a Republic that declares all men to be free and equal.[62]

Yet, Rose noted, when the wife passed away the result was quite different,

> all that is left is her husband's; there is no interference of the law, no change is made, no stranger intrudes on his home and his affliction; no one dares to ask a question concerning the things which she, whom he loved, has left behind her. But it is otherwise when the husband dies - strangers assume authority denied to the wife and mother; the sanctuary of affliction and sorrow must be desecrated, everything ransacked and assessed by the agents of the law."[63]

In the following month Rose traveled to Cleveland to attend the fourth national convention on women's rights where her activism led the *Cleveland Plain Dealer* to report that she was "decidedly the master spirit of the convention."[64] On the way home from the meeting Rose and Lucretia Mott spoke in Buffalo, New York, to an audience that included many who opposed their views. A reporter for the *Buffalo Commercial Advertiser* characterized the two reformers as "The Old Girls from New York," adding that Rose was "a female fillibuster" who "went off like an overloaded musket and was evidently disposed to kick."[65] Moving on to Rochester, Rose spoke at yet another meeting where she was introduced to the abolitionist orator Sallie Holley. Holley described Rose as "a charming woman and at times playful. She is far before any woman speaker I ever heard. She is splendidly clear and logical. But oh! I cannot give any idea of the power and beauty of her speech. I can only stammer about it a little."[66] A Boston newspaper concurred, describing Rose as "an excellent lecturer, liberal, eloquent, witty, and decidedly handsome." Indeed, by the middle of the decade of the 1850s Rose's notable oratorical skill had earned for her the appellation "Queen of the Platform."[67]

By the mid-1850s, support for the women's rights movement was growing in both number and activism. When the New York State women's rights movement met for two days in Albany in 1854, public interest stretched the gathering to a full two weeks during which Rose and the movement's other leaders spent considerable time testifying before legislative committees and lobbying with individual members

---

62. *Proceedings of the Woman's Rights Convention Held at the Broadway Tabernacle in the City of New York, on Tuesday and Wednesday, Sept. 6th and 7th, 1853* (New York: 1853).
63. *Ibid.*
64. Suhl, 148.
65. Suhl, 152.
66. Suhl, 152; John White Chadwick, ed., *A Life for Liberty: Anti-Slavery and Other Letters of Sallie Holley* (New York: Negro University Press, 1969 reprint of 1899 original), 127.
67. Gurko, 88–89.

of the Senate and Assembly. The *Albany Transcript* reported that "Mrs. Rose is the queen of the company. On the educational question in particular she rises to a high standard of oratorical power. When speaking of Hungary and her own crushed Poland, she is full of eloquence and pathos, and she has as great a power to chain an audience as any of our best male speakers."[68]

"Gentlemen," Rose began when speaking before the Assembly, "these are not the demands of the moment or the few; they are the demands of the age; of the second half of the nineteenth century. The world will endure after us, and future generations may look back to this meeting to acknowledge that a great onward step was here taken in the cause of human progress." According to reporters who were present, her statement was met with loud applause.[69]

Yet, influential doubters remained. The *Albany Register* lamented:

> While the feminine propagandists of women's rights confined themselves to the exhibition of short petticoats and long-legged boots, and to the holding of conventions, and speech-making in concert-rooms, the people were disposed to be amused by them, as they are by the wit of the clown in the circus, or the performances of Punch and Judy on fair days, or the minstrelsy of gentlemen with blackened faces, on banjos, the tamborine and bones. But the joke is becoming stale. People are getting cloyed with these performances, and are looking for some healthier and more intellectual amusement. The ludicrous is wearing away, and disgust is taking the place of pleasurable sensations, arising from the novelty of this new phase of hypocrisy, and infidel fanaticism. People are beginning to inquire how far public sentiment should sanction, or tolerate these unsexed women, who make a scoff of religion, who repudiate the Bible and blaspheme God; who would step out from the true sphere of the mother, the wife, and the daughter, and taking upon themselves the duties and the business of men, stalk into the public gaze, and by engaging in the politics, the rough controversies, and trafficing of the world, unweave existing institutions, and overturn all the social relations of life.
>
> It is a melancholy reflection, that among our American women who have been educated to better things, there should be found any, who are willing to follow the lead of such foreign propagandists as the ringleted, glove-handed exotic, Ernestine L. Rose. We can understand how such *men* as the Rev. Mr. May, or the sleek-headed Dr. Chalmers may be deluded by her to becoming her disciples. They are not the first instances of infatuation that may overtake weak minded men, if they are honest in their devotion to her and her doctrines. Nor would they be the first examples of a low ambition that seeks notoriety as a substitute for true fame, if they are dishonest. Such *men* there are always, and honest or dishonest their true position is that of being tied to the apron strings of some "strong minded woman," and to be exhibited as rare specimens of human wickedness, or human weakness and folly. But, that one educated American woman, should become her disciple and follow her infidel and insane teachings, is a marvel.

68. Suhl, 154.
69. *Albany Register*, March 6, 1854.

An 1857 drawing of the "ringleted" Mrs. Rose by Grozlier
Courtesy of the Jacob Rader Marcus Center of the American Jewish Archives.

Ernestine L. Rose came to this country, as she says, from Poland, whence she was compelled to fly in pursuit of freedom. Seeing her course here, we can well imagine this to be true. In no other country in the world, save possibly one, would her infidel propagandism, and preachings in regard to the social relations of life, be tolerated. She would be prohibited by the powers of government from her efforts to obliterate from the world the religion of the Cross—to banish the Bible as a text-book of faith, and to overturn social institutions that have existed through all political and governmental revolutions from the remotest time. The strong hand of the law would be laid upon her, and she would be compelled back to her woman's sphere. But in this country, such is the freedom of our institutions, and we rejoice that it should be so, that she, and such as she can give their genius for intrigue full sway. They can exhibit their flowing ringlets and beautiful hands, their winning smiles and charming stage attitudes, to admiring audiences, who, while they are willing to be amused, are in the main safe from their corrupting theories and demoralizing propagandism.

The laws and the theory of our government suppose that the people are capable of taking care of themselves, and hence need no protection against the wiles of domestic or foreign mountebanks, whether in petticoats or in breeches and boots. But it never was contemplated that these exotic agitators, would come up to our Legislature and ask for the passage of laws upholding and sanctioning their wild and foolish doctrines. That was a stretch of folly, a flight of impudence which was hardly regarded as possible. It was to be imagined, of course, that they would enlist as their followers, here and there one among the restless old maids and visionary wives who chanced to be unevenly tempered, as well as unevenly yoked. It was also to be assumed, as within the range of possibility, that they might bring within the sphere of their attractions, weak minded restless men, who think in their vanity, that they have been marked out for great things, and failed to be appreciated by the world, men who comb their hair smoothly back and with fingers locked across their stomachs speak in a soft voice, and with upturned eyes. But no man supposed they would abandon their "private theatricals" and walk up to the Capitol, and insist that the performances shall he held in legislative halls. And yet it is so.

This Mrs. Ernestine L. Rose, with a train of followers, like a great kite with a very long tail, has, for a week, been amusing Senatorial and Assembly committees, with her women's rights performances, free of charge, unless the waste of time that might be better employed in the necessary and legitimate business of legislation, may be regarded as a charge. Those committees have sat for hours, grave and solemn as owls, listening to the outpourings of fanaticism and folly of the Polish propagandist, Mrs. Ernestine L. Rose, and her followers in pantalets and short gowns. The people outside, and especially those interested in the progress of legislation, are beginning to ask one another how long this farce is to continue. How long this most egregious and ridiculous humbug is to be permitted to obstruct the progress of business before the committees and the Houses, and whether Mrs. Ernestine L. Rose, and her followers, ought to be satisfied with the notoriety they have already attained. The great body of the people, regard Mrs. Rose and her followers, as making themselves simply ridiculous, and there is some danger that these legislative committees will make themselves so too.[70]

Rose responded to the *Register's* commentary with a letter to the editor, noting that:

In your paper of Monday the 6th inst., I perceive you pass judgment upon the Woman's Rights Cause, upon those engaged in it, and particularly upon myself—how justly, I leave to your conscience to decide.

---

70. *Albany Register,* March 6, 1854.

Every one who ever advanced a *new idea,* no matter how great and noble, has been subjected to criticism, and therefore we too must expect it. And in accordance with the spirit of the critic, will be the criticism. Whether dictated by the spirit of justice, kindness, gentleness and charity, or by injustice and malice, rudeness, and intolerance, it is still an index of the man. But it is quite certain that no true soul will ever be deterred from the performance of a duty by any criticism.

But there is one thing which I think even editors have no right to do, namely: to state a positive falsehood, or even to *imply* one, for the purpose of injuring another. And, as the spirit of charity induces me to believe than in your case it was done more from a misunderstanding than positive malice, therefore, I claim at your hands the justice to give this letter a place in your paper.

In the article alluded to, you say, "Ernestine L. Rose, came to this country, as she says, from Poland, whence she was compelled to fly in pursuit of freedom." It is *true* that I came from Poland; but is *false* that I was *compelled to fly from my country,* except by the compulsion, or dictates of the same spirit of "propagandism," that induced so many of my noble countrymen to shed their blood in the defense of the rights of this country, and the rights of man, wherever he struggles for freedom. But I have no desire to claim martyrdom, which does not belong to me. I left my country, *not flying* but *deliberately.* I chose to make this country my home, in preference to any other, because if you carried out the theories you profess, it would *indeed* be the noblest country on earth. And as my countrymen so nobly aided in the *physical struggle* for Freedom and Independence, I felt, and still feel it equally *my* duty to use my humble abilities to the uttermost in my power, to aid in the *great moral struggle* for Human Rights, and Human Freedom.

Hoping that you will accede to my (I think) just claim to give this a place in your paper.

I am, very respectfully,
Ernestine L. Rose[71]

What Rose and her colleagues sought was an extension of the rights they obtained earlier. Particularly, they sought the right of a married woman to own in her own name the property and money she accumulated during marriage. They sought the legal right for married women to buy, sell, sign contracts, and otherwise engage in business without the permission of their husbands, and the right of mothers to legal custody of their children. They also sought the right for women to sue, to be tried by a jury, to serve on juries, to vote, and to hold elective office. To achieve these goals, Rose and her associates renewed their efforts to increase pressure on the legislature by organizing meetings and petition drives in every county in the state with Anthony serving as the principal organizer and Rose the primary speaker. After one such address in Bath, New York, a local reporter pronounced Rose "one of the best speakers we have ever heard," adding that "we can only regret

71. *Albany Register,* March 10, 1854.

that a woman of such brilliant intellect should be wasting her energies in a cause for which there is not a shadow of hope."[72]

Through 1855 and 1856 the reform efforts continued with Rose speaking across New York State, while also taking time out for tours to address audiences in Massachusetts, Michigan, and Pennsylvania. Finally, physically exhausted from her unrelenting schedule, she was forced to leave in May, 1856, for a six-month vacation in Europe to restore her health. "Whether I shall be able once more to see my own poor native land, Poland, I know not," she wrote before leaving. Four days after her return she took up the gauntlet once more, speaking at the national women's rights convention meeting in New York City.[73]

The national convention in 1858 met once again in New York City, convening at Mozart Hall with Rose among the featured speakers who included Lucy Stone, Wendell Phillips, and William Lloyd Garrison. "Formerly," she began,

> all that was deemed requisite in the education of woman was that she should be able to sign her name to the marriage contract, and even that could be dispensed with for she could use her "x" mark. Arithmetic was deemed entirely superfluous for, what, indeed, had woman to count? Her children she could count on her fingers! But that time is passed and the fact is that the Press, as often the led as the leader, the Bar, still oftener led than leading, and the Pulpit, always in the rear of public opinion, are all together, at last, pleading for the education of women.[74]

In 1860 Rose's long crusade for the extension of the women's property rights act finally met success. On March 20 the New York State Legislature passed an *Act Concerning the Rights and Liabilities of Husband and Wife*. The act granted almost everything in the women's petitions except suffrage. Under its provisions, women could own both property held before marriage and that acquired during marriage, and could "dispose of them as she pleased without her husband's interference." A married woman "could make investments, engage in business enterprises, [and] sign contracts." On the important question of child custody, the act proclaimed that "Every married woman is hereby constituted as the joint guardian of her children, with her husband, with equal powers, rights, and duties in regard to them, with the husband."[75] Of Rose's contribution to the stunning victory, William Lloyd Garrison wrote that she was "one of the most remarkable women of the age . . . as the advocate of the rights of her sex, she has no superior."[76]

---

72. Suhl, 157–159.
73. Suhl, 179, 186.
74. Suhl, 199–200.
75. Gurko, 313; Hymowitz and Weissman, 120; quote from Suhl, 200.
76. Suhl, 247.

On May 12, 1860, the leaders of the women's rights movement met at the Cooper Institute in New York City to begin their tenth national convention. In New York, at least, victory was theirs, and they all felt the remaining battle, the elective franchise, was only a matter of time. Few would have believed it would be another sixty years before the ratification of the Nineteenth Amendment finally gave women the right to vote in 1920.

In the intervening years, Rose took a leading part, along with Elizabeth Cady Stanton and Susan B. Anthony, in an unsuccessful attempt to change the wording of the Fourteenth Amendment to extend the right to vote to women. An active member of the Women's Loyal National League during the Civil War, she was a prime mover behind the postwar American Equal Rights Association before returning with her husband to England in 1869. Although she visited the United States to participate in the National Woman's Suffrage Association meeting in 1873, she took little further part in the struggle for women's equality in America, refusing even an offer by Susan B. Anthony to write a portion of *The History of Woman Suffrage*. Instead, Rose lived out the remainder of her years in England, passing away in Brighton on August 4, 1892 at the age of eighty-two.[77] At her funeral, George Jacob Holyoake, a leader in the English cooperative movement, said in his graveside oration that she had

> the fire of Judith in her, and her passion was to see women possess civil and social equality, and to inspire women and men with self-helping sense, not taking religion, politics or social ideas second-hand from their 'pastors and masters,' but choosing principles of belief, government and conduct for themselves. . . . Mrs. Rose took truth for authority, not authority for truth. . . . The slave she had helped to free from the bondage of ownership, and the minds she had set free from the bondage of authority, were the glad and proud remembrances of her last days. . . .
>
> When the more prominently known leaders of the later women's rights movement came to the cause, Ernestine L. Rose's activities and speeches were among the factors that attracted them. She was on the scene *before* Lucretia Mott, Elizabeth Cady Stanton, and Susan B. Anthony.[78]

Although the legal battles were not yet over at the time of her death, the groundwork for gender equality before the law had been laid in New York State due in no small part to the tireless work of the daughter of a Polish rabbi. L. E. Bernard

77. Mary Stetson Clarke, *Bloomers and Ballots: Elizabeth Cady Stanton and Women's Rights* (New York: The Viking Press, 1972), 182; Gurko, 313; National Women's Hall of Fame, misc. papers. Five years before her death, Rose summarized her career in a letter to Rev. Edward F. Strickland on August 30, 1887 (American Jewish Archives). She wrote (in her own spelling): "For over 50 years I have endeavored to promote the rights of Umanity [humanity] without distinction of sex, sect, party, contry or coller [color]."

78. Morris U. Schappes, "Ernestine Rose, Queen of the Platform," *Jewish Life*, March, 1949, 7, 10.

summed up her contribution thusly: "How much freedom they now enjoy, the women of America owe to the noble Polish woman, cannot be estimated, for moral influences are too subtle for measurement. Those who sat with her on the platform in bygone days will remember her matchless powers as a speaker, and how safe we all felt while she had the floor, that neither in manner, sentiment, or repartee, would she in any way compromise the dignity of the occasion."[79]

In the fight for women's rights she focused most of her efforts on legal issues. "Emancipation from every kind of bondage is my principle," she stated in a speech on the anniversary of the emancipation of slaves in the West Indies. "I go for the recognition of human rights, without distinction to sect, party, sex, or color."[80] Her forte in the fight for equality was clearly her oratorical ability. "Probably the most fiery orator that the early days of the woman's suffrage cause produced, the Patrick Henry of the movement, was Ernestine L. Rose," declared Lillie Devereaux Blake. "[T]all and dignified in figure, with keen dark eyes, curling black hair and a brilliant complexion," the *Boston Intelligencer* described her as "an excellent lecturer, liberal, eloquent, witty, and, we must add, decidedly handsome—the Rose that all were praising. . . . [S]he thrilled the audience by the electric force of her words, and her dark eyes flashed as her voice rose in the fiery earnestness of her eloquence. . . . The liberal laws which we now live under are due to the tireless exertions of this gifted woman, and never ought the women of New York to forget the debt of gratitude they owe to Ernestine L. Rose."[81]

Among her contemporaries she was respected as a pioneering leader in the movement for women's rights. To Lucretia Mott, Rose was "one of our best." To Theodore Tilton, she was "a kind of Thomas Paine among her sisterhood." To Susan B. Anthony she was the "brave[est] and [most] fearless of all women." To William Lloyd Garrison she was "one of the most remarkable women, and one of the ablest and most eloquent public speakers, in this country." Her colleagues in the movement thought so much of her that when Susan B. Anthony, Elizabeth Cady Stanton, and Matilda Joslyn Gage edited the history of the women's rights movement, they attributed its initial formation to two pioneers, Frances Wright, a Scottish noblewoman, and the woman biographer Yuri Suhl characterized as "the beautiful and exotic Polish lady," Ernestine Potowska Rose.[82]

79. Lewis, "Ernestine Rose—First Jewish Advocate of Women's Rights."

80. Jacob Rader Marcus, *The American Jewish Woman: A Documentary History* (New York & Cincinnati: Ktav and American Jewish Archives, 1981), 167.

81. "A Jewess the Pioneer of Woman Suffrage," *American Hebrew*, XLV, No. 7 (December 19, 1890), 172. The *Hebrew Leader* for May 21, 1869, considered her "the best female lecturer in the United States."

82. Suhl, 35, 48, 49; Garrison quote from *The Liberator*, March 23, 1855.

Documents

Document 1

Letter, Ernestine Potowska Rose to Elizabeth Cady Stanton, May 17, 1880, Regarding the Woman's Suffrage Convention to be Held in Chicago on June 2, 1880.

London, May 17, 1880

Dear Mrs. Stanton,

You know me too well to require my assurance that it would give me great pleasure to be with you at your meeting on the second of June. But as that is impossible, I send my voice across the Atlantic to plead for Human rights without distinction of sex, and to swell the grand chorus in the demand of Justice to Woman by declaring her right to the suffrage and proclaim her a citizen.

But the suffrage is not only a badge of citizenship but a mental and moral elevator which raises the possesser to self respect and dignity, and prepares him for greater usefulness and higher and nobler aims in the progress of Humanity.

Success to our cause and love to the Friends devoted to it.

Yours effectionately
Ernestine L. Rose

Document 2

Women's Rights Lecture Presented by Ernestine Potowska Rose at Cochituate Hall, Boston, October 19, 1851.

My FRIENDS: The observing and reflecting mind that casts its vision far beyond the panoramic scenes of every day life, must perceive that our present age is fast ripening for the most important changes in the affairs of man. The desire for freedom has shaken Europe to its very centre. The love of Liberty has convulsed the nations like the mighty throes of an earthquake. The oppressed are struggling against the oppressors. Kings and priests are called upon to give an account of their stewardship, for man no longer believes in the divine right of force and fraud.

Yet great as these signs of the times are, they are not new. From the time of absolute despotism to the present hour of comparative freedom, the weak had ever to struggle against the strong, right against might. But a new sign has appeared in our social zodiac, prophetic of the most important changes, pregnant with the most beneficial results that have ever taken place in the annals of human history. And to him who can trace the various epochs in human life, it is as cheering as it is interesting to mark the onward movement of the race towards a higher state of human progression—that while nations strive against nations, people against people, to attain the same amount of freedom already possessed in this country, WOMAN is rising in the full dignity of her being to claim the recognition of *her* rights. And though the first public demonstration has been here, already has the voice of Woman in behalf of her sex been carried, as it were, on the wings of lightning to all parts of Europe, whose echo has brought back the warmest and most heartfelt responses from our sisters there.

Among the many encouraging letters received at the recent Woman's Convention at Worcester, there was one exceeding all the rest in the soul-stirring interest it created. It spoke, through the dungeon walls, the cheering and encouraging words of sympathy from two incarcerated women of Paris, to the hearts of their sisters in America. The cause of their imprisonment was their practically claiming the fulfillment of that glorious motto, "Liberty, Equality, and Fraternity," destined to shake the thrones, break the sceptres, and bow down the mitres of Europe. One of them presented herself as candidate for Mayor of an Arrondissement, the other (to the honor of the genuine Republicans of Paris, be it said,) was nominated by the Industrial Union, consisting of two hundred and twenty Societies, as a member of the Assembly. For these offences they were cast into prison. Oh! France, where is the glory of thy revolutions? Is the blood thy children poured out on the altar of freedom so effaced, that thy daughters dare not lift their voices in behalf of their rights? But so long as might constitutes right, every good cause must have its martyrs. Why, then, should woman not be a martyr to *her* cause?

But how can we wonder that France, governed as she is by Russian and Austrian despotism, does not recognize the higher laws of humanity in the recognition of the rights of woman, when even here, in this far-famed land of freedom and of knowledge, under a republic that has inscribed on its banner the great truth that all men are created free and equal, and are endowed with inalienable rights to life, liberty, and the pursuit, of happiness a Declaration wafted like the voice of Hope on the breezes of heaven to the remotest parts of earth, to whisper freedom and equality to the oppressed and down-trodden children of men,—a Declaration that lies at the very foundation of human freedom and happiness, yet in the very face of that eternal truth, woman, the mockingly so-called "better half of man," has yet to plead for her rights, nay, for her life. For what is life without liberty? and what is liberty without equality of rights; and as for the pursuit of happiness, she is not allowed to pursue any line of life that might promote it; she has only thankfully to accept what man, in the plenitude of his wisdom and generosity, decides as proper for her to do, and that is, what he does not choose to do himself.

Is woman, then, not included in that Declaration? Answer, ye wise men of the nation, and answer truly; add not hypocrisy to your other sins. Say she is not created free and equal, and therefore, (for the sequence follows on the premises) she is not entitled to life, liberty, and the pursuit of happiness. But you dare not answer this simple question. With all the audacity arising from an assumed superiority, you cannot so libel and insult humanity as to say she is not; and if she is, then what right has man, except that of might, to deprive her of the same rights and privileges he claims for himself?

And why, in the name of reason and justice, I ask, why should she not have the same rights as man? Because she is woman? Humanity recognizes no sex—mind recognizes no sex—virtue recognizes no sex—life and death, pleasure and pain, happiness and misery, recognize no sex. Like him she comes involuntarily into existence; like him she possesses physical, mental, and moral powers, on the proper cultivation of which depends her happiness; like him she is subject to all the vicissitudes of life; like him she has to pay the penalty for disobeying Nature's laws, and, far greater penalties has she to suffer from ignorance of her far more complicated nature than he; like him she enjoys or suffers with her country. Yet she is not recognized as his equal. In the laws of the land she has no rights; in government she has no voice, and in spite of another principle recognized in this Republic, namely, that taxation without representation is tyranny, woman, is taxed without being represented; her property may be consumed by heavy taxes, to defray the expenses of that unholy and unrighteous thing called war, yet she cannot give her veto against it. From the cradle to the grave, she is subject to the power and control of man,—father, guardian, and husband. One, conveys her like some piece of merchandize over to the other.

At marriage she loses her entire identity. Her being is said to be merged in her husband. Has Nature there merged it? Has she ceased to exist or feel pleasure and pain? When she violates the laws of her being, does he pay the penalty? When she breaks the laws of the land, does he suffer the punishment? When his wants are supplied, is it sufficient to satisfy the wants of her nature? Or when, at his nightly orgies, in the grog-shop, the oyster cellar, or the gaming table, he spends the means she helped by her co-operation and economy, to accumulate, and she awakens to penury and destitution, will it supply the wants of her children to tell them that owing to the superiority of man she has no redress by law, and that as her being was merged in him, so also ought theirs to be?

But it will be said that the husband provides for the wife, or, in other words, he is bound to feed, clothe, and shelter her. Oh! the degradation of that idea! Yes, he keeps her; so he does his horse. By law both are considered his property; both can, when the cruelty of the owner compels them to run away, be brought back by the strong arm of the law; and, according to a still extant law of England, both may be led by the halter to the market place and sold. This is humiliating, indeed, but nevertheless true, and the sooner these things are known and understood, the better for humanity. It is no fancy sketch. I know that some endeavor to throw the mantle of romance over the subject, and treat woman like some ideal existence not subject to the ills of life. Let those deal in fancy that have nothing better to deal in. We have to do with sober, sad realities, with stubborn facts.

But again it will be said, the law presumes the husband would be kind, affectionate, and that he would provide for and protect the wife; but I ask, what right has the law to presume at all on the subject? What right has the law to intrust the interest and happiness of one being to the power of another? And if this merging of interests is so indispensable, then why should woman always be on the losing side? Turn the tables; let the identity and interest of the husband be merged in the wife, think you she would act less generous towards him than he towards her?—that she would be incapable of as much justice, disinterested devotion, and abiding affection as him?

Oh! how grossly you misunderstand and wrong her nature. But we desire no such undue power over man. It would be as wrong in her as it now is in him; all we claim is our own rights. We have nothing to do with individual man, be he good or bad, but with the laws that oppress woman. Bad and unjust laws must in the nature of things make man so too. If he acts better, if he is kind, affectionate, and consistent, it is because the kindlier feelings instilled by a mother, kept warm by a sister, and cherished by a wife, will not allow him to carry out the barbarous laws against woman; but the estimation she is generally held in, is as degrading as it is unjust.

Not long ago, I saw an account of two offenders brought before a Justice in New York; one, for stealing a pair of boots, for which offence he was sentenced to six months imprisonment; the other, for an assault and battery on his wife, for which offence he was let off with a reprimand from the Judge! With my principles I am entirely opposed to punishment. I hold to reforming the erring, and removing the causes, as being much more efficient, as well as just, than punishing; but the Judge showed the comparative value he set on these two kinds of property. But you must remember that the boots were taken by a stranger, while the wife was insulted by her legal owner. Yet it will be said that such degrading cases are few. For the sake of humanity I hope they are, but as long as woman is wronged by unequal laws, so long will she be degraded by man.

We can hardly have an adequate idea how all-powerful law is in forming public opinion, in giving tone and character to the mass of society. To illustrate this point, look at that inhuman, detestable law, written in human blood, signed and sealed with life, and liberty, that eternal stain on the statute books of this country, the Fugitive Slave Law. Think you that before its passage you could have found any in the free States, except a few politicians in the market, base enough to desire such a law? No, no! Even those that took no interest in the subject would have shrunk from so barbarous a thing; but no sooner is it passed, than the ignorant mass, the rabble of the self-styled Union Safety Committee, found out we were a law-loving and law-abiding people. Such is the magic power of law; hence the necessity to guard against bad ones, and hence also the reason why we call on the nation to remove the legal shackles from woman.

Set her politically and civilly free, and it will have a more beneficial effect on that still greater tyrant she has to contend with, public opinion. Carry out the Republican principle of universal suffrage, or strike it from your banner, and substitute freedom and power to one half of society, and submission and slavery to the other. Give women, then, the elective franchise. Let married women have the same right to property that man has; for whatever the difference in their respective occupations, the duties of the wife are as indispensable and far more arduous than the husband's. Why, then, should the wife, at the death of her husband, not be his heir to the same extent that he is to her?

In this legal inequality there is involved another wrong. When the wife dies, the husband is left in the undisturbed possession of all, and the children are left with him. No change is made, no stranger intrudes on his home and his affliction; but when the husband dies, not only is she, as is too often the case, deprived of all or at best receives but a mere pittance, but strangers assume authority denied to the wife and mother. The sanctuary of affliction must be desecrated by executors, everything must be ransacked and assessed, lest she should steal something out of her own house, and, to cap the climax, the children are taken from her and placed under guardians. When he dies poor, no guarantee is required; the children are left with the mother to care and toil for them as best she may; but when anything is left for the maintenance and education of the children, then it must be placed in the hands of strangers for safe keeping, lest the mother might defraud them. The whole care and bringing up of the children are left with the mother, and safe they are in her hands; but a few hundred or thousand dollars cannot be intrusted with her.

But it will be said, that in case of a second marriage, the children must be protected in their possession. Does that reason not hold as good in his case? Oh! no! for when he marries again he still retains his identity and power to act, but she becomes merged once more into a mere non-entity, and therefore the first husband must rob her to prevent the second from doing it. But we say, make the laws regulating marriage, if *any* are required at all, equal for both, and all these difficulties would be obviated. According to a late act, the wife has a right to the property she brings at marriage, or received in any way after marriage. Here is some provision for the favored few, but for the laboring many there is none. The mass of the people commence life with no other capital than the head, hearts and hands. To the result of this best of all capital, the wife has no right. If they are unsuccessful in married life, who suffers more the bitter consequences of poverty than the wife? But if successful, she cannot call a dollar her own. He may will every dollar (of his personal property) and leave her destitute and penniless, and she has no redress by law; and even when real estate is left, she receives but a life interest in a third part of it, and at her death she cannot leave it to any of her relations; it falls back even to the remotest of his relations.

This is law, but where is the justice of it? Well might we say, that laws were made to prevent, but not promote, the ends of justice. Or, in case of separation, why should the children be taken from the protecting care of the mother? Who has a better right to them than she? How much do fathers generally do towards the bringing them up? When he comes home from business, and the child is in good humor and handsome trim, he takes the little darling on his knee and plays with it; but when the wife, with the care of the whole household on her shoulders, with little or no help, was not able to put them in the best order and trim, how much does the father do towards it? Oh! no? Fathers like to have children good-natured, well-behaved, and comfortable; but how to put them in that desirable condition is out of their philosophy. Children always depend more on the tender, watchful care of the mother, than the father. Whether from nature, or habit or both, the mother is more capable of administering to their health and comfort than the father, and therefore she has the best right to them; and where there is property, it ought to be divided equally between them with an additional provision from the father towards the maintenance and education of the children.

Much is said about the burdens and responsibilities of married men. Responsibilities there are, if they only felt them; but as to burdens, what are they? The sole province of man seems to be centred in that one thing, attending to some business. I grant that owing to the present unequal and unjust reward for labor, some have to work too hard for a subsistence; but whatever his vocation, he has to attend to it as much before as after marriage. Look at your bachelors, and see if they do not strive as much for wealth, and attend as steadily to business as married men. No; the husband has little or no increase of burden, and every increase of comfort after marriage, while all the burdens, cares, pains, and penalties of married life fall entirely on the wife. How unjust and cruel, then, to have all the laws in, his favor! If any difference ought to be made by law between husband and wife, reason, justice, and humanity, if their voices were heard, would dictate it in her favor.

It is high time, then, to denounce such gross injustice, to compel man by the might of right to give woman her political, legal, and social rights. Open to her all the avenues of emolument, distinction, and greatness; give her an object for which to cultivate her powers, and a fair chance to do so, and there will be no need to speculate as to her proper sphere. She will find her own sphere in accordance with her capacities, powers, and tastes; and yet she will be woman still. Her rights will not change, but strengthen, develop, and elevate her nature. Away with that folly that her rights would be detrimental to her character—that if she is recognized as the equal to man, she would cease to be woman!—Have *his* rights as a citizen of a republic, the elective franchise with all its advantages, so changed his nature that he has ceased to be a man? Oh! no! But woman could not bear such a degree of power; what has benefitted him would injure her; what has strengthened him would weaken her; what prompted him to the performance of his duties would make her neglect hers!

Such is the superficial mode of reasoning, if it deserves that name, that is brought against the subject. It reminds me of two reasons given by a minister of Milton, on the North River. Having heard I had spoken on the rights of woman, he took the subject up the following Sunday, to prove that woman ought not to have equal rights with man,—first, because Adam was created before Eve; and secondly, man was compared to the fore wheel, and woman to the hind wheel of a wagon! These reasons are about as philosophical as any that can be brought on the subject. Man forgets, or he never knew, that our duties spring from our rights, and in proportion to the rights we enjoy are the duties we owe, and he that enjoys the most rights owes in return the most duties; though until now, while man enjoys the rights, he preaches all the duties to woman.

But, say some, in point of principle we grant it is right enough, but would you expose woman to the contact of rough, rude, drinking, swearing, fighting men at the ballot-box? What a humiliating confession lies in this plea for keeping women in the back-ground! Is the brutality of some men, then, a reason why woman should be kept from her rights? If man, in his superior wisdom, cannot devise means to enable woman to deposit her vote without having her finer sensibilities shocked by such disgraceful conduct, then there is an additional reason, as well as necessity, why she should be there to civilize, refine, and purify him, even at the ballot-box. Yes, in addition to the principle of right, this is one of the reasons why women should participate in all the important duties of life; for, with all due respect to the other sex, she is the true civilizer of man. Without her, he is at best but a semi-barbarian. From my very heart do I pity the man who has grown up and lives without the benign influence of woman!

Even now, in spite of being considered the inferior, she has a most beneficial effect on man. Look at your annual festivities where woman is excluded, and you will find more or less drunkenness, disorder, vulgarity, and excess to be the order of the day. Compare them with such where woman is the equal participant with man, and you will find rational social enjoyment and decorum prevail; and if this is the ease now,—and who can deny it?—how much more beneficial would be her influence, if, as the equal to man, she would take her stand by his side, to cheer, counsel, and aid him in the drama of life, in the Legislative Halls, in the Senate Chamber, in the Judge's chair, in the Jury box, on the Forum, in the Laboratory of the Arts and Sciences, and wherever duty would call her for the benefit of herself, her country, her race? In every step she would carry a humanizing influence.

And why, I would ask, should she not occupy all these stations? Why should one half of the race legislate for the other? In this country it is considered wrong for one nation to enact laws and enforce them against another. Does the same wrong not hold good of the sexes? Is she a being like him? Then she is entitled to the same rights, is she not? Then how can he legislate rightfully against a being whose nature he cannot understand, whose motives he cannot appreciate, and whose feelings he cannot realize? How can he sit in judgment and pronounce a verdict against a being so entirely different? No, there are no reasons for it, but there are deep-rooted, hoary-headed prejudices against her.

The main cause of them is, that pernicious falsehood propagated against her being, viz.: that she is inferior by her nature. Inferior in what? What has man ever done, that woman, under the same advantages, could not be made to do? In morals, bad as she is, she is generally considered his superior. In intellect, give her a fair chance before you pronounce a verdict against her. Cultivate that portion of the brain as much as that of man's, and she will stand his equal, at least. Even now, where her mind has been called out at all, her intellect is as bright, as capacious., and as powerful as his.

Will you tell me, we have no Newtons, Shakespeares, and Byrons? Greater natural powers than even these possessed, have been destroyed in woman, for want of proper culture—a just appreciation and reward for merit, as an incentive to exertion and freedom of action, without which, mind becomes cramped and stifled. It cannot expand under bolts and bars; and yet, under all these blighting, crushing circumstances, confined within the narrowest possible limit, trampled upon by prejudice and injustice, from her education and position forced to occupy herself almost exclusively with the most trivial affairs—in spite of all these difficulties, her intellect is as good as man's.

The few bright meteors in man's intellectual horizon could well be matched by woman, were she allowed to occupy the same elevated position. There is no need of naming the De Staels, the Rolands, the Somervilles, the Wollstonecrafts, the Wrights, the Fullers, the Martineaus, the Hemanses, the Sigourneys, the Jagiellos, and the many more of modern as well as ancient times, to prove her mental powers, her patriotism, her heroism, her self-sacrificing devotion to the cause of humanity—the eloquence that gushes from her pen or from her tongue. These things are too well known to require repetition. And do you ask for fortitude of mind, energy, and perseverance? Then look at woman under suffering, reverse of fortune, and affliction when the strength and power of man has sunk to the lowest ebb, when his mind is overwhelmed by the dark waters of despair. She, like the tender plant, bent but not broken by the storms of life, not only upholds her own hopeful courage, but, like the tender shoots of the ivy, clings around the tempest-fallen oak, to bind up the wounds, speak hope to his faltering spirit, and shelter him from the returning blast of the storm.

Wherein, then, is man so much superior that he must forever remain her master? In physical strength? Then allow me to say that the ox and the elephant is his superior! But, even on this point, why is she the feeble, sickly, suffering being we behold her? Look at her most defective, irrational education, and you will find the solution of the problem. Is the girl allowed to expand her limbs and chest in healthful exercise in the fresh breezes of heaven? Is she allowed to inflate her lungs and make the welkin ring with her cheerful expanded voice, like the boy? Whoever heard a girl committing such improprieties? Strongly developed limbs in a girl is unfashionable—a healthy, sound voice is vulgar—a ruddy glow on the cheek is coarse; and when life within her is so strong as to show itself in spite of bolts and bars, then she has to undergo a bleaching process, eat lemons and slate pencils—drink vinegar, and keep in the shade!

And do you know why these irrationalities are practiced? Because man wishes them so, and whatever he mostly admires in woman will she possess. That is the influence man has over woman, for she has been made to believe that she was created for his benefit only.—"It was not well for man to be alone," therefore she was made as a plaything to pass away an idle hour, or a drudge to do his bidding; and until this falsehood is eradicated from her mind—until she feels that the necessities, services, and obligations of the sexes are mutual—that she is as independent of him as he is of her; that she is formed for the same aims and ends in life that he is;—until, in fact, she has all her rights equal with man, there will be no other object in her education except to get married, and what will best promote that desirable end will be cultivated in her.

When a boy arrives at the age of twelve or so, the parents consult as to the kind of education that shall best fit him for all the purposes of life, to enable him to become a useful, respectable, independent member of society; and in accordance with the knowledge and means of the parents, and the capacities of the boy, so do they direct his education to make him a farmer, mechanic, merchant, lawyer, doctor; or, if the boy is not bright enough for any of these callings or professions, then he is destined for the ministry. But for what purpose is the girl educated? Do parents ever direct the education of a daughter for any such purposes? Oh! no! The rich man's daughter is taught to dance, to play on the piano, to draw and paint, (which she sometimes practices on her own face,) to speak a little bad French, &c., &c., not for the intrinsic value and beauty of these accomplishments, but to attract, and ultimately catch a beau and get married; for no sooner is she married than these things are all laid aside as some idle things to be thought of no more. How many ladies past the age of fifty use these accomplishments from a pure love of them, and the gratification of the family around them? Among the musical nations of Europe you may find some, but here these accomplishments are acquired as a means to an end;—that end once obtained, there is no further use for them.

The working classes educate their daughters in accordance with what would now be required of them namely, to cook a dinner good enough for a poor man, darn his stockings, sew on buttons, &c. Now these things are all very good in themselves; every girl ought to know them, and know them well, yet it is not enough for a healthy, happy, rational, intellectual life, but then it is all man now requires of woman. When he will look for higher and nobler mental accomplishments and powers, she will possess them.

Do you not yet understand what has made woman what she is? Then see what the sickly taste and perverted judgment of man now desires in woman. Not health and strength of body and mind, but a pale, delicate face; hands too small to grasp a broom, for that were treason in a lady; a voice so sickly, sentimental, and depressed, as to hear what she says only by the moving of her half-parted lips; and, above all, that nervous sensibility that sees a ghost in every passing shadow—that beautiful diffidence that dare not take a step without the arm of a man to support her tender frame, and that shrinking (mock) modesty that faints at the mention of the leg of a table! I know there are many noble exceptions that see and deplore these irrationalities, but as a general thing it is so, or else why set up the hue-and-cry of "mannish," "unfeminine," "out of her sphere," &c., whenever she evinces any strength of body or mind, and takes part in anything deserving a rational being?

Oh! the crying, injustice towards woman! She is crushed in every step she takes, and then insulted for being what a most pernicious education and corrupt public sentiment has made her. But there is no confidence in her powers nor principles. After last year's Convention of women, I saw an article in a Unitarian paper edited by the Rev. Mr. Bellows of New York, where, in reply to a correspondent upon the subject of woman's rights, in which he strenuously opposed her taking part in anything in public, he said, "Place woman unbonneted and unshawled before the public gaze, and what becomes of her modesty and her virtue?" In his benighted mind, the modesty and virtue of woman is but shawl deep, and, when in contact with the atmosphere, evaporates like chloroform. But I refrain to comment on the subject; it carries its own condemnation with it. When I read the article, I earnestly wished I had the ladies of his congregation before me to see whether they could realize the estimation their pastor held them in; yet I hardly know which sentiment was strongest in me, contempt for such foolish opinions, or pity for the writer; for a man that has such a degrading opinion of woman, of the being that gave him life and sustenance—that sustained his helpless infancy with her ever-watchful care, and laid the very foundation for the little mind he may possess—of the being he took to his bosom as the partner of his joys and sorrows—the one whom, when he strove to win her affections, he courted as all such men court woman, like some divinity—such a man deserves our pity, for I cannot realize that man purposely and willingly degrades his mother, sister, wife, and daughter.

No! my better nature, my best knowledge and convictions forbid me to believe it. It is from ignorance, not malice, man acts as he does. In ignorance of her nature, and the interest and happiness of both, he conceived ideas, laid down rules, and enacted laws concerning her destiny and her rights. The same ignorance, strengthened by age, sanctified by superstition, ingrafted into his being by habit, makes him still carry them out to the detriment of his own as well as her happiness; for is he not the loser by it? Oh! how severely he suffers! Who can fathom the depth of suffering and misery to society from the subjugation and injury inflicted on woman? The race is elevated in excellence and power, or kept back in progression, in accordance with the scale of woman's position in society. The attainment of woman's co-equality with man, is, in itself, not the end, but the means towards a still higher elevation of the race, without which, it never can attain. But so firmly has prejudice closed the eyes of man to the light of truth, that though he feels the evils, he knows not the cause. Those that have their eyes already open to these facts, earnestly desire the restoration of her rights, to enable her to take her proper position in the scale of humanity. If all could see it, all would desire it as they desire their own happiness, for the interest and happiness of the sexes cannot be divided. Nature has too closely united them to permit one to oppress the other with impunity, and therefore I can cast no more blame or reproach on man than on woman; for she, from habit based on the same errors, is as much opposed to her interest and happiness as he is. Yes, I will do man the justice to say, that I never mentioned the subject to any man capable of reflection, but he acknowledged the justice of it; and how long is it since any of us have advocated this righteous cause?—how long since any of us have come out of the darkness into the light of day? The longest period is but as it were since yesterday, and why? From the same reason that so many of both sexes are opposed to it yet—ignorance. Both have to be aroused from that deathly lethargy in which they slumber. That worse than Egyptian darkness must be dispelled from their minds before the pure rays of the sun can penetrate them.

And therefore, while I feel it my duty—aye, a painful duty, to point out the wrong done to woman and its evil consequences, and would do all in my power to aid in her deliverance, I can have no more ill feelings towards him than for the same errors towards her. Both are the victims of error and ignorance, and both suffer; and hence the necessity for active, earnest endeavors to enlighten their minds; hence the necessity to protest against the wrong and claim our rights, and in doing our duty we must not heed the taunts, ridicule, and stigma cast upon us. We must remember we have a crusade before us far holier and more righteous than led warrior to Palestine—a crusade not to deprive any one of his rights, but to claim our own; and as our cause is a better one, so also must be the means to achieve it. We therefore must put on the armor of charity, carry before us the banner of truth, and defend ourselves with the shield of right against the invaders of our liberty. And yet, like the knights of old, we must enlist in this holy cause with a disinterested devotion, energy, and determination never to turn back until we have conquered, not indeed to drive the Turk from his possession, but to claim our rightful inheritance for his benefit as well as our own.

To achieve this great victory of right over might, woman has much to do. She must not sit idle and wait till man inspired by justice and humanity will work out her redemption. It has well been said, "He that would be free, himself must strike the blow." It is with nations as with individuals, if they do not strive to help themselves no one will help them. Man may, and in the nature of things will, remove the legal political, and civil disabilities from woman, and recognize her as his equal with himself, and it will do much towards her elevation; but the laws cannot compel her to cultivate her physical and mental powers, and take a stand as a free and independent being. All that, she has to do. She must investigate and take an interest in everything on which the welfare of society depends, for the interest and happiness of every member of society is connected with that of society. She must at once claim and exercise those rights and privileges with which the laws do not interfere, and it will aid her to obtain all the rest. She must, therefore, throw off that heavy yoke that like a nightmare weighs down her best energies, viz., the fear of public opinion.

It has been said, that "The voice of the People is the voice of God." If that voice is on the side of justice and humanity, then it is true, if the term God means the principle of Truth and of Right. But if the public voice is oppressive and unjust, then it ought to be spurned like the voice of falsehood and corruption; and woman, instead of implicitly and blindly following the dictates of public opinion, must investigate for herself what is right or wrong—act in accordance with her beat convictions and let the rest take care of itself, for obedience to wrong is wrong itself, and opposition to it is virtue alike in woman as in man, even though she should incur the ill will of bigotry, superstition, and priestcraft, for the approval of our fellow-being is valuable only when it does not clash with our own sense of right, and no farther.

The priests well know the influence and value of women when warmly engaged in any cause, and therefore as long as they can keep them steeped in superstitious darkness, so long are they safe; and hence the horror and anathema against every woman that has intelligence, spirit, and moral courage to cast off the dark and oppressive yoke of superstition. But she must do it, or she will ever remain a slave, for of all tyranny that of superstition is the greatest, and he is the must abject slave who tamely submits to its yoke. Woman, then, must cast it off as her greatest enemy; and the time I trust will come when she will aid man to remove the political, civil, and religious evils that have swept over the earth like some malignant scourge to lay waste and destroy so much of the beauty, harmony, and happiness of man; and the old fable of the fall of man through a woman will be superseded by the glorious fact that she was instrumental in the elevation of the race towards a higher, nobler, and happier destiny.

The Role of Women in the Polish Migration to the Rhein-Westphalia Industrial Region at the Beginning of the Twentieth Century

Jan Molenda

translated by Robert E. Blobaum

Existing Research and Sources

Despite the already substantial literature on Polish migration to the Ruhr Basin before 1918, the subject of women still awaits separate treatment.[1] To date there has been little reference to or information about women and their role in Polish migration to western Germany. Of the more recent publications, works by Wojciech Chojnacki,[2]

This article is an expanded version of a paper delivered at the V World Congress for Central and East European Studies which met in Warsaw August 6–11, 1995. I wish to thank Professor Robert Blobaum for organizing the panel "What's New in Polish Social History," which inspired my work on this topic, and for his translation of this article into English. Research for this article was made possible by a six-month grant provided by the Gerda Henkel Foundation in Düsseldorf. I also wish to thank the late Professor Peter Huttenberger and Professor Hans Fecker of the Heinrich Heine University Düsseldorf for their kind assistance, as well as the staff of the Düsseldorf Press Office.

1. The geographical range of this work embraces the specific area comprised of the Düsseldorf, Münster and Arnsberg regencies. Considering the numerous ties, especially the economic, linking these three regencies, this area is commonly referred to as the Rhein-Westphalia industrial region. Here is where the largest community of Poles in western Germany was located. The statistical data presented in this article also comes from these three regencies. At times I refer to the region as the Ruhr Basin, although the Ruhr encompasses an area larger than the three regencies mentioned.

2. Wojciech Chojnacki, "Bibliografia czasopism i kalendarzy wydawanych w języku polskim w Westfalii i Nadrenii w latach 1890–1918" [Bibliography of Periodicals and Calendars Published in Polish in the Rhein-Westphalia Region, 1890–1918], *Studia Migracyjne – Przegląd Polonijny* [Migration Studies – Review of Polish Diaspora] vol. 3, no. 1(5) (1977), pp. 191–200.

From *The Polish Review*, vol. 42, no. 3 (1997), pp. 317–338.

Christoph Klessmann,[3] Jerzy Kozlowski,[4] John J. Kulczycki,[5] Krystyna Murzynowska,[6] and Valentina Maria Stefanski[7] are certainly worthy of attention in regard to the larger theme of Polish migrants in the Ruhr. Stefanski points to an inadequate source base as the main reason for the lack of interest in women.[8] My own research confirms that the sources on women are fewer than on other aspects of Polish activities in the Ruhr. There are especially large gaps in the statistical data while other surviving source materials are dispersed and difficult to locate. Extremely scant documentation was left by the women themselves.

What remains are primarily police records and press accounts. Of the former, the most important regarding women are contained in the annual reports of the Central Office for Surveillance of the Polish Movement in Bochum.[9] This office, established by order of the Minister of Internal Affairs on July 22, 1909, encompassed the three regencies of Düsseldorf, Münster and Arnsberg. It also collected and compiled questionnaires completed by Polish organizations, including those of organized women's groups, during the process of their registration. The annual

3. Christoph Klessmann, *Polnische Bergarbeiter im Ruhrgebiet 1870–1945: Sozial Integration und nationale Subkultur einer Minderheit in der deutschen Industriegesellschaft* [Polish Miners in the Ruhr, 1870–1945: The Social Integration and National Subculture of a Minority in German Industrial Society] (Gottingen: 1978).

4. Jerzy Kozłowski, *Rozwój organizacji społeczno-narodowych wychodźstwa polskiego w Niemczech w latach 1870–1914* [The Development of Social and National Organizations of the Polish Migration in Germany, 1870–1914] (Wrocław: 1987). See also his "Rozwój organizacji społeczno-narodowych wychodźstwa polskiego w Niemczech przed I wojną światową" [The Development of Social and National Organizations of the Polish Migration in Germany Before the First World War] in *Organizacje polonijne w Europie Zachodniej: Współczesność i tradycje. Materiały z konferencji naukowej w dniach 2 i 3 kwietnia 1987 r. w Poznaniu* [Polish Organizations in Western Europe: Past and Present. Materials from the Academic Conference of April 2–3, 1987, in Poznań], Barbara Szydłowska-Cegłowa and Jerzy Kozłowski, editors (Poznań: 1991), pp. 75–92.

5. John J. Kulczycki, *The Foreign Worker and the German Labor Movement: Xenophobia and Solidarity in the Coal Fields of the Ruhr, 1871–1914* (Oxford/Providence: Berg, 1994).

6. Krystyna Murzynowska, *Polskie wychodźstwo zarobkowe w Zagłebiu Ruhry w latach 1880–1914* [Polish Wage Migration to the Ruhr Basin, 1880–1914] (Wrocław: 1974). This work also appeared in German translation under the title *Die polnischen Erwerbsauswanderer im Ruhrgebiet während der Jahre 1880–1914* (Dortmund: 1979).

7. Valentina-Maria Stefanski, *Zum Prozess der Emanzipation und Integration von Aussenseitern: Polnische Arbeitsmigration im Ruhrgebiet* [The Process of Emancipation and Integration of Foreigners: Polish Labor Migrants in the Ruhr] (Dortmund: second edition, 1991).

8. Stefanski, p. 4.

9. For more on the surveillance of Poles, see Wojciech Chojnacki, "Nadzór policyjny niemiecki nad polską prasą i działalnością narodową w Westfalli i Nadrenii w latach 1861–1924" [German Police Surveillance of the Polish Press and National Activity in the Rhein-Westphalia Region, 1861–1924), *Przegląd Zachodni* [Western Review], vol. 36, no. 1 (1980), pp. 122–134.

reports, which cover all aspects of Polish life in the region for the years 1909–1914 and 1919–1930, contain the most important statistical data regarding the general numbers of women, their family status, women's organizations, readership of the Polish press, and mixed Polish-German marriages. The questionnaires contain sections which were continually updated by new information on the names and headquarters of organizations, their expressed aims and appended statutes, their forms and methods of work, their level of activity, lists of executive board members, size of memberships, and evaluations of their practical impact.

Significant information is also contained in the records of German institutions and organizations, whether lay or religious, which had contact with the Poles, including firms employing Polish female labor and various administrative and judicial offices. Historians of Polish migration frequently avoid the data contained in these records, however, due to the time consumed in their compilation and analysis.

The Polish press is another important source for examining Polish affairs, including those related to women's roles, in the Ruhr Basin. Among the dozen titles, published simultaneously in the Rhein-Westphalia industrial region from 1909 to 1914, only one was designated specifically for women.[10] It first appeared as a supplement to *Wiarus Polski* [The Polish Veteran] under the title *Polka* [The Polish Woman]. Among the tens of titles of the Polish press published outside the region, but which circulated among subscribers in the Ruhr, only two women's publications have been identified, as well as one each for families and youth (see Table 4).[11] It should be emphasized, however, that in eleven of the locally published titles and supplements, the role of the family, education, and child-rearing in a national spirit was strongly accented, often in the mottoes.[12] Women were assigned a special place in these activities.

---

10. Chojnacki, "Bibliografia . . . ," pp. 191–200.

11. In 1913, Poles in the Ruhr subscribed to *Głos Wielkopolanek* [The Voice of Women of Great Poland] from Poznań (69 subscriptions), *Wieczory Rodzinne* [Family Evenings] from Stargard (65 subscriptions), *Gazeta dla Kobiet* [The Newspaper for Women] from Poznań (one copy), and *Przyjaciel Dzieci* [The Children's Friend] from Ostrów (one copy).

12. For example, *Narodowiec* [The Nationalist], published in Herne from 1909 to 1924, took the following quotation from Juliusz Słowacki as its motto: "Let the living not lose hope, but hand on the torch of learning to the people." *Ojczyzna* [The Fatherland], published in Bochum from 1908 to 1914, carried the subtitle: "A National Weekly Devoted to Learning and Recreation." Its supplement, *Pismo dla dzieci i młodzieży* [Periodical for Children and Youth] (Bochum, 1908), termed itself "The National Classroom." *Przewodnik Związkowy* [Union Leader], the organ of the Union of Mutual Aid of Polish Catholic Associations Abroad and published in Bochum during the years of the First World War, contained the motto "Love! Education! Work!" *Tydzień* [The Week], published in Oberhausen in 1912–1913, referred to itself as a "Periodical for Polish Families." The main newspaper of the Polish migration in the Ruhr, *Wiarus Polski* [The Polish Veteran], published in Bochum from 1891 to 1923, after 1904 carried the subtitle: "A Popular Daily for Poles Abroad Devoted to Learning, as well as to National, Political, and Labor Issues."

Unfortunately, large gaps also exist in the Polish press of that era.[13] Many articles and informational materials (for example, reports of the activities of Polish organizations) are contained in issues which are no longer extant in Polish but are partially preserved in German translation in *Gesamtüberblick über die polnische Tagesliteratur* [General Overview of the Polish Press] (published in Poznań from 1892 to 1918), *Übersetzungen aus dem "Wiarus Polski"* [Translations from *Wiaros Polski*] (published in Arnsberg beginning in 1897), *Übersetzungen aus westfälischen und anderen polnischen Zeitungen, 1907–1914* [Translations from Westphalian and Other Polish Periodicals, 1907–1914].[14] It is necessary to remember, however, that these police publications made selections from the Polish press according to their own needs, with a particular focus on the "Polish danger." The translations contained therein, similar to other police sources, presented the Polish movement, as well as the women associated with it, in a one-sided manner.

Finally, the articles which appeared in the Polish press were frequently written by the leaders of Polish organizations and, therefore, had mainly an instructional flavor. They expressed the views of the elite and not those of the "average" Polish worker in the Rhein-Westphalia industrial region. The press, as a source, also provides little information on actual popular perceptions of the recommendations and instructions, published by the editors of particular newspapers and periodicals, save for the information which may be culled from their correspondence sections.

The Role of Women in the Family

The most complete statistical data on women are confined to their numbers in the general population and, more narrowly, to their employment and marital rates. These data have already been thoroughly analyzed in the literature on Poles in the Ruhr, especially in the works of Klessmann and Murzynowska.[15] The occupational structure of the Polish population is characterized in Table 2.

Available statistical information on the number of marriages is even more limited. According to Christoph Klessmann, sufficiently detailed data exist only for the year 1893. At that time, of the 20,494 non-Germans employed as miners in the Reich (of whom almost 18,000 spoke Polish as the native tongue), 9,160 (44.7 percent) had not married, 4,619 of those who did marry lived with their families (22.5 percent), and 2,626 (12.8 percent) had left their families behind.[16]

---

13. The most complete information regarding the state of the preserved Polish press is provided in Chojnacki, "Bibliografia . . . ."

14. For more information on this topic, see "Niemieckie tlumaczenia z prasy polskiej 1858–1958" [German Translations From the Polish Press, 1858–1958] *Przegląd Zachodni*, vol. 6 (1958), pp. 382–398.

15. Klessmann, pp. 21, 41–41, 68, 268–269; Murzynowska, pp. 20–40.

16. Klessmann, p. 42.

Table 1: Population in the Arnsberg, Düsseldorf and Münster Regencies, 1910–1912

Year	Total Population	Polish Population	Men	Women	Children under 14
1910	4,642,032	267,347	92,884	57,417	117,047
1912	4,866,410	297,322	98,506	63,272	135,544

Of Which Polish Men Were Categorized As (Table la):

Year	Family Heads and "Sons Employed in Their Parents' Households"	"Boarders"
1910	54,867	35,793
1912	63,020	35,486

And Polish Women Were Categorized As (Table 1b):

Year	Single (Including Widows and Domestic Servants)	Wives and Daughters Over 14 in "Their Husbands' or Fathers' Households"
1910	8,371	49,046
1912	6,301	56,971

Note: Neither the tables nor my analysis include Mazurians, male or female. The Mazurian question, given its specific nature, requires separate discussion. Source: Statistical Data on the Polish Population of the Rhein-Westphalia Industrial Region, signed by the Police President Gerstein, Bochum, March 15, 1913, Nordrhein-Westfälisches Staatsarchiv, Münster (North Rhein-Westphalia State Archive in Münster) (NWStAM), Regierung Münster [Münster Regency] (Reg. MS), VII-37, 1:254–275.

Table 2: Employment of Professionally Active Population from the Eastern Provinces in the Rhein-Westphalia Region as of June 12, 1907.

	Total Employed	Men	Percent of Total	Women	Percent of Total
A. Agriculture	8,881	4,184	48	4,697	52
B. Industry	185,837	179,399	97	6,348	3
C. Commerce	13,457	13,547	83	2,810	17

Note: Here the "eastern provinces" refer to East Prussia, West Prussia, and Poznania. Upper Silesia is not included.

Source: Murzynowska, p. 37.

These data come from a time when predominantly single persons came to the Ruhr from the eastern provinces, especially men in search of temporary wages with the thought of eventually returning to their native parts and purchasing land. When, at the beginning of the century, the price of arable land increased, which was then followed by the restrictions imposed by the Prussian authorities in 1904 and 1908 on new Polish residential construction in the eastern provinces, the migrants began to tie their fate to and locate their savings in their new place of settlement. One manifestation of these phenomena, as indicated in Table 1, is the rapid growth in the total number of Polish women, even more so of children, and the simultaneous decline in the percentage of single persons of both sexes, but particularly of single women.

Taken together, these factors promoted growth in the number of Polish marriages in the Ruhr. Unfortunately, more specific data in this regard are unavailable and what follows below is based only on estimates. Moreover, while scholars agree on the relatively large size of Polish families in the Rhein-Westphalia industrial region, some of them believe that the estimate of five to six children per family is exaggerated.[17] If one can therefore assume that the average family contained three children and there were 135,544 Polish children under the age of fourteen in 1912, it is possible to estimate the number of Polish families at over 45,000. On the other hand, if one takes a figure of four children per family, the total number of families is reduced to 34,000. The increase in the number of Polish migrants who established and maintained families (nearly 56 percent) is also confirmed by Murzynowska's data, although they refer only to the province of Westphalia.[18]

In any event, the data in Table 1 suggest that children and young people, as well as approximately 90 percent of the women, already lived in established family groupings. The relatively small proportion of single women would also indicate that Polish girls in the Ruhr had greater marital possibilities than they would have had in their native land.

Despite the still relatively high proportion of single men, recognizable in the category of "boarders" in Table 1, their percentage had declined significantly when compared with Klessmann's data in 1893. The group of "boarders" contained primarily single men as well as husbands whose families remained behind in the country. In comparison to 1893, the number of the unaccompanied husbands and fathers certainly declined by several percentage points.

---

17. Klessmann, p. 42.

18. Murzynowska, p. 44; according to provincial data for Westphalia in 1906, of a total number of 80,981 Poles living in the province, 45,145 maintained families, while 35,836 were single. See also F. Schulze, *Die polnische Zuwanderung in Ruhrrevier und ihre Wirkungen* [Polish Migration to the Ruhr Basin and Its Effects] (Munich: 1909), p. 42, table VI.

The stable and numerically large group (over 35,000 in 1910–1912) of "boarders" requires further examination, not only because their existence provided women with additional employment and an opportunity to increase family incomes, which has frequently been noted by historians.[19] It is also necessary to consider the significance of family interactions, particularly for young boarders. In other words, these young men could seek support not only in Polish organizations but also in families with whom they had daily contact and shared meals. Moral support provided by a family was especially important for new arrivals acclimatizing to different customs and cultural conditions. The family gave them a sense of security which the seasonal migrant worker otherwise lacked.

Employment data on women in the Rhein-Westphalia region are significantly more limited than for men. Table 2 demonstrates above all the generally low level of employment among Polish women. In 1907, 13,855 women worked on the whole outside of agriculture in industry, commerce and artisanal shops, but in 1912 that number had declined to 10,174.[20] If we assume that the employment of women in agriculture remained at relatively the same level as in 1907 (4,697) and that the number employed as domestic servants held steady at around four thousand (see Table 1), then the general employment of Polish women in the Ruhr in 1912 can be estimated in the vicinity of 19,000, or about 30 percent of all women.

The data presented in Table 2 show that the employment of women in industry, relative to men, was barely 3 percent (6,348), and this mainly in the textile and garment industries. This proportion grew significantly during the years of the First World War. As men were called to military service, women took up various occupations, particularly those requiring moderate physical exertion. For the war years, only partial and descriptive information exists regarding the changes in the employment of women. Unfortunately, a more complete compilation and closer analysis of that evidence, which would certainly shed greater light on the wartime employment of Polish women, is beyond the scope of this article.

Agriculture employed the highest percentage of women compared to men (52 percent). Such employment, according to Murzynowska, had an "improvised and seasonal" character.[21] To support her opinion, Murzynowska cites information from a date on the calendar (June 12) which, she believes, usually witnessed the more intensive demand for labor in agriculture. The first half of June, however, was not a time when female field labor was especially required. Instead, women were involved in the spring weeding of beets, and from the end of June to August (taking into account slight variations in particular years) in various reaping tasks. In the

19. Murzynowska, pp. 37, 44.
20. Murzynowska, p. 43.
21. Murzynowska, p. 37.

autumn they harvested root crops. It is possible that the demand for women's labor by agriculture in the Ruhr was not only seasonal but also required more permanent employment.

A fairly substantial group of Polish women (2,810 or 17 percent relative to men) were also employed in commerce, especially in grocery stores established from the savings of their fathers and husbands.[22] In addition, the employment of women as domestic servants declined somewhat from 1910 to 1912 (see Table 1) and had a composition similar to female employment in agriculture. Both of these sectors only slightly exceeded, and then in 1910–1912 gave way to industry, commerce and handicraft production in terms of the numbers of employed working women. In light of these data, Murzynowska's argument that in the Ruhr "women were employed above all in agriculture and as domestic servants" is obviously incorrect.[23]

In a situation whereby barely 30 percent of all women (19,000) were employed in 1912, the question of taking in boarders assumes a particular significance which has not been properly appreciated in the existing literature. Considering both the size and continuity of this phenomenon, the income derived from boarding 35,000 people in 1910–1912 significantly affected the domestic budgets of women, as well as older daughters and sons, who occupied themselves with this economic activity.

The fact that the previously mentioned "Central Office for the Surveillance of the Polish Movement" in Bochum collected statistical data on boarding is yet another indication of its importance. Those data not only embraced "boarders" but also the people occupied in their maintenance, that is, wives and daughters over fourteen years old in "their husbands' or fathers' households" as well as "sons employed in their parents' households" (see Tables 1a and 1b). Maintaining boarders was made much easier by the fact that the majority of Polish migrant wives, particularly of the numerous group of miners in the Ruhr, were primarily engaged in traditional domestic duties and household management.

The position of woman in family and public life is usually connected in the literature to their professional activity. The available evidence seems to indicate that in the period under discussion, the real position of married women was not determined so much by their occupation or profession as by the relatively better material existence resulting from marriage as well as by the effect and even pressure of organized opinion in the Polish community on determining their family and public roles.

This is not the place to discuss the material situation of Polish families in the Ruhr, but it should be noted that living standards were much better than in their

22. Murzynowska, pp. 37–38.
23. Murzynowska, p. 41.

native land.[24] Wages in the Ruhr's heavy industry were among the highest in the entire Reich. The majority of Polish migrants were employed precisely in the mining and steel industries (61,751 and 24,589 workers, respectively). This constitutes approximately 83 percent of all Poles employed by industry in the three Rhein-Westphalia regencies in 1912.[25]

The wives of these well-paid workers were not forced by economic circumstances to take up wage labor since their husbands' earnings were sufficient to maintain the entire family. There was even enough income for savings and investment, the result of which was the rapid growth of a Polish middle class. In 1912 the number of Polish merchants, shopowners and small entrepreneurs already stood at 2,073 persons, and over a thousand families owned their own homes.[26] Due to the favorable material situation, Polish families in Germany could also designate part of their savings for the development of Polish education, to press subscriptions, and to the payment of membership dues in Polish organizations and associations which sponsored various musical, theatrical and sporting ensembles as well as library collections.

Similarly, the legal and political status of Polish migrants in the Rhein-Westphalia industrial region exerted an influence on shaping the position of the family in society and the role of women in the family. Therefore, in the deteriorating situation affecting the activity of Polish associations as a result of the measures undertaken by the Prussian authorities after 1908, families assumed part of their public functions.[27] Families, and especially mothers, also took charge of the instruction of children in the Polish language, an activity which could not be accomplished in a practical sense outside the home.

The fashioning of women's tasks not only in public life, but also in the family was taken up by Polish organizations as well as the local Polish language press.[28] A Congress of Polish Organizations in the Ruhr, which met on November 1–2, 1913, in Winterswijk, Holland, devoted special attention to this matter. According to the German political police, the congress was attended by 1,200 delegates

24. See Klessmann, pp. 55–56, and Murzynowska, pp. 45–63.

25. NWStAM, Reg. MS Vll-37, 1:262–266. For more on the employment of Poles in the Ruhr, see Klessmann, pp. 37–55, and Murzynowska, pp. 36–45.

26. NWStAM, Reg. MS Vll-37, 1:259–260, 267–268.

27. According to Murzynowska, "The police authorities observed with alarm a new system of agitation in the Polish community, namely, numerous and otherwise banned meetings disguised as social gatherings as well as an increasing resort to various forms of agitation based on the home, which involved significantly wider circles of Poles in community work than had the old public meetings"; Murzynowska, p. 199. On the conditions faced by Polish organizations, see Kozłowski, *Rozwój . . .*, pp. 234–236.

28. Stefanski, p. 4.

and several hundred guests, or approximately two thousand participants. Among the four reports presented, one was entitled "Women in Our National Work" and another "Our Work Among Youth." Special resolutions were also passed which placed considerable emphasis on the role of the family and "Polish mothers" not only in public life but also in the rearing of children at home in a Polish spirit; the latter was treated as if it were a civic responsibility.

The resolution on Polish youth contained the following appeal:

> To guarantee that Polish children receive the necessary guidance, the Polish Congress in Winterswijk of November 1–2 calls upon parents, especially Polish mothers, to make a greater effort to insure that their children not only can read and write in the Polish language, but that in the home they speak and sing only in Polish, say their prayers in Polish, attend only Polish masses, and use only Polish catechisms. Furthermore, the father or the mother at every commemoration, every performance, every important event which has a bearing on our national life should instruct their children in an appropriate way of the significance of the event or the performance for Poland.[29]

Polish organizations were also obliged by the resolution to collaborate with home and family in the rearing of children:

> The assembly furthermore calls upon our unions, especially those which possess a librarian and a standard-bearer, to elect an irreproachable person as a patron of children and Polish youth, whose task should be to keep watch over Polish children, to visit Polish homes, to assemble the children in a special room on the occasion of commemorations and performances, and there to sing and play together with them in Polish.[30]

The resolution, after stating that "the German schools completely exclude reading and writing in Polish," appealed to parents, and particularly to selected associations, to provide or donate books to Polish elementary schools and to otherwise encourage children to study the native language. To achieve this aim, Polish teachers were called upon to organize excursions and summer camps during school vacations

29. Report of Police President K. Gerstein in Bochum to the Minister of Internal Affairs in Berlin, November 9, 1913, NWStAM, Reg. MS Vll-35a, 1:233. The resolutions of the Congress, as well as two of the four reports presented to it (namely, "The Importance of Polish Unions and Their Division of Labor" and "On the Germanization Efforts of German Clergy and the Significance of Polish Unions in the Preservation of the Polish Language and the Catholic Faith") have been published in *Die Polen und die Kirche im Ruhrgebiet, 1871–1919: Ausgewählte Dokumente zur pastoral und kirchlichen Integration Sprachlicher Minderheiten im Deutschen Kaiserreich* [The Poles and the Church in the Ruhr, 1871–1919: Selected Documents on the Pastoral and Ecclesiastical Integration of a linguistic Minority in the German Empire], edited by H. J. Brandt et al., (Münster: 1987), pp. 275–281.

30. Brandt et al. . . . , p. 281.

and to establish libraries for children. The resolution also obliged the Congress to elect "a committee for the patronage of children living abroad and empower it with the right to raise funds and to implement existing resolutions.[31]

In the discussion of the report "The Polish Woman in National Work," women themselves participated,[32] pointing to the clear priority assigned to the role of mothers in teaching children the Polish language and raising them in a Polish national spirit: "Since the future of Poland resides in its young people, the Polish mother whose primary calling is child-rearing has therefore an obligation to ensure that her children are raised in a genuine Polish spirit."[33]

The Prussian authorities, informed of the resolutions and recommendations of the Congress in Winterswijk in the area of elementary Polish language instruction among migrant families, also perceived the special role of women.[34] Karl Gerstein, the Police President in Bochum, even ascribed to Polish private instruction in the home, which was placed under police surveillance, the character of underground education. He was particularly alarmed by its planned nature, without the knowledge and legal approval of the authorities, and its requirement of children to maintain secrecy.[35] Nonetheless, the information collected by the police provides considerable evidence about the range of private instruction, its organizers, and its subject matter.

The elementary schooling of children in Polish families took place in the cities of Osterfeld, Wanne, Herne, Solingen as well as "in numerous other places."[36] Gerstein ascribed the rapid growth in the private instruction of Polish children to the

---

31. Brandt et al. . . . , p. 281.

32. Gerstein's report of November 9, 1913, on the Winterswijk Congress refers specifically to one Kwaśniewska. The former was the wife of Ignacy Kwaśniewski, the founder and owner of *Zgoda* [Harmony], published in Wanne in 1908–1909. The latter, a teacher from Cracow, attended the Congress as a representative of the Cracow Women's Defense Office. NWStAM, Reg. MS VII-35a, 1:234.

33. Gerstein . . . , Reg. MS VII-35a, 1:235.

34. Police President Gerstein, in his reports from Bochum to the Münster and Arnsberg regency presidents, informed them: "The Polish Congress in Winterswijk, as is known, has passed a resolution which requires Polish parents, and especially Polish mothers, to strive to teach their children to read, write and speak in Polish, and to identify with the Polish nation." "Regarding Private Polish Instruction," May 23, 1914, NWStAM, Reg. MS VII-31, 64.

35. Gerstein . . . , pp. 64–65. According to Gerstein, "It has become known that the Poles are planning to introduce on a mass basis private elementary instruction for their children without taking the appropriate measures of notifying the authorities." In the same report, Gerstein continues, "Polish pupils are forbidden [in Wanne - J.M.] to associate with German children, among themselves they are obliged to speak only Polish. If questioned, they have been told to declare that they are practicing their church hymns."

36. Gerstein . . . , pp. 64–68.

numerous women's organizations created after the Winterswijk Congress.[37] With their participation, "Polish instruction was introduced by Mrs. Szymanowska" in Wanne, and in Heme "a Polish kindergarten" was established under the direction of Jadwiga Pankowska. The organization "Samopomoc Zenska" [Women's Self-Help] was also created in Heme "in which already educated young women were entrusted with the direction of elementary instruction of the Polish language."[38] This instruction most frequently involved speaking, reading and writing in the Polish language. Children also learned Polish songs from books published in Cracow but forbidden by the Prussian and Russian authorities as well as Polish poetry copied in notebooks.

Women's Organizations and Their Roles

Jerzy Kozłowski's previously cited work on social and national organizations of the Polish migration in Germany has already devoted considerable attention to the associations in the Ruhr that are of interest to us here. Therefore, what follows is confined to a few general remarks based on the preliminary results of my own research.

Among the most characteristic qualities differentiating Polish society, as well as its women, in the region under discussion before the outbreak of World War I, is the development on a scale unprecedented in other Polish communities of its own organizations (see Table 3), its own press (see Table 4), and other forms of public activity. Contemporary observers were already aware of the unique nature of the development of the Polish community in the Ruhr. Despite progress in researching that community, there are still gaps in our knowledge regarding the formation of both central and local structures of Polish organizations, the leading cadres, not to mention the role of women in these (and not only specifically women's) organizations.

Relatively more is known about the size of the Polish organizations, which before the First World War contained as many as 120,000 members, and about the circulation of the local press, which exceeded runs of 82,000 copies.[39] In addition, over 25,000 subscribed to Polish language periodicals published outside the region (see Table 4). When one considers, however, that Poles in the Ruhr frequently

---

37. Gerstein . . . , p. 64. According to Gerstein, "Following the rapid progress of the organization of Polish women under the leadership of the agitator Ruszczyńska, evidence of the 'national education of children' has multiplied, as it has come under the effective jurisdiction of the women's unions." He also noted that other Polish organizations were involved in the training and raising of children.

38. Gerstein . . . , pp. 65–69.

39. According to Table 3, membership in Polish organizations had reached 111,444 by 1912. The figure of 120,000 is based on Kozłowski's estimate; Kozłowski, *Rozwój* . . . , p. 181.

Table 3: Polish Organizations in the Rhein-Westphalia Industrial Region, 1909–1914

Year	Number of Polish Organizations	Number of Members	"Polish Women's Unions"		Rosary Fellowships	
			#	Members	#	Members
1909	841	-	2	-	22	-
1910	969	61,861	2	65	32	-
1911	1,147	-	5	-	77	-
1912	1,278	111,444	15	674	93	16,297
1913	1,471	-	60	-	93	-
1914	-	-	80	6,270*	-	-

*Membership in the "Polish Women's Unions" in 1914 is estimated.
Source: Annual Reports of the Central Office for the Surveillance of the Polish Movement in Bochum, 1909–1914, NWStAM, Reg. MS VII 35a, 1:87–121, 167–198, Vll-31:2–34, 35–62, 71–100.

Table 4: The Polish Press in the Rhein-Westphalia Industrial Region, 1909–1914

Year	Number of Titles of the Local Polish Language Press		Circulation	Number of Women's Titles Published Locally	Polish Language Press Published Outside of the Ruhr but Circulating in the Region			
		(a)			(b)	(c)	(d)	(e)
1909	12	4	61,300	-	63	2	21,354	61
1910	12	5	51,600	-	63	2	21,211	51
1911	16	6	60,400	-	71	2	21,211	38
1912	17	5	67,200	-	73	2	20,877	81
1913	26	13	82,200	-	88	2	25,038	70
1914	-	-	-	1	-	-	-	-

a = supplements, b = total number of titles, c = women's titles, d = total subscribers, e = subscribers to the women's press.
Source: Addenda to the Annual Reports of the Central Office for Surveillance of the Polish Movement (see Table 3).

belonged to more than one organization, actual total membership has been estimated at around 60,000.[40] This matter, of course, requires much closer analysis. Suffice it to say that the estimate of 60,000 organized Poles is very conservative, and may be increased to as many as 80,000, a figure based on the circulation of and subscriptions to the local press.

Looking at the development of an organized women's movement in the Rhein-Westphalia industrial region, certain similarities with the homeland can be observed.

40. Kozłowski, *Rozwój . . .*, p. 189.

Its far-ranging specificity, at home and in the Ruhr, is particularly striking. Generally speaking, in both places mass women's organizations developed with considerable delay in comparison with other, predominantly male, organizations. In addition, at the beginning they had the character of religious associations and fellowships. Secular women's organizations arose later. The earlier and greater mass membership of women in church-related organizations was motivated not only by traditional religious customary norms, but also by the fact that the right of women to belong to secular social and national associations was not recognized until May 15, 1908, in a new law on associations.[41]

The distinguishing feature of Polish religious organizations in the Ruhr in contrast with their counterparts at home, beyond their purely spiritual and self-help activities, was the absence of a community of interest in terms of citizenship and nationality between their Polish members and the German clergy who exercised pastoral care over them. On Polish lands, priests involved in religious organizations often identified with the national strivings of their members. In Germany, according to Kozlowski,

> those German clergy who were involved in pastoral work among the Poles were generally far removed from germanization tendencies, but were convinced nonetheless that this process would proceed in a natural way.[42]

Indeed, only part of the German clergy actually embraced the Prussian policy of germanization. However, only a few actively opposed it, while most spoke out against the continually renewed demands to improve pastoral work among the migrants, particularly by bringing in Polish priests. Public discussion of these issues, which became particularly intense at the beginning of the twentieth century, introduced an element of mutual distrust between the German and Polish sides. This led to an unintended politicization in the character of Polish Catholic organizations and the restriction of German clerical influences within them.

These processes also affected the rosary fellowships which grouped Poles and were the most religious of the associations. The rosary fellowships were among the largest Polish organizations. In 1912, they counted 16,297 members (see Table 3).[43]

The proportional participation of women in these fellowships as well as the degree of their dependence on the German clergy are questions that specifically

41. For more on the legal bases of the activities of associations, see Kozłowski, *Rozwój . . .*, pp. 206–208.

42. Kozłowski, *Rozwój . . .*, p. 189. For the most complete analysis of the pastoral activities of German clergy among Poles in the Ruhr, see *Die Polen und die Kirche . . . .*

43. Kozłowski, *Rozwój . . .*, p. 208; Klessmann, p. 103.

require further elaboration. Kozłowski maintains that "women as well as men" were members of the rosary fellowships.[44] Klessmann, on the other hand, perceives them as women's organizations.[45] Evidence contained in the annual police reports as well as reports and resolutions of the Polish Congress in Winterswijk distinctly support the latter view. In my own opinion, even if the rosary fellowships cannot be treated as exclusively women's organizations, they were certainly dominated numerically by women.

More problematic is the issue regarding the influence of the German Catholic clergy on the rosary fellowships. Klessmann emphasizes that they were "purely religious" organizations.[46] Kozłowski, for his part, maintains that they were "completely subordinate to the influence of the German clergy."[47] Only the resolutions of the Polish Congress in Winterswijk partially support these opinions which are strongly contradicted by police sources. In any event, it is necessary to remember that both views, albeit for different reasons, are equally one-sided in their evaluation of the rosary fellowships.

Significantly, the annual reports of Bochum Police President Gerstein indicate a process of emancipation of the rosary fellowships from the influences of the German clergy. Gerstein's reports even accused the fellowships of using religious symbols for conducting agitation in a Polish national spirit. Moreover, these perceptions were formed several years before the Winterswijk Congress, which is usually considered the starting point for the emancipation of Polish women from the influences of the German clergy.[48]

Thus, in Gerstein's report for 1910 one reads:

> The rosary fellowships created for Polish women and girls exist in great number and in almost every community with a considerable Polish settlement. In contrast to the rosary fellowships in the east, which mainly limit themselves to common prayer meetings, in the west the existing associations have developed a type of activity, which in reality differs only slightly from that of the so-called Polish Catholic male associations. They hold meetings twice a month outside the Church which are devoted to "learning," and as is often evident from the Polish press, participate in the amusements of other associations; thus they do not confine themselves to the purely Catholic religious tasks of rosary fellowships. Surpluses from their treasuries are deposited in the Polish Bank of the eastern territories. Attempts of the clergy

---

44. Kozłowski, *Rozwój* . . . , p. 208.
45. Klessmann, p. 99.
46. Klessmann, p. 99.
47. Kozłowski, *Rozwój* . . . , p. 208; see also Murzynowska, p. 199.
48. See the statements on this question by Kozłowski, *Rozwój* . . . , p. 208, Klessmann, p. 99, and Murzynowska, pp. 198–199.

> to lead Polish women and girls in the existing German rosary fellowships are met with strong opposition.[49]

In subsequent years, the trend of Polish national activity in the rosary fellowships spread further, according to the annual police reports. The German clergy, moreover, could not contain the movement.[50] Starting in 1912, individual rosary fellowships began to declare their subordination to the Union of Polish Catholic Organizations.[51]

Meanwhile, the report and resolution of the Winterswijk Congress in 1913 regarding the women's movement recognized the service of women in Catholic organizations and in the development of the Polish national movement. However, Polish women were criticized for being too pervious to the influence of the German clergy who used the religiosity of female members for germanizing aims and in the interest of the Center Party, and which led to the setting of wives and daughters against the national activities of their husbands and fathers.[52] In Gerstein's accompanying commentary, we read: "This resolution is especially directed against the Polish rosary fellowships, so long as they remain under the guidance of the German clergy."[53]

---

49. Gerstein's annual report of April 1, 1911, NWStAM, Reg. MS VII-35a, 1:176–177. Gerstein went on to provide specific examples: "In Erie bei Buer, the Poles and the clergy have come into conflict for this very reason. One community member wrote in a newspaper article: 'It would be shameful for us to participate in the German rosary fellowships and voluntarily give up our language. We best praise God and the Holy Mother when we are allowed to participate in Polish rosary fellowships.' In Gelsenkirchen-Schalke, the rosary fellowship divided into two parties over the question of whether it should remain under the leadership of the clergy. The moderate direction follows Father Grüne, while the radicals have seceded and have formed a separate fellowship under secular leadership." Already a year earlier, in his report of May 6, 1910, Gerstein called attention to the growing discord in the rosary fellowships grouping "Polish women and girls." Gerstein, p. 96.

50. In his report of April 22, 1912, Gerstein wrote: "The rosary fellowships serve the Polish national movement inasmuch as Polish women and girls stay aloof from German associations of a similar kind and in their invariable "learning" are ever more estranged to the German idea. The German clergy, for the most part, are no longer in a position as patrons of the rosary fellowships to preempt the national currents inside them; the least attempt to do so makes them appear as 'Germanizers' in the eyes of the Poles and deprives them of consideration and influence among part of their parishioners." Gerstein, Reg. MS VII-31: II.

51. In his annual report of May 3, 1913, Gerstein maintained: "The Polish national movement has not changed its promotional activity. The fact that individual fellowships have subordinated themselves to the Union of Polish Catholic Organizations serves as an example as well as further evidence of the homogeneity of aims." Gerstein, p. 45.

52. Gerstein, Reg. MS VII-35a, 1:234.

53. Gerstein, Reg. MS VII-35a, 1:234.

How does one explain such significant differences between the Polish Congress and the German police in their respective evaluations of the rosary fellowships? Apparently, in the period 1909–1914 these fellowships had already reached such a state of internal differentiation that both sides were capable of finding evidence in support of their arguments. The German authorities had particular reasons for alarm since the Polish emancipation processes cropping up in the fellowships restricted the possibility of having an impact on the only mass women's organization of that time, and through it on Polish families, indeed, on the entire Polish community.

Both the German and Polish sides were in agreement on the particular role played by women in this regard, although they drew contrary conclusions from their evaluation of that role. Hence, the resolution of the Polish Congress in Winterswijk maintained:

> Considering that the mother exerts a decisive influence on the development and well-being of the community and mainly determines the nationality of the offspring, we treat the organization of women in separate associations as a compelling necessity.[54]

The German authorities also noted the greater attachment of women, compared to men, to Polish traditions and customs. Thus they explained the dominant role of women in the rearing of children in a national Polish spirit in migrant families; they even perceived a threat to German nationality in mixed marriages involving Polish women. Regarding the collected information on mixed marriages from 1910 to 1912, Gerstein commented:

> In the first instance [of marriages between Polish men and German women]. it can be anticipated with some confidence that despite exceptions the male will assimilate and the children will be brought up as Germans. In the opposite case (of marriages between German men and Polish women), especially if the wife was not born and raised in the west, the German nationality of the family fares less well.[55]

The resolutions of the Winterswijk Congress pointed in the direction of greater centralization of Polish associations. They placed prohibitions on accepting German members in them and on Polish participation in German organizations or in organizations directed by Germans. The latter proscriptions mainly had in mind the rosary fellowships, which frequently were headed by the clergy. Henceforth, clergy were only to be permitted to influence "unions and their members in a religious and moral spirit."[56]

54. Gerstein, Reg. MS VII-35a, 1:234.
55. Annual Report of Gerstein of May 3, 1913, in Gerstein, Reg. MS VII-31:39.
56. Gerstein, Reg. MS VII-35a, 1:231.

It is difficult to determine, based on the present state of research, to what extent the influences of the German clergy on the rosary fellowships declined in conjunction with the strengthening of the Polish national current within them. The data presented in Table 3, demonstrating a rapid growth in the number of rosary fellowships from 1909 to 1912, suggests that the alarmist opinions of Polish President Gerstein about the curtailment of German clerical influences in the fellowships tend to exaggerate the phenomenon. Only a slowing of the growth of the rosary fellowships in 1913 could have signaled a strengthening of Polish national tendencies in them.

These conclusions are indirectly supported by the numerical data in Table 3 about the growth at this time in the number of "Polish Women's Unions." In 1909 to 1911, that growth was still slow, but in the following three years the increase was rapid. In addition, it is necessary to note that the police authorities treated the development of these organizations as a competitive alternative to the rosary fellowships.

We continue to know very little about the genesis of the "Polish Women's Unions." It can only be stated that the decision to create them, despite prevailing scholarly opinion, was made not at the Polish Congress in Winterswijk in November 1913, but earlier and in any event no later than 1909.[57] Convincing evidence for this revised chronology comes from Gerstein's annual reports and the appendices attached to them for the years 1909 to 1914. In contrast to the previous labels given women's organizations such as "Christian Women's Associations," "Women's Christian Associations" or "Rosary Fellowships," the new organizations were called "Women's Unions," "other Women's Associations" or "Polish Women's Unions."

The first Polish women's organizations arose in Dortmund and Essen in 1909, if not earlier, and by the following year counted 65 members. Two more were organized in Wettenscheid and Solingen in 1911. In 1912, seven new organizations were created in Duisburg, Hamborn, Benrath, Oberhausen, and Düsseldorf. The tempo then accelerated in 1913 with the founding of 45 organizations. The movement peaked in the first five months following the Winterswijk Congress, as 80 more "Polish political women's organizations" were established. Thus by World War I, there were 140 in existence. If we can assume that the size of their memberships was similar to those fifteen for which we have data (see Table 3) and contained 674 members in 1912, then it is possible to estimate total membership in May 1914 as around 6,270. The rapid growth of an independent women's movement came to a momentary halt at the beginning of the First World War. In the end, however, this trend emerged strengthened after the war, influenced by new factors, a discussion of which cannot be undertaken here.

---

57. See Klessmann, p. 99, Murzynowska, p. 198, and Kozłowski, *Rozwój* . . . p. 208.

In these organizations, despite the lack of a central directing body, strong unifying tendencies appeared already before the Winterswijk Congress. The annual police report of May 3, 1913, contained the following information:

> According to their statutes, their purpose is to support Poles who require assistance, to foster the native language, and to emphasize child-rearing and contemporary learning through lectures and evening entertainment.

In addition, aside from the two associations directed by priests,

> the other unions stand outside the Church and carry on activities which in reality differ very little from those of Polish political associations.[58]

The Winterswijk Congress confirmed the aforementioned goals and directions of action of the "Polish women's organizations" and, for its part, accelerated their organizational development and began to introduce central structures.[59] An important step in this direction occurred when the Congress called for the creation of "a department of women's affairs" and "a secretariat for women's affairs."[60] Their tasks were to oversee the implementation of the resolutions of the Congress and the development of the women's organizations.

Maria Ruszczyńska, an activist from Cracow mentioned earlier in this article (see footnotes 35 and 40), directed work on the new structures of the women's organizations in the first months of their existence and received financial support for this purpose from the National Council. Ruszczyńska, according to the police, was involved in the training of "women and girls" for directing the work of the rapidly developing organizations. After her departure, Jadwiga Pankowska took over direction of the department for women's affairs. These activities were crowned in May 1914 with the establishment of a central "League of Polish Women's Unions in Western Germany."[61]

Relatively less is known regarding the participation of women in organizations not defined by gender in the Ruhr. There are enough individual pieces of evidence, however, which could add to our knowledge about this important arena of women's

---

58. NWStAM, Reg. MS VII-31:45.

59. Gerstein's annual report of May 4, 1914, notes: "Besides [the activities of the rosary fellowships], 'Polish women's unions' have been formed in recent years which are devoted to fostering the native language and child-rearing and have practically placed themselves in opposition to the German clergy. . . . Since November 1913, the Polish women's unions' aim has been to remove the Polish women brought together in the first kind of association from German clerical influences." Gerstein, p. 81; see also Klessmann, p. 99.

60. Gerstein's report of May 4, 1914, NWStAM, Reg. MS VII-31:81; see also Murzynowska, p. 198, and Kozłowski, *Rozwój* . . . , p. 208.

61. Klessmann, p. 99.

public activity. Since this evidence is dispersed, long and time-consuming research would be required for its analysis. Here, I would only like to indicate the types of organizations in which, according to my own preliminary calculations, it is possible to document women's participation. The first consistent information is derived from the years 1908–1909. This coincides in time, therefore, with the creation of separate Polish women's organizations and relates specifically to the participation of women in meetings of Polish associations. They took part in discussions and were elected, albeit infrequently, to executive committees. This type of women's activity can be noted particularly in economic, cultural-educational, electoral, youth, and temperance organizations.

The Winterswijk Congress registered an appreciation of women's involvement in its recognition of the principle of equality of responsibility for organizational membership of both men and women:

> It is the duty of every Pole over the age of 18, whether male or female, to belong at the very least to a Polish national association recognized by our supreme elected bodies and by the National Council. We call upon all associations to accede to the appropriate league without fail.[62]

It is also necessary to note that women's involvement in mass strikes in the mining industry, and particularly in social demonstrations in the last years of World War I, were other important aspects of their participation in public life.

• • •

The statements and conclusions presented in this article have a preliminary character and require further, more penetrating research. Despite significant gaps in the source base, the preserved materials do permit such a possibility. They have enabled us to know more about the employment of women, particularly in managing the family household and the taking in of "boarders," as well as the assistance women provided their husbands and fathers in commerce.

Polish women in the Rhein-Westphalia industrial region, despite their seemingly weak occupational position, particularly in industry, nevertheless managed at the beginning of the twentieth century to play the dominant role in the family, in the teaching of children to read and write in their native language, as well as in the raising of children in a Polish national spirit. Such roles were made possible by relatively good material conditions and particularly by the places assigned to women by Polish organizations and their influential press. The legal-political status of Poles insured that the family would have to take on some obligations of a public character.

---

62. Gerstein's report on the Polish Congress in Winterswijk of November 9, 1913, NWStAM, Reg. MS 35a, 1:231.

It has also been possible to establish that the rosary fellowships in the Ruhr, despite the prevailing opinion of a number of historians, were typically women's organizations and after 1909–1910 no longer restricted themselves to exclusively religious and self-help activities. They were also involved in work of a national Polish character and began to emancipate themselves from the social influences of the German clergy.

Finally, new assessments and conclusions regarding the Union of Polish Women are now possible. It can be determined that the origins of separate Polish women's organizations in Rhein-Westphalia go back at least as far as 1908–1909, therefore earlier than the existing literature on the subject had indicated.

Women, Work & Family

Polish, Italian and Eastern European Immigrants in Industrial Connecticut, 1890–1940

Laura Anker

This paper explores the central role of women in the migration of Southern Italian and Eastern European families to Connecticut cities. An analysis of over two hundred immigrant life histories, largely of women, and of demographic, industrial and institutional data compiled by the Connecticut Federal Writers Project in the late 1930's reveals women as active agents, not passive victims of the transformation from pre-industrial to industrial culture.[1] Women were engaged in every aspect of the migration process: from decisions about whether to emigrate and where to go, to considerations of who should work and in what jobs, where to live, how to accommodate, when, where and how to resist.[2] The WPA oral histories record

1. The life histories in this paper are taken from the archives of the WPA, Federal Writers' Project Connecticut Ethnic Survey, housed in the library of the University of Connecticut, Storrs, Conn. I wish to thank William D'Antonio, Bruce Staves and Vaneta D'Andrea for facilitating my use of this material. I have a large debt to Rand Jimerson and the staff of the Collections Department, University of Connecticut Library, for their generous help in guiding my access to the archive. A larger collection of Connecticut WPA materials can be found in the State Library in Hartford, but it is not usefully catalogued. A handlist of the Storrs collection is provided in Appendix I of my Ph.D. Dissertation: Schwartz, Laura Anker, *Immigrant Voices From Home, Work and Community: Women and Family in the Migration Process 1890–1938* (Stony Brook, NY: State University of New York Press, 1983), p. 780–816. The autobiographies in the archive were elicited by WPA interviewers who were usually themselves members of ethnic communities. The life histories were written from the interviewers most often verbatim notes since they did not have tape recorders.

2. See also Isabelle Bertaux-Wiame, "The Life History Approach to the Study of Internal Migration," in Daniel Bertaux (ed.), *Biography and Society* (Beverly Hills, CA: Sage, 1981), 253. Miriam Cohen, "Italian-American Women in New York City, 1900–1950" in Milton

From *Polish American Studies*, vol. 45, no. 2 (Autumn 1988), pp. 23–49.

the actions of ordinary immigrants from various ethnic groups and disclose both the commonality and specificity of women's experiences and perspectives. They transcend abstract notions of ethnic difference or cultural superiority to reveal the concrete processes by which women fabricated life strategies in response to specific conditions. They do not simplify or romanticize women's lives. Rather they demonstrate the constraints under which women labored and the ambiguities and complexities of their responses.

By recounting the stories of particular Polish, Hungarian, Slovak, Italian and Jewish families in Europe and in the specific industrial contexts of Bridgeport, New Haven, Hartford and New Britain, the WPA oral histories provide a detailed and concrete description of the overlapping worlds of family, community and work and of the confrontation between ethnic familial cultures and the exigencies of American urban life. They demonstrate the crucial role of women in creating and maintaining the kinship and social networks that structured immigration and adaption. Not only

---

Cantor and Bruce Laurie (eds.) *Class, Sex, and the Woman Worker* (Westport, CT: Greenwood Press, 1970), 120–143; and "From Workshop to Office: Italian Women and Family Strategies in New York City, 1900–1950" (Ph.D. Dissertation, University of Michigan, 1978); Elizabeth Ewen, *Immigrant Women in the Land of Dollars, 1890–1920* (New York: Monthly Review Press, 1985); Carol Groneman, "'She Earns as a Child, She Pays as a Man': Women Workers in a Mid-Nineteenth-Century New York City Community," in Richard L. Ehrlich (ed.) *Immigrants in Industrial America, 1850–1920* (Charlottesville: University Press of Virginia, 1977), 33–46; Herbert Gutman, *Work, Culture and Society in Industrializing America: Essays in Working Class and Social History* (New York: Knopf, 1976); Tamara Haraven, "The Dynamics of Kin in Industrial Communities: The Historical Perspective," *American Journal of Sociology* 84 (1978 supplement), S151-S182; "Family Time and Industrial Time: Family and Work in a Planned Corporation Town, 1900–1914" in Tamara Haraven (ed.) *Family and Kin in Urban Communities, 1700–1930* (New York: New Viewpoints, 1971); "The History of the Family as an Interdisciplinary Field," *Journal of Interdisciplinary History* 2 (1971), 399–414; "The Laborers of Manchester, New Hampshire, 1912–1922: The Role of Family and Ethnicity in Adjustment to Industrial Life," *Labor History* 16 (1975), 249–265; Elizabeth H. Pleck, "Two Worlds in One: Work and Family," *Journal of Social History* 10 (Winter 1976), 178–195; Joan W. Scott and Louise A. Tilly, "Women's Work and the Family in Nineteenth-Century Europe," *Comparative Studies in Society and History* 17 (1975), 36–64; Judith E. Smith, "Our Own Kind: Family and Community Networks," *Radical History Review* 17 (Spring 1978), 99–120; *Family Connections: A History of Italian and Jewish Immigrant Lives in Providence, Rhode Island 1900–1940,* New York, SUNY Press, 1985; Joan W. Scott and Louise A. Tilly, "Women's Work and the Family in Nineteenth-Century Europe," *Comparative Studies in Society and History* 17 (1975), 36–64; Louisa A. Tilly and Joan W. Scott, *Women, Work, and Family* (New York: Holt, Rinehart and Winston, 1978); Virginia Yans-McLaughlin, *Family and Community: Italian Immigrants in Buffalo, 1880–1930* (Ithaca: Cornell University Press, 1978); "A Flexible Tradition: Immigrant Families Confront New Work Experiences," *Journal of Social History* 17 (Summer 1974), 429–445; "Patterns of Work and Family Organization: Buffalo's Italians," *Journal of Interdisciplinary History* 2 (1971), 299–314.

were women's lives embedded within the household and kinship ties they utilized to actively influence and alter their new environments, but contrary to the familiar American myth, immigrant men did not move about as "rugged individuals."

The WPA narratives offer more than additional nuggets of information; they raise new questions and suggest fresh interpretations from the previously neglected standpoint of ordinary immigrants, about what they believed mattered in their lives. The possibility of a more integrated synthesis emerges from their narration and description of the interior dimension of immigrant life.

The Connecticut WPA Ethnic Survey oral histories are rare first person accounts which reflect the immediacy of experience still fresh in the subjects' minds, articulated and interpreted within the value context in which the events took place and recollected from the special vantage of ongoing ethnic community life. They are life histories of immigrants conducted mainly by immigrants; biographies of residents of ethnic neighborhoods recorded in those communities by compatriots who shared a similar past and a common present. Many interviewers spoke Polish, Italian, Yiddish, Russian, or Hungarian and could interview their neighbors in their native tongues. Because they talked to immigrants in their kitchens and on their doorsteps, as well as in small shops, factories, and ethnic halls, project workers, many of whom were women themselves, they collected an unusual number of women's biographies. "We interviewed women," recalled Pearl Russo, because "we wanted to and because they were at home." "Most people wanted to talk," she explained: "We were part of a whole culture of story telling. . . . Now people would rather watch television. . . . When we were growing up, the city (Bridgeport) was vibrant. . . . It had all these nationalities . . . and we knew each other. . . . Today we could live together and be strangers."[3]

The WPA oral histories record the subjective experiences of broad historical transformation, bringing us back from the grand patterns of history to the awkwardly individual lives that are its basis. Take for example Helen Doneski's recollection of the changes that led her to leave her "little home" in Russian Poland: "Besides my mother and father, there were four sisters and two brothers in my family. Our home was small and so was our acreage. Once there were over sixty acres to our little estate, but . . . these areas were divided into smaller ones and given to those of the family who were married. . . . On this little farm of ours there was also little

3. Author's interview with Pearl K. Russo, Feb. 16, 1983. I am particularly indebted to Pearl Russo, not only for her wonderful oral histories, but for the memories and analysis of the Connecticut Ethnic Survey she shared with me in many hours of discussion over the last few years. For a detailed discussion of the significance, history, politics and methodology of the Connecticut WPA Ethnic Survey, see Schwartz, *Immigrant Women. op. cit.*, specifically Chapter III.

food to be had at times. . . . There was no income whatever in terms of money. We were all there, and what subsistence we received was done so through the toil of the earth. Out of this . . . we had to pay Russian taxes. . . . Nothing happened of great significance that made me desirous of leaving my little home in Poland. Nothing except the fact that we were growing up and were becoming poorer. Economic conditions, you might call them here. No money and little land."[4]

Such testimony offers valuable evidence about the intimate arenas in which immigrants assessed their alternatives and possibilities, reached decisions and pursued their hopes. It allows the historian to analyze specific choices and actions together with the networks of social relations that allowed them to take place.

The perspective of women reveals the collective and familial context of immigrant life, focusing attention on the ways individual experience is embedded in complex fabrics of social organization.[5] The women interviewed by the Connecticut Federal Writers Project spoke of the people around them and of their relationships of those people, contextualizing social processes in a way that men did not. From women's narratives emerged the outlines of biographies of husbands, children, sisters, brothers, neighbors, and more distant kin and the relational networks which tied them together. Men more frequently spoke about their actions and decisions as solely *their* own. For example, Morris Shapiro, a Jewish immigrant to Hartford in 1923, made the journey from Russia to the United States with money from his father and the help of his sister, who had preceded him. Upon his arrival in New York, he was met by an aunt, who directed him to Hartford where he went to live with his sister and brother-in-law. They, in tum, settled him in a place to live and helped him find a job. Yet he described his migration as a series of self-induced events. Asserting his individualistic self-reliance, he explained: "For the first time in my life, I was actually on my own. . . . No family, no relations, and very few friends."[6]

4. "Personal History of a First Generation Pole" (Mrs. Helen Gadomska Doneski, pseud.), interviewed by Stanley Dabkowski (box 87; 187:7b; 28p), p. 2–3, 12. References are to names of subjects, name of interviewer, box, folder number, and to the number of pages in the life history. Since many of the subjects are referred to by initials, I have assigned them fictional names to facilitate references to them in the text These names are provided after their initials. See Schwartz, *op. cit.* Bibliography, section I, pp. 726–737 for the complete cross reference of pseudonyms and full life histories in the archives.

5. Carol Gilligan, *In A Different Voice: Psychological Theory and Women's Development* (Cambridge, MA: Harvard University Press, 1982), 28. See also, Paul Thompson, *The Voice of the Past, Oral History;* "Life Histories and the Analysis of Social Change." Isabelle Bertaux-Wiame, *op. cit.*

6. Morris Shapiro, interviewed by Morris Tonkin (box 61; 157:le; 25p.)

Immigration was itself a familial, not an individual act, one of many steps taken by impoverished European families to make survival possible.[7] By the late 19th century southern Italian and Eastern European peasant and artisanal households had been increasingly drawn into a complex nexus of market relationships. Access to money became imperative to meet the exigencies of daily existence.[8] Families responded by developing strategies that modified preindustrial cultural patterns to defend their way of life.[9] At the center of preindustrial households, women, especially mothers, were often the authors or organizers of new and intensified modes of family co-operation. These included sending daughters, as well as fathers and sons, out of village economies into the world of wage labor. As local sources of employment became saturated or pogroms forced permanent departure, the field of migration increased to include the United States. Immigration, thus, became a rational familial response to the economic dilemmas of individual households.

Contradictory realities engulfed the migration process. The very bonds that united families in a common battle for survival led mothers to send daughters to America, often resulting in their permanent separation. Forty years after leaving her village in Poland Julia Karbowsky still struggled to comprehend the forces that led to her departure and the conflicting familial and individual contexts of love that separated her girlhood in Europe from her adulthood in the United States. She recalled: "Then one day we talked about America. My parents thought it would be a good idea if I went there to make some money and then eventually to return. You mustn't get the wrong impression about my mother wishing me to go. You mustn't

7. Robert F. Harney, "Men Without Women: Italian Migrants in Canada, 1885–1930," in Betty B. Caroli, Robert F. Harney, and Lydio F. Tomasi, *The Italian Immigrant Woman in North America* (Toronto: Multicultural History Society of Ontario, 1978), 79–102; Anthony Leeds, "Women in the Migratory Process: A Reductionist Outlook," *Anthropological Quarterly* 49 (Jan. 1976), 69–76; Jacob Mincer, "Family Migration System," *Journal of Political Economy* 86:5 (1978), 749–774; Tilly and Moch, *op. cit.*

8. Josef Barton, *Peasants and Strangers: Italians, Rumanians and Slovaks in an American City, 1880–1950* (Cambridge, MA: Harvard University Press, 1975), p. 27–47; John W. Briggs, *An Italian Passage: Immigrants to Three American Cities, 1890–1930* (New Haven: Yale University Press, 1978), 1–14; Irving Howe, *The World of Our Fathers* (New York: Harcourt Brace Jovanovich, 1976), 15–24; Ezra Mendelsohn, *Class Struggle in the Pale: The Formative Years of the Jewish Workers' Movement in Tsarist Russia* (Cambridge, Eng.: Cambridge University Press, 1970), Chapter 1; Smith, *op. cit.* Family Connections, Chap. 2; Golab, Caroline, *Immigrant Destinations,* Philadelphia, 1977.

9. Barton, *op. cit.,;* Briggs, *op. cit.;* Louise A. Tilley and Joan W. Scott, *Women, Work, and Family, op. cit.;* Smith, *op. cit.* 125–136; Charlotte Chapman. *Milocca, A Sicilian Village* (Cambridge, MA: Schenkinan, 1971), Chapters 2, 4, 5; Leonard Covello, *The Social Background of the Italo-American School Child* (Leiden, NJ: E. J. Brill, 1967, reprint of 1944 edition), Chapters 5 and 7; Mark Zborowski and Elizabeth Herzog, *Life is With the People* (New York: Schoeken, 1969, reprint of 1952 edition), pp. 291–307.

think that just because your parents wanted you to do that they didn't love you. Oh no. Underneath, they were thinking of me, and of the entire family's welfare. It is something you have to contend with when you grow older."[10]

Emigrants embarked upon a voyage of estrangement from family and traditional culture with the immediate intention of preserving their former ways of life. Women ran households in Europe while men traveled near and far in search of work. Often years passed before husbands returned or sent for their wives and children. After her husband left for America to earn money in the mines, Frank Kovalauskas' mother bought and ran a farm. For sixteen years she headed her household in Lithuania, supporting four children.[11] Agnes Bonsza, a Hungarian women who ultimately emigrated to Bridgeport, recalled: "My father . . . was coming back and forth, back and forth. He'd come home, leave a child, then go back to America. Every two, three years he was doing that. And my mother was taking care of the farm. My father never made money—he was all the time spending what he saved for the passage."[12]

Although husbands usually sent money home, many families relied upon the entrepreneurial, wage labor, and management skills of women for survival. The experience of women as formal heads of households sometimes altered internal family relationships when husbands and wives reunited. When she was single, Mary Kycinski ran a cooperative store in Poland. After marriage, her husband came to America where Mary planned to join him shortly, but World War I interrupted their plans. Mary explained: "I stayed with my mother and, in October, my first child was born. In December I opened a grocery store of my own . . . I used the money my husband sent me with some of my own to start the store. . . . I was interested in business. We all worked together for six years, mother, father, and three sisters."[13]

Mildred Hecht worked as a tailor in a small factory to support her aging mother, father, and younger siblings after her older brothers and sisters left for America. Her work introduced her to new ideas of labor organization and socialism that undermined her father's patriarchal authority: "My father was a very Orthodox Jew. He used to get mad at me because I didn't believe in those things. He used to say when I come home, 'Nu, here's the revolutionerka.' He was the head of the house and bossed everybody . . . a regular Kahan. . . . When I was small, I used to be

---

10. "Polish Woman #1," (Julia Karbowski, pseud.) interviewed by Stanley Dabkowski (box 87; 187:7b; 6p), p. 1–3.

11. Frank Kovalauskas (Lithuanian), interviewed by Albert S. Kayeski (box 64; 158:1, 7p), p. 1–2.

12. Mrs. B (Hungarian; Agnes Bonsza. pseud.) interview by P. K. Russo (box 21; 109:11; 21p), 3. See also Sebastian Scalo, quoted in Frazzetta, "Survey of an East Side Block," 2.

13. Mary Kyc (Polish; Kycinski, pseud.), interviewed by Bishop (box 85; 187:3; 10p), 5.

afraid of my father . . . but when I went to work and supported the family, I wasn't so afraid."[14]

Antoinetta Scavono made the difficult decision to leave the home which her family had occupied for generations and join her husband in Bridgeport, where he emigrated in search of work three years earlier. While Mr. Scavano was employed at various "pick and shovel" jobs in America, she had labored tirelessly in Sicily on a small garden patch they owned, refusing to "leave even 10 square meters fallow. . . . But everything we had to buy was expensive," she explained. Even with her husband's earnings, they could not maintain their already scanty holdings, let alone buy the additional land necessary to subsistence.[15]

Wives traveled to the United States to join husbands. They made the arrangements for departure and managed the complexities of the journey with young children. They participated in the deliberations and were sometimes the moving force in family migration or the decision to send household members abroad. They ran their households while their husbands were gone, under conditions of increasing scarcity and turmoil. Daughters accompanied mothers and siblings or came to Connecticut by themselves. These immigrant women had years of valuable experience accessing networks of mutuality and support, managing family economies, and organizing family enterprises. These skills not only allowed women to negotiate the migration process itself, but also enabled them to muster the resources and create the networks to deal with more years of hardship and struggle in a new land.

Traditional familial norms of mutual assistance were strengthened and kinship ties were extended to handle both the economic insecurities which enveloped households and the vicissitudes of migration itself. The story of Nuola Obretsky, a Polish woman who finally emigrated to New Haven, exemplifies how individuals survived economic, religious and political upheaval in Europe and negotiated the migration process through the help of non-household kin who provided services, monetary aid, and links to new jobs. Nuola was seven when her mother died and eight when her father was drafted into the Russian army, never to return. She moved in with an uncle, but he, too, was drafted. An overlapping circle of close and distant kin and family friends cared for her during World War I. Finally, after the war, an aunt in New Haven sent money for the voyage and provided her with a permanent home.[16]

14. M.H. (Jewish; Mildred Hecht, pseud.), interviewed by Rahel Mittelstein (box 61; 157:1e), 1.

15. Antoinetta Scavono, quoted in Vincent Frazzetta, "Italians in Bridgeport" (box 22; 109:13a; 99p), 62.

16. N. O. (Polish; Nuala Obretsky, pseud.), interviewed by Rahel Mittelstein (box 61; 157:le), 1–3.

A village-wide collection helped pay for John Lukasavius's passage to the United States: "A day or two before I was to leave for America, we had a big party at my house. My mother prepared many dishes and the two village musicians played for dancing. All the village came to the party and everybody donated as much money as they could spare for the journey. . . . Everybody was glad that I was able to go and I remember that night, I made several promises of presents to my friends after I was working in America."[17]

At least sixty-three percent of the people interviewed by the Connecticut WPA relied directly on kinship or village ties to manage migration and resettlement Of those who arrived after 1900 (well over half the sample), ninety-one percent utilized such networks, seventy-eight percent came through relatives and thirteen percent through village connections. For women, the ties were even tighter, since early migrants tended to be men. Of twenty-seven women, twenty-five came to husbands, close relatives or more distant kin; the two exceptions came to friends. Furthermore, seventy-two percent of immigrants relied upon resources from parents, siblings, or children to finance their migration, and another eleven percent received money from friends, cousins, aunts and uncles. Only the remaining seventeen percent paid for their own passage. While women were more deeply embedded in these bonds of mutual assistance—ninety-six percent relied upon family, kin, and friends, fully seventy-four percent of the male immigrants also received such assistance.[18]

For those immigrants who arrived without direct kinship ties or letters of introduction, ethnic communities and organizations often provided the link to kin or acquaintances and therefore to jobs and lodging. Julia Karbowski arrived in America at seventeen years of age with no one to meet her, but found her way with the assistance of fellow Poles to the St. Joseph's Home in New York City. The minister there had connections to the Polish community in New Britain where she soon located a forgotten distant relative who provided her with lodging and got her a job as a domestic.[19] Weaker, more extended ties were often the most crucial for reaching out to jobs and lodging in distant immigrant destinations. Catherine

17. John Lukasavicius (Lithuanian), interviewed by Albert Kayeski (box 64; 158:1; 10 p.), p. 4.

18. These figures are based on tallies from oral histories in the W.P.A. archives. See Schwatz, *op. cit.*, Chap. 5, p. 209. The Immigration Commission (Volume 20, *Statistical Review of Immigration*, 360–361) found that nearly three-fourths of immigrants told American immigration officials that they, not relatives, had financed their voyages. This discrepancy seems to derive from the anxiety of immigrants that insolvency might result in exclusion. See, for example, George M. Price (translated by Leo Shpald), "The Russian Jews in America," in Abraham Karp (ed.), *The Jewish Experience in America;* Vol. IV, *The Era of Immigration* (New York: KTAV Publishing, 1969), 345. Price estimates that 75 percent of Jewish emigrants in 1890 came with tickets sent by, or financed by, relatives in the U.S.

19. "Polish Woman #1" (Julia Karbowski, pseud.), *op. cit.*

Soika, from Galicia, used village networks to obtain work in New Haven. "When I came to America," she recalled, "[I] went to live in Shelton with some people I knew from the village. I knew a lot of girls who lived in New Haven so I came here and got a job."[20]

Mary Osochowsky's aunt reached New Haven through village ties, then sent for her niece: "I came to New Haven because my aunt lived here. She lived here, I suppose, because many of our people from the village were here."[21]

Carrie Leisaski left alone, but went directly to her brother in Terryville, New York. The day after her arrival: "I went to a factory with another girl and got a job. It was easy, just like that." Within a year, a visit to distant relatives in New Britain resulted in a better paying job at the Stanley Works.[22] Her story illustrates the process by which single women immigrants were transformed into permanent residents of Connecticut's cities. Carrie came to New Britain to earn wages to help her family and then return to her "little village in Russian Poland."[23] But, working at various factory jobs from the moment of her arrival, she quickly became integrated into New Britain's growing "Polonia" and, like many of her friends, found a man she wished to marry.[24] Likewise, Mrs. Joseph Barbello came to New Haven "to make money," and "go back," but marriage intervened: "I was eighteen years old when I came here, and I got married when I was twenty. One year later, I got a baby and I couldn't go back."[25] Women with children were most often permanent migrants from the outset. The migration of women enabled the completion of family units and the creation of household economies that depended on their labor at home and in factories. The very existence of extensive wage earning opportunities for women in Connecticut's cities encouraged permanent settlement and the persistence of ethnic communities.[26]

While the networks and resources provided by kin made migration possible, immigration also disrupted and altered family relationships. Husbands usually left before wives; parents were often separated permanently from the children they sent

20. Catherine Soika (pseud), quoted in Rahel Mittelstein, "Ukrainians in New Haven" (box 92; folder 262:2; 21p), 5.

21. Mary Osochowsky (pseud.), quoted in *ibid.*, p. 5.

22. "Polish Woman #3" (Mrs. Carrie Lesiaski, pseud.) interviewed by Stanley Dabrowski (box 85; folder 187:4 5p), p. 3.

23. *Ibid.*, p. 1

24. *Ibid.*, p. 6.

25. Mrs. Joseph Barbello, quoted in Vincent Frazetta, "Survey of An East Side Block" (Hallett St. & Pembroke St.) (box 27; 109:23b; 15p), p. 3.

26. Caroline Golab, "The Impact of Industrial Experience on the Immigrant Family: The Huddled Masses Reconsidered" in Richard L. Ehrlich (ed.), *Immigrants in Industrial America 1985–1920* (Charlottesville: University Press of Virginia, 1977), p. 3, makes the same point about immigrant communities in Philadelphia.

to America. Tabulations from the Connecticut survey show that some seventy-five percent of those who immigrated as adults left their parents behind.[27] Women were especially affected, since they were less able to depend upon their mothers for domestic instruction or, more importantly, for childcare. The absence of vertical ties had the paradoxical effect of forcing them out of the household, extending family ethics of mutuality and reciprocity into ties with more distant kin and neighbors.

Connecticut's immigrants brought with them European patterns of family, kinship and village organization that had already been partially transformed and expanded to cope with the very forces that engendered emigration. This process of adaptation continued in Connecticut's cities as kin and village ties became the basis for complex ethnic communities that developed within the interstices of city life. Between households flowed relatives, boarders and mutual assistance, all lending substance to a dense collective life. The daily demands of existence, of finding and keeping a job and a place to live were mediated through overlapping networks of family, kinship, and ethnicity. These ties provided the structural foundation for the preservation and extension of ethics of mutual support and reciprocal obligation into new strategies of adjustment and resistance.[28]

New arrivals could turn to brothers, sisters, cousins, uncles and aunts for information and sociability, but more importantly for lodging and jobs. Tabulations from the WPA oral histories indicate that seventy-eight percent of immigrants entered the American job market through kin and friendship networks. Less than twenty-two percent found jobs without such direct ties. Eighty-four percent of new arrivals lodged with relatives or friends from Europe. Only eighteen percent lived alone or with strangers. Whereas households in Eastern Europe and Southern Italy customarily had been limited to nuclear families and an occasional aging parent, Connecticut households were transformed to include married siblings, cousins, nephews, nieces, aunts, uncles or friends. The possibility of sharing wages, services and other income sources was enhanced by this tendency of Connecticut immigrant families to live in extended households, or in close proximity to relatives. It also eased the problem of childcare for many immigrant women who, like Barbara Orosz, left her mother behind in Hungary, but could depend on her sister-in-law to watch her infant.[29]

---

27. More than three-fourths of immigrants to the U.S. were under forty years old. Frank Thistlewaite, "Migration from Europe Overseas in the Nineteenth and Twentieth Centuries," in Stanley Katz and Stanley Kutler (eds.), *New Perspectives on the American Past,* Vol. 2 (Boston: Little Brown, 1969, pp. 67–77), p. 74.

28. Schwatz, *op. cit.,* Chap. 6.

29. M. G. Sayers and P. K. Russo, "Survey of Reminton City with Interviews" (Bridgeport) (box 27; 109:23b; 8p), p. 3.

Women did most of the small acts of mutual aid that solidified kinship and neighborhood ties and expanded bonds of reciprocity outward. "Gossip" told where jobs were available, what stores to avoid, how to act and what to learn if one was to avoid being a "greenhorn."[30] The neighborhood activities of women sometimes bridged ethnic differences or hostilities in Connecticut's medium-sized cities where various groups lived in closer proximity to each other than they did in great metropolises like New York or Chicago.

The realities of low wages and irregular employment patterns required immigrant families to rely on the work of more than one household member in the United States, as they had in Europe.[31] Contrary to images of family breakdown,

---

30. See for example Morris Tonken, Jewish Autobiography (box 61; 157:le; 18p). *Ibid.*, Vincent Frazzetta, "Survey of an East Side Block." "Italian Community in Bridgeport," 30, 39. Jeremy Brecher, Jerry Lombardi, Jan Stackhouse and The Brass Workers History Project, *Brass Valley* (Philadelphia: Temple University Press, 1982), p 30. This point has been made in a number of important contexts. See Elizabeth Bott, *Family and Social Network* (New York: 1957; reprinted, New York: Free Press, 1971); Miriam Judith Cohen, "From Workshop to Office: Italian Women and Family Strategies in New York City, 1900–1950," (Ph.D. Dissertation, University of Michigan, 1978), 192–93; Corrine Azen Krause, "Oral History in Pittsburgh—Women, Ethnicity, and Mental Health: Rational, Procedure and Methodology," in Betty B. Caroli, Robert F. Harney and Lydio F. Tomasi (eds.), *The Italian Immigrant Woman in North America* (Toronto: The Multicultural History Society of Ontario, 1978), 260–268; and *Grandmothers, Mothers and Daughters: An Oral History Study of Ethnicity, Mental Health, and Continuity of Three Generations of Jewish, Italian, and Slavic-American Women* (New York: American Jewish Committee, 1978); M. Estelle Smith, "Networks and Migration Resettlement: Cherchez La Femme," *Anthropological Quarterly*, 49 (January, 1976), 20–27; and Louise A Tilly and Joan W. Scott, *Women, Work and Family* (New York: Holt, Rinehart and Winston, 1978), 143–210; Anzia Yezierska, *The Breadgivers* (1925; reprinted, New York: George Braziller, 1975), 14–15; Mario Puzo, *The Fortunate Pilgrim* (New York: Lancer Books, 1973), 9. See also "Choosing a Dream: Italians in Hell's Kitchen," in Thomas Wheeler (ed.), *The Immigrant Experience* (Baltimore: Penguin, 1973). The Italian wife "must share everything about her," wrote settlement worker Lillian Betts. "A tenement hall in New York is a substitute for the village road, where she and her neighbors can communicate." Lillian Betts, *The Italians of New York* (University Settlement Studies, Vol. 1, No. 3; New York: University Settlement Society, 1908), 94.

31. Howard Woolston, "Wages in New York City," *Survey*, 34 (1915), 510; Paul H. Douglas, *Real Wages in the U.S. 1890–1926* (New York: Houghton Mifflin, 1930; reprinted, New York: A M. Kelley, 1966), 584; Golab, *op. cit.*, p. 136–39, offers similar figures for Pennsylvania. Winifred D. Wandersee, *Women's Work and Family Values, 1920–1940* (Cambridge: Harvard University Press, 1981), 9–14; Wandersee reviews a number of studies (including Douglas) which indicate that for most families a single wage could not produce even poverty level subsistence. Among those cited are: Karl De Schweinitz, "Are the Poor Really Poor," *Survey*, 59 (January 15, 1928), 517, who found that in 1925, 88 percent of a sample of Philadelphia men earned less than the subsistence standard of $38 for a family of five; and Leila Houghteling,

new industrial necessities intensified family interdependence. Immigrants transferred the concept of a family wage economy to Connecticut's cities, adapting and realigning household work relationships in accordance with the needs and demands of industrial labor.[32]

The main issue confronting immigrant mothers was how to maintain an economically viable family life. The elimination of home agricultural and craft production, available at least as a limited resource in Europe, made money the key to survival. But the conditions of paid female labor in the United States made it harder for mothers to combine domestic responsibilities and work tasks. Furthermore, they found that the handskills they had learned and applied in Europe to earn income at home had lost their value in competition with machine-made products. In America their crafts became self-consumed luxuries. Lucia Salanto explained: "In Italy . . . if the girl . . . learn to embroidery and to sew dresses . . . then they could do this work

The Income and Standard of Living of Unskilled Workers in Chicago (Chicago: University of Chicago Press, 1927), who found, in 1925, that fewer than one-third of a sample (n=467) of Chicago heads of families earned enough to provide for a minimum standard of living. Through women's work, which was often "arduous," the population reaching subsistence was raised to about 50 percent. See also, New York State Investigation Commission, *Fourth Report, Volume IV, Report on the Cost of Living* (1915); Arcadius Kahan, "Economic Opportunities and Some Pilgrims' Progress: Jewish Immigrants from Eastern Europe in the U.S., 1890–1914," *Journal of Economic History*, 38 (March, 1978), 250; George M. Price, "The Russian Jews in America," translated by Leo Shpall, in Abraham J. Karp (ed.), *The Jewish Experience in America: Volume IV, The Era of Immigration* (New York: KTAV Publishing, c1969), 287; and Robert Chapin, *The Standard of Living Among Workingmen's Families in New York City* (New York, 1909; reprinted, New York: Arno, 1971). Katherine Anthony, "The Family," in H. E. Stearns (ed.), *Civilization in the U.S.* (New York: Harcourt Brace, 1922), which is based on national figures. See also Wandersee, *op. cit.* Louise C. Odencrantz, *Italian Women in Industry* (New York: Russell Sage Foundation, 1919; reprinted, New York: Arno Press, 1977), 119–20, 212–213.

32. Joan W. Scott and Louise Tilly, "Women's Work and the Family in Nineteenth-Century Europe," *Comparative Studies in Society and History*, 17 (1975), 36–64, especially 42–43; Louise A. Tilly and Joan W. Scott, *Women, Work and Family* (New York: Holt, Rinehart and Winston, 1978), 104–105, 227–230, 232; Judith Ellen Smith, "Remaking Their Lives: Italian and Jewish Immigrant Family, Work and Community in Providence, Rhode Island, 1900–1940" (Ph.D. Thesis, Department of History, Brown University, 1981), 28–29; Tamara Hareven, "Family Time and Industrial Time: Family and Work in a Planned Corporation Town 1900–1914," in Tamara Hareven (ed.), *Family and Kin in Urban Communities 1700–1930* (New York: New Viewpoints, 1977); Miriam J. Cohen, "From Workshop to Office: Italian Women and Family Strategies in New York City, 1900–1950" (Ph.D. Dissertation, University of Michigan), 1978, 12; and John Bodnar, "Immigration and Modernization: The Case of Slavic Peasants in Industrial America." *Journal of Social History*, 10 (1976), 57–58.

for money. That's all I was doing in Italy. I still do that, but I can't get no work like this, because in this country you could buy all these things in the store."[33]

Despite these constraints, wives in Connecticut found ways to work, as they had in southern and eastern Europe. The WPA oral histories reveal the varying strategies women organized, integrating and alternating their own labor—paid and unpaid, inside and outside the household, with their husband's and children's wage contributions. Different employment patterns and choices emerged from the complex interplay of inherited cultural traditions, new relationships of production, and changing social roles. For women, job preferences were sometimes determined by their particular stage in the life cycle. Polish women, many of whom were single and alone when they arrived in the United States, were more likely to work as domestics than Jewish women, who came with their families or Italian women, who came to join husbands or fathers who had emigrated earlier.[34]

The particular opportunities for paid labor in American cities and economic necessity altered southern and eastern European work preferences. For example, Mary Huda claimed that domestic service was a preferred way for Slovak women to earn wages in Europe and therefore when young single girls first migrated to Connecticut cities, they went directly to such jobs, which frequently had been arranged before their arrival. Mrs. Huda had herself worked as a domestic when she first came to Bridgeport, but later, like many other Slovak women, she took factory jobs, first at Warner Corset and then at Acme Shear because they paid higher wages and offered predetermined hours. She explained: "When I would get home (from her job as a cleaning woman), I used to have my lady friend in the next house come to my house and we would talk about her work and my work. She used to tell me that she worked in the Corset Co., on bench work. . .that it would be better if I worked in the factory instead of house work. She said that the work wasn't hard and that in the night time you were like free. I told her that in Europe our people all worked on the farms and when there was a chance for a young girl to work in the house of some rich people, it was like work on the other side. I said that the Slovak people think that there is more respect to work in the house instead to work in the factory.

33. Mrs. L. Salanto (Italian, Lucia. pseud.) interviewed by Vincent Frazzetta (box 23; 109:13b; 3p), p. 2.

34. Virginia Yans-McLaughlin and others who argue that Italian women did not take jobs as domestics (or even factory workers) because patriarchal cultural traditions forbade them from working in such close proximity to men who were not their husbands or children, do not address the contradiction posed by the prevalence of often male boarders in Italian households. Why was it acceptable for Italian women to take men in as boarders but not to go into other people's homes or factories? The danger of increased sexual contact was at least as great in the woman's home as in a factory. See Yans-McLaughlin, "Italian Women and Work: Experience and Perception," p. 113.

She said that the old country was the old country, and in this country the people think it is better for the woman to work in the factory."[35]

Mothers tended to work, not when they had the most time on their hands, but rather when their income was most critical to family survival. These were usually the years when their children were young and unable to contribute to the family economy, years when they also had the greatest child care responsibilities.[36] For this reason, they often chose to earn wages doing piecework, caring for boarders, or working in artisanal shops, rather than entering factories. Immigrant communities provided unique opportunities for first generation mothers to integrate domestic chores and wage earning activities as they had, under different circumstances, in Europe. When these opportunities declined and male income increased, second generation women adopted very different work patterns, more frequently working when their children were older, in school, or able to take care of themselves.

WPA interviews reveal that more than forty percent of first generation wives and mothers were engaged in income-generating work at home, tending boarders and lodgers, washing clothes, doing piecework or working alongside their husbands or other household members in small artisanal and retail stores.[37] Hermina Lovasz ran a grocery business with her mother and brother; Maria Esposito's mother cooked much of the food sold in the family's small delicatessen, and also assisted her husband with customers in the store.[38] One Jewish daughter recalled that it was her mother who had the real "head" for business and was therefore the central figure in the family butcher shop.[39] Many women ran small neighborhood shops on their own. Mrs. Julia Satamory found that the working day was too long in the factories, restaurants and hospitals where she had labored and the distance from home too great to accommodate her domestic responsibilities. She, therefore, opened a small

35. Mrs. Mary Huda (Slovak) interviewed by Vincent Frazzetta (obtained by author from Mr. Frazzetta. 10p), p. 2–3. During World War I, Slovak women left domestic work in droves for better paying jobs in shops like Bridgeport Brass, Acme Shear, Singer Manufacturing Company, Holmes and Edwards Silver, United Metalic Cartridge and other factories in and around the Eastside Slovak community.

36. Smith, "Remaking Their Lives," *op. cit.*, 95; and Cohen, "From Workshop to Office," *op. cit.*, 114f. Tilly and Scott, *Women, Work and Family*, make a similar point about differing conditions of women's work in Europe.

37. This is an underestimate, since women were counted as not working if no such work was mentioned.

38. Miss A. (Hungarian; Miss Hermina Lovasz, pseud.) interviewed by P. K. Russo (box 21; 109:11; 19p); Marie Esposito (Jewish), *loc. cit.* See also N Family (Polish; Novakowski, pseud.) interviewed by Stanley Dabkowski (box 87; 187:7b; 28p). Mrs. Honi Mendelson (Hungarian Jew) quoted in George Fisher, "Magyar Interviews, #7, #8 and #34–43" (box 27; folder 109:23c; 20p).

39. Author's interview with Pearl K. Russo, Feb. 10, 1983.

Hungarian restaurant in the West End of Bridgeport. Her family lived in two rooms behind the tiny establishment.[40]

Industrial homework also provided Connecticut immigrant women with cash-producing employment that could be fit into their domestic routine. Michelangelo Russo recalled his whole family sitting at their kitchen table in Bridgeport helping his mother to sew garters, work brought home from Warner Corset and other smaller shops.[41] Other factories provided jobs finishing garments, stringing beads, linking chains, and filling cards with pins or buttons. In the brass manufacturing center of New Britain, the most common production work done in immigrant households was attaching brass snap fasteners to the cards on which they were sold. Women also took in washing, ironing, and sewing. Kalya Greenberg had learned to be a skilled dressmaker in Russia. She then "started working at home as a dressmaker when I came [to New Haven], and I am still working."[42]

More commonly, however, Connecticut immigrant mothers earned money at home by cooking and cleaning for boarders and lodgers. An Italian woman recalled: "I had to take care of the house and we had four boarders and I had to cook for them. When I first came here I didn't want to do this because everybody wants to have their own house. Well, I change my mind because everybody was doing this thing."[43]

Boarding and lodging provided a familial atmosphere in which immigrants from the same country, region, village or family, speaking the same language, and

---

40. Mrs. Julia Satamory (Hungarian) interviewed by P. K. Russo (box 21; 109:11; 10p), 2–3. See also, "History of a Lithuanian Immigrant" (John Wasclauskaas, pseud.) interviewed by Albert Kayeski (box 64; 158:1; 8p), 7.

41. Pearl Kosby and Michaelangelo Russo, interview, Feb. 26, 1983. Jeremy Brecher, Jerry Lombardi, Jan Stackhouse and the Brass Workers' Project, *Brass Valley* (Philadelphia: Temple University Press, 1982), 64. See also Mary Vankleeck, *Artificial Flower Makers* (New York: Survey, 1913), 38. See also Jerre Mangione, *Mount Allegro: A Memoir of Italian American Life* (New York: Columbia University Press, 1942), 39–40; and Vincent Panella, *The Other Side: Growing up Italian in America* (Garden City, NY: Doubleday, 1979), 62. U.S. Senate, *Report on the Condition of Women and Child Wage Earners* (61st Congress, 1st and 2nd Sessions, 1908–1910, Senate Document 645), vol. 2, 255f. See also Cohen, *op. cit.*, p. 188; Odencrantz, *op. cit.;* and Caroline Golab, "The Impact of Industrial Experience on the Immigrant Family: The Huddled Masses Reconsidered," in Richard L. Ehrlich (ed.) *Immigrants in Industrial America, 1850–1920* (Charlottesville: University Press of Virginia, 1973), 23.

42. K. G. (Jewish; Kalya Greenberg, pseud.) interviewed by Rahel Mittelstein (box 61; 157:le; 14p); Mrs. C. (Hungarian; Bella Chornoy, pseud.), *loc. cit.*, Mrs. Kurmay (Hungarian; Bessie, pseud.), *loc. cit.;* Mrs. Kurmay (Hungarian; Bessie, pseud.), *loc. cit.* See also Judith Smith, "Our Own Kind: Family and Community Networks," *Radical History Review,* 17 (Spring, 1978), 99–120.

43. Sixty-seven year old woman, quoted in Vincent Frazzetta, "Italians in Bridgeport" (box 22; folder 109:13a; 40p), 18–19.

often sharing the same skills and occupations, could collectively face their first encounters with American society.[44] Joint residence acted as a kind of mutual aid, extending the bonds of assistance to new arrivals. A Polish woman explained: "I paid my sister out of my earnings. She also had about five other borders in her home. A lot of other Polish people also had many boarders at that time. Most of them were single, without much money, and since they only paid four or five dollars a month for board, outside of food, of course, they could save money that way. They didn't want to go anywhere else because they could only speak in Polish and they wanted to be with their own people."[45]

Such collective living arrangements were rational economic choices for both lodgers and the women who housed them. Women, who worked outside the home, were seldom paid more than $5 or $6 a week by Connecticut shops before 1915. If each of five boarders paid $4 to $5 a month, married women could earn as much or more working at home as in factories. Women who had worked before marriage took in boarders while children were young and then returned to factory work when their children grew older.[46] Boarding and lodging also provided needed income when older children no longer contributed their paychecks to the family economy.

Economic necessity forced many mothers to seek employment in the factories, textile mills and machine shops which skirted Connecticut's immigrant neighborhoods. By the late 1930s, the declining availability of home-based sources of income and male unemployment pushed even more women out of their homes into

---

44. John Modell and Tamara K. Hareven, "Urbanization and the Malleable Household: An Examination of Boarding and Lodging in American Families," in Tamara Hareven (ed.), *Family and Kin in Urban Communities 1700–1930* (New York, 1977), 167–68. Robert Smuts estimated that in 1890, 20 percent of the families in N.Y. State had boarders and 50 percent of the working class households in New York City contained boarders and lodgers. Robert W. Smuts, *Women and Work in America* (New York: Columbia University Press, 1959; reprinted, New York: Schaeken, 1971). See also Odencratz, *op cit.*, p. 21. Miriam Cohen *(op. cit.*, p. 109) estimated that 25 percent of the Jewish and 33 percent of the Italian households she studied had boarders. In Steelton, John Bodnar found that 57 percent of Slovenian and Croatian immigrant households had boarders and that 89 percent of all Slavic immigrants were living with boarders; John Bodnar, *Immigration and Industrialization: Ethnicity in an American Mill Town, 1870–1940* (Pittsburgh: University of Pittsburgh Press, 1977), 26–32. See also Jane Synge, "Labor and Analysis in the Planning and Interpretation of Research Using Life Histories," in Daniel Bertaux (ed.), *Biography and Society* (Beverly Hills, CA: Sage, 1981), for similar rates in Canada.

45. Mrs. Mary Gadomska (Polish), *loc. cit.*, p. 4. See also Frazzetta Family (Italian) autobiography of Vincent Frazzetta (box 23; 109:13b; 13p), 4. "Polish Woman #1" (Julia Karbowski, pseud.) interviewed by Stanley Dabkowski (box 87; 187:7b; 6p), 6. Bella Chornoy complained that the main furniture in her house had been beds for boarders (Mr. C. [Hungarian]), *loc. cit.*

46. See for example The N Family (Polish; Novakowski, pseud.), *loc. cit.*, p. 18. Joseph Julianelle (Italian interviewed by Frank Nolan (box 23; 109:13b; 8p), 5.

factories, retail stores and personal service industries. In Connecticut's diversified industrial cities, women were employed in machine and tool manufacturers, brass and metal factories, electronics and munitions plants and other "male" industries. Their employment was not limited to traditional areas like textiles, garment manufacture, and domestic service which could be seen as an extension of their household roles or which encapsulated them in a distinct "feminine" mentality. In Bridgeport, women worked on assembly lines at Warner's Corset and other garment factories, but also at Bryant Electric, the Graphone Co., Bridgeport Brass, Acme Shear, Singers Manufacturing Co., Holmes and Edwards Silver, Starr Tool, Salt Textiles, Remington Arms, the Frisbee Pie Company, Union Metalic Cartridge, Casco's and at various lock and small metal ships. In New Haven immigrant women worked at the L. Candee Rubber Shop, the New Haven Clock Company, munitions manufacturers, electrical plants, corset, garment and other factories. They also shucked oysters for Row and Mansfield. In Waterbury, immigrant women found jobs in the various factories such as Scovill, American Brass, Waterbury Manufacturing and Mattaluck Manufacturing, which comprised and developed around the country's foremost brass industry.[47]

Cross-sectional tabulations of the percentages of women who worked at any one time hide the enormous significance of paid labor outside the home for immigrant women.[48] By providing a glimpse of the entire life cycle, oral histories enable us to perceive the integration of the spheres of unpaid family labor and wage work in women's lives. Analysis of the Connecticut WPA life histories reveals that ninety-two percent of the women interviewed, who were single when they arrived in the United States, worked outside the home before they were married. A majority continued to work until the birth of their first child. Although most labored at home, while their children were young, sixty-five percent of the women, including those who were married in Europe, returned to jobs outside the home for substantial periods in their later lives. Work outside the home was clearly an acceptable and viable alternative for first generation mothers. Immigrant women left the workforce

---

47. See Tilly and Scott, *Women, Work and Family,* 88f, for a critique of the view that women's wage labor was an extension of their household responsibilities.

48. Twenty-six percent of all Connecticut women were working in 1929, and immigrant women were always more likely to be in the workforce than their native-born sisters, but these numbers do not capture the reality of women's work experience. Harold Bingham, *History of Connecticut, Volume II* (New York: Lewis Historical Publishing, 1962), 850; Hill, *op. cit.,* pp. 269–70. See also Joan Younger Dickinson, "The Role of the Immigrant Women in the U.S. Labor Force, 1890–1910" (Ph.D. Dissertation, University of Pennsylvania, 1975); Loaraine Pruette, *Women Workers Through the Depression* (New York: MacMillan, 1934). See Chapters 2 and 4 for a more detailed discussion of women's participation in the work force. Joseph Hill, *Women in Gainful Occupations 1870–1920* (Census Monograph 9; Washington, D.C.: Government Printing Office, 1929), 13, 19, 67, 105, 123. See also Cohen, *op. cit.,* p. 10–11.

usually expecting to return. They lived and perceived the trajectories of their lives as part of an immigrant working class world in which the arenas of family, work and community would not be separated.

"The husband is the boss of the house and . . . everything that he says is to be obeyed. . . . The man in the family should be the only worker. . . . The woman is not made for work."[49] These dogmas pervade the WPA narratives, proclaimed by men and sometimes echoed by women, but they do not capture the flavor or reality of immigrant life. Actions more often contradicted articulated attitudes, and the exigencies of material existence gradually altered the values themselves. A case in point was the joint interview of Mr. and Mrs. Carpati, an impoverished Polish couple with many children. Although Mr. Carpati assured the interviewer that his wife had stopped factory work immediately after their marriage because he believed married women should stay at home, Mrs. Carpati corrected him and explained that she had not quit at all, but had been laid off. Thereafter, she continued to work intermittently.[50]

Both women and men expressed ambivalent attitudes about wives working outside the home. The traditional European division of labor required women to work hard indoors and alongside husbands in fields and shops, but the place of men at the head of the pre-industrial family had been firmly grounded in their control over the land and skills which provided subsistence. Once land ownership and artisanal status were undermined, wages became both the major means of family support and the main foundation for male superiority. But women's work outside the home implicitly threatened traditional role relationships. Employer practices which pitted male against female workers could cause this contradiction to erupt into overt hostility.[51] When the income of husbands and children was sufficient,

49. Pasquale Gruci (Italian) interviewed by Vincent Frazzetta (box 23; 109:13b; 18p), 8.

50. Mr. and Mrs. C. (Polish; Carpati, pseud.) interviewed by Tanna Sayers and P. K. Russo (box 25; 109:19; 13p), 6.

51. See, for example, Mrs. Gergely (Hungarian), *loc. cit.;* Mrs. B. (French-Canadian: Marie Bertagne, pseud.), *loc. cit.;* Mrs. Q. (Jewish; Pauline Bartram, pseud.) interviewed by P. K. Russo (box 24; 109:14; 6p). For questionnaire responses see W. P. A., "Industrial Workers in New Britain" (box 27; folder 109:23d). This pattern has occurred in a variety of historical contexts. For an incisive discussion of this issue, see Harold Benenson, "Skill, Degradation, Industrial Change and the Family and Community Bases of U.S. Working Class Response," paper delivered to 9th Annual meeting of Social Science History Association (Bloomington, Indiana, Nov. 1982), 12. See also Alan Dawley, *Class and Community: The Industrial Revolution in Lynn* (Cambridge, MA: Harvard University Press, 1976), 92–94; David Montgomery, *Worker's Control in America: Studies in The History of Work, Technology and Labor Struggles* (Cambridge, England: Cambridge University Press, 1979), 23; and David Brody, *Steelworkers in America: The Non-Union Era* (Cambridge. MA: Harvard University Press, 1980), 73–75.

married women themselves often preferred to remain at home, rather than take the low-paid, exhausting, often dangerous jobs available to them. But many women did not have this choice; they worked outside the home because their wages were crucial to family survival.[52]

Married women's entrance into the industrial workforce could be rationalized as an extension of their traditional role at the center of the pre-industrial household. Lucia Salanto insisted on working in a laundry after marriage. To her husband's objections, she responded that such work was simply a continuation of Italian customs and practices: "In Italy, when the husband don't make enough money the wife she have to work, too . . . they have to pick fruits and everything—that's hard."[53] Although she stopped working when her first baby was born, Mrs. Salanto returned to work when the child was only three years old. She claimed: "Italian girls they are always knowing that they have 'responsibilita' of the house and they want to help."[54] Ironically, Mrs. Salanto portrayed the refusal of some non-Italian women to work outside their homes as the real break with traditional culture: "The girls from the other nationalities . . . they want everything they own way. They work when they are single, but when they marry, they expect the husband to support. . . . The Italian girls, even the ones that born in this country . . . understand when the husband is not working or he makes little money they have to help, this is the way I believe."[55]

If the *"responsibilita"* of women in traditional Italian culture provided a value system within which Mrs. Salanto could adapt to, and actively influence, her new industrial environment, the experience of work itself transformed and altered these attitudes themselves. She refused to stop working when her husband got a better job, claiming that she now would stay on to ease bill paying. Mrs. Salanto had grown used to working. While she began her employment at the laundry to make possible the family's subsistence; by the late 1930s, she was working to improve their standard of living.[56]

---

52. See, for example, Slovak woman, foreperson at Frisbie Pie Company, quoted by Vincent Frazzetta, "Slovak Community in Bridgeport" (box 18; folder 109:4; 80p), 51–52. Doris Gumkowski quoted in Frazzetta, "Polish Community in Bridgeport," 84. Mr. and Mrs. C. (Polish; Carpati, pseud.) interviewed by M. G. Sayers and P. K. Russo (box 25; 109:19; 13p). Quoted in Frazzetta, "Slovak Community in Bridgeport," 50.

53. Mrs. L. Salanto (Italian; Lucia, pseud.), *loc. cit.*, p. 2. See also Geza Vecsey (Hungarian) interviewed by P. K. Russo (box 21; 109:11; 31p), 27.

54. *Ibid.*, p. 2.

55. *Ibid.*, pp. 2–3.

56. *Ibid.*, p. 3.

Mildred Hecht bitterly complained of her dual exploitation as a working wife, and yet she did not want to stop working . . .[57] She described the independence and power that contributing wages to the family gave women within the home. Work, entered into within the familial values of traditional patriarchal culture, had the potential to subvert that culture: "Still there is advantage to working. It makes me independent. You see, I am a hot communist and my husband isn't and is against communist. . . . He reads the *Forward*, that's the trouble. I read the *Freiheit* . . . I got angry and told him he can't stop me from going where I want to go. I couldn't talk like that if I wasn't working."[58]

Women's power within the family lay in their control over the pay envelope and the disposition of the family resources as well as in their direction of the children's labor and their own wage contributions.[59] Wives had to develop the complex budgetary skills necessary to balance the income of family wage earners against the needs of its members as consumers. One Slovak man explained: "My wife is the boss of the house, running all the details of the home, buying, cleaning, upholding. I just bring home the pay, get a certain weekly allowance while she pays all the domestic bills."[60]

---

57. M. H. (Jewish; Mildred Hecht, pseud.), *loc. cit.*, p. 3.

58. *Ibid.*, p. 6.

59. Tilly and Scott, *Women, Work and Family*, 6, 106, 142–44, 205. Mario Puzo, *Fortunate Pilgrim* (1964; reprinted, New York: Lancer Books, 1973), 15. See also Cohen, "From Workshop to Office," 180–90; Scott and Tilly, "Women's Work and the Family in Nineteenth-Century Europe," 48–49; and Ann Cornelisen, *Women of the Shadows: The Wives and Mothers of Southern Italy* (New York: Vintage Books, 1977), 219–22. Cornelisen concludes: "In the end I cannot. I believe that the social structure of Southern Italian villages, archetypical peasant societies, is matriarchal, and that the social structure of most other poor, relatively isolated Western communities in countries where the Catholic Church either dominates or is an outright state religion, is matriarchal. It is a de facto system, one that is felt by everyone, that functions every day, but is not codified and does not have to be recognized. It is simply there. There are no large decisions to be made by the men and day-by-day existence is left to the women, who unconsciously take over all the practical aspects of life. There are no others. Once a woman has power, however slight, her influence appears to be outside the family, she consolidates it into a hold over her sons stronger than that famous boast of the Jesuits. Only death will loosen it, but already her daughter-in-law has learned the art of day-by-day living and day-by-day power and has tied her sons to her as firmly as though they were still swaddled. She has also slowly replaced her husband's mother, and he, accustomed as he is to the strength of women, does not notice it. He would, in fact, insist with aggressive pride, 'In casa mia, comando io!'" (p. 219). See also "First Generation Interview" (Polish; Andro Vojcak, pseud.) interviewed by Stanley Dabkowski (box 87; 187:7b; 15p), 12.

60. "First Generation Interview" (Polish; Andro Vojcak, pseud.) interviewed by Stanley Dabkowski (box 87; 187:7b; 15p), 12.

Housekeeping in immigrant apartments, where the legendary "American conveniences" had not penetrated, was a continuous battle.[61] But since women's domestic labor was unpaid, it often went unnoted. One mother complained: "The only time a woman is the center of attention is when she gets married and when she has a baby, and then everything goes the same old way."[62] Nevertheless, women expressed pride in their mastery of skills necessary for efficient household management. Another woman explained: "I'm the carpenter, I'm the electrician, I'm the painter, plumber, everything around here. I fix cords, change sockets, fix lamps, put in curtain rods. Sure I'm good. I'm the jack of all trades. . . ."[63]

Women's unpaid labor in the home permitted working class immigrants to withstand low wages, unsatisfactory housing, frequent unemployment and the complex logistics of managing many workers in a single family. But it also provided an indirect support to an oppressive industrial order, enabling families to endure below-subsistence incomes and unemployment by sweating women's labor in the household.[64] Agnes Bonsza, a Hungarian C.I.O. activist, argued against a friend who, in times of distress, increased her own work load and never complained. "I always tell her, 'If all the people was like you, the capitalists give the people hay.' Then they never have to give the people anything."[65]

If men took money from their pay envelopes for entertainment, smoking or alcohol, the family still had to be fed, clothed and lodged. When corners had to be cut, women's own comfort was frequently the only resource they could access or over which they had control. In many families there were, in fact, two levels of subsistence, one for wives and one for husbands and children. An immigrant

61. Mrs. Mary Gadomska (Polish) interviewed by Stanley Dabkowski (box 87; 187:7b), 5. See also M. H. (Jewish; Mildred Hecht, pseud.) interviewed by Rahel Mittelstein (box 61: 157:le). Mrs. Mary Huda (Slovak) interviewed by Vincent Frazzetta (obtained from Frazzetta, 10p), 6. Mrs. Blizman, quoted in Robert C. Goulden, "Growth of Hell's Kitchen" (box 28; folder 109:23e; 12p), 1–2. See also Mrs. B. (French-Canadian; Mrs. Marie Bretagne, pseud.) interviewed by P. K. Russo and M. G. Sayers (box 19; 109:7; 16p), 12. See Andrew Greeley, "Ethnic Miracle," *Public Interest, 45* (Fall, 1976), 20–36, for descriptions of similarly horrendous conditions in Polish neighborhoods in Chicago. See also Mrs. Donato Verrilli (Italian) interviewed by Emil Napolitano (box 23; 109:13b, 11p), 3. Mrs. B. (Hungarian; Agnes Bonsza, pseud.) interviewed by P. K. Russo (box 21; 109:11; 21p); Mrs. C. (Hungarian; Bella Chornoy, pseud.), *loc cit.*

62. "#10" (Jewish) unsigned interview (box 61; 157:le; 20p), 15. See also Mrs. Donato Verrilli (Italian), *loc. cit.*, p. 3.

63. Mrs. C. Hungarian; Bella Chornoy, pseud.), interviewed by P. K. Russo (box 21; 109:11; 41p).

64. Susan Kleinberg, "Technology and Women's Work: The Lives of Working Class Women in Pittsburgh, 1870–1900," *Labor History,* 17 Winter, 1976), 58–72.

65. Mrs. B. (Hungarian; Agnes Bonsza, pseud.), *loc. cit.*, p. 3–4.

mother of seven described the tragic consequences of her desperate self-sacrifice in an attempt to stretch her husband's meager earnings. "[My youngest child] is a year old now, and doesn't make any attempt to get up. I wasn't getting the proper nourishment when I was carrying her. What I had, I gave to the children, and didn't take it for myself. I cheated her to feed the others. Somehow you don't think of the one that isn't there yet. . ."[66]

Mothers attempted to enforce traditional codes of mutual support and responsibility on all family members. Husbands were valued for diligent labor and for the delivery of the pay envelope undepleted by a costly stopover at the neighborhood saloon. Nevertheless, patriarchal prerogatives allowed fathers and sons to retain substantial portions of their pay envelopes for themselves. One son explained: "My parents felt that the family was an economic unit. I felt the family was a group of individuals. . . . I was expected to tum in what money I earned [but] I felt that I should be allowed to keep part of it."[67] Under such circumstances mothers came to depend heavily for family support on their daughters, who could be called upon as dedicated and loyal lieutenants, even when loyalty meant active self-deprivation. One daughter recalled: "Whenever I got some money, I useta' give it to my mother, I useta' make some money helpin' the neighbors. Anything over two penny, I'd always give it to my mother. When I was workin' in Harvey and Hubbell's I useta' give my mother my whole pay. . . . I never kept any of it for myself."[68]

Since most grandparents remained behind in Europe, mothers came to rely upon their daughters for aid in domestic chores and childcare as well as for the wages they earned outside the home. Daughters were socialized early to assume dual family and work responsibilities.

It was not the size of the daughter's contribution so much as its reliability that created her mother's dependence on her earnings. Daughters brought home only half the wages of their fathers and brothers, seldom more than seven dollars a week. But the very insufficiency of women's earnings caused by sexist wage differentials meant that mothers could count on their daughters' commitment to the family economy. Young women, unlike their brothers, could not afford to live separately

---

66. Mrs. B. (French-Canadian; Marie Bretagne, pseud.), *loc. cit.*, p. 2. See also Louise A. Tilly and Joan W. Scott, *Women, Work and Family* (New York: Holt, Rinehart and Winston, 1978), 59, 132.

67. Paul Kubisek (Slovak) autobiography (box 18; 109:4; 8p), 7.

68. Mrs. C. (Hungarian; Bella Chornoy, pseud.) *op. cit.*, 139. See also Cohen, "From Workshop to Office"; "Italian-American Women and Their Daughters in Rhode Island: The Adolescence of Two Generations, 1900–1950," in Betty B. Caroli, Robert F. Harney and Lydia F. Tomasi (eds.), *The Italian Immigrant Women in North America* (Toronto: The Multicultural History Society of Ontario, 1978), 191–205.

from their parents; they simply did not earn enough.[69] Whereas mothers were afraid to enforce familial obligations too stringently on sons who might be pushed into leaving altogether, daughters were as dependent on their families as their mothers were on them.

Work outside the home by immigrant daughters was seldom an expression of independence from family obligation; it was primarily aimed at augmenting inadequate family income. But for unmarried women who entered factories within the ideological framework of the home, the factory itself opened up new possibilities for comradeship and self-sufficiency. "Americanization" and rebellion by these young women was a contradictory consequence of the innovative application of traditional values of mutual obligation. As in migration, mothers sent their daughters out of the family to preserve the family; and, like migration, this process created both new bonds and tensions.

Women frequently suffered under the yoke of the very traditions they upheld. Girls were sent to work to provide money so that their brothers could continue their educations; working daughters were denied the autonomy in spending money and leisure time that was granted to husbands and sons. Whereas men could socialize in saloons and clubs, or on street corners, married women were kept home by chores, childcare, homework, jealousy, and traditional values which barred them from public places without their husbands. Bella Chornoy's husband was frequently away socializing from Friday to Monday night "among his Polacks, Russians, Slavs. Do you wonder why I don't like them?"[70] Yet he resented her going out on her own, even to pray, and certainly not to dance in a tavern. Yet she stayed with him despite frequent beatings. "It's hell to live that way," she explained, "but my husband is a good saver. . . . He's like me that way."[71]

While urban conditions and wage labor frequently exacerbated the contradictions between male dominance and the familial values of reciprocity, they also provided a context within which women resisted the constraints of patriarchal traditions, taking advantage of the new chances for self-sufficiency created by job opportunities and the broadened support provided by extended kinship and neighborhood ties. Annie Borkowski, for example, finally left her morose and stingy husband because she found a job and could leave her young children in a nursery.

---

69. Odencrantz, *op. cit.*, p. 176, 179. See also Hewes, *op. cit.*, p. 65; p. 76; Scott and Tilly, "Women's Work and the Family in Nineteenth-Century Europe," 54, and Cohen, "From Workshop to Office," p. 164.

70. Mrs. C (Hungarian; Bella Chornoy, pseud.) *loc. cit.*, p. 7.

71. *Ibid.*, p. 15. Despite her unhappiness, Mrs. Chornoy remained married to her husband until at least 1971, when their names disappeared from the Bridgeport City Directory. See also Mrs. M. (Polish; Bertha Macej, pseud.), quoted in Frazzetta, "Polish Community in Bridgeport," 74.

Later her married daughter contributed to her support.[72] Mrs. Michalowski endured years of beatings from an alcoholic husband, working throughout her marriage to maintain her family of seven children. But when she finally separated from her husband, she acknowledged the satisfaction she felt in her self-sufficiency: "For me, I be like this all the time. I don't want nobody supportin' me so long that I have health and I could work all myself."[73]

The values of mutual support and communal responsibility that women upheld in their households provided a powerful moral stance from which to challenge the low pay and high prices that undermined the family wage economy. In 1915 women in Hartford mobilized the community for a strike by bakers which linked wage demands to calls for stable or lower prices. Their support led the strikers to hold out until they had not only won their wage demands, but had exacted a promise from employers that bread prices would remain the same.[74]

Immigrant working class organization was embedded in household economies which depended on women's labor at home and in factories. Family solidarity, kinship ties and community cohesion sustained ethnic associations and labor organization creating an intense social and ethical basis for militant resistance rooted in the defense of an entire way of life. Women's perception of the individual worker as part of a greater collectivity was often translated into their fierce and steadfast defense against employer practices which threatened, not just their own livelihood, but also that of their family or community.

Matilda Broca described the militance of Italian immigrant working girls on strike at the Flossie dress shop in Stamford: "We grabbed the foreman. . . . We pulled his pants down and made him stay that way in his undies. We laughed like hell. He got pushed back and forth along the picket line, in his underwear. . . . He begged us to let him go, and said he would join the union the next day. We told him never mind tomorrow, but to come down to the union hall right then and there in his underwear. . . . The next day he came down to the union with the forelady. She was Italian, too. They both joined the union and everything was settled. We were like one big happy family together."[75]

---

72. Mrs. B. (Polish; Annie Burkowski, pseud.), p. 77.

73. Mrs. Michalowski, quoted in Frazzetta, "Polish Community in Bridgeport," 37.

74. *Hartford Daily Courant* (Wed., May 5, 1916), p. 21.

75. Matilda B. (Italian; Broca, pseud.), unsigned interview (box 89; 195; 9p), 1–6. See also Sayers and Russo, "Survey of Remington City: with Interviews" (box 27; folder 109:23b; 8p), interviews with Mr. Andrew Vassie, the head of the company union at GE and Frank Frazekas, head of the competing UERMWA. Two-thirds of the workers were women. A union worker claimed that "it is easier to get the foreign language speaking groups to join the union than the Americans of 'Limies'. . . . The English are too well educated; they got a raw deal. The others come from the old country and know what hard times are" (p. 3). See also, charter of the Ladies Brass Workers of Waterbury, in Brecher, et al., *op. cit.*, p. 77.

As a young tailor in Russia, Mildred Hecht had first been exposed to radical ideas. Her experiences as a factory worker in Connecticut deepened her involvement in Jewish oppositional circles in New Haven and enmeshed her in a growing left political culture. She recalled her anger at the degradation of her tailor's craft by American industrial practices. "I was a tailor in Russia and a good one, too. I liked my work. I liked it like a painter likes his work. When I used to finish making a coat, it was good and I would get much pleasure from it I would look at it and feel good all over like I made a beautiful sculpture. I used to think that in America human beings are like machines, and I wasn't fooled. In America, when I went to work in a factory, I felt like a machine. Here is a bigger speed-up, hurry-up. I wasn't enthusiastic about . . . America."[76]

Mary Rakici Young took a factory job at Casco's to support her children. Once there, she participated in a sit-down strike and subsequently joined the C.I.O. "Since I'm in the C.I.O. I haven't much time for recreation. I give a couple of nights a week for that. I don't like the sound in the West End theatre anyway."[77]

Industrial labor stretched and burst ethnic boundaries. Union activity then propelled many women into a new meta-family. While the intrusion of new patterns of industry and consumption was undermining the structural basis for the ethnic community, industrial unionism was building networks which could supplant ethnic and kin ties and enable women to forge a new consciousness of their worlds and their lives. Mrs. Young explained: "I'm glad I'm in the union, though. Through the union I've met a lot of wonderful people I wouldn't have met otherwise. . . . People that know what they're talking about. As I said, I never belonged to any organizations before. The people I've been meeting have a much wider variety of knowledge than I do."[78]

Immigrant women achieved a means of survival and even betterment under conditions that they did not create and could not entirely control. Their actions were conditioned both by the defense of a familial culture of mutual obligation and the transformation of that culture by the immigration process and their own strategies for adaptation and resistance. The different work patterns of immigrant women from diverse ethnic groups cannot be contained within the simple rubric of cultural preference. They were created by the complex interaction of many factors: household need, European background, particular stage in the life cycle, skills, available employment opportunities and the existence of familial, friendship or ethnic ties to specific jobs. Premigration patterns were not were not rigidly preserved; they persisted and evolved because they were useful in Connecticut cities. New

76. M. H. (Jewish; Mildred Hecht, pseud), *loc. cit.*, p. 3.
77. Mrs. Z. (Hungarian; Mary Rauci Young, pseud.), *loc. cit.*, p. 6.
78. *Ibid.*, p. 6

strategies arose from the interaction of customary practices and new economic realities. Household needs sent women into the paid workforce in immigrant households not yet affected by the possibilities of single-income support or Victorian domesticity. Their jobs, in tum, altered family relationships, introducing new arenas of oppression and new possibilities for liberation.

The strength and resourcefulness of immigrant women who managed their families in difficult situations should not blind us to the constraints under which they labored. Persistent patriarchal values and American industrial practices imposed stultifying limitations on immigrant mothers and their daughters. Pearl Russo, perhaps the most talented WPA interviewer, cautioned against the creation of a new tradition of happy endings for "the world of our mother's." She warned against substituting for the ideology of success a false perception that reifies preindustrial values. In contrast, she recalled her own perspectives in recording the life histories of her immigrant neighbors and friends: "We could not be nostalgic about the lives of our neighbors. Why would we, when we lived them. In your generation you see this sort of roseate picture. . . . It's not true at all. These (actions) were the exigencies that the situation demanded and they came naturally to you because you came from poor people."[79]

79. Interview with Pearl K. Russo, Feb. 16, 1983.

Purity and Power
Chicago Polonian Feminists, 1880–1914

William J. Galush

At the turn of the century a Polonian feminist lamented that many women were still bound by the old saying: "She lived purely, spun wool and stayed at home."[1] Yet in the face of traditional passivity, a dynamic minority among Polish American women sought entrance to the corridors of power and status in the new land. The particular nature of their background conditioned the thrust of their effort. Uncomfortable with the American language and culture, and ignored by most native-born female activists with their middle-class orientation, the newcomers expressed their concerns in an ethnic context. Though conservative, they were definitely feminists. These women sought not merely marginal participation in the organized life of Polonia but recognition as equals. When denied this, they showed no hesitation in forming appropriate structures under their control, grounded in an ideology of equality and voiced in an ethnic rhetoric. Functionally, this was the equivalent of the suffrage movement.[2] Since Chicago had the greatest immigrant concentration and the most extensive development of feminist activity, it will form the focus of the essay, but as the references indicate, such concerns were echoed in other settlements in American Polonia.

The environment for the emergence of feminist consciousness among Polonian women was not promising in the late nineteenth century. They were typically

---

1. *Głos Polek* [Voice of the Polish Woman], I (July 1902) p. 7. "Polonia" in this essay refers to a concentration of Poles outside the homeland, with further definition provided by context,

2. In the categories defined by N. Cott, Polonian women partook of the first (social concern, drawing from the allegedly special caring talents of women) and the second (equal rights), but did not press for the radical third ("emancipation" from conventions enforced by law and custom). Their ethnic status largely confirmed their demands to the Polish immigrant group; thus "civic" rights were essentially those permitting equal participation in the organized life of Polonia. Nancy Cott, *The Grounding of American Feminism* (New Haven, 1987), p. 16.

From *Polish American Studies,* vol. 47, no. 1 (Spring 1990), pp. 5–24.

ill-educated and usually married by age twenty to men whose lack of marketable skills placed them at the lowest rungs of the occupational and income ladder.[3] With their homes filled with children and often boarders, such women had little time or energy for concerns which were not practical or immediate. If single, they usually had to support themselves with physically demanding labor over long hours, with similar effects on outside interest.[4] Yet within Polish settlements, most notably Chicago, an ethnic middle class emerged which offered its female members some possibilities for leisure—or leadership. Likewise, a few educated women, sometimes durably single, came to America and supported themselves by a combination of special skills and impressive determination. It was disproportionately the wealthier women of Polonia who fostered the feminist impulse.[5]

---

3. Information from prewar marriage records from the large Cleveland parish of St. John Cantius showed that almost two-thirds of women married at 20 or less, with four-fifths of the brides 22 or younger. There is no reason to see this as atypical. William J. Galush, "Forming Polonia: A Study of Four Polish-American Communities, 1890–1940" (University of Minnesota: Unpublished Ph.D. Dissertation, 1975), p. 109. Fertility was high, with an average of over 5 children per family, compared to a U.S. average of 3.4 in 1910. *Ibid.*, pp. 110–111.

A broad survey of male Polonian occupational structure c. 1900 is by Krzysztof Groniowski, "Struktura społeczna-zawodowa Polonii amerykanskiej" ["The Social and Occupational Structure of American Polonia"] in Hieronim Kubiak (ed.), *Polonia amerykańska: przeszłość i współczesność* [American Polonia: Past and Present] (Warsaw, 1988), esp. pp. 100–107. For more extensive studies of major localities, see John Bodnar, *Lives of Their Own: Blacks, Italians and Poles in Pittsburgh, 1900–1960* (Urbana, IL, 1982), p. 64; Caroline Golab, *Immigrant Destinations*, (Philadelphia, 1977), p. 103 for Philadelphia; Galosh, "Forming Polonia," p. 115 for Cleveland, Minneapolis and Utica, N.Y.

4. Doris Weatherford, *Foreign and Female: Immigrant Women in America, 1840–1930* (New York, 1986), pp. 106–107, 120–123.

5. Information on Polish economic activity is scanty. Individuals such as John Smulski (banker) and Peter Kiolbasa (notary) were major community figures in early Chicago Polonia, as were the saloonkeepers, grocers and other petty entrepreneurs out of scale to their numbers. Polonian communities evolved a middle and upper ethclass which had a role and status disproportionate to its economic scale as measured by the general society. Yet businesses such as saloons and other petty entrepreneurial activities were often short-lived. Their significance is as much evidence of dynamism and assertiveness as it is actual higher income. Edward Kantowicz, *Polish American Politics in Chicago, 1880–1940* (Chicago, 1975) pp. 45–46, 60–64; Groniowski, "Struktura," p. 101.

For a discussion of the relationship of ethnicity and class (ethclass), see Milton Gordon, *Assimilation in American Life: The Role of Race, Religion and National Origins* (New York, 1964), pp. 51–54.

In terms of marriage patterns, the female physicians in Chicago seem to be an example of those who married late or not at all. In his stimulating study of American feminism, William O'Neill notes that many leaders were dilatory in marrying, more prone to divorce and had fewer children. See William O'Neill, *Everyone Was Brave* (New York, 1969, 1976) p. 22.

Despite the above, the first exclusively female organizations had traditional roots and appeared among the immigrant masses. These were pious societies of women attached to parishes, whose ancestry was long a part of homeland rural life.[6] In Chicago the first arose in 1874 at St. Stanislaus Kostka Church, the original Polish congregation. In addition to prayer and work for the church, the group provided rudimentary mutual aid through sick support and bore funeral costs of dues-paying members.[7] The latter function was more characteristic of urban homeland parishes and suggests a parallel development. More important for our concerns, members were no longer "silent as fish," to use the evocative phrase of an historian of Polonia.[8] Such societies allowed women to debate issues, elect their own leaders and generally control an organization. Yet these religious associations were more an example of "cultural baggage" than innovation; they did not address the evolving concerns of Polonia life so much as provide a comforting reminder of the homeland village.

One of the first groups to break with the pious society model was the short-lived "Pennies for Poland" (PFP; Grosz Polski), founded in mid-1886 in Chicago. It emerged on the twin bases of patriotic and social concern. The PFP sought to collect money for the purchase of land in Prussian Poland to counter the German Colonization Commission's efforts to dispossess Polish farmers, and also to build a home for poor Polish working girls in the city. Very unusual for the time, the society included both men and women. Its female shelter project likely derived from the women's perceptions of a need for protection of single girls, an enduring concern of female societies. But men held the top posts and women saw them as domineering, and after a few months Pennies for Poland split along gender lines.[9] The movement towards independent existence was led by Theophila Samolińska, a Polish-born poet and ardent patriot. She had come to Chicago in the seventies and had worked diligently with—but was never allowed membership in—the Polish Commune (Gmina Polska, f. 1866) Society, one of the first two ethnic organizations in the city. Never a shrinking violet, she carried on a public dispute with an Anastasius Skowronski in the columns of *Wiarus* [Veteran] prior to the Pennies

6. William I. Thomas and Florian Znaniecki, *The Polish Peasant in Europe and America*, I (New York, 1958 reprint), pp. 279–280.

7. "Album Pamiątkowe z Okazji Złotego Jubileuszu Parafii Św. Stanisława Kostki, 1867–1917" [Jubilee Book on the Occasion of the Fiftieth Anniversary of St. Stanislaus Kostka Church] (Chicago, 1917); *Głos Polek*, I (June, 1903), p. 3.

8. Arthur L. Waldo, *Sokolstwo przednia straż narodu: dzieje idei i organizacji w Ameryce* [The Falcons, Advance Guard of the Nation: A History of their Conception and Organization in America] (Pittsburgh, 1953), I, p. 309.

9. *Głos Polek*, I (June, 1903), p. 3; *Wiarus* [Veteran], November 4, 1886, p. 5.

for Poland's formation. Now she appeared as secretary of a committee to set up a women's society, which in March of 1887 became the Central Association of Polish Women (CAPW; Centralne Towarzystwo Polek).[10] At the organizational meeting at her southside home, Samolińska was elected president of a body essentially duplicating the structure and purposes of an ethnic fraternal. The proposed society advocated mutual aid, work for patriotic goals, help for Polish orphans, widows, cripples and elderly and the diffusion of ethnic culture. These ambitious goals, combining nationalism with social concern and using the proven framework of fraternalism, indicated the future orientation of Polonian women activists. I shall term this "patriotic feminism."[11] With the occasional addition of a stated Catholic connection, a broadly defined nationalism provided the ideological lever to open the door to more extensive female participation in the life of American Polonia.

The development of the Central Association was less extensive than Samolińska and other initiators wished. It never became the basis for a federation of women's organizations on the model of the Polish National Alliance, but instead remained a single local group with a smattering of unaffiliated imitators and sometimes rivals. For despite their essential moderation and generally Catholic membership, in entering the field of fraternalism the Association also entered Polonian politics. Polish Americans, meaning males, had split into two "camps" (obóże) by 1880,

10. For the controversy, see *Wiarus*, May 27, 1886, p. 2; June 17, 1886, p. 2. The announcement of the proposed organization came in *ibid.*, December 30, 1886, p. 1. Hieronim Derdowski, editor of *Wiarus*, was a typically strong-willed ethnic editor with no hesitation about engaging in public controversy and supporting a novel movement which struck his fancy. His openness at this period to women's participation in public life was attested to in his joining the first U.S. Falcon organization, a society open to women as well (see p. 6). At this time his weekly, published in the small town of Winona, Minnesota, enjoyed a national readership due in part to the paucity of Polish journals in the 1880s.

11. Steven Buechler identifies several varieties of American feminism: "domestic"—seeking to extend women's traditional responsibilities, rights and obligations to society at large; "moral"—solving social problems by applying absolute moral principles; and "professional"—oriented to upward mobility, individual opportunity, and career advancement Steven Buechler, *The Transformation of the Woman Suffrage Movement: The Case of Illinois, 1850–1920* (New Brunswick, N.Y., 1986), pp. 121–122. Broadly speaking, these may be considered forms of "social feminism" in O'Neill's sense, since they sought to advance broad social reforms instead of a narrow focus on women's rights, his "extreme" feminists. See William O'Neill, *Everyone was Brave* (New York, 1969, 1976) pp. ix–x, 50–53. Polish American women did not overtly challenge existing familial relationships; they did seek an enlarged role for themselves outside the home in the pattern of social feminists.

embodied in the leading mutual aid federations.[12] Samolińska's long association with the secularist Polish National Alliance (f. 1880) and similar unwillingness to bar non-Catholics stigmatized her movement in the eyes of those who conceived of Polishness as inseparable from Catholicism—the religionists. Soon letters to *Wiarus* complained of opposition from the leading local cleric, Father Vincent Barzyński, a Resurrectionist and pastor of the gigantic parish of St. Stanislaus. Outspoken and authoritarian even by the standards of his peers, Barzyński had been a founder of the leading religionist federation, the Polish Roman Catholic Union (f. 1873).[13] He denounced the new society as "pagan" from his pulpit.[14] Yet the pastor was shrewd enough not to attack the idea, and soon his parish had a competing "Polish Women's Association" (Stowarzyszenie Polek) dedicated to patriotic activity and led by Leocadia Kadow, a stalwart of women's organizations for decades to come.[15] Though the St. Stanislaus-based society was not durable, in Chicago and elsewhere there was a flowering of women's organizations in the late 1880s. Formation of female associations was local and uncoordinated, with little impact in that decade on the larger

12. A useful and compact history of fraternalism is Frank Renkiewicz, "The Profits of Non-Profit Capitalism: Polish Fraternalism and Beneficial Insurance in America" in Scott Cummings (ed.), *Self-Help in Urban America: Patterns of Minority Business Enterprise* (Port Washington, NY, 1980), pp. 113–129. For a more recent and extended history of the Polish National Alliance, see Donald E. Pienkos, *PNA: A Centennial History of the Polish National Alliance of the United States of North America* (Boulder, CO, 1984). The Polish Roman Catholic Union awaits its history in English, but useful to Polish readers is Mieczysław Haiman, *Zjednoczenie Polskie Rzymsko-katolickie w Ameryce, 1873–1948* [The Polish Roman Catholic Union in America, 1873–1948] (Chicago, 1948).

The nature of nationalism in the fraternal movement has been the subject of considerable discussion. Victor Greene developed the word "religionist" to characterize the identification of Catholicism with Polish identity (the PRCU) and applied the term "nationalist" to those who more strongly advocated patriotism and did not give it a specific religious content (the PNA). This derives from readings of the national press and ignores local variations in which religionist societies could affirm a (religiously-enclosed) patriotism as fully as the others. For this reason I prefer the more neutral "secularist" as the alternative to religionist. Victor Greene, *For God and Country: The Rise of Polish and Lithuanian Ethnic Consciousness in America, 1860–1910* (Madison, 1975), pp. 66–90. An evaluation similar to Greene for 19th century Polonia may be found in Andrzej Brożek, *Polish Americans, 1854–1939* (Warsaw, 1985), pp. 60–64.

13. A good summary of his career in Chicago is in Joseph J. Parot, *Polish Catholics in Chicago, 1850–1920* (DeKalb, IL, 1981), esp. pp. 59–132. St. Stanislaus had a membership of about 50,000 by 1890, which probably made it the largest Roman Catholic congregation in America. *Ibid.*, p. 91.

14. *Wiarus*, March 17, 1887, p. 1.

15. *Ibid.*, March 3, 1887, p. 1.

ethnic society.[16] Groups such as the CAPW were too small to compel the attention of the much larger male organizations in the eighties, but their very existence and articulation of aspirations of the "silent" half of Polonia was to bear more impressive fruit in the next decade.

The choice of a fraternal format by innovating women was hardly accidental. They had the mutual aid example exhibited before them in all communities, since typically a fraternal society was the first organized expression of a Polish presence. Adoption was not merely imitative, however. Unlike middle-class American women who could afford to join a club and support it for its own sake or for charitable or reform purposes, these predominantly lower-class newcomers needed the concrete protection offered by mutual insurance. Moreover, the nationalism characteristic of Poles in America was their single universal point of agreement; its advocacy by women could only evoke praise. Other activities such as social concern or cultural improvement were all traditional female functions and now could be defined as elements of patriotism. The leaders of the societies were disproportionately middle ethclass, usually married to men with small businesses or skilled blue collar jobs.[17] At least somewhat removed from the pressures of economic scarcity, such women sometimes had more extensive education and certainly an unusual determination which fostered their pioneering activities. While the immense Polish influx of the nineties brought thousands of newcomers, these women were more settled and affluent a decade later, and in the last years of the century more overt challenges to masculine dominance, buttressed by superior organization, and arose to enrich the field of Polonian feminism.

---

16. In New York City a "Women's Society" (Towarzystwo Polek) without specified aims existed in 1886, but the name was not characteristic of a pious society. Late that year a Mrs. T. Kraemer founded the National Treasury Society (Skarb Narodowy), a religionist body promoting nationalism and aid to the unfortunate. *Wiarus,* Oct. 21, 1886, p. 7; Oct. 28, 1886, p. 7. Women were also at least considering action in Milwaukee, and even in a small Polonia like Grand Rapids, Michigan a Pennies for Poland Society was founded soon after its Chicago namesake fragmented. *Ibid.,* Feb. 3, 1887, p. 5. Doubtless there were others, but lack of newspapers, let alone a specifically feminist press, made publicity hard to obtain and formation of a federation very difficult.

17. Information on women's occupations is virtually absent unless they were single or happened to be unusually literary, so the material below is typically for their husbands and derived from city directories. For the first officers of the Central Association of Polish Women, President Theophila Samolińska was married to a machinist, Vice-president Julianna Pokrzywińska to a small businessman, Recording Secretary Prakseda Kosmowska to a laborer, Financial Secretary Anna Morzyńska to a driver and Treasurer Michilina Ciesielska to either a grocer or skilled worker. With the exception of the laborer, such jobs were much above the average for the Polish community in Chicago. *Chicago City Directory,* 1887 and 1888; cf. with Parot, *Polish Catholics,* pp. 219–220.

The drive for recognition through competing organizations may also have been undercut by the simultaneous appearance in Chicago of a novel form of society, one which was unprecedentedly open to women. This was the Falcons (Sokol). Begun in Austrian Poland in 1881 and drawing from German and Czech models, it was a gymnastic society with patriotic and military overtones. In Galicia the urban middle-class dominated the Falcon movement.[18] The same class bias obtained among the early Falcons of Chicago. Of the male members in the founding year of 1887, three-fifths were in white collar occupations, and only one was a common laborer.[19] This was a remarkable contrast to the overwhelmingly lower blue collar profile of local Poles. This youthful, confident and successful group had the example of female participation before them from Galicia and promptly opened their ranks here. Theophila Samolińska was among the first to join, along with twenty-eight other women, making the society about a third female at its inception. But the Falcons remained under male control and the proportion of men grew over the years. By 1897 a committee composed of Samolińska, Stefania Chmielewska, Gabriela Laudon and Maria Rokosz protested to the governing board about the limits on their status. They alleged restrictions on voting, subordinate status within nests and other complaints. The officers listened politely and countered with the presumably crushing argument that since women could not be soldiers, they were not entitled to equality in a semi-military organization. Amidst the common feminine disappointment, Samolińska urged expansion of the Central Association of Polish Women.

18. The first "nest" (lodge) was in 1881 in the Galician capital of Lwów (Lemberg), and at least to 1892 all nests were in larger towns or cities. The elevated social status of the membership is suggested by the example of the Tarnow branch, which in 1886 was composed of 7 physicians, 3 physical education teachers, 3 elementary teachers, 5 property owners, 14 lawyers, 16 engineers, 5 merchants, 28 artisans and a priest. All officers listed for the Nowy Sącz and Wadowice nests were titled "doctor" or "professor" in the pre-1900 period. Waldo, *Sokolstwo,* I, pp. 86, 172–73.

19. The information comes from a membership list in Waldo and city directory information found for 28 of 55 male members. In comparison with the Tarnow nest, however, the Chicago Falcons were more marginally white collar. The Chicago group had only 2 professionals (physicians) in this category, with the remaining number owners of small stores, disproportionately saloons. As noted previously, the durability of such enterprises was questionable, but in comparison with other local Poles the Falcons still were at the upper levels of the Polonian ethclass structure. Waldo, *Sokolstwo,* II, p. 519; *Chicago City Directory,* 1888.

% UWC	#	% LWC	#	% SKL	#	% SER	#	% LAB	#	TOTALS	
7	(2)	54	(15)	29	(8)	7	(2)	4	(1)	101%	(28)

UWC—upper white collar; LWC—lower white collar; SKL—skilled workers; SER—service/semi-skilled; LAB—unskilled workers

The occupational categories are from Stephan Thernstrom, *The Other Bostonians: Poverty and Progress in the American Metropolis, 1880–1970* (Cambridge, 1973), pp. 290–292.

The others rejected the specific suggestion, but soon (without Samolińska) formed the first Polish fraternal federation for women.[20]

Women in the homeland were also developing ideas and organizations, in fact more elaborately and diversely than in America. Even in the early nineteenth century women in societies such as "Piątek" [Friday] promoted patriotism. The leaders were almost all of noble or intelligentsia background, highly educated and patriotic, but with few ties to the masses of peasant women. In the seventies middle-class women began to press, with increasing success, for admission to higher education and even manual training, since changes in the economy forced some to seek work and others simply wanted to enter professions.[21] By this time three orientations emerged: radicals, wanting full equality in education and jobs, often associated with the socialist movement; moderates, sympathetic to some changes but disinclined to alter familial relationships and likely to enter traditional female occupations; and finally conservatives, asserting that women should remain at home. Liberation of women became linked with liberation of the nation, not dissimilar to Polonian women's conceptions. The increasingly extensive women's press served a largely middle and upper-class audience, with some more radical publications further enlarging the range of periodicals, offering information and stimulation unavailable in America before 1900.[22] In the eighties and nineties societies for cultural improvement, both mixed and female, became popular outlets for women of means to reach both peasant women and the slowly growing urban lower classes. Groups like the Popular School Society's (Towarzystwo Szkoły Ludowej, f. 1891) Ladies Circle (Koło Pań, f. 1892) had funding from donations and consciously sought to help their "sisters under the thatch," a viewpoint characteristic of a much more stratified society.[23] During the nineties a series of women's congresses met to discuss programs and actions, bringing together leaders of education and often sophisticated ideological

20. Waldo, *Sokolstwo*, I, pp. 119–120. Given the subsequent support for the Polish Women's Alliance from Samolińska, there was an apparent lack of enmity. Her absence among the PWA founders may be attributed to their desire for a new and independent organization (implying some effort to exclude her), but more likely she simply would not join a movement which was unwilling to subordinate itself to her.

21. Dionizja Wawrzykowska-Wierciochowa, *Od prządki do astronautki: z dziejow kobiety polskiej jej pracy i osiagniec* [From Spinners to Astronauts: A History of Polish Women in their Work and Aspirations] (Warsaw, 1963), pp. 196–197; 234–235.

22. *Ibid.*, pp. 238–240.

23. Dionizja Wawrzykowska-Wierciochowa, *Wysłouchowa: opowieść biograficzna [Mrs. Wyslouch: A Biography]* (Warsaw, 1974), pp. 313–317; 321–324. For additional discussion of feminism and village "enlightenment," see Eugenia Podgorska, "Szkolnictwo elementarne" ["Elementary Education"], in Stanisław Michalski, *Dzieje Szkolnictwa i Oświaty na Wsi Polskiej do 1918* [A History of Education and Enlightenment in the Polish Villages to 1918] (Warsaw, 1982), I, esp. pp. 290–291.

orientation. This occurred in conditions of conspiracy and threat of arrests in the Russian and German partitions, since the authorities feared—with reason—that even educational gatherings were covers for nationalism.[24] Around 1900 Polish feminists had a varied and vigorous movement, but rent by ideological and attitudinal conflicts. In the years before World War I, the development of Polish socialism gave greater coherence to the radicals and their contacts with non-Poles increased significantly. They advocated not merely legal and political equality but also a different structure of family relationships. Struggling for political equality under often oppressive governments, leftists sometimes allied with liberal middle-class women. But the homeland movement remained more divided and competitive than that in emigration, and no orientation at home forged formal ties with Polish women in America.[25]

• • •

The advent of the Polish Women's Alliance [Związek Polek] in 1898 was crucial to the elaboration not only of organizational form but to the stimulation of consciousness as well. In developing a more sophisticated structure, Polonian women also thought more deeply about their role in ethnic and American society.

The overt reason for the PWA's formation was insurance. Women could only be insured in existing fraternal federations through their husbands, ignoring single women and barring married ones from full participation in the most important ethnically-controlled organizations. Solitary mutual aid societies were financially much less secure and offered no sense of belonging to a larger association, nor could they support a publication. But more compelling was desire for dignity and recognition. Reflecting on PWA formation in 1910, the Alliance organ *Glos Polek* [Voice of Polish Women] asserted: "Mixed organizations . . . today do not provide an independent, self-reliant field for female thought and work-men always dominate. This occurs, even from the men's side, with the best of good will." Thus, "only in their own organizations, only in organizations controlled by women, will their own ideas, feelings and wishes reign."[26] The initial announcement of the new body was more restricted in rhetoric, perhaps to avoid criticism. The first appeal came not in a Chicago paper, despite the impetus deriving from that city, but from *Kuryer Polski*

---

24. Wawrzykowska-Wierciochowa, *Od Przadki*, pp. 240–241, 302.

25. *Ibid.*, 270–275. This situation existed from the other side as well. *Głos Polek* reprinted with vigorous approval the "10 National Commandments" by P. Kozak of Detroit's *Dziennik Polski* [Polish Daily News], the first of which was to maintain continuous contact with the homeland, but there was no effort to establish organizational links to supplement occasional communications. See *Głos Polek*, September 21, 1911, pp. 8–9.

26. *Głos Polek*, Oct. 24, 1910, pp. 1–2.

[Polish Courier], a Milwaukee daily with a liberal and anti-clerical reputation.[27] The declaration stressed insurance benefits, "maintenance of the Polish spirit" and nationalist work, especially among the young (American-born). Such useful generalities were acceptable to most immigrant women—and to men also. But the desire for independence was there, and its expression became more public and defined over time. It is clear that federation was more than a device to get insurance; it was a way to sustain and enlarge a distinctive role in the ethnic society in which they wished to participate.[28]

The founders were not typical immigrant women. They all had experience in the Falcon movement and perhaps other societies as well. Their socio-economic status was unusually high. The husband of the committee president, Mary Rokosz, was a saloonkeeper and vice-president of the Polish National Alliance. Stephania Chmielińska, the secretary and subsequently PWA president, was independently employed as a florist. The other three were married to service or skilled workers.[29] The PNA connection was not only by way of Rokosz's spouse, but also through T.M. Helinski, PNA national secretary, who gave advice at the first meeting of the three constituent groups. The new women's federation arose from three Chicago female fraternals, but by 1900 had attracted several other societies outside the city. Though the Central Association of Polish Women (CAPW), still led by Samolińska, did not join, its leaders supported the effort.[30] Due to the support from CAPW and PNA leaders, the new federation unwillingly acquired an association with the secularist camp, upon which it expended much effort to shed in the coming years. Like all fraternals it wanted an organ. First it used the columns of the local *Dziennik*

---

27. The publisher of the *Kuryer* was Michael Kruszka, a fascinating figure of considerable complexity, interested in what he saw as progressive causes. Anthony Kuzniewski carefully discusses his critical stance towards Catholicism and argues persuasively that he had a "utilitarian view of the Church as a sort of national resource which would keep Poles together while they waited for an opportunity to unify around a restored Polish state." At the time, religionists viewed him simply as anti-clerical. Anthony Kuzniewski, S.J., *Faith and Fatherland: The Polish Church War in Wisconsin, 1896–1918* (Notre Dame, 1980), p. 41; also pp. 126–128.

28. The Polish Women's Alliance may be seen a part, though a highly distinct and unusual one, of a broader movement to create separate women's institutions in the United States. In turn this helped foster a unique female identity. See Estelle Freedman, "Separatism as Strategy: Female Institution Building and American Feminism, 1870–1930," *Feminist Studies*, V (Fall, 1979), pp. 512–529.

29. Information on persons comes from the *Chicago City Directory* for 1900; Rev. Francis Bolek (ed.), *Who's Who in Polish America* (New York, 1970, reprint of 1943); Pienkos, *PNA*, Appendix C.

30. *Telegraf* [Telegraph], November 8, 1899, p. 2.

Narodowy [National Daily News], followed in mid-1902 by its own *Głos Polek.*[31] Once established, the young association grew steadily, answering needs felt by a significant minority of Polonian women.

Scarcely a year later, the overt *raison d'etre* of the PWA was challenged by the established federations. In 1899 *Naród Polski,* organ of the Polish Roman Catholic Union, welcomed "with open arms" the founding of the exclusively female St. Joseph's Lodge in Schenectady, N.Y. and stressed that women could now get insurance on equal terms with men. The Polish National Alliance followed in 1900, and both set up a "Women's Department" [Wydział Kobiet], and elected women to national posts by 1915.[32] But the intensified competition did not destroy the fledgling federation, which resisted calls to join the PNA *en masse,* though it may have slowed its growth. The Polish Women's Alliance increased from 264 members in eight lodges in 1900 to 5,812 in 78 lodges in 1910, and almost tripled by World War I.[33]

The successful establishment of an ethnic women's fraternal federation was part of the larger process of development of a range of legitimate activities outside the "domestic sphere." By asserting the primacy of women not only in childrearing and moral concern, but also as instillers of Polishness [Polskość] in the formative years, ethnic feminists could logically justify enlarged involvement in the affairs of Polish America.[34] Under their direction patriotic feminism assumed a wide variety of forms.

31. *Głos Polek,* I (June, 1903) pp. 4–5; Jadwiga Karlowiczowa, *Historia Związku Polek w Ameryce* [History of the Polish Women's Alliance of America] (Chicago, 1938), I, p. 30. For regretful comments on the continuing reluctance of pious women to join the PWA as late as 1903, see the federation history in *Głos Polek,* I (June, 1903), p. 3.

32. *Naród Polski* [Polish Nation], January 11, 1899, p. 2. Pienkos, *PNA,* 393; Stanisław Osada, *Historya związku narodowego polskiego, 1880–1905,* [A History of the Polish National Alliance] (Chicago, 1957, I, p. 531; Haiman, *Historya,* pp. 183, 217.

33. *Głos Polek,* I (June, 1903), p. 5; Karlowiczowa, *Historia,* pp. 62, 85; Haiman, *Zjednoczenie,* pp. 183, 187–88; Stanisław Osada, *Historia Związku Narodowego Polskiego, 1880–1905* [A History of the Polish National Alliance] (Chicago, 1957 reprint of 1905), I, pp. 497–499; Pienkos, PNA, pp. 93–94.

34. This had the advantage of congruence to clerical views, which themselves underwent an evolution. Thus in 1886 a priest typically urged mothers to raise their children carefully in a moral, religious and Polish-speaking household, while by 1902 another cleric defined their role as that plus improving society and participating in nationalistic work. See *Wiarus,* May 6, 1886, p. 1; *Głos Polek,* I (July 1902), p. 2.

It also drew on homeland sources. The woman most prominently featured in the journal from the fatherland was Maria Konopniczka, a poet and writer, who in 1902 stressed that Polonian women must not only cultivate patriotism in themselves but had a duty as mothers to pass it on to their children. Thus the favored Polish figure advocated a rather conservative feminism. Konopniczka was in fact in the "bourgeois" camp. *Głos Polek,* I (November 1902), p. 3.

One drew on the possibilities of the new federation. The Polish Women's Alliance founded an "Education Department" [Wydział Oświaty] by 1902, which soon organized lectures and essay competitions, promoted plays and reading while requesting lodges to form their own committees for the same purposes. The PWA also founded a library, and only after much agonizing about financial constraints did the young federation regretfully not establish a stipend for higher education in 1903. *Głos Polek* also gave much publicity to educational achievements of both ethnic and American women, doubtless prodded by intellectuals such as Samolińska and the several female physicians who were active members of the PWA.[35] By 1910 Drs. Anna Krygier and Anna Wyczolkowska led discussion evenings, such as "the very important and interesting" topic of "Women and Work," concerning women in factories, participation in strikes and equal rights.[36] Increasingly mindful of the growing number of female members, the PRCU and PNA began special sections for women in their official organs. But the content of *Naród Polski*'s and *Zgoda's* material for women was more domestically oriented, with much less information on women in professions or politics.[37]

Another broad field, not confined to fraternals, was social concern. One important aspect of this was charity. While mutual aid was the preferred means of dealing with misfortune among Poles, there was some recognition of the need for benevolence also.[38] Into the 1890s, ethnic charity was the preserve of males, but during that decade women began to enter such work. The short-lived Organization of Patriotic Polish Women promoted by Father Barzyński at St. Stanislaus, gave as one of its

---

35. *Głos Polek,* I (August 1902), p. 1 on Education Department formation. For references to culture, higher education and local activity, examples are found in *ibid.,* I (July 1902), p. 5; I (September, 1902), pp. 7, 9; I (October 1902), p. 9. By 1910 the PWA's reputation for concern with enlightenment was such that it occasionally received requests for assistance from foundering male-run cultural bodies. E.g., *ibid.,* December 15, 1910, pp. 6–7.

36. *Głos Polek,* Jan. 19, 1911, p. 6. The topic was particularly timely since 1911 was the year of a major textile strike in Chicago, an industry with a considerable Polish female contingent However, while some coverage was given to the strike, in a broadly sympathetic vein, it was not a major concern. There was no evidence of any organized relationship with the union.

37. E.g. "Dzial dla Kobiet" in *Naród Polski.* This section appeared by 1904. *Zgoda's* "Wydanie dla Kobiet" (Women's Edition) appeared c. 1902 for a few years. In 1909 the PNA elected its first female national officer. Pienkos, *PNA,* pp. 91–92, 393, also Appendix C. The PRCU did not have a woman in national office until 1915. Haiman, *Zjednoczenie,* p. 288.

38. For a more extended treatment of charity among Poles in Chicago, see William Galosh, "God Will Repay: Polish Charity in Chicago, 1870–1940" (unpublished paper delivered at the Polish Institute of Arts and Sciences Conference; June, 1988 in Washington, D.C.). This essay breaks with the traditional emphasis on the work of religious communities in Polonian charity with lay persons in the passive role as donors to examine the development of active lay participation.

goals "charitable activity in the broadest range," with particular attention to women.[39] More durable was the project for a Polish hospital. As early as 1891 several immigrant physicians led by Dr. Boleslaus Klarkowski began campaigning for an ethnic hospital, and his wife Anna had a prominent role in the successful effort Along with several other female activists, she was also important in the PWA founded some years later.[40] After the turn of the century another Chicago meliorative body, the St. Elizabeth Charity Society (Towarzystwo Dobroczynności pod Opieką Św. Elzbiety), instituted a free clinic in 1905 with the aid of Franciscan nuns and distributed goods and funds to the Polish poor. By 1912 it had day care centers in several parts of the city, frankly recognizing the need of many Polonian women to work.[41] By the early 1900s the clergy had come to accept and even desire the presence of laywomen on charitable bodies. Hence when the first Polonian bishop, Paul Rhode, formed the Polish Charities Organization of Chicago (Polskie Stowarzyszenie Dobroczynności w Chicago), at the parish level a woman as well as the pastor and a laymen were to be officers. Even the nine-person governing board had the same tri-partite division.[42]

---

39. *Dziennik Chicagoski* [Chicago Daily], Jul. 7, 1893, p. 1. In 1897 a similar society formed "at the initiative of the pastor" at Holy Trinity Church in Chicago, but disappeared after a short time. "Pamiątnik Parafii Sw. Trojcy w Chicago, Ill., 1893–1918" [Jubilee Book of Holy Trinity in Chicago, Ill.] (n.p., 1918). Even in a small community like Bay City, Michigan, Polish women formed a benevolent organization at this time. *Dziennik Chicagoski,* December 12, 1893, p. 4. Doubtless the depression of the early 1890's was a stimulus to such efforts.

In this connection, it is worth noting that Catholicism played a role similar to that of Protestantism in legitimating women's "social assertions," a point ignored by N. Cott in her important overview of feminism. Cott, *Grounding of American Feminism,* p. 17. It was important to these typically pious immigrant laywomen that their Church bless and encourage efforts in benevolence, which enlarged their social role and stressed their allegedly superior moral character.

40. Karlowiczowa, *Historia,* I, p. 21. Klarkowska subsequently headed the Ladies Society (Towarzystwo Pań), a fund-gathering organization to support the hospital. See *Dziennik Chicagoski,* Jan. 3, 1905, p. 8.

41. *Ibid.,* Jan. 19, 1905, p. 8; Oct. 10, 1914, p. 3; Oct. 22, 1914, p. 8. The president for many years was the indefatigable Leocadia Kadow, an officer of the Central Association of Polish Women in the 1880s and likewise prominent in the PWA.

Women's organizations, mainly pious but sometimes mutual benefit, were the most consistent donors to the Polish orphanage, which existed under several names. *Sierota* [Orphan], December 15, 1900, p. 16; *Dziennik Chicagoski,* September 2, 1905, p. 5. *Głos Polek* maintained that the PWA always supported the St. Elizabeth Society, at least indicating the federation's perception and preferred self-image. *Głos Polek,* December 15, 1910, p. 8.

42. Rev. Thomas Bona, "Polskie Stowarzszenia Dobroczynności w Chicago" [Polish Charity Society of Chicago], *Przegląd Kościelny* [Church Review], IV (April 1916) pp. 254–257.

On the eve of the war, Polonian women had an acknowledged and growing role in ethnic benevolence.[43]

Another dimension of social concern was improvement of society. The temperance movement, so important among mainstream Protestants of the day, had a weak echo among Poles.[44] From its early years, the PWA denounced liquor as a "poison" and praised women for their lower level of consumption, evidence of a "higher morality." Later it also urged support for the small abstinence movement led by the Chicago Resurrectionist, Father Ladislaus Kwiątkowski, himself a strong supporter of equality for women.[45] Yet the modest and rather unimpassioned advocacy of a movement so powerful among American women prevented these immigrants from using it to forge links with social feminism in the general society.

If temperance failed to arouse strong feelings, competition by non-Polish fraternals for potential members did. Beginning in the eighties, the Catholic Order of Foresters enrolled many Poles in its "courts" (lodges), based on ethnic parishes.[46] Since the Foresters ("Foresterzy" in Polish American) enrolled Polish women beginning in 1894, they preceded Polish federations, and in the bitter words of *Głos Polek*, "grew like mushrooms after rain," reaching 2,200 members in eighteen courts by 1903. The PRCU and PWA both denounced such membership as a betrayal of

---

43. A dissenting note on the virtue of charity came from the socialists. They denounced it as a palliative which fostered a false sense of moral superiority. Since most immigrant women saw charitable work as both useful and spiritually uplifting, such a stance could only alienate most of their intended audience. *Dziennik Ludowy*, January 6, 1911, p. 1.

44. Standard interpretations lump Poles with Catholic immigrants and place them in opposition to temperance. While broadly correct, this ignores an articulate minority among these East Europeans who advocated abstinence, though not necessarily legal prohibition. This awaits study among Poles. For traditional views see Norman H. Clark, *Deliver Us from Evil: An Interpretation of American Prohibition* (New York, 1976), esp. pp. 88–90, 135–163; Jack S. Blocker, Jr., *American Temperance Movements: Cycles of Reform* (Boston, 1989), pp. 109–110.

45. *Głos Polek*, I (April, 1903), p. 2; November 10, 1910, pp. 9–10. Prominent papers such as *Naród Polski* or *Dziennik Chicagoski* occasionally denounced drinking, and by 1911 Father Kwiątkowski founded *Abstynent* [Abstainer] to publicize his cause. He promoted various clerical and lay male abstinence societies, but also appealed to the allegedly higher moral standards of women to combat drinking. See *Abstynent*, I (December, 1911), pp. 1–2.

For a warm reference to both the priest and his cause, see *Głos Polek*, September 28, 1911, pp. 9–10.

46. Even by 1890 there were at least eighteen Polish courts for men in this multi-ethnic federation, and beginning in 1894 the COP became active among Polish women. *COF Guide*, II (January 1890), pp. 6–7; *Głos Polek*, I (June 1903) pp. 3–4.

ethnicity.[47] Even more galling, though essentially a local challenge, were organizations such as the German Catholic "Gesellschaft Katolischer Damen" [Society of Catholic Women], which attracted some Polish members in Chicago. The ethnic press regularly attacked Germany as an oppressor of Poland and such societies were portrayed as another Teutonic plot to denationalize Poles.[48] But the conflicts with non-Polish fraternals, while irritating, were also another means to affirm ethnicity and to foster ties with male-dominated federations. The vehemence of the Polish Women's Alliance not only served their own interests but demonstrated another dimension of their patriotism.

The rise of feminine participation in organized Polonia can be measured most broadly through the numerous efforts to transcend the fraternal federations. These normally took the form of umbrella organizations premised on nationalism, and just as regularly foundered due to lack of support, quarrels over the definition of Polishness and organizational rivalry. One of the first was the Polish League [Liga Polska] of 1894, promoted by the religionist camp and inevitably undercut by the secularist Polish National Alliance, which aspired to lead U.S. Polonia.[49] Women as individuals or groups were never part of this. The congress movement, which attempted to avoid PNA opposition by excluding it from the outset, sought to bring more cohesion to the religionist camp through periodic conventions. Three were actually held—in 1896, 1901 and 1904—with commissions to consider various topics, but women again were not in the organization nor were their concerns

47. *Ibid.*, I (June 1903), p. 4; I (March 1903), p. 4; *Naród Polski*, January 11, 1899, p. 2. In some instances, the PWA organ wrote favorably of non-Polish fraternals. Frequently and generally favorably cited was the Czech Women's Alliance (Jednota Ceskych Dam, f. 1878), though it had a few Polish members. Apparently it was seen as a stimulating and essentially noncompetitive example of a successful Slavic women's group. See *Głos Polek*, I (September 1903), p. 2.

The Foresters used organizers and defined a superior one as a "pusher," aggressively seeking members among the Catholic "new immigrants." The COF stressed its Catholicism and episcopal appropriation, much to the annoyance of religionist Poles. Some immigrants may have perceived it as a higher status mutual benefit organization, American Catholic but flexible enough to accommodate ethnicity on the lodge level. Its sickness and death benefits were higher than Polish fratemals in the early nineties, though possibly dues were higher also. The COF organ published announcements in this period in several languages, including Polish. *Catholic Forester*, November 6, 1893, p. 1; March 5, 1896, p. 1.

48. *Głos Polek*, (March 1903), p. 4. The irritation at competing German organizations here became bitterly hostile in coverage of German women's organizations which promoted "Prussian" nationalism at the cost of Polish interests and cultural identity in the German partition. E.g., an article on the "League of German Women" meeting in Bromberg (Bydgoszcz). *Ibid.*, November 24, 1910, p. 11. Such sentiments would likely have made any collaboration with German women here more difficult.

49. Andrzej Brożek, *Polish Americans, 1854–1939* (Warsaw, 1985), pp. 74–75.

considered worthy of specific examination.[50] Given the religionist initiative in the above ventures, the inclination to place the PWA among the secularists in its first years may explain the group's exclusion; the absence of Roman Catholic women was a more telling indication of the conservatism of the religionist camp. In fact, the PWA tried to stay out of factional conflicts, and its increasing size brought in more and more women who were drawn to a religionist vision of Polishness, an evolution which became obvious by 1913.[51]

A modest beginning towards transcending camp divisions was an initiative from the Polish Women's Alliance itself. In 1902, to mark the 25th anniversary of the noted homeland author Maria Konopniczka's commencement of poetic work, the PWA's celebration in Chicago included speakers from both camps.[52] A more important harbinger of change, due to its male origins, was the inclusion of selected women in the Pulaski Monument project in Washington, D.C. The "Polish National Congress" (Kongress Narodowy Polski), held there in 1910 to unveil the monument, included not merely a few delegates from the small number of PNA women's lodges, but the entire national board of the PWA. Several women also gave addresses at the meeting.[53] Even more striking was the feminine participation the following year at

---

50. *Niedziela* [Sunday], VI (March 26, 1896), p. 208; *Naród Polski,* October 16, 1901, pp. 4–5; October 23, 1901, p. 5; October 30, 1091, p. 2 for 1901; *ibid.*, August 31, 1904, p. 4; October 12, 1904, p. 4 for 1904. Particularly striking is the absence of women from the Education Commission, as well as no reference to them (save for nuns improving their educational qualifications) among the recommendations for 1904. See *ibid.,* November 9, 1904, p. 4. Women were similarly unrepresented in the stillborn Federacja Polaków Rzymsko-katolicków w Stanach Zjednoczonych Półń. Am. [Federation of Polish Roman Catholics of the United States of North America], promoted in 1902 by activist clergy. See Haiman, *Zjednoczenie,* pp. 193–195.

51. *Głos Polek,* I (June 1903), p. 3 for comments on the leadership's problem with this identification. In fact, the PWA tried to avoid linkage with either orientation, but under the circumstances it wished to stress its compatibility with the faith of the vast majority of Poles. An important aspect of this strategy was the periodic national convention, held annually and then biennially through 1914, normally at a major parish. This customarily included an address by the pastor, who invariably spoke highly of the association. Karlowiczowa, *Historia,* I, pp. 34, 39, 45, 47, 50, 69–70, 77, 81, 85. Information on Convention II is lacking.

From another perspective, the Polish Socialist Party organ *Dziennik Ludowy* had nothing to say about the PWA or *Głos Polek* in its special issue on women in 1911, suggesting at least that it did not consider them in the secularist camp, in which it sought with some difficulty to include itself. *Dziennik Ludowy* [People's Daily], Feb. 25, 1911.

52. Brożek, *Polish American, 1854–1939,* p. 82. Brożek notes an uneven but generally increasing pattern of collaboration among the leading religionist and secularist groups after 1900.

53. Romuald Piatkowski, *Pamiętnik Wzniesienia i Odsłonięcia Pomników Tadeusza Kościuszki i Kazimierza Pułaskiego* [Commemoration of the Elevation and Unveiling of the Monuments to Thaddeus Kościuszko and Casimir Pułaski] (Chicago, 1911), pp. 111, 113–117; 369–384; 515–520. Some of these were women from the homeland.

a convention of the Journalists and Writers Society (Towarzystwo Dziennikarzów i Literatów). Stefania Laudyn, editor of the PWA's *Głos Polek,* was elected president of the assembly and gave an address on the "Woman Question" (Kwestja Kobiet), raising the topic in a highly publicized setting.[54] In late 1912, the formation of the first inclusive patriotic association, the Committee of National Defense (Komitet Obrony Narodowej) included the PWA from its inception, a striking contrast to the Polish League eighteen years previously. In the rupture of June 1913, the PWA followed the religionists into the competing Polish National Council (Polska Rada Narodowa), where it played an active though minor role.[55] Its larger significance was achievement of the ethnic equivalent of enfranchisement. Women's organizations or female officials in mixed societies had acquired a recognized voice in the activities of Polonia. By the eve of World War I, patriotic feminism had at last become an accepted part of the general nationalist movement.

• • •

The development of a feminist consciousness among these immigrant women derived primarily from their own aspirations and examples in the ethnic environment. Though not so stringently barred from work outside the home as their Italian American contemporaries, Polonian women were nonetheless seen by their men as homemakers.[56] Challenges to the domestic sphere came largely from the minority of women in better economic circumstances. Such persons had greater amounts of free time, or at least less pressing economic concerns, and sometimes better education as well. Before them was the ubiquitous model of the fraternal, a flexible structure which could offer not only the practical protection of insurance but pursue multiple additional goals as well. The universal aspiration for Polish independence, most diligently promoted through mutual aid structures, offered an obvious basis for entering the attractive world of ethnic activity. Patriotic feminism was elastic, stretching to include benevolence and cultural improvement. The effect was to democratize what was at home largely the concern of upper and middle class

---

54. *Głos Polek,* September 28, 1911, pp. 10–11; October 5, 1911, pp. 1–4.

55. Mirosław Frančić, *Komitet Obrony Narodowej w Ameryce, 1912–1918* [The Committee of National Defense in America] (Wrocław, 1983), pp. 39–40, 49–50; Karlowiczowa, *Historia* I, pp. 84, 91; *Naród Polski,* December 25, 1912, p. 4. The PNC and linked organizations formed the dominant element in Polonian wartime activity.

56. Virginia Yans-McLaughlin, *Family and Community: Italian Immigrants in Buffalo, 1880–1930* (Urbana, IL, 1982), pp. 168–174; John J. Bukowczyk, *And My Children Did Not Know Me: A History of the Polish-Americans* (Bloomington, 1987), pp. 23–25.

women into organizations of persons derived overwhelmingly from peasant extraction. Initiated by an innovative elite, these associations fostered an alternative to the fatalism of traditional homeland rural society and slowly expanded the mental horizons of Polonian women.[57] In so doing, the female leaders joined the ethnic elite in one of its most important functions, defining what it meant to be a "good Pole" in America.[58] After the turn of the century male leaders began to recognize the need to include women and legitimized their entrance by allowing them into positions of prestige and even authority, symbolized by their inclusion in umbrella organizations and the older fraternal federations.

In this evolution homeland influences were secondary. Women of superior education and status, such as Theophila Samolińska, brought new ideas and attitudes to American Polonia, but this was individual and idiosyncratic. The rich, varied and contradictory feminist movement in the Polish lands was little known before 1900 in America. The development of a socialist perspective after this time received little attention since the feminist press was tiny and too conservative to be attracted to it The underdevelopment of Polonian socialism meant that the few leftist periodicals had small circulations and evinced a sympathetic but still superficial interest in women's causes.[59] Publicity in the women's press went instead to homeland

57. An editorial in *Głos Polek* entitled "Lepsze Jutro" (A Better Tomorrow) captured this, urging that instead of complaining, "we must work for a 'better tomorrow'" because the future is ". . . largely in our, that is, women's, hands." *Głos Polek*, I (October 1902), p. 1. In a larger sense, the incessant calls to activism and participation were an expression of optimism, of the possibility for desirable change.

58. For a useful discussion of the defining role of ethnic elites, see Phillip Gleason, "The Crisis of Americanization," *Contemporary Catholicism in the United States* (Notre Dame, 1969), pp. 4–7.

59. There were only two durable Polish socialist periodicals in the prewar era: *Robotnik Polski* [Polish Worker] and *Dziennik Ludowy* [People's Daily]. Up to 1903 there was only abortive effort to establish a socialist women's organization, and in 1911 still only one "section" (oddział) of women in the Polish Socialist Alliance. Jan Wepsiec, *Polish American Serial Publications, 1842–1968* (Chicago, 1968), pp. 40, 137–138; *Głos Polek*, I (June 1903) p. 4; *Dziennik Ludowy*, Jan. 6, 1911, p. 4.

Dziennik Ludowy asserted that socialism stood for equal rights for women, but after saying that placed them within the system of class exploitation which would be eliminated by the triumph of socialism. There seemed to be small appreciation of the unique problems of women. This was not confined to Polish socialists; the American party suffered from a similar perception. *Dziennik Ludowy*, January 1, 1911, p. 3; February 24, 1911, pp. 2–3; Mari Jo Buhle, *Women and American Socialism* (Urbana, 1981), pp. 207–208.

manifestations of nationalism, benevolence, suffrage and uplift, but without the development of organic ties.[60]

Even less significant among these immigrant women was American feminism. Polonian women typically had a weaker knowledge of English than their menfolk, and aside from some Poles in unions, they had no direct exposure to organized American women. Given the weak relations of the largely middle class suffrage movement to organized labor c. 1900, personal contacts were few. After 1902 *Głos Polek* did report regularly but with little depth on American and foreign feminist activities, and was sympathetic to unions as well, but there was no formal or deep connection to either.[61] A sympathetic but distant interest characterized these ethnics.

The insularity of Polish American women was grounded in their definition of their movement. The wholesale adoption of patriotic feminism fostered ethnocentrism. While such an orientation made them more acceptable to Polonian men, it encouraged disinterest in the concerns of women in the larger society and erected barriers against collaboration across ethnic lines. Moreover, their location in an basically conservative ethnic society with greater possibilities for personal advancement than at home undermined the attraction of a more radical critique. Quite to the contrary, the efforts of the Polish Women's Alliance to be seen as respectable by clerics and pious women alike made drawing from radical ideas unlikely. Still, they discussed new ideas and forged novel organizations with a range of activities unknown a generation before. A woman was still supposed to live purely, but she no longer had to stay at home.

---

60. E.g., *Ibid.*, I (July 1902), p. 12; November 10, 1910, p. 11. "Kronika Kobieca" (Chronicle of Women) or "Z Ruchu Kobiecego" (From the Women's Movement) or similarly titled columns regularly gave information in brief items.

As such, *Głos Polek* existed from mid-1902 to mid-1903, and then on a permanent basis from 1910 onward. In the interim there was a regular feature in *Dziennik Narodowy*, no longer extant for that period, but almost certainly less extensive than an entire periodical in its coverage of women's affairs.

61. Such material was customarily part of the above columns, with very occasional special articles. There was Polish female participation in unions in Chicago, but it was very limited. James R. Barrett, *Work and Community in the Jungle: Chicago's Packinghouse Workers, 1894–1922* (Urbana, IL, 1987), pp. 136–137, 176.

An Act of Devotion

The Polish Grey Samaritans and the American Relief Effort in Poland, 1919–1921

Robert Szymczak

For Polish Americans the establishment of independent Poland in November 1918, after a century and a quarter of dismemberment, was cause for unrestrained joy. Polonia could look with pride on the contributions and sacrifices made from afar toward the resurrection of the Polish state. The aid rendered to the cause by these recent immigrants in the forms of money, men, and moral and political support was quite significant. But when the celebrations subsided, the world was shown an old and battered nation reconstituted as a democratic republic without secure, guaranteed borders and suffering from a severely depleted agricultural system which was unable to feed its war-weary citizens. The problem of malnutrition was so severe that the very future of the country appeared to hang in the balance. Immediate relief measures were necessary, especially to save Polish children from starvation.

American relief agencies and charitable organizations answered the call, as did Polonia, which responded with financial aid, clothing, and a most remarkable group of young women known as the Polish Grey Samaritans whose dedication to the cause of humanity in the immediate post-war years in Poland constitutes a little-known but truly admirable chapter in Polish American history. What follows is a discussion of the origins, goals, achievements, and effects of the work of the Polish Grey Samaritans in Poland from 1919 to 1921, crucial years during which the fate of the new republic was often in doubt.

The tradition of support for the homeland among Polish Americans was well-established by the time that the Polish Grey Samaritans were created. Polish Nationalist leaders, ably assisted by the oratorical skills of the famed pianist and patriot Ignacy Jan Paderewski, had, since 1914, beseeched their ethnic compatriots in the

From *Polish American Studies*, vol. 43, no. 1 (Spring 1986), pp. 13–36.

United States for financial assistance and the application of political pressure for the cause of an independent Poland. The response exceeded all expectations. In a few short years, Polish peasant immigrants from German, Austrian, and Russian sections of the homeland, who had not previously been known as patriots or nationalists, had taken such an interest in the affairs of their native land that they came to be identified as the "fourth province of Poland." According to Helena Znaniecki Lopata, "Polish immigrants and their children were easily convinced that their status in the motherland would be improved by their known sacrifices during the struggle for political independence" as would their prestige as a group if they remained in the United States. "The emotional fervor aroused in Polonia by these arguments," writes Lopata, "is documented in reports of meetings, the Polish language press, and constitutions and congresses of various groups."[1]

Thus Polish immigrants, most of whom arrived at Ellis Island impoverished, supported Polish independence to the tune of millions of dollars in both personal contributions to relatives and through political committees. Chicago banker Jan Smulski, the president of the Polish National Department [*Wydział Narodowy*] during World War I, reported that Polonia had donated over fifty million dollars in goods and money for Polish independence and relief, in addition to $67,000,000 in American Liberty Bonds purchases.[2] With the cooperation of the French and American governments, a Polish volunteer army of 28,000 men, the bulk of them from the United States, was organized in 1917 for service on the Western Front.[3] All this represented considerable sacrifice for an ethnic group estimated at between two and one-half to four million people. As Znaniecki Lopata notes, Polish Americans

> contributed to Poland's political rebirth through intensive efforts and willingness to part with money that was being saved for their most important status symbols—land and durable property. Their action was a reflection of political patriotism and an emotional response to dynamic leadership, despite the fact that they did not identify with the parties, ideologies or internal struggle in Poland. They were simply interested in restoring Poland as a nation protected by a political state [and] in helping victims of the war. . . .[4]

---

1. *Polish Americans: Status Competition in an Ethnic Community* (Englewood Cliffs, New Jersey, 1976), p. 23.

2. See Joseph A. Wytrwal, *Poles in American History and Tradition* (Detroit, 1969), pp. 321–22 for the contributions of Smulski's National Department.

3. The Polish volunteer force, known as the "Blue Army," fought in France under General Józef Haller; after the armistice, the unit was pressed into service during the Russo-Polish War of 1919–1920.

4. Znaniecki Lopata, *op. cit.*, p. 24.

When Polish independence became a reality, Polonia was elated. Parades and mass rallies were held in New York, Chicago, Cleveland, Buffalo, Pittsburgh, Milwaukee, and Detroit. The national anthem was sung in halls and churches in demonstrations of sheer joy that for the first time since the eighteenth century a Polish national state had reappeared on the map of Europe in the wake of the defeat of Poland's oppressors. One observer noted that

> In view of such feelings among the Poles in America it is not surprising that when a Polish consulate opened in New York after World War I, pilgrimages from all over America began to make their way there, merely to see the Polish flag and the White Eagle over the building. It reached such a point that the New York Police had to close the street to traffic, since it was always crowded with Pilgrims, sometimes kneeling to pray and weep.[5]

Such is the background which spawned the Polish Grey Samaritans, thirty young Polish American women whose selfless dedication to their work in a land fraught with hardship and despair stands as a symbol of Polonia's continued concern for the motherland once the cheering stopped. The Poland to which the Greys would soon be dispatched was a bleak, desolate land filled with hunger, deprivation, misery, and danger after four bloody years as a major battleground for the empires engaged in World War I. When the first American Relief Administration mission, headed by Dr. Vernon Kellogg, arrived in Warsaw on January 4, 1919, the group painted an almost hopeless picture of destitution in its reports to ARA director Herbert Hoover. "Here were about 28,000,000 people," Hoover recorded in his memoirs,

> who had for four years been ravished by four separate invasions during this one war, where battles and retreating armies had destroyed and destroyed again. . . . Many hundreds of thousands had died of starvation. The homes of millions had been destroyed and the people in those areas were living in hovels. Their agricultural implements were depleted, their animals had been taken by armies, their crops had been only partly planted and then only partly harvested. Industry in the cities was dead from lack of raw materials. The people were unemployed and millions were destitute. . . . The railroads were barely functioning. The cities were almost without food; typhus and diseases raged over whole provinces. Rats, lice, famine, pestilence—yet they were determined to build a nation.[6]

The first American food shipment arrived in early January 1919 and continued in significant increments until the fall harvest, by which time 751,135 tons of foodstuffs had reached the country. Used military clothing, medical supplies, and 60,000,000

---

5. Quoted in Wytrwal, *op. cit.*, p. 349.
6. *The Memoirs of Herbert Hoover: Years of Adventure, 1874–1920* (New York, 1951), p. 356.

pounds of raw cotton were also dispatched, along with $176,541,079 in credit and charity.[7]

Among the charitable organizations working with Hoover's ARA was the Young Women's Christian Association, through whose War Work Council aid had been sent to war victims throughout Europe. In late 1918 the YWCA received a request from Laura de Turczynowicz, the American-born wife of a Polish aristocrat from the Poznań area and the head of the Polish Reconstruction Association, for assistance in the matter of Polish relief. Madame Turczynowicz, who was not of Polish ancestry, suggested that the YWCA "select and train a unit of Polish girls in America for social service in their own communities in preparation for reconstruction work in Poland."[8] The National War Work Council of the YWCA thought highly of the proposal, for the language barrier had proved to be a hinderance to the group's charitable work in the past.

The YWCA, having accepted Madame Turczynowicz's suggestions, immediately set out to secure the cooperation of Polish American leaders in every major Polish community in the United States. Polish physicians were enlisted to train the young women who volunteered for service in Cleveland, Trenton, Rochester, Chicago, Milwaukee, Detroit, Buffalo, and Pittsburgh. Three hundred young women had answered the call; two hundred were sent back to their home towns to work as nurse's aides in Polish settlements. Ninety girls, all judged as having the necessary qualities for the rigors that lie ahead, were separated from the rest and were dispatched to New York City for further instruction at the Polish Grey Samaritans School operated by the YWCA.[9] Departure for New York was delayed, however, as the Grey Samaritans, so named because of their nurses' uniforms, were pressed into service during the great influenza epidemic in the last months of 1918. One Samaritan, Eugenia Panek, died of the disease while assisting Polish flu victims in

7. *Ibid.*, p. 358. Hoover expressed great dissatisfaction with Polish political bickering during this period, reporting that Dr. Kellogg has recommended that Józef Piłsudski, a leader of the Polish wartime resistance to both the Central Powers and Russia, "be put on a pedestal" and that the internationally known pianist Ignacy Paderewski, be appointed prime minister in order to "close up the factions." Unless this was done, Kellogg informed Hoover, the Poles ought to be told that "American cooperation and aid were futile." Hoover supported Kellogg's recommendations in conference with President Wilson. "As a result," writes Hoover, "Pilsudski was elevated to the position of Chief of State," and Paderewski became Prime Minister on January 16th." American aid thus continued. (pp. 357–358).

8. *Emergency Services: A Statement of the Services Rendered By the Overseas Committee of the American YWCA in Ten Countries During and Following World War I* (War Work Council of the Board of Young Women's Christian Associations, 1917–1920, n.d.), p. 1.

9. *Ibid.*, pp. 1–2. A partial list of Polish physicians involved in the training and selection of the Polish Grey Samaritans includes Drs. Konrad of Cleveland; Tadeusiak of Trenton; Nawrocki of St. Louis; Heller and Krzyszko of Milwaukee; Sadlowski, Pasternacki, and Cyman of Detroit; and Ricker of New York.

The Grey Samaritan recruits from Rochester, N.Y., pictured above in their white nurses uniforms, received three months of training in nursing at the Homeopathic Hospital before departing for New York City. Photo courtesy of Mrs. Leon Lustyk with the assistance of Ms. Kathleen Urbanic.

Perth Amboy, New Jersey. Others became ill but recovered in time to report for training in New York on January 17, 1919.[10]

According to Martha Graczyk Gedgowd of Rochester, one of the original Samaritans selected for a YWCA scholarship in New York, the women received welfare training in the slums of the city, attended lectures at the New York School of Philanthropy, and were given Red Cross courses in cooking, health, and hygiene. Additional lessons in business principles and arts and crafts at Teacher's College, Columbia University and YWCA lectures in social manners rounded out the six-month program.[11] In early June, 1919 seventy-five Polish Grey Samaritans graduated from the training course and were sent home to await their assignments. "Theirs had not been an easy task," Gedgowd writes of the YWCA counselors. "Managing a group of young girls, some not more than 18 years old . . . required women who understood the life of just such a group of girls, some foreign born, others with much of the native customs of their ancestors."[12]

10. Statement of Marta Graczyk Gedgowd, undated, in Polish Grey Samaritans Records, 1919–1965, in the Hoover Institution on War, Revolution, and Peace, box 1. Hereafter cited as Gedgowd Collection, PGS Records, H.I.

11. *Ibid.*

12. *Ibid.*

Grey Samaritan volunteers in training at the New York School of Philanthropy. Photo courtesy of Mrs. Leon Lustyk with assistance from Ms. Kathleen Urbanic.

Meanwhile, the YWCA's War Work Council had delegated a commission to make advance arrangements for the Polish Grey Samaritans in Europe. In Paris the delegation met with Polish Premier Ignacy Paderewski and his wife, both of whom expressed great interest in the project. "As a result," a YWCA pamphlet recorded, "the Polish Government in conjunction with American Relief Administration . . . cooperated in all arrangements and gave every needed facility."[13]

The initial plan, worked out among representatives of the YWCA, the Polish Government, and the ARA, was to place twenty Grey Samaritans in nurseries and hospitals as nurses' aides, "and to send them out as social workers to help in the investigation of cases through home visits and in the distribution of food and clothing" in order "to set a standard for child welfare, and to build up scientific social service. . . ."[14] Travel instructions were issued to the first Grey Samaritan contingent to sail for France on July 17 on the French liner *SS Rochambeau.* Expenses were paid by the YWCA for the journey, but Madame Paderewska and the Polish Versailles delegation were to make further arrangements for lodging and transportation to Poland. Under the provisions of the YWCA-Polish agreement, the YWCA was to pay for the first three months' maintenance and half the maintenance for the second three months in Poland. Afterwards, Madame Paderewska was to make financial

13. *Emergency Services, YWCA, op. cit.,* p. 1.
14. *Ibid.,* p. 2.

arrangements. The women were to receive thirty dollars a month salary in addition to the living expenses for one year's service, during which time an American YWCA secretary "will be in absolute charge and all her instructions must be obeyed."[15]

Before making the ocean voyage, the volunteers were required to take the Polish Grey Samaritan Pledge:

> I, ____________, in accepting the Polish Grey Samaritan uniform, pledge myself to uphold the highest ideals of womanhood in every action of my life;
> To be faithful in the fulfilment of the duties of a Polish Grey Samaritan;
> To be obedient to the orders of my Superiors;
> To serve the cause of Poland;
> To allay suffering and bind up the wounds of those by the wayside;
> Believing that in so doing I serve the cause of humanity.[16]

To oversee the Grey Samaritan project, the YWCA assigned Amy Pryor Tapping of Utica, New York, a long-time YWCA secretary. Recalling the reception of the unit in Warsaw, Tapping wrote in her journal of the pride she felt in her charges:

> This afternoon Madame Paderewska gave an audience to the Polish Grey Samaritans in her room. She wore khaki with a red cross on the sleeve and spoke to them in Polish, welcoming them to Poland. She calls them *szary kotki,* little grey kittens. For so do they look in their blue-grey uniforms. And . . . they are my job, these Polish American girls; I wish that you might know them in their youth and their enthusiasm. They are Poles and to be a Pole is to be a patriot. They have been in America and America has given them something to bring back to their newly reconstructed country. And here they are, ready to serve, my basket of *szary kotki.*[17]

The success of the group became readily apparent within a month of their initial assignments. According to the YWCA, those assigned to case work visited 150 destitute Polish families, securing relief and clothing for the needy and recommending a number of them for hospitalization, while the Samaritans posted to nurseries had, through their care, reduced the death rate by fifty percent. As word spread of their work, calls came from many cities, towns, and villages for a least one Grey Samaritan to organize welfare work, compelling the YWCA to cable New York for a second contingent of volunteers. The second group, numbering ten, arrived in January 1920, raising the total number of Greys in Poland to thirty.[18]

The ARA's Children's Fund requested the Grey Samaritans for its relief work in Lwów, Pińsk, Wilno, Lublin, Kielce, Lódź, and other locations as needs arose.

---

15. Gedgowd Collection, PGS Records, HI, *op. cit.*

16. *Ibid.*

17. Personal recollection of Amy Pryor Tapping, undated, in Polish Grey Samaritans Records, 1919–1965, in the Hoover Institution on War, Revolution, and Peace, box 2. Hereafter cited as Tapping Collection, PGS Records, HI.

18. *Emergency Services, YWCA, op. cit.*, p. 2.

The first contingent of Grey Samaritans on the docks in New York directly prior to embarking on the *SS Rochambeau*. Photo courtesy of Mr. Ted Perkowski.

Sent to these places in teams of four to six, the Polish Greys were charged with the distribution of 700,000 outfits of children's clothing and the feeding of 1,200,000 Polish children in January alone. These volunteers were made responsible for all ARA distribution outside Warsaw.[19]

One of the Greys, Martha Graczyk, was assigned to Wilno, where 40,000 children were being fed by the ARA, in order to supervise the distribution of food and 12,000 sets of children's clothing. Her orders from W. P. Fuller, Jr., the Children's Fund director in Warsaw, stated that she "should take such steps as may be feasible to make sure that distribution is carried on without any discrimination whatsoever, and totally regardless of race, politics, religion, or inability to pay. The need of the child should be the sole test."[20] Such instructions were deemed prudent especially for relief work

19. *Ibid.* The Polish Grey Samaritans working under the auspices ARA inspectors in the field in January 1920 were Maria Andrzejewska, Helena Chmielewska, Anna Czaban, Zofia Kosobucka, Felicia Krutewicz, Anna Michalowska, Leokadia Myszynska, Józefina Tarkowska, Krystyna Zduleczna, Helena Cichowicz, Katarzyna Ciesicka, Józefina Czarnik, Annette Friebe, Maria Goch, Marta Graczyk, Helena Gustowt, Stanisława Kendzierska, Anna Kopec, Katarzyna Krzyzanowska, Stella Lysakowska, Helena Mielczarek, Stanisława Mucha, Helena Piotrowska, Karolina Sławinska, Walentyna Smentkowska, Franciszka Sobczynska, Waleria Staszko, Waleria Tomasik, Eleonora Wasilewska, and Eugenia Winckiewicz.

20. Letter from W.P. Fuller, Jr., ARA Children's Relief Fund, Warsaw, to Marta Graczyk, December 19, 1919. Gedgowd Collection, PGS Records, HI, *op. cit.*

in Poland's eastern regions, where Lithuanians, White Ruthenians (Byelorussians), Ukranianians, Jews, and Poles lived in close but not necessarily harmonious proximity.

The Polish Grey Samaritans also worked closely with the Polish relief organization known as the *Polsko-Amerykanski Komitet Pomocy Dzieciom* [PAKPD], created under ARA auspices for the distribution of relief material from the United States, as well as that contributed locally. Often the Greys' task was to organize children's kitchens and administer them for a time, turning them over to the PAKPD, before moving on to another area. For this reason, all records of Grey Samaritan field work were kept in Polish.

Officially, the feeding program was a joint venture of the ARA and the PAKPD; the United States government supplied the funds for food under Hoover's ARA, provided the transportation to Danzig, and assigned the personnel for distribution while the Poles paid for the transportation from the port of entry to their clearing house in Warsaw and finally to the kitchens. At every step of the way, however, ARA officials or Polish Grey Samaritans supervised the shipments and organized the distribution. According to a Polish Grey Samaritan statement,

> The children are charged 15 pfennings per portion and only the very poorest children in the community are allowed to buy. This money is used for the upkeep of the kitchens. In some of the cities of Poland many hundreds of children are fed at each kitchen every day while in small villages the numbers are only a few. The charge at 15% of our rate of exchange might be about one-fifth of a cent. . . .
>
> The standard ration is 160 grams. . . . The ration is a bit different for Christians and Jews and therefore the children of these races are fed in separate kitchens. It is estimated that the ARA is feeding every day in Poland 2 of the 3 needy children and one-fourth of all the children in Poland.[21]

In each locality, the small teams of Polish Greys faced different situations. Upon entering a new area, the woman reported to the local Polish authorities, determined the needs of the vicinity, and quite often planned the work of the Polish relief committee. On occasion, when the Greys learned of pilferage problems, they secured guards to protect the ARA material. In some cases the Greys themselves sat on bales of clothing as they were transported from warehouse to storeroom to insure the safety of the goods. Travel from town to town was an often difficult, if not dangerous proposition. Military transportation for the Greys was arranged when possible, but more often than not such a journey meant box-car accommodations. Trips to small towns and villages were usually made in horse-drawn hay wagons. Upon arrival, the Greys often discovered that no accommodations were available, in which case they were housed in orphanages or churches.

21. Unsigned typewritten statement dated 1920, Tapping Collection, PGS Records, HI, *op. cit.* (This writer believes that there is a strong possibility that this typescript memoir was written by Amy Pryor Tapping.)

As bleak as the situation and conditions were, humorous episodes indeed occurred. One diminutive Grey Samaritan, ordered to proceed to a small town in central Poland, telegraphed the municipal authorities that she was to arrive the following day. Since no Grey had visited the area before, she thought it wise to sign the dispatch "American Mission." After bouncing unceremoniously into town on a haycart, she could find no one. The entire town, she finally learned, had repaired to the train station with flags flying and a band blaring out the "Star Spangled Banner" to royally welcome the "American Mission." In another small town the Polish relief committee, comprised of local citizens, was placed in charge of a shipment of ARA cocoa. Puzzled as to the identity and use of the substance, the committee met to discuss a number of theories after which it was determined that the powdery stuff was to be used to plaster the walls of the relief kitchen. "There it stays," wrote a Polish Grey, "a lasting tribute to the work of the ARA in that community."[22]

In a few short months, the Polish American relief brigade had earned glowing tributes for their dedication and efficiency. In a report to his ARA superiors in London, Fuller wrote that

> In my opinion the Polish Greys have increased the efficiency of the clothing program by 50%, that is, probably 50% more children had received outfits than otherwise if the girls had not supervised. A certain loss of clothing by theft and other causes had been figured on but the girls greatly decreased that. Their effect on the local committees was very beneficial. (1) They stimulated the Poles themselves to help (2) They stimulated the interest that made the Poles feel that America was there to put through an American job (3) They insured a fair distribution without discrimination of race or religion (4) They gave a good example of American organization. . . .[23]

Just as the ARA and the Grey Samaritans appeared to be solving some of the tremendous logistical problems inherent in the distribution of vast quantities of food and clothing to the destitute, the Russo-Polish War, which had begun in 1919 with the clash of Polish and Bolshevik troops in the disputed eastern border region, turned into a full-scale conflict. In April 1920, Marshal Józef Piłsudski, the Polish Chief of State, sent Polish forces crashing into the Ukraine. Determined to restore Poland's pre-partition eastern border and to establish an anti-Bolshevik federation of Ukrainians, White Ruthenians, Lithuanians, and Poles, Piłsudski had caught the Western Allies and Hoover's ARA by surprise. Conditions in 1920, although improved, were nevertheless deplorable. Nearly a million tons of ARA food had been shipped to the stricken country by the spring of 1920; the records for that year

---

22. *Ibid.*, pp. 4–5.

23. Report of W.P. Fuller, ARA, Warsaw, to ARA London office, March 30, 1920. Tapping Collection, PGS Records, HI, *op. cit.*

also show 34,000 cases of typhus and nearly a million and a half Polish children being fed daily by the ARA. For a poor nation in these horrible straits to launch a major military offensive against Soviet Russia was "a fantastic enterprise," according to George F. Kennan.[24]

By the beginning of the summer of 1920, the Polish attack had become a retreat. A powerful Soviet counteroffensive had driven the Poles out of Kiev in May, pushing Piłsudski's troops back and creating a massive refugee problem that added more woes to the harried ARA and Grey Samaritan field workers' normal complement of troubles. White Ruthenians, Ukrainians, and Poles from the eastern territories poured into refugee camps with the Red Army only a few miles behind them. Typhus, smallpox, cholera, dysentery, and tuberculosis rampaged through the camps. ARA doctors estimated the death rate at fifty percent. "Surgeons had no anesthetic," the YWCA reported, "doctors no medicine," and hunger stalked everywhere. "One relief worker, noticing the strange absence of birds around the camps, was told by a Polish child: "We have killed them to eat."[25] Malnourished children abounded throughout Poland, even in Warsaw. Despite the ministrations of the ARA and the Grey Samaritans, the death rate among the young was estimated at twenty-five percent. The entire program initiated by the ARA and its adjuncts appeared to be in grave jeopardy. A YWCA secretary, writing in 1920, explained some of the problems faced by the ARA and the Grey Samaritans:

> The food is shipped from Danzig [Gdánsk] to one of eight regional warehouses and from there . . . to the 190 [Polish relief] committees and thence through the 500 local subcommittees to the kitchens and then to the children. It is "Big Business" this seeing that 1,300,000 children in Poland receive every day their meal from the Americans; and only one who has glimpsed even ever so casually the possibilities of delay of transportation in a country where possibly every month or so all the trains are held up for ten days, where freight cars are used to transport troops, where a strike [by pro-Soviet German dockworkers] at Danzig hinders for days the unloading of a transport already weeks overdue . . . can appreciate even ever so little what it means to keep every little village supplied with rations for its starving children. . . .[26]

Although the Polish Greys continued to administer ARA kitchens for children, they often took the time to visit military hospitals filled with wounded Polish soldiers evacuated from the war front. Some of these facilities were mere tents only a

---

24. George F. Kennan, *Russia and the West Under Lenin and Stalin* (New York, 1961), pp. 158–159. For the best account to date of the Russo-Polish War and its effect on the Polish population, see Norman Davies, *White Eagle, Red Star: The Polish-Soviet War of 1919–1920* (London, 1972), *passim.*

25. *Emergency Services, YWCA, op. cit.*, p. 1.

26. Unsigned typewritten statement, Tapping Collection, PGS Records, HI, *op. cit.*

few miles from the nearest Bolshevik line. The women helped to treat the wounded whenever they could. One Grey, Josephine Tarkowska of Cleveland, described such a visit in a letter to ARA Warsaw Mission Chief Fuller:

> We girls visited a military hospital. I call it a death trap; [we] went into one room and found seventeen dead soldiers—in another, 23 dying from lack of food and proper care. Very sick soldiers get a piece of black dry bread and a cup of black bitter so-called coffee for breakfast. The rest I will not state. They have no sheets, no blankets; some soldiers here are lying for weeks with bullet wounds and the doctors have no instruments to operate.[27]

In July, Lenin decided to order Soviet forces to capture Warsaw and impose a Communist government on the nation. The swift Soviet advance, a three-pronged movement, caused an initial collapse of Polish defenses; the road to Warsaw lay open to the Bolsheviks, whose drive to the capital had exacerbated the already serious refugee problem. YWCA secretary Tapping recorded the sight of displaced persons in eastern Poland during this period in the following terms:

> Can you imagine the sight, wagons that looked like the immigration of the 40's back in America with prairie schooners line after line and mile after mile ever and anon. . . . It was a most pathetic sight—the coming to an end of possibly five-year wanderings; and with no hope of finding their land, no seed, no home, no machinery, no cattle. War-weary they looked, these humble travelers, and tired, bundled in the rage, leading their weary horses while the little children rode on the loads and the women walked behind. I shall never forget it—never.[28]

With Warsaw threatened by the advancing Red Army, the safety of ARA, YWCA, and Polish Grey Samaritan field workers became a matter of concern to the American authorities. In July, the American minister in Warsaw, Hugh Gibson, somberly advised the YWCA to make plans to leave Poland, in a hurry if necessary. "With as little fanfare as possible, so as not to frighten our loyal Polish friends," remembered Amy Tapping, "we quietly sent all the trunks, including those of the Polish Greys through Danzig to Antwerp, keeping only suitcases and duffle bags."[29] The United States Legation was to announce the order for all American women to evacuate Poland as soon as the Soviets crossed the River Bug.

When the Greys discovered that preparations for their departure had been undertaken, they protested to their YWCA superiors that Poland needed them. They wished to remain regardless of the danger in order to complete their work. As

---

27. Letter, Josephine Tarkowska to W.P. Fuller, ARA Children's Relief Fund, Warsaw, February 18, 1920. Marta Graczyk Gedgowd Collections, PGS Records, HI, *op. cit.*

28. Personal recollection of Amy Pryor Tapping, Russo-Polish War period, Tapping Collection, PGS Records, HI, *op. cit.*

29. *Ibid.*

Allied missions and diplomatic personnel fled Warsaw to escape what they believed to be a certain Soviet victory, Christine Zduleczna, a Grey from Pittsburgh, wrote to YWCA headquarters in the capital, imploring her superiors not to order the unit home:

> Do not take to heart the Bolshevik invasion. I am sure it will not come. There is too much of our youth going into Poland not to make a turn in this drive. I cannot understand what curse is on Poland that she has to bleed and suffer for her freedom.[30]

The precarious position of the Poles and their attitude toward the Bolshevik threat was noted by the Greys' immediate superior, Amy Tapping, who noted on July 7:

> Situation more critical. For the first time in the paper the Poles admit that there have been defeat and losses. Since the taking of Kiev the Bolo [Bolshevik] army has been advancing at the rate of 7 miles a day. Whatever the mistake in military tactics may have been I am sure that no spirit could be finer than the desire of the men and women of the country to serve it. Patriotism, always the ruling passion of these people, has risen to the fore and they are inspired to save their land even after six years of warfare. Thousands of men enlist every day.[31]

The fine Polish spirit notwithstanding, the American Legation and the ARA decided that the Grey Samaritans could work safely, for the time being, only in the Kraków district in southern Poland. Should Warsaw fall—as was expected—the women would be evacuated immediately to Western Europe. Each Grey was made fully aware of the gravity of the situation and given a choice: Temporary assignment in the relative safety of the Kraków vicinity, or immediate passage to the United States. Four Greys availed themselves of the opportunity to leave; the remaining twenty-six elected to stay throughout this crucial period.[32]

Warsaw indeed appeared to be doomed. By early August the northern wing of the Soviet offensive commanded by the famed General Mikhail Tukhachevsky stood before the gates of Warsaw. On August 6, the American Legation ordered the evacuation of all remaining American women from the capital as thousands of Poles dug trenches in a defensive perimeter on the city's outskirts. In an amazing turn of fortune, however, Piłsudski launched a sudden counterattack and drove a wedge between the Soviet lines; the Red Army, stunned by this bold mid-August action, beat a quick retreat. Warsaw—and Polish independence—had been saved by

---

30. Letter, Christine Zduleczna to Amy Pryor Tapping, YWCA, Warsaw, no date. *Ibid.*

31. Personal recollection of Amy Pryor Tapping, Russo-Polish war period, Tapping Collection, PGS Records, HI, *op. cit.*

32. *Ibid.*

this remarkable victory, thwarting Lenin's revolutionary dreams of a Polish-Soviet Republic and a gateway to Germany. As the Polish people toasted Piłsudski as the greatest national hero since Tadeusz Kosciuszko, the women of the Polish Grey Samaritans learned that they could remain to resume their duties toward the poor and the hungry.

Under the Treaty of Riga in 1921, Poland's eastern frontier was officially extended to include parts of the Ukraine and White Russia. While much of the territory also included Poles, the settlement placed within the Polish state several million non-Polish people who inhabited a devastated land. The Grey Samaritans were dispatched to this Polish hinterland to confront the problems of feeding and clothing the victims of war. In January 1921, the journalist Coningsby Dawson toured eastern Poland and reported scenes of destruction that he, a veteran war correspondent, found shocking. "Mention devastated areas," he wrote, "and it conjures a picture of the kind of destruction that happened in France. But in Poland," he continued,

> the problem of devastation is quite different. It is almost true to say that the whole of Poland is devastated. In France the destruction was intensely concentrated in a narrow belt of the country where battles were fought. In Poland, with its tremendous distances, the depth of devastation rarely is less at any point than two hundred miles.[33]

As Dawson traversed the rough terrain from Brześć to Kowel, he described a panorama of "eloquent misery." Passing grave yards and solitary crosses, he stopped to view the ruins of villages. "Tenanting these ruins," he reported, "are gaunt human beings who hurry out of sight like pariahs. . . . They wore no shoes, their feet swathed in sodden rags. They bore a hunted look and gave us wide berth as though they feared our cruelty." In Kowel, Dawson met his guide, Grey Samaritan Christine Zduleczna, the Pittsburgher who had worked in the vicinity of Kowel for two years. Impressed with the dedication of the Greys, the journalist noted that

> All of them can talk the Polish language, and most of them are old enough to remember the land of their birth at the time when they emigrated. Because of their dual nationality they are invaluable as liaisons between the need of the country and the American authorities. Their self-effacement is a sight to make more comfortable people blush. They practice the sacrifice of saints and the fearlessness of soldiers.[34]

Describing Kowel as "a wretched hovel of a town," Dawson was amazed that Zduleczna had survived in such a place so "unsanitary," permanently splashed with mud, inhabited by Jews and White Russians" and so horrible that "nothing that

---

33. Cablegram copy of news article by Coningsby Dawson, Warsaw, to ARA office in New York, January 12, 1921. Tapping Collection, PGS Records, HI, *op. cit.*

34. *Ibid.*

Anna Badura, a volunteer from Rochester, N.Y. Photo courtesy of Mrs. Leon Lustyk with assistance from Ms. Kathleen Urbanic.

Gorki or Tolstoy has described is more accursed or Godforsaken." As Zduleczna and Dawson toured the countryside, the latter noted that

> There is not a solitary sign of human habitation . . . yet people lived there. How? In timbered dugouts . . . in shell holes. They lived like foxes . . . And what did they feed on? In many parts of the devastated region they are eating grass as though they are cattle. They boil it into a kind of soup. Where they have no flour of any sort, they bake bread out of a mixture of bark and acorns. But our Grey Samaritans informed us that there are mostly no ruined villages that we had passed where American children's relief stations had not been established. [Zduleczna] knew for she had established them, that was her job.[35]

35. *Ibid.*

Zduleczna took Dawson to visit Polish and White Ruthenian families in the area, where he was told on each occasion that all the children in the village would have died were it not for American aid. "Whoever dies in Poland," he stated, "children can be saved as long as America recognized the necessity." Parting company with Zduleczna on the return trip to Kowel, Dawson expressed some misgivings about leaving her alone to face her tasks. "We left her in her mouldly room in the dingy den of the Bellevue which looks more like a thieves' kitchen than a hotel. She parted with us with a cheery smile—she loved her people and her work. . . . But I for one felt like a coward leaving her alone to carry such a burden."[36]

In March 1921, Philip S. Baldwin, ARA Children's Fund chief in Warsaw, recommended that the Greys be given one month's leave to visit the United States "in view of their long continued service in Poland," but stated that ". . . it is exceedingly desirable that at least twelve competent Grey Samaritans be engaged in work in the field."[37] Several of the Greys journeyed home at this juncture, while others were reassigned to new posts in the field. Meanwhile, Amy Tapping had already pronounced the Greys' mission a success. In a letter to the ARA office in London, she cited Herbert Hoover's call for more Samaritans.[38]

But the YWCA's funds were at this time nearly depleted. Cyril J. C. Quinn, the newly-appointed ARA mission chief in Warsaw, addressed this issue in a letter to his superiors in London, stating that continued YWCA-Grey Samaritan work in Poland was contingent on the YWCA's ability and willingness to raise new funds. Should new funds not be forthcoming, Quinn estimated that the YWCA would be compelled to cease operations in Poland by January 1922. The mission director also seemed to be concerned about the role played by the YWCA in Catholic Poland:

> While we are willing and heartily recommend the retention of the Gray [sic] Samaritans in Poland in view of the work they are to do until the completion of our operations in the Spring, we do not feel justified in recommending that the YWCA continue the work it is now carrying on in Poland. From our point of view the only American organizations which should remain in Europe are those meeting the primary need of emergency relief, and that with the present economic situation in America no other appeal to the charity of America is justified. This is entirely apart from the obvious considerations of an organization of character of the YWCA working in a Catholic country and other contingent considerations which are obviously no concern of ours.[39]

---

36. *Ibid.*

37. Confidential Memo, Philip S. Baldwin, ARA Children's Fund, Warsaw, to ARA office, London, March 1, 1921. Tapping Collection, PGS Records, HI, *op. cit.*

38. Letter, Amy Pryor Tapping, YWCA headquarters, Warsaw, to Walter Lyman Brown, ARA office, London, February 8, 1921. *Ibid.*

39. Letter, Cyril J.C. Quinn, ARA Mission, Warsaw, to ARA office, London, Confidential No. 1082, September 14, 1921. Gedgowd Collection, PGS Records, HI, *op. cit.*

To be sure, Poland was a strange land to non-Polish Americans, as Amy Tapping discovered on more than one occasion. While there is no solid evidence that cultural differences between Protestant ARA and YWCA officials and their Polish hosts actually hindered the distribution of relief material, anecdotal commentary and reminiscences from the period found among the statistical information suggests that at times American efforts to understand the Pole could indeed be frustrating. Here is YWCA Secretary Tapping on the Polish penchant for observing religious holidays:

> I am so mad! I can scarcely see! And at whom am I mad? St. Peter and Paul! And why am I mad? They are being honored in Poland tomorrow. How many holidays do you suppose Poland celebrated during the year including Sundays? Four hundred seventeen! Honest Injun—they love to celebrate and can plan a holiday for anything and hang their best rugs out the windows as decoration and call a band in and march through the streets. They celebrate everybody's going to heaven and all the saints coming to earth and everything in the life of everybody who lived in Bible times, I really believe, and all the Polish notabilities and everything. . . .[40]

At Baranowicze, the teetotalling Tapping found herself the object of "toast after toast" at a celebration honoring the Polish Grey Samaritans and American relief. She recounted this Polish drinking episode in a report to ARA headquarters:

> I tried to say 'Thank you' for Mr. Harding, Mr. Hoover, all America, and incidentally the ARA. I clicked glasses with the bishop and the mayor over those toasts but I remained a patriotic American and let them do the drinking![41]

While Amy Tapping and ARA officials displayed great sympathy for the Poles and their plight—especially during the Russo-Polish War—some Poles, although grateful for American assistance, complained that too many Protestant organizations had come to Poland ostensibly to dispense charity, but were, in reality proselytizing for their particular sects. In May 1921, this problem was addressed by no less a figure than Prince Adam Sapieha, the Archbishop of Kraków, who, in a pastoral letter read to congregations all over Poland took great care to thank Herbert Hoover, the ARA, the American Red Cross, the YWCA and the Polish Grey Samaritans, and Jan Smulski's Chicago-based Polish National Department, but bitterly attacked other American church-based charity organizations. "We cannot but notice," the Archbishop wrote, "that some of these organizations have not made charity their only aim."

> We therefore have the right to request of those who come, to state clearly and honestly the designs that brought them here. Among organizations which have come, there are religious ones, mostly Protestant or Schismatics, who wish to imbibe in

40. Letter, Amy Pryor Tapping, YWCA headquarters, Warsaw, to unnamed correspondent, July 1920. Tapping Collection, PGS Records, HI, *op. cit.*

41. Report, Amy Pryor Tapping to ARA office, Warsaw, from Baranowicze, October 28, 1921. Tapping Collection, PGS Records, HI, *op. cit.*

> us their religious beliefs. . . . They act secretly, and we know of them only through their speeches, their writings . . . and the distribution of tracts. . . . Not only every good Catholic, but every good Pole must be made indignant by . . . these tracts which besmirch with the mud of blasphemy things that are holy. . . .[42]

Sapieha singled out the YWCA for praise of their willingness to work with the Polish church and their use of the Greys, but condemned the YWCA for its refusal to follow the example of its sister organization. He marked the Protestant "Bible Searchers" for particular rebuke, but also castigated the Polish National Catholic Church of the United States for its missionary activities in Poland undertaken, according to Sapieha, under the guise of charity work. In the strongest possible terms, the Archbishop urged the Polish people to reject the entreaties of such groups.[43]

The fact that Sapieha included the YWCA on his list of bona fide charitable organizations whose assistance to Poland was to be deeply appreciated bespeaks much of that association's efforts to employ Poles wherever possible in its relief efforts. Certainly the Polish American volunteers who had served with such distinction throughout this period made some difference. Not only did they serve as interpreters for YWCA and ARA officials, but acted as ambassadors between two disparate cultures. The ability of the Greys to bridge the cultural chasm did not go unappreciated. "Over and over," Amy Tapping remembered, "they patiently answered the same questions of how they happened to come to Poland, that America was not paved with gold, and that they were only trying to give back to Poland what she and America had given them . . . the girls were constantly interpreting America as no non-Polish American ever could."[44]

The Polish Grey Samaritans served in Poland for almost three years, earning the praise of American relief officials and the Polish people alike. Originally financed for the first few months by the YWCA and $10,000 contributed by the Polish Reconstruction Fund, they became the sole responsibility of the Polish government through the YWCA Warsaw office. Attached to the ARA from the beginning, they were the only relief workers to serve in Poland without regular pay. "Their work," the YWCA said, "was an act of devotion to the land of their ancestors."[45]

In the fall of 1921, at the conclusion of their long service in Poland, Herbert Hoover commended the Greys for their contribution to the American relief effort to serve the children of Poland:

> I would like to take occasion to express the gratitude we all owe and the appreciation we hold for the extraordinary service of the Grey Samaritans in Poland. The

---

42. Pastoral letter of Prince Adam Sapieha, *Czas* (May 22, 1921), p. 1.

43. *Ibid.*

44. Personal recollection, Amy Pryor Tapping, Tapping Collection, PGS Records, HI, *op. cit.*

45. *Emergency Services, YWCA, op. cit.*, p. 2.

> hardships they have undergone, the courage and resource they have shown in sheer human service is a beautiful monument to American womanhood.[46]

According to Amy Tapping, who supervised her basket of *szary kotki* with affection and devotion, the YWCA "took a long chance in training and sending back for work overseas such a group of women younger than any other group of war workers in the world."[47] Never before had an American Protestant organization worked so closely with Catholic Polonia. Tapping was justifiably proud of her charges and was aware of the precedent established by the YWCA in organizing the Greys:

> One wonders what the effect will be in the years to come; whether the venture will start a new department in Americanization possibly. In them the present stock of Poland has come to flower. Possibly as this new republic rights itself before the world and is able to undertake the large problems of education of its peoples, these girls will be a unique reminder of what education has done for its humbler classes.[48]

The YWCA saw the Polish Grey Samaritans as both Polish *and* American. The fact that they were dealing with an unknown quantity is shown time and again by Tapping's early reports to headquarters. While the young women were always considered to be Polish, they were constantly reminded to uphold the "ideals of American womanhood" as perceived by the YWCA. That they did so is reflected in the same sources. To the hundreds of thousands of Polish children served by the Greys, the unit came to symbolize the United States and the "fourth province" of Poland, American Polonia. The Greys' knowledge of the Polish language, customs, and mentality served the group, the YWCA, and the ARA very well. Their duties took them all over Poland; they withstood great hardship with stoic resolve and proudly wore a Polish eagle badge on their horizon blue uniforms as they ministered to the needy. One of the Greys, Martha Graczyk, accidently strayed over the Lithuanian border and was arrested and held until American authorities secured her release; another, Anna Kopec, died of tuberculosis she contracted at a children's refuge in Poland. The wretched conditions in which the group worked posed a constant hazard to mind and body. Not only did the Samaritans persevere, they actually triumphed over such adversity by their skill and dedication to the cause. They believed that in so doing, they served both Poland and the United States.

---

46. Letter, Herbert Hoover, ARA headquarters, New York, to Polish Grey Samaritans YWCA, Warsaw, August 15, 1921. Tapping Collection, PGS Records, HI, *op. cit.*

47. Personal recollection, Amy Pryor Tapping, Tapping Collection, PGS Records, HI, *op. cit.*

48. *Ibid.* Several of the Greys elected to remain in Poland to continue their work under the PAKPD.

Sidney Brooks of ARA headquarters, looking back from several years' perspective, stated that

> One of the most interesting phases of the child relief was the work of the Polish Grey Samaritans. We all feel that their devotion and service, given under the most trying and difficult conditions, forms a record which has no equal in American relief work in all the countries of Europe since the Armistice.[49]

Neither the successive Polish government of the interwar period nor the Polish people forgot the significance of the American relief efforts in Poland in those grim few years after World War I. Hoover was immortalized with a square in Warsaw, avenues in Kraków and Lwów, several statues, honorary doctorates, and a flood of letters, telegrams, and resolutions from Poland each year on the occasion of his birthday.[50]

When the ARA finished its mission in Poland on June 1, 1922, a government proclamation issued to Philip S. Baldwin stated that the American relief effort "has meant health and life to more than one and a half million children, thus preserving a generation for Poland, which in large part otherwise would have perished during the hard days through which our country struggled after the war."[51] At that time the Polish Parliament, by unanimous consent, made Herbert Hoover an honorary Polish citizen.

As an integral part of the American relief operation in Poland, the Grey Samaritans also shared in the outpouring of gratitude for the United States. Commended by the Polish Republic, the ARA, and the YWCA, the women returned home to the applause of Polonia, after which they resumed their lives in America.

As Polonia turned inward in the 1920s and 1930s, the Greys appeared forgotten. Nevertheless, the Polish Grey Samaritans remain a strong symbol of the role played by American Polonia in the resurrection and rehabilitation of Poland. Their contributions within the framework of the American relief program in newly independent Poland from 1919 to 1921 constitute a largely forgotten chapter in the history of Polonia which deserves to be remembered for what it surely was: an act of devotion.

---

49. Statement of Sidney Brooks, ARA headquarters, New York, September 7, 1924, in Tapping Collection, PGS Records, HI, *op. cit.*

50. Wytrwal, *op. cit.*, p. 352.

51. *Ibid.*, p. 353.

Wayward Wives and Delinquent Daughters

Polonia's Second-Generation Flappers in the Novels of Melania Nesterowicz

Karen Majewski

In the interwar years American Polonia faced a crisis of loyalties as Polish independence forced the immigrant community to reassess its relationship to the old country and to the United States. It was during this important period that Buffalo journalist Melania Nesterowicz focused several popular novels on the careers and love affairs of second-generation Polish-American *"flaperki."* Through these novels of manner Nesterowicz fashioned a dynamic model of American Polishness in which the threats of modernization and Americanization were rechanneled in order to empower the local community and reinforce ethnic loyalties. Nesterowicz's heroines, the daughters of Polish immigrants, are the first to venture out of their neighborhoods and into the commercial world, where they are seduced by materialism and embrace a new social independence. While their pursuit of an imagined America of wealth, glamour, and status compromises their connection to family and community, Nesterowicz also offers these secretaries, salesgirls, and nurses a way back to an ethnic home of their own creation. Her novels offer a contemporary, insider's view of Polonia's struggle for a cultural identity in the crucial period between the wars.

Nesterowicz's interest in the future of Polonia, particularly as shaped by Polish American women, grew out of her professional and personal experience. She was born Melania Habdank-Białobrzeska in Warsaw in 1876. After finishing teacher's training she intended to study medicine in Switzerland, specializing in mental illness, but instead in 1894 she married Stefan Nesterowicz, an adventurer, world

---

This article is a revised version of a paper delivered at the annual meeting of the Polish American Historical Association in Atlanta, Georgia, January 5, 1996.

From *Polish American Studies*, vol. 53, no. 1 (Spring 1996), pp. 5–16.

traveler, pharmacist, and newspaperman twenty-five years her senior. The couple and their two children emigrated first to Brazil, and finally, sometime before 1907, to the United States, where both began working for the notorious Antoni Paryski on his Toledo, Ohio-based newspaper, *Ameryka-Echo.* In the years leading up to World War I, editorials by Melania Nesterowicz appeared regularly in the paper, often signed with the pseudonym "Jan Kłos." In these years, too, her first published fiction appeared, in both newspaper serialization and in pamphlet form. Generally speaking, these were short exemplary works with titles like "Siódme przykazanie" [The seventh commandment], *Pan Krzywda,* and *Życia analfabety* [From the life of an illiterate], all published between 1907 and 1908. In this last-mentioned work a gum-chewing salesclerk rejects her immigrant suitor, humiliating him in front of her newfound American friends when he reveals that, despite his best efforts, he has never learned to read or write. Her character is a precursor of the heroine who would in various shapes continue to inhabit Nesterowicz's full-length novels of the 1920s and 1930s—the second-generation career woman in her often misguided search for love, success, and social status.

In 1917 Nesterowicz began work for Buffalo's *Dziennik dla Wszystkich,* which she edited from 1921–33, and with which she continued to be affiliated into the 1940s. Although her husband returned to Poland in 1922, dying in Lwów nine years later, Nesterowicz remained in the United States. In the 1930s, the Polish government awarded her the *Polonia Restituta.* She also received the Independence Cross, the Legionnaire's Cross, and the Polish Academy of Literature's silver Laurel of Merit. After leaving *Dziennik dla Wszystkich,* Nesterowicz lived with her daughter's family in Wilkes-Barre, Pennsylvania, until her death in 1951.

It was in the pages of *Dziennik dla Wszystkich* during her tenure there that Nesterowicz serialized the full-length novels which the rest of this paper will discuss. The first of these, and in many ways the richest, was *Stella z Buffalo* [Stella from Buffalo], published in 1926–27. *Hot-Cha-Cha* appeared in 1934. But the most popular of Nesterowicz's novels was probably *Sprzedawaczka z Broadwayu* [The Salesgirl from Broadway], which was serialized in 1932 and reprinted in 1933 in the monthly literary magazine *Jaskółka,* affiliated with Stevens Point, Wisconsin's *Gwiazda Polarna. The Salesgirl from Broadway* was also turned into a radio play, and in 1937 was published in book form. In fact, Detroit's *Tygodnik Swiat Polski* reserialized this novel in 1993–94, when an old copy of it fell serendipitously into the editor's hands. Nesterowicz may be the author of other novels as well—also attributed to her is *Tajemnice Nieślubnego Dziecka* [The Secret of the Illegitimate Child], which suggests the general flavor of Nesterowicz's subject matter. All of her novels in *Dziennik* were printed anonymously, like many of the other works serialized in the paper. About Nesterowicz's tendency to leave her works unsigned or to use a male pseudonym, Detroit's *Dziennik Polski* speculated in the 1940s that

Melania Nesterowicz
Courtesy of Basia Kocyan McCoy of Wilkes-Barre, Pennsylvania.

"Maybe it was a female inferiority complex. Maybe she lacked the manly courage to look the cruel demands of life bravely in the eye."[1] This explanation is especially ludicrous considering Nesterowicz's controversial subject matter and the barriers and prejudices her female characters confront, as well as her own professional struggles. Nesterowicz herself was not interested in artistic recognition. In her own words:

> I didn't care at all about any kind of renown as a novel writer. I cared primarily about a pedagogical goal, to instruct our people on how they should live and advance in the great circumstances of life. From my journalistic experience I know that at every step in our emigrant affairs mistakes are made and faults committed which

1. J. K., "Los pracownicy pióra," *Zgoda*, June, 1947 [repr. from *Dziennik Polski*, Detroit]. All translations are my own.

> harm us, but which are caused by ignorance. But if a handful of readers benefit by my writing, that's a great reward for me.[2]

Certainly as a journalist (and particularly as a journalist apprenticed under Paryski, that master at reading—and perhaps at writing—his public), Nesterowicz was aware of her audience's interests and concerns, and of the social problems of their day-to-day lives. Under her editorship, the pages of *Dziennik dla Wszystkich* reflect those interests, with plenty of stories of divorces, love triangles, criminal trials, and the lives of the rich and famous, the same material that fills her novels. She also provided a voice to Polonia's leftist elements, with which she was herself involved, although overtly political questions are rarely readable in her fiction.

Her newspaper work also provided the inspiration for her storytelling. "Generally," she explains, "after returning from the editorial office if I didn't have a meeting or some pressing work, I wrote the chapter of a novel treating what I had seen or heard in the course of the day."[3] The haphazardness of this literary technique is apparent in sometimes abrupt shifts in characterization and rambling story lines. At times she seems even to have forgotten what names she has given her characters. On the other hand, it's hard to see how even the secrets to which a journalist is privy could have inspired some of her more fanciful turns of plot, such as the conclusion of *Hot-Cha-Cha,* in which to spare him the prejudices he would confront in America, the heroine takes her mixed-race son to the south sea island of his father's ancestors in order to establish an outpost of Polishness, a New Poland. Here is a re-telling of the immigrant epic, in which the founding myth is rewritten in recognition of America's troubled pluralism. Without ceasing to love America or the American Polonia of her parents, a second-generation woman envisions an alternative world of tolerance in which one's roots in varied soils can be honored and nurtured. When he gets old enough, she vows, her son will learn the Polish language and travel with her to Poland, where his dark skin will presumably be no obstacle. Likewise, new emigrants will not only find a home on this Polish colony, but the original inhabitants will welcome them as linked to themselves by new ties of blood.

Behind this remarkable scenario is the theme that unites these novels, and which Nesterowicz saw as a primary issue for her readership—the second generation's ongoing struggle with identity and direction, which she focused through the prism of the ethnically-charged romance. In all these novels the heroines use romantic relationships to refashion their identities, playing out alternative ethnic scenarios before "finding themselves" in their Polishness, before making a Polish

2. Artur L. Waldo, *Zarys historii literatury polskiej w Ameryce: Szkic bibliograficzny* (Chicago: Nakł. Dziennika Zjednoczenia, 1938), 33.

3. *Ibid.*

home for themselves and their families. This pattern stands in stark contrast with the canonical paradigm described by scholars of ethnic literature like Mary Dearborn.[4] Concerning English-language immigrant fiction, the accepted wisdom has favored assimilationist, mediated readings, noting the recurrence of inter-ethnic marriages which carry the immigrant into American society and interpret ethnic culture for American readers. On the other hand, the Polish-language fiction, that is, the literature written within and for the immigrant and ethnic community itself, overturns this pattern.

Specifically, despite the second generation's attraction to and engagement within the world outside the ethnic enclave, particularly in terms of career and consumer-driven romance, it is only through marriage within the ethnic group that one becomes a better Pole and a better American, or, to use Nesterowicz's preferred term, a better American of Polish descent. The "material girl" of *The Salesgirl from Broadway*, for example, after treacherous associations with American men, learns to love her Polish-American husband and takes her place in the community which is itself changing under the influence of her generation. Stella, despite a scandalous past, finds purpose and true love on a trip to Poland during its turbulent early days of independence. And Róża, nicknamed "Hot-Cha-Cha" by her American dance-hall companions, makes a disastrous marriage with an American millionaire before recreating herself as the Mother of a New Poland.

It is clear that in Nesterowicz's case the Polish Academy of Literature's Laurel of Merit was not based on artistic strength alone, but must rather have been awarded in recognition of the author's work on behalf of Poland as a political reality and as a cultural ideal. Her colleagues, the writers and journalists of the great wave migration, had in the years leading up to the First World War used literature to help create a Polish national identity among their former peasant readership. After Polish independence, Nesterowicz refocused this journalistic mission. At the same time that a disoriented Polonia was forced to reconsider its relationship to the European homeland and to the America of which it was now a part, a new, native-born generation was coming of age in a dizzying society which seemed to many to have lost its moral guideposts. Nesterowicz addresses the question of Polonia's future in such a society through ethnic soap operas which conflate family and nation in order to create a model of second-generation Polish identity. She takes her heroines along a trajectory that leads farther and father away from home—from Buffalo's Polish east side, from family and familiar ethnic touchstones. But for Nesterowicz the path is circular, and propelled by undeniable ties of blood her characters can find fulfillment only by reconstructing and reinhabiting their ethnic selves.

4. See Mary Dearborn, *Pocahontas' Daughters: Gender and Ethnicity in American Culture* (New York: Oxford University Press, 1986).

Historian Thaddeus Radzilowski asks that we recognize the second generation's active role in the fabrication of much of what we have come to think of as American Polonian culture, through its synthesis of oppositional new and old world influences.[5] He cautions against characterizing the second generation as the dupe of materialism, trading its birthright for a spot of lawn and a new Ford. But Nesterowicz's characters are drawn dangerously close to this trap, and her treatment of their treacherous relation to the sources of money and power is ambiguous and troubling.

American men, particularly the recurring figure of the penniless ne'er-do-well from a respectable and powerful family, prey on the affections and passions of the Polonian young women who see in them the key to the American ancestral mansion. As might be expected, these men more often than not deceive and abandon their lovers, taking their money, their virtue, and their good names. Irena, the salesgirl from Broadway, is tricked by an old flame into handing over thousands of dollars in exchange for a fake movie contract and a few kisses. Róża deceives her Polish American husband by continuing to work for her former beau, the millionaire who still pursues her and who eventually marries and deserts her. Stella's liaison with an American under the thumb of his powerful family leads to the secret birth and death of an illegitimate child, and to charges of murder against Stella. These relationships, holding the promise of a life outside Polonia, of the Americanization through marriage so prominent and so positive in the general discussion of ethnic literature, are not only doomed to failure, but even in their best moments threaten the second-generation's relationship to family, to community, and to their own better selves.

Of course, the impoverished young man from a prominent family is certainly a type that had its counterpart in Polish society as well. Such a character occurs only once in Nesterowicz's novels, under very odd circumstances. The first husband of former party-girl Róża, a poor but noble-hearted Polish American musician and composer with the unlikely-sounding name of "Dżordż Kolt," is discovered to come from a royal family which has lost its lands to the Bolsheviks. Although he and Róża enjoy some short-lived notoriety ("Here in America a princely title has great significance," Dżordż assures his wife in all seriousness)[6] and although they briefly entertain the hope of riches, this subplot is barely developed before being dropped altogether. Interestingly, although a leftist, Nesterowicz is uncritical of the Polish nobility, while unmitigatingly disapproving of the American rich. In fact, it

---

5. Thaddeus Radzilowski, "The Second Generation: An Unknown Polonia." *Polish American Studies,* Vol. 43, No. 1 (1986), p. 8.

6. Melania Nesterowicz, "Hot-Cha-Cha: Opowiadanie z życia młodzieży polskiej w Buffalo," *Dziennik dla Wszystkich,* June 18, 1934.

appears to be his noble blood that provides Kolt with his artistic sensibilities. But Nesterowicz insistently links American wealth not with the mythical drive, determination, and creative vision of the legendary self-made man, but with inherited privilege perpetuated through bigotry and resulting in arrogance, corruption, and dishonor.

On the other hand, while unequivocally representing the heartbreak and disruption of the social order that results from these exogamous relationships, Nesterowicz also allows Polish-American women, their ethnic communities, and Poland itself to reap very real benefits from them, not simply in terms of money, but in the use to which American wealth can be put. Róża's divorce from her second husband, the American with the Polynesian princess for a great-great-great grandmother—more specifically, her triumph over his charge that their dark-skinned child is a product of Róża's own adultery—guarantees millions of dollars for her and her baby son. It is with this money that she is able to create a Polish island paradise. The death of Stella's long-time admirer leaves her millions with which to aid the newly-independent Poland and Buffalo's Polonia. America's inherited wealth is made clean through its use in service to Poland and to Polonia, as it is rechanneled into the development of a more socially responsible ethnic community and the reconstruction of the ancestral homeland. This becomes possible only when the second generation is able to create a balance between what are inherently unequal, power-driven relationships—between men and women, between wealth and poverty, between American and Pole.

What attracts these women to American society is not only the romance of the high life and the hope of material gain. A range of conditions and attitudes pull them toward what they imagine to be American life at the same time that they are pushed away from ethnic identification by American prejudice and by Polonia's own failings. The second generation is shown to be painfully aware of the low regard in which Poles are held within America-at-large, of "the poisonous propaganda of the one hundred percenters against the 'undesirable' immigrants from eastern and southern Europe [which] revealed itself at every step."[7] Nor, they discover, is American birth a passport to nativeness. "I was born in America," Stella keeps reminding people, who despite surprise at her perfect English never manage to see her as anything but a foreigner.[8] American-born Stan realizes that the opportunity for professional training he received when he left his country for the society of the Polish intelligentsia in Paris would not have been given him in America, where he

7. Melania Nesterowicz, "Stella z Buffalo: Powieść na tie życia polsko-amerykańskiego," *Dziennik dla Wszystkich*, April 12, 1927.

8. *Ibid.*, December 18, 1926.

was always considered an outsider. It was his "good Polish name" that opened doors for him in Europe, the same name that closed those doors in the land of his birth.

But the fault is not all with American nativism. Although the immigrant parents of her heroines are always honorable and good people, even if "a little backward,"[9] they are also implicated in their daughters' mistakes. In their misguided desire to give their children easier lives than they have had, they fail to give them the skills and values necessary for good character. Rather, the immigrant parents stand in awe of their attractive, American-born children, unable to believe that these lovely creatures are their own creations. Their deference not only leaves the second generation ill-equipped for adulthood, but it places these sons and daughters on the margins of family life. The Polish-American "princesses" whose hands are thought too delicate for the housework of their mothers, grow up with little sense of responsibility or accountability. The self-absorbed Irena not only employs an African-American maid (unfortunately named "Sambo"), but even hires her own mother to keep house for her! Her attempt to make a place in what she perceives to be American well-to-do society causes her to violate her rightful place within her family. In fact, she refuses to recognize herself as either wife or daughter, turning both relationships into commercial ones which can, presumably, be exchanged or renegotiated for more favorable terms. The danger is that the second generation's marginality, which allows them to function in more than one social world, prevents them from belonging unequivocally to any of those worlds. Without that belonging, without that sense of one's rightful place in relation to others and without, Nesterowicz reminds us over and over, the influences of neighborhood gossip and finger-pointing, social controls break down. Such is the case for the orphan Róża who, as a well-paid stenographer, lives in a boardinghouse, and who "could go where she wanted and with whom she wanted, not needing to consider the opinion and criticism of a mother or father, brother or sister."[10] But without those social controls these young women are endangered as they maneuver in the unfamiliar territory they know mainly from advertisements and movie fantasies.

Nesterowicz was no moral conservative, however. About Stella's pregnancy by her American lover the narrator says, "Human feeling isn't shameful. . . . It's not a crime that, because of a burst of passion for the man she loves, Stella will become a mother. But it's terribly reckless, bordering on the criminal, that Stella will give life to a child under such conditions, and sentence such a defenseless little creature to life's cruel battle."[11] Nesterowicz operates within the material dreamworlds of her readers, exciting and deflating their Hollywood-fed romantic fantasies, and bringing

---

9. "Stella z Buffalo," *Dziennik dla Wszystkich,* December 8, 1926.
10. "Hot-Cha-Cha," *Dziennik dla Wszystkich,* May 21, 1934.
11. "Stella z Buffalo," *Dziennik dla Wszystkich,* March 7, 1927.

them back to the consequences of their actions, consequences which are played out not just in the broken hearts of her heroines, but in the home, in the community, in the nation, and in the larger world.

Collectively, Nesterowicz suggests, immigrant Polonia has been judged inadequate by its second generation—intellectually, culturally, and materially—and has failed to provide an attractive alternative for its educated and worldly children. At the same time, she exhibits sympathy toward the struggles of working-class rust-generation immigrants like Irena's mother, who "cleaned offices downtown" when she arrived from the old country[12] and like Stella's, who "for thirty-odd years . . . had not stirred beyond Buffalo."[13] The moral voice in Nesterowicz's novels belongs to these immigrants, and is echoed by the second-generation young women who do marry neighborhood boys and whose struggles with poverty are sweetened by their love for their husbands and for their children. Like Stella herself, her American lover fails to recognize the virtues and attractions of such a life: "What to do?" wonders Stef Mitchell, "Move in with the Kowalskis. Marry Stella and every morning eat the breakfast her mother makes, put my 'luncz' in my pocket and go to work with my wife. And at night head to the saloon for a beer with her father and listen to him tell stories about Piłsudski in broken English."[14]

Stella's father, broken English and all, is shown to be the infinitely more honorable character. At the same time, Nesterowicz clearly understands the dreams and ambitions that entice the wayward daughters of working-class Polonia away from this life. It is their experiences in the white-collar workforce that open their eyes to these alternatives. After beginning to earn her own living as a stenographer in a downtown office, Stella announces, "I'm a free woman, independent of my father and mother."[15] Not only does she rebel against her parents' "old-fashioned" ways, refusing to carry a bag lunch to the office or to bring her American beaus into the house, she also rejects the "life 'in Poland'" she sees ahead of her on the East Side:

> a life like the one her girlfriends led. Children, a poor apartment, furniture bought on installment, with no possibility of rising to the sphere of millionaires, where sensation and amusement make life pleasant, where you don't have to worry about trifles, where even though women don't have a slough of children they still manage to be happy.[16]

While Nesterowicz paints Americans like "Stef" with a stiff brush, treating them as largely interchangeable symbols of threatening and seductive social and

12. "Sprzedawaczka z Broadwayu," *Dziennik dla Wszystkich,* November 14, 1932.
13. "Stella z Buffalo," *Dziennik dla Wszystkich,* February 7, 1927.
14. *Ibid.*, February 28, 1927.
15. *Ibid.*, December 15, 1926.
16. *Ibid.*, December 22, 1926.

economic forces, she is sensitive and sympathetic to the varied voices within American Polonia, and to its own social hierarchies. For instance, at Irena's wedding to Dr. Patocki, who belongs to Polonia's *śmietanka,* recognizable but not uncrossable lines are acknowledged between the families of the bride and groom: "What are we doing here with such educated, high class people," [Irena's parents] asked each other. "Irena will get along fine as their daughter-in-law. That girl knows how to look after herself. But we won't try to win their favor. They're not *that* rich."[17] And the discomfort of Irena's old friends suggest alternative, concurrent Polonian experiences: "What a wedding!" a bridesmaid complains. "If all great people get married like this, I prefer to marry Piotr. His father is only a *buczer,* but I'm sure our wedding will last three days and everybody will have a good time."[18]

Eventually, whatever its faults and failings, however annoying its gossip and scrutiny, this Polish neighborhood pulls Nesterowicz's heroines back to the fold. It finally proves all the more attractive in contrast to the strange places through which these young women have wandered, even as Polish-American husbands become all the dearer in contrast to the American admirers who fail the tests of mature and responsible love. The new commitment to their Polish American lovers and husbands translates into a parallel commitment to American Polonia, including the old ethnic neighborhood, which is refigured through these unions into the hope of Poland and America. Stella Kowalski's father describes a future in which Polish-Americans are Buffalo's "dominant element":

> There will be as many of us in Buffalo as sands on the banks of Lake Erie, and we will become a cohesive group which will not break its ties with Poland, but will cooperate closely with the former homeland in cultural and artistic affairs. Our Polish genius will emerge in all the fields of science, art, industry, and business. . . .
>
> In the future our Stella and Stan will take the position they deserve in the American homeland. And the sooner they become educated, the quicker it will happen.[19]

What has brought Stella's father to this conviction, and brought Stella and Stan together, is their renewed love for Poland. Nesterowicz's characters are bound not just to Buffalo's Polish east side but finally, they must realize, to Poland itself, the neglected lover who always lingers in the background. Nesterowicz's heroines all come to reclaim their Polishness, nowhere more visibly than in *Stella from Buffalo,* in which the heroine falls in love simultaneously with Poland and with the former Buffalo "sheik" whose perspective was once limited to mechanics and sports, but who has been turned into a "serious, soulful soldier, with exquisite manners" by his

17. "Sprzedawaczka z Broadwayu," *Dziennik dla Wszystkich,* November 15, 1932.
18. *Ibid.,* November 15, 1932.
19. "Stella z Buffalo," *Dziennik dla Wszystkich,* May 21, 1927.

participation in Poland's struggles for independence.[20] Looking about her on the streets of Warsaw, Stella sees both a nation and a family: "These people were not foreigners—they were her people, close to her. They were the brothers she hadn't seen for so long, and had now rediscovered."[21]

But the love for Poland which Nesterowicz idealizes does not alienate the second generation from the America which has seduced and disappointed them. Rather, it underscores their fundamental claim there, not as foreigners, but as natives whose dedication to Poland infuses America with noble purpose. "Already I love Poland," Stella marvels, "and what's even stranger is that when I began to feel this love for the newly-discovered homeland of my parents, my love for America was awakened."[22] At the same time, their experience as Americans brings not only much-needed dollars, but democratic idealism to the reborn nation. When in the turmoil of Poland's first days of independence the doctors and nurses at Warsaw's hospital are ordered not to treat Piłsudski's wounded soldiers, Stella wraps herself in the American flag she has brought from Buffalo and "as an American citizen" rallies others to the soldiers' aid: "Long live Stella!" they cry. "Long live the United States! Long live the Brightest Republic! Long live Marshall Piłsudski!"[23]

Nesterowicz's work held out the hope that education and upward mobility, rather than alienating the second generation from the ethnic community, could awaken a deeper appreciation for Polonia and a stronger love for Poland—that not only could America turn out patriotic Poles, as it had in the days of Poland's subjugation, but that the love of Poland could encourage American patriotism in Polonia's youth. For Nesterowicz the two were complementary, and their combination offered the best hope for Poland and for Polish America. "You young Americans of Polish descent . . . must finally understand," Stella's father points out, "that the bonds of blood are not easily broken, and in fact there is no reason to break them."[24] Stan articulates Nesterowicz's model for proper Polishness in America: "We'll return to our American homeland," he says. "But the memory of Poland will remain in our hearts, and we'll visit Poland as often as we can, in order to replenish our patriotic spirit and make ourselves glad with the sight of the reborn Homeland of our ancestors."[25]

Nesterowicz's characters wander over an uncertain map, drawing it as they go, but this map inevitably leads them, if not permanently back to Europe, then to a self-created, newly-designed Polish colony which can exist in Polynesia as well

20. *Ibid.*, May 10, 1927.
21. *Ibid.*
22. *Ibid.*, May 11, 1927.
23. *Ibid.*, May 12, 1927.
24. *Ibid.*, May 14, 1927.
25. *Ibid.*, May 12, 1927.

as on Buffalo's East Side. But, Nesterowicz admonishes her readers, Poland is the compass point by which they should navigate. At a time in the 1920s and 1930s when disillusionment about the resurrected Polish state had already set in and the fever of return had subsided, Nesterowicz's novels challenge readers to integrate Poland into their American world, to re-embrace Poland, and to dedicate themselves to service on behalf of both the ethnic community and the old country. It is only through this service, made possible by unequivocally embracing their identity as Americans of Polish descent, that the second generation can build a home for itself and give birth to the generation to follow. Polonia must love Poland, Nesterowicz suggests, in order to love and reproduce itself. "All my hopes are fulfilled, and my sorrows have flown," rejoices Stella, the new bride. "It's Poland that did that," Stan answers. "You're right," says Stella. "It's Poland."[26]

26. *Ibid.*

Scouting for Identity

Recruiting Daughters to Save the Traditional Polish Family During the Interwar Years

Lori A. Matten

A sampling of articles from the Polish Roman Catholic Union's newspapers during the 1920s suggests a serious concern about Polish girls' waywardness. Two typical comments read as follows:

> There exists in Chicago a girls' club called the "Flappers." The Polish definition given to them is "blockheads in the highest degree," because they are persons opposed to dignity and respect. They wear short skirts or dresses and want everyone to speak about them. Our clergy preaches a great deal about them, denouncing their style and cautions Polish girls to shun those "blockheads."[1]

• • •

> We have written many times before about our girls strolling around the city, lingering at hotels of questionable character, and their frequenting all kinds of Venetian gardens in the company of the worst type. . . . The object of this article is not to convert the already fallen girl—although it is never too late to reform—but to warn and save other young girls from the same fate and to warn mothers who do not realize the dangers to which their daughters are exposed by going out with strangers. Therefore, we appeal to mothers, especially to those who are fascinated by their daughters' beautiful faces and who dress their daughters far beyond their means, but never criticize their behavior, permitting them to go out with all kinds of "fine beaux". . . . Who is to blame—these naïve girls who chase the glittering trifles of life? No, a hundred times, No! The whole fault lies with those parents who suffer with the delusion of grandeur and to whom a Pole [as a suitor] means nothing.[2]

---

1. As cited and translated in John Radzilowski, *The Eagle and the Cross: A History of the Polish Roman Catholic Union of America, 1873–2000* (Boulder: East European Monographs, 2003), 191. Original citation, *Dziennik Zjednoczenia*, April 19, 1922.

2. As cited and translated in Radzilowski, *The Eagle and the Cross*, 192. Original citation, Editorial, *Naród Polski*, January 19, 1921, CFLPS IB3b. Brackets added by Radzilowski.

From *Polish American Studies*, vol. 71, no. 1 (Spring 2014), pp. 5–36.

Such anxiety about Polonia's youth was a common refrain during the 1920s and 1930s. Polish girls' flirtation with mainstream American culture—especially the dance halls and slick American men associated with the flapper, or "flaperki," lifestyle—was particularly alarming, as it called into question their ability to sustain the traditional Polish family. What sort of mothers would these "flaperki" make? What if they chose not to marry Polish men? How could Polonia continue to thrive without the Polish family, its most basic building block? Could it maintain its distinctiveness as an ethnic community? Or would it simply blend into the great American melting pot?

That these fears of assimilation were projected onto young Polish girls perhaps suggests that gender played a significant role in Polonia's attempt to grapple with its interwar identity crisis. An investigation of Polish scouting, one of the most popular youth programs during this era, supports this contention. Because it allows for comparison of sex-segregated ethnic youth organizations to each other as well as to their American counterparts, Polish scouting serves as a particularly useful case study. More specifically, the development of the Polish Roman Catholic Union's program of scouting for girls in the 1930s—Córy Zjednoczenia (Daughters of the Union)—suggests a concerted effort to retard the process of assimilation by encouraging young girls to embrace their Polish heritage, thereby preserving the traditional Polish family.

Chicago's Polonia: From "Poles in America" to "Polish Americans" (Late Nineteenth Century–World War I)

Following their arrival to Chicago in large numbers in the late nineteenth century, Polish immigrants have engaged in debates about the essence of their identity. The majority of these immigrants left behind lives as rural peasants in partitioned Poland in search of new economic opportunities in the New World. Political émigrés of the gentry class, however, continued to remain more invested in the affairs of the mother country, viewing Polonia as the "fourth partition of Poland" rather than as a fresh start in an adopted country.[3] These "nationalists," with their singular focus on the goal of achieving Poland's independence, were bound to conflict with the "religionists" who equated true Polishness with Roman Catholicism.

That these early debates about identity would coalesce around religion should come as no surprise as the majority of these immigrants brought with them a fierce loyalty to their Roman Catholic religion. For rural peasants living in a partitioned nation, religion went beyond the spiritual, taking on a political meaning as a "symbol

3. Edward R. Kantowicz, *Polish-American Politics in Chicago, 1888–1940* (Chicago: University of Chicago Press, 1975), 8.

of resistance to the partitioning powers."[4] Their devotion to Roman Catholicism continued in the United States where parishes were among the first institutions that they established. The majority of the immigrants readily aligned with the "religionist" camp led by clerics who argued that religious identity trumped any nationalist sentiments associated with their mother country. As Victor Greene contends, "The religionists insisted that a Pole could only be Roman Catholic, and that the primary function of the community in America was to maintain that identity."[5] In contrast, the "nationalists" contended that the primary goal of Polonia was to work toward the independence of Poland. As Greene summarizes, "Thus, as the work of the nationality was mainly political, a member's religion was of secondary importance; a Pole could be Jew, Protestant, Greek Catholic, or Roman Catholic."[6] Although the nationalists showed considerable strength initially, the religionist argument eventually shaped the course of Polonia's history, resulting in the marginalization of non-Catholics from most studies of Polish immigration.[7] The founding of rival fraternal organizations—the Polish Roman Catholic Union (PRCU) in 1873 and the Polish National Alliance (PNA) in 1880—ensured that the debate surrounding Polish identity would linger in Polonia.[8]

In the midst of these discussions about identity, Polish immigrants established ethnic institutions to address their needs, the top priority of which was the parish. For the Polish immigrants, the parish church meant more than simply a place to worship; it was a community center.[9] From baptism to last rites, the parish managed every stage of life.[10] By the 1930s, Chicago alone counted forty-four Polish Roman

---

4. James S. Pula, *Polish Americans: An Ethnic Community* (New York: Twayne, 1995), 20.

5. Victor Greene, *For God and Country: The Rise of Polish and Lithuanian Ethnic Consciousness in America, 1860–1910* (Madison: The State Historical Society of Wisconsin, 1975), 67.

6. Greene, *For God and Country*, 67.

7. John J. Bukowczyk, "Polish Americans, History Writing, and the Organization of Memory" in *Polish Americans and Their History: Community, Culture, and Politics*, ed. Bukowczyk (Pittsburgh: University of Pittsburgh Press, 1996), 8.

8. A third faction, "independentism," emerged in Polonia in the mid-1890s, which focused on the issue of control of parish resources. Whereas most Polish pastors contended that local church assets should be controlled by them and their non-Polish superiors, independents argued that the ethnic congregation should be in charge of parish resources. Ultimately, this movement resulted in the founding of the Polish National Catholic Church (PNCC). The religionist camp obviously viewed this movement with great concern, referring to the establishment of PNCC congregations as a "schism." See Greene, *For God and Country*, ch. 6.

9. Kantowicz, *Polish-American Politics in Chicago*, 30.

10. Lizabeth Cohen, *Making a New Deal: Industrial Workers in Chicago, 1919–1939* (Cambridge: Cambridge University Press, 1990), 85.

Catholic parishes.[11] Once the parish was founded, the community worked diligently to set up the parish school. These schools, staffed by women of Polish religious orders, emphasized the Polish language and Polish heritage.[12] As historian James S. Pula notes, "[T]he purpose of the parish school was *not* to speed assimilation; rather, its goal was to preserve cultural and religious values."[13] As such, English was taught as a foreign language. After founding the parish and school, the Polish immigrants proceeded to create self-sufficient communities that mitigated the need, at least initially, to learn English.

Whereas Edward Kantowicz contends that Polonia created isolated ethnic enclaves, Dominic A. Pacyga suggests that Chicago's immigrant neighborhoods are best described as "spatially integrated, but socially segregated."[14] Polish immigrants may have had occasion to interact with other ethnic groups at work or in the neighborhood, but most were able to satisfy their needs within their own community. They lived, worshipped, and fraternized within walking distance of their homes. Beyond the family, the neighborhood—the *okolica*—was central to the Polish immigrant's identity, for it was here that one's reputation was known. Indeed, fear of damaging one's honor served as an effective mechanism for controlling behavior.[15] The peasant culture's traditional attachment to land, when combined with this concern for status, translated into a strong desire for homeownership in the Polish immigrant community. To assist in the process of home ownership, they formed neighborhood building and loan associations.[16] Offering additional support to the immigrants were the fraternal organizations, which initially provided death benefit insurance but eventually expanded their services to meet the evolving needs of the community. While the fraternals and the expanding Polish press connected Polish neighborhoods across the city, the most significant relationships remained in the *okolica*.

Thus, prior to the outbreak of World War I, Chicago's Poles developed thriving and insular communities. Rather than being completely uprooted, these immigrants managed to create institutions in the United States that preserved their most

11. Frederick J. Augustyn Jr. "Together and Apart: Lithuanian and Polish Immigrant Adult Literacy Programs in Chicago, 1890–1930," *Polish American Studies* 57, no. 2 (Autumn 2000), 38.

12. Thaddeus C. Radzilowski, "Family, Women, and Gender" in *Polish Americans and Their History: Community, Culture, and Politics*, ed. John J. Bukowczyk (Pittsburgh: University of Pittsburgh Press, 1996), 74.

13. Pula, *Polish Americans*, 21.

14. Dominic A. Pacyga, *Polish Immigrants and Industrial Chicago: Workers on the South Side, 1880–1922* (Chicago: University of Chicago Press, 1991), 56; Kantowicz, *Polish-American Politics in Chicago*, 26.

15. Pula, *Polish Americans*, 23.

16. Greene, *For God and Country*, 39.

treasured cultural values from the Old World. Such "institutional completeness in Polonia"[17] mitigated the need for them to assimilate into the host society. Indeed, some even remained open to the possibility of returning to Poland given a change in the political situation. Because Polish immigrants in Chicago successfully transplanted so much of their Old World culture, they most readily identified as "Poles in America." As Victor Greene notes, "Few incoming Poles after 1900 needed to suffer cultural shock in this city where over 150,000 of them lived in the so-called 'American Warsaw.'"[18]

World War I, however, was a turning point for American Polonia. With the outbreak of the war, the Polish immigrant community united to aid the mother country. In addition to financial and moral support, nearly 40,000 Polish Americans volunteered to fight in the Polish Army, eventually coming under the command of General Józef Haller.[19] With the U.S. entry into the war and President Wilson's explicit support of Polish independence—the thirteenth of his famed "Fourteen Points"—opportunities for Polish Americans to contribute to the war effort increased. Far exceeding their proportion of the population, over 200,000 Polish Americans served in the U.S. Army during the war.[20] Aid to Poland continued in the postwar years as a variety of organizations, both within Polonia and in the broader American society, raised funds to rebuild wartorn Europe. The YMCA trained ninety bilingual Polish American girls—the "Grey Samaritans"—to work as nurses in postwar Poland.[21] In short, the war created new roles for Polish immigrants.

With the end of hostilities, Polonia had two reasons to celebrate: the Allied victory and the prospect of a re-created Polish nation. Once Poland finally achieved its independence—the nationalists' dream for decades—returning to the mother country suddenly became a viable option. While some members of Polonia did return to Poland, most of their reports suggested disillusionment with the difficult postwar economic situation. Indeed, many of these postwar hopefuls eventually reimmigrated back to the United States. In addition, many grew increasingly frustrated by Poland's paternalistic attitudes toward Polonia. For these reasons, the Polish immigrant community finally resolved to stay in the United States for good.

Accordingly, Polonia turned its attention to the domestic scene in the interwar years, particularly the arduous work of working out a new identity. As the promise of successful resettlement in Poland faded, so too did the Polish immigrants' use of the term "Poles in America." Indeed, newspapers in Polonia shifted from use of the

17. This phrase is attributed to Frank Renkiewicz as cited in Pula, *Polish Americans*, 38.
18. Greene, *For God and Country*, 58.
19. Pula, *Polish Americans*, 60.
20. Ibid., *Polish Americans*, 59–60.
21. Ibid., 62.

terms "We Poles" or "Poles in America" to "Polish-Americans."[22] As the community worked out the exact meaning of its hyphenated identity, disagreements about the degree and pace of assimilation inevitably surfaced.

"Polish Americans" in the Interwar Years: The "Youth Problem" Forges a Cultural Mosaic

The debates about assimilation during the interwar years reveal typical cleavages between the first and second generations. While the former resisted assimilation, the latter more willingly accepted the inevitability of this process. Both camps, however, expressed a common concern for the problems plaguing Polonia's youth: juvenile delinquency, morally remiss "flaperki" girls, and Polish cultural illiteracy. Much of the blame for the youth problem was placed on the parents who were failing to establish proper Polish homes. Some in Polonia sought to resolve this crisis by reaffirming the Polishness of Polish American families. In doing so, they advanced a culturally pluralistic vision of the United States.

Long-standing prejudices against "new immigrants" and perceived deficiencies in the Polish family shaped the debates about assimilation during the interwar years. Although some of the earlier criticism was deflected by the loyal service of immigrants during the war, the drive for 100 percent Americanism nonetheless continued well into the 1920s, epitomized by the enactment of a series of restrictive immigration laws. The nativists' disregard for Polish Americans was rooted in three areas: religion (mainstream Protestants had a long-standing intolerance for Catholics), racism (eugenics-based language favored Anglo-Saxons/Teutonics over Slavic Poles), and a general resentment of immigrants as economic competitors.[23] Moreover, the 1919 study by sociologists William I. Thomas and Florian Znaniecki promulgated the image of the dysfunctional Polish immigrant family and its delinquent youth.[24] While some members of Polonia responded to these external forces by rejecting assimilation, others attempted to "Americanize."

This "Americanization" of Polish Americans was most notable in the increased use of the English language. Polish-language newspapers during the interwar years typically included more English and "American" elements such as sports sections, crossword puzzles, and comic strips.[25] Moreover, the Chicago Society, an organization

22. Kantowicz, *Polish-American Politics in Chicago*, 163, 169.

23. Janice E. Kleeman, "Polish-American Assimilation: The Interaction of Opportunity and Attitude," *Polish American Studies* 42, no. 1 (1985): 11–16.

24. William I. Thomas and Florian Znaniecki, *The Polish Peasant in Europe and America* (Boston: Richard G. Badger, 1918–1920; and ed. Eli Zaretsky (Urbana: University of Illinois Press, 1984).

25. Pula, *Polish Americans*, 73–74; Kantowicz, *Polish-American Politics in Chicago*, 170.

composed of successful second generation "elites," willingly embraced the English language, preferring to conduct meetings in it rather than in Polish. Their advocacy of English literacy as a necessary precursor for social mobility aligned them with contemporary Anglo Progressive reformers.[26] The increasing use of English among the second generation was particularly irksome to the established leadership of the fraternals. The PRCU leadership was accused of "making 'a pariah out of any young Polish boy or girl' unable to speak fluent Polish" and using "'the language barrier as a means of retaining control of the organization.'"[27] The increasing preference for English, therefore, heralded the assimilation of Polish Americans and triggered fears about the continued existence of a distinctive Polish community.

Inevitably, these fears prompted an alternative response: fierce resistance to assimilation. Not surprisingly, the most vehement attempt to reject assimilation involved Polonia's most treasured resources: its parishes. In order to protect Chicago's Catholic Church in an era of increasing nativism, Archbishop Mundelein attempted to Americanize the ethnic Catholic parishes. His assault on the Polish parishes, particularly their use of the Polish language and their school curricula, generally failed and unintentionally strengthened Polish identity.[28] Indeed, Lizabeth Cohen notes that Mundelein's actions actually prolonged the survival of Polonia during the 1920s. Polish pastors discouraged people from moving out of neighborhoods so as to protect the ethnic church from absorption into the Catholic fold.[29] Not surprisingly, Polish religious leaders generally opposed assimilation as it challenged their *raison d'être*. In 1928, Father Wacław Kruszka, a prominent priest in Wisconsin, rejected an invitation written in English to a social event sponsored by the Milwaukee Society, a derivative of the Chicago Society. He was particularly disturbed by the invitation's use of the term "Americans of Polish descent," a moniker that implied a significant degree of assimilation.[30] Clearly, the new crop of leaders emerging out of elite organizations, like the Chicago and Milwaukee Societies, challenged the authority of the old guard as they competed for the role of ethnic spokesperson.[31] In these instances, opposition to assimilation appears to have been predicated on fears about the loss of autonomy and relevance for the traditional leaders of Polonia's ethnic institutions.

---

26. Augustyn, "Together and Apart," 44.

27. As cited in Radzilowski, *The Eagle and The Cross*, 189–90. Radzilowski's citation notes original location in PRCUA Presidential Papers, 1934–1944, PMAA.

28. Cohen, *Making a New Deal*, 84–87.

29. Ibid., 87.

30. William Galush "City Societies and Commercial Clubs: Embourgoisment Among Second Generation Polish Americans," *Polish American Studies* 56, no. 2 (Autumn 1999): 5.

31. Ibid., 12.

Although motivated by different factors, friends and foes of assimilation both agreed that Polonia had a serious "youth problem." Concerned that the "good name of Polonia was being denigrated," the Chicago Society directly addressed the issue of juvenile delinquency.[32] Indeed, sociologist Frederic Thrasher's 1927 study of gangs identified Polish Americans as having twice the number one might expect based on their proportion of the population.[33] In response to this growing problem, the Chicago Society established the Polish Welfare Association in 1922 and an Educational Fund in 1927. A 1922 article in the *Chicago Daily News* explained the intent of the former:

> The purpose of this society is the protection and aid of adolescent boys and girls who are brought into court for violation of the law and who lack sufficient legal assistance. The Association will try to protect these boys and to lead them from crooked ways to the straight path of life.[34]

In a 1928 article advertising an upcoming benefit ball, the association once again reminded readers of its goal of assisting the "tens of thousands of underprivileged Polish children and youths, many of whom get their training in the streets without guidance."[35] Taking aim at the dysfunctional family of the underclass, the article concluded: "Therefore, the Polish Welfare Association takes the place of the home which is negligent in taking care of the children."[36] Thus, the more assimilated Chicago Society focused its energies on working through the American legal system to mitigate the problem of juvenile delinquency that resulted from the breakdown of the family.

The discussions surrounding the Polish "flaperki"—the cause of much anxiety in Polonia during the interwar years—also implied that something was amiss in Polish families. Religious leaders were especially alarmed by this development: "'Our clergy preaches a great deal about them [*flaperki*], denouncing their style and cautions Polish girls to shun those "blockheads."'"[37] "Flaperki" girls, with their short hair and skirts, seemed more interested in frequenting dance halls and cavorting with questionable men than in becoming the devoted Polish wives and mothers

32. Ibid., 10.

33. As cited in Radzilowski, "Family, Women, and Gender," 64.

34. "Meeting of the Polish Welfare Association" in *Dziennik Chicagoski*, February 8, 1922, in Chicago Foreign Language Press Survey: Polish Reel; available at http://www.archive.org/stream/5423968_7/5423968_7_djvu.txt (accessed February 2, 2012).

35. "Benefit Ball for Polish Welfare Association Planned," *Dziennik Chicagoski*, January 7, 1928 in Chicago Foreign Language Press Survey: Polish Reel; available at http://www.archive.org/stream/5423968_7/5423968_7_djvu.txt (accessed February 2, 2012).

36. Ibid.

37. As cited and translated in Radzilowski, "Family, Women, and Gender," 191. Original citation, *Dziennik Zjednoczenia*, April 19, 1922.

Polonia expected them to be.[38] Such defiance challenged the safeguards Polonia had devised to protect its daughters. As Helena Znaniecki Lopata notes, "[E]ach family exerted strong patriarchal control over the children, particularly the daughters. A girl's reputation affected her marriage chances and the family status."[39] The family, and by extension the *okolica*, attempted to closely guard a girl's honor, especially since few alternatives existed outside of marriage save life in a religious order. This need for supervision often limited a girl's educational attainment and employment choices. If employed, work as a domestic servant was much preferred to factory work as it was thought to prepare daughters for their future roles as wives and mothers. If a young woman did work in a factory, the location was typically close to home so that the *okolica* could keep tabs on her.[40]

Despite these precautions, city life included many temptations for the daughters of Polonia, at least as portrayed in popular culture. The dance halls were particularly troublesome. Since the late nineteenth century, antiprostitution reformers had been cautioning against the dangers lurking in dance halls, especially for immigrant girls. H. W. Lytle and John Dillon's 1910 tract *From Dance Hall to White Slavery* recounted the tragic story of Stefania Zradska, an immigrant from Poland whose life came to a tragic end because of her frequent visits to dance halls.[41] The work of Melania Nesterowicz, a Buffalo journalist who wrote a series of novels in the 1920s and 1930s on the careers and love lives of second-generation "flaperki," echoes this theme of poor judgment.[42] In her most popular tales—*Hot-Cha-Cha*, *The Salesgirl from Broadway*, and *Stella from Buffalo*—Nesterowicz offers her protagonists a clear remedy for their poor decision making: reconnecting with their Polish culture and family. The author calls particular attention to the young women's pursuit of relationships with "American" men from dance halls. In contrast to the disappointment her protagonists inevitably experience with these men, Nesterowicz offers up the Polish American husband as the ideal. As Karen Majewski contends, these novels offer insight into the interwar identity crisis by providing:

> a contemporary, insider's view of Polonia's struggle for a cultural identity in the crucial period between the wars. . . . The danger [presented in the novels] is that the second generation's marginality, which allows them to function in more than one

38. Radzilowski, "Family, Women, and Gender," 191.

39. Helena Znaniecki Lopata, *Polish Americans: Status Competition in An Ethnic Community* (Englewood Cliffs, NJ: Prentice Hall, 1976), 99.

40. As cited in ibid., 99.

41. Leslie Hahner, "Practical Patriotism: Camp Fire Girls, Girl Scouts, and Americanization," *Communication and Critical/Cultural Studies* 5, no. 2 (June 2008): 118.

42. Karen Majewski, "Wayward Wives and Delinquent Daughters: Polonia's Second Generation Flappers in the Novels of Melania Nesterowicz," *Polish American Studies* 53, no. 1 (Spring 1996): 5.

> social world prevents them from belonging unequivocally to any of those worlds. Without that belonging, without that sense of one's rightful place in relation to others and without . . . the influences of neighborhood gossip and fingerpointing, social controls break down.[43]

Clearly, Polonia feared its daughters' pursuit of activity outside the parameters of the *okolica*. Nesterowicz's prescription for redemption—reconnecting to one's ethnic roots—held great promise to those anxious about assimilation's detrimental effects on Polonia's girls, as we will see in the case of *Córy Zjednoczenia*.

In addition to juvenile delinquency and "flaperki," Polish Americans during the interwar years also worried about the increasing Polish cultural illiteracy among its youth. In response to nativist sentiment, Polonia attempted to foster a positive image by commemorating two of its own—American Revolutionary War heroes Casimir Pułaski and Thaddeus Kościuszko—in the naming of numerous monuments, parks, and streets. While such efforts may have introduced these ethnic heroes to mainstream America, Polish youth apparently were too busy to notice. A survey conducted in Buffalo in the 1920s found that more Polish youngsters were able to identify George Washington and Abraham Lincoln than Kościuszko; even fewer were able to identify the president of newly independent Poland (52.6 percent).[44] A 1926 cartoon published in a Polish newspaper in New York poignantly demonstrates the youth's lack of Polish cultural literacy. In the cartoon, General Kościuszko looms large in the background as he looks down upon three Polish youth: an inebriated "Old Sport" who is leaning against a pole with a bottle of moonshine, a flapper girl, and a young man identified as "Polish sheik" with whom the flapper is dancing. In response to the flapper's inquiry as to the identity of the general, the young man mistakenly identifies him as an actor. The caption at the top reads: "Look, Kościuszko, look at the way some of our countrymen are carrying on."[45] In order to remedy this situation, both the PNA and PRCU developed youth programs during the late 1920s and 1930s that aimed to inculcate an appreciation of Polish heritage. By "Polonizing" the youth, these programs aimed to reverse the Americanization process that had wreaked such havoc on the Polish family.

Thus, the intense debates about identity during the interwar years reveal uncertainty as to what it meant to be called a "Polish American." Pula suggests that the classic symptoms of the "marginal man"—one who lives in a state of ambiguity as he struggles to satisfy the expectations of two cultures—began to appear in Polonia.[46] Moreover, Kantowicz describes Polish Americans in this era in a "state

43. Ibid., 6, 12.
44. As cited in Kantowicz, *Polish-American Politics in Chicago*, 169–70.
45. As cited and translated in Pula, *Polish Americans*, 82.
46. Ibid., 81.

of maximum tension" as they continually negotiated their Polish past with their American future.[47] As Majewski astutely observes, this was particularly confusing for the second generation:

> At the same time that a disoriented Polonia was forced to reconsider its relationship to the European homeland and to the America of which it was now a part, a new, native-born generation was coming of age in a dizzying society which seemed to many to have lost its moral guideposts.[48]

William Galush notes that the Chicago Society's approach—one that demonstrated its members' acceptance of mainstream American culture while still maintaining ties to their ethnic group—reflects the "dynamism and flexibility of ethnicity."[49] Others note that the outcome of this debate was the development of a progressive ideology that rejected the melting pot theory of assimilation in favor of a new conceptualization long before it was popular to do so. As Lopata contends, once Poland's independence made the "fourth partition" argument moot, Polish Americans were searching for a new paradigm to justify their continued existence as a distinct community. In the process of this search, they managed to reject the melting pot theory and reconceptualize America as a cultural mosaic in which they figured prominently.[50] In this pluralistic vision, Polish Americans could be proud of their cultural heritage while freely borrowing from other elements in the mosaic without fear of losing their distinct identity. Significantly, the Polish community retained a modicum of control in this model. The PRCU's newspaper summed it up best when it called for "Americanization of Poles *by* the Poles" (emphasis added).[51] Programs for Polish youth developed during this era, especially scouting, reflect the internalization of this mantra.

Programming for Polish Youth: Boys Can Be Boys, Girls Must Act Like "Daughters"

In the creation of extensive programming for youth during the interwar years, the established fraternals addressed two concerns: the Polish youth problem and their own declining membership. For the first time, membership drives targeted Polonia's youth, offering them the opportunity to purchase insurance. Furthermore, membership provided the youth an opportunity to participate in wholesome activities such

47. Kantowicz, *Polish-American Politics in Chicago*, 163.
48. Majewski, "Wayward Wives and Delinquent Daughters," 10.
49. Galush, "City Societies and Commercial Clubs," 17–18.
50. Lopata, *Polish Americans*, 73, 144.
51. As cited in John F. McClymer, "Gender and the 'American Way of Life': Women in the Americanization Movement," *Journal of American Ethnic History* 10, no. 3 (Spring 1991): 7. Citation notes original reference as *Dziennik Zjednoczenia* 36, no. 112 (May 13, 1922).

as athletics and scouting. The latter—the "lifeblood of Polish culture"—emerged as a major vehicle for the transmission of Polish culture.[52] The careful consideration given to the name of the PRCU's girl troops suggests that gender played an essential role in this process of "Polonization."

• • •

As was the case when Lord Baden-Powell launched the British Scouts in 1906, the youth departments of the PNA and PRCU initially focused their efforts on organizing troops of boys. Inspired by the establishment of the Boy Scouts of America (BSA) in 1910 and their counterparts in Poland in 1911, Polonia developed an early interest in promoting scouting. While some troops were formed prior to World War I, scouting fever did not hit Polonia until the 1920s and 1930s. The PNA *Harcerstwo* movement, initially modeled on the Boy Scout Movement in Poland, began in 1931 but was short-lived because of internal disagreement and a refusal to affiliate with the BSA. Because of the PNA's insistence on complete autonomy over its program and its refusal to pay dues, the BSA encouraged the PNA troops to remove "boy scouts" from their name and alter their program so as to avoid confusion.[53] Ultimately, the PNA scouting program came to an end in 1939. Although in existence less than a decade, the PNA's program aspired to inculcate an appreciation of Polish culture in its young members, most notably in its sponsorship of trips to Poland for its most exemplary scouts.

In contrast to the PNA's refusal to affiliate with the BSA, the PRCU Boy Scout troops organized in the early 1930s chose to formally join the BSA on condition that they could freely use the Polish language in their program.[54] As early as 1935, the PRCU had ninety-seven registered Boy Scout units in twelve states.[55] Indeed, the cooperation of the PRCU in organizing its troops was noted in the 1936 BSA "Report of the Commission on Inter-racial Activities, Section on White Nationality Groups."[56] In 1934, the PRCU published a scouting guidebook in Polish that placed great emphasis on the need for the youth to reconnect with their Polish cultural heritage. In his introduction, the president of the PRCU wrote:

> This handbook is designed to inculcate into our children obedience to parents and superiors, a loyalty to land and religion of our ancestors, a consciousness of belonging to our great association, the Polish Roman Catholic Union in America;

52. As cited in Radzilowski, "Family, Women, and Gender," 184.

53. Saul Scheidlinger, "A Comparative Study of the Boy Scout Movement in Different National and Social Groups," *American Sociological Review* 13, no. 6 (December 1948): 745.

54. Ibid., 746.

55. Ibid., 746–47.

56. As cited in Radzilowski, "Family, Women, and Gender," 185. The citation notes that an annotated copy of this report is located in the PRCUA Presidential Papers, 1934–1941 (PMA).

> to make them better future citizens of this country, conscious of their origin and willing to respect the ideals and tradition of the nation from which they spring.[57]

In the same vein, the preface to the scouting guidebook contains "An Unwritten Law for Polish Scouts," which again stresses the importance of the boys' Polishness in very sentimental language:

> In this handbook you will find 12 Scout Laws which indicate to you how to act in order to become the pride of your parents and an asset to the community in which you live. . . . You are an American Boy Scout of Polish origin! It is, hence, your duty to be loyal to your homeland, America. Your Polish extraction requires of you a second duty, toward the land from which your parents came, toward Poland. This "Unwritten Law" of the Polish Scout in America is engraved in your Polish heart. You need only knock on it and it will whisper to you that in it Polish blood is flowing; that the first word your mother spoke to you was the Polish word; that the tunes she sang when putting you to sleep were Polish; that your childhood's first prayer was Polish. . . . This "Unwritten Law" engraved in your heart orders you to feel as a Pole everywhere and always to emphasize your Polish origin; it calls upon you to learn the beautiful Polish tongue, the great history, literature and traditions of the Polish nation from which you originated. . . . In standing guard for the Catholic faith and for "Polishness" you are opening the doors for others and yourselves for a better and a greater future.[58]

Clearly, transmission of the Polish culture, faith, and language was an essential element of the PRCU scouting program for boys. The rest of the guidebook includes topics one would expect in a typical scouting manual—scout laws and vows, first aid techniques, knot tying, and flag protocol. In addition, the PRCU scouts were expected to have knowledge of both the U.S. and Polish flags as well as the national anthems of both countries. According to a survey of scoutmasters conducted in the late 1940s, troop meetings were conducted in English while songs, prayers, and the occasional skit were recited in Polish.[59] Wearing uniforms similar to those of the BSA, most troops were organized out of the local parishes where they held their meetings. Once the boy scouts were up and running, the PRCU turned its attention to organizing girl troops, a topic that initially engendered much debate.

Beginning in 1933, the Women's Department of the PRCU took an active role in organizing its program for girls—Córy Zjednoczenia. Like the boys' programs,

---

57. As cited and translated in Scheidlinger, "A Comparative Study," 747. The citation notes the title as *Scout Handbook for Polish Roman Catholic Union Troops in the United States* (Chicago, 1934), 1.

58. As cited and translated in Scheidlinger, "A Comparative Study," 747; *Scout Handbook for Polish Roman Catholic Union Troops*, 8.

59. Scheidlinger, "A Comparative Study," 747. Sheidlinger conducted the survey for his research and comments in a footnote about the small sample size. Of the twelve questionnaires he sent to the most successful troops, only six were returned.

Figure 1: Córy members practice their first aid techniques. Courtesy of Natalie Stefański Budzikowski.

Córy provided wholesome activities to serve as an antidote to Polish cultural illiteracy among the youth. Notably, while the PRCU's boy scout program affiliated with the BSA, its counterpart for girls chose not to affiliate formally with an American scouting program.[60] This decision suggests that the girls' program was held to a different standard than the boys'.

That the stakes were higher for the girls' program is most obvious in the spirited discussion that occurred over the naming of the troops. Whereas the boys were always known by the generic title of "Polish Boy Scouts," their girl counterparts were given a more provocative name—"Daughters of the Union." This name, which beat out several equally interesting contenders, was finally chosen after a "lively discourse" on the topic and at least one deferment of the matter in the Executive Council of the PRCU.[61] Heeding the advice of PRCU Scoutmaster John Troike who cautioned in 1933 that "it is best to proceed slowly in order to insure [*sic*] the best

60. Despite choosing not to affiliate with an established American program, by the early 1940s Córy proved to be more popular than the boys' program, perhaps because boys had more outlets from which to choose. Whereas in 1934 Córy counted fifteen troops, by 1941 it included 109 troops in addition to nine Junior Daughter troops and two Senior Daughter troops. See Radzilowski, "Family, Women, and Gender," 186–87, 284.

61. Minutes of the Executive Council, July 17–18, 1933, p. 15, and March 20, 1934, p. 67, Polish Roman Catholic Union of America, Chicago.

results" when organizing the girl scouts, the Executive Council carefully considered an appropriate name for the girls.[62]

Although ultimately adopting the name "Daughters of the Union," the Executive Council considered four other names. During a meeting of the Executive Council March of 1934, three possible names were mentioned: "Samaritans," "Guides," and "Kaliny."[63] The "Samaritans" most likely referenced the Grey Samaritans, the bilingual Polish American young women who donned gray uniforms in their service as nurses in Poland in the aftermath of World War I. Interestingly, the Grey Samaritans' pledge parallels some of the language used in scouting:

> I, ________, in accepting the Polish Grey Samaritan uniform, pledge myself to uphold the highest ideals of womanhood in every action of my life; To be faithful in the fulfillment of the duties . . . ; To be obedient to the orders of my Superiors; To serve the cause of Poland; To allay suffering and bind up the wounds of those by the wayside; Believing that in so doing I serve the cause of humanity.[64]

That the PRCU would consider a name with such strongly religious and service-oriented overtones should come as no surprise. Similar themes were associated with the term "guides" used in the British scouting program for girls. These "Girl Guides" were distinguished in name from their male counterparts—"Scouts"—so as to affirm their role as helpmates. Interestingly, the Girl Guides' participation in World War I rallies in which they demonstrated their competency in drill and signaling led some newspapers to describe them as the "'anti-thesis of flapperdom.'"[65] "Guides" was also the term commonly used for girls' troops in Poland, although scouting there took on even more militaristic overtones in the wake of two world wars. The final name under consideration at this meeting was "Kaliny" which referred to both a geographic region in Poland as well as a type of guelder rose, a deciduous shrub whose white flowers eventually turn into red berries. Either meaning suggests a symbolic reference to gender by invoking a location in the motherland or a plant that bears fruit.

By July 1934, the Executive Council had eliminated these three names and forwarded two more for consideration: "Daughters of the PRCU" and "Rainbow Girls."[66] Unlike the "Samaritans," "Guides," or "Kaliny," this latter option is particu-

---

62. Ibid.

63. Minutes of the Executive Council, March 20, 1934, p. 67, Polish Roman Catholic Union of America, Chicago.

64. As cited in Pula, *Polish Americans*, 62.

65. As cited in Tammy M. Proctor, *Scouting for Girls: A Century of Girl Guides and Girl Scouts* (Santa Barbara, CA: Prager, 2009), 27.

66. Minutes of the Executive Council, July 9–10, 1934, pp. 29–30, Polish Roman Catholic Union of America, Chicago.

larly striking in its lack of reference to any specific element of scouting, service, or Poland. Rather, it seems to imply the troops' work would be merely decorative. At this July meeting, the council finally agreed on the "Daughters of the PRCU," although the minutes are silent as to the logic behind this decision.[67] All of the names considered suggest something about the types of qualities that the PRCU hoped to inculcate in its young girls. That they selected "daughters" perhaps provides insight into the state of gender roles in Polonia at this time.

Gender in Polonia: Tradition and Change in the Polish Family

As was the case in agrarian Poland, the family remained the basic economic and social unit in Polonia.[68] Despite the challenges that accompanied immigration and assimilation, the traditional Polish family, headed by a strong patriarch, proved remarkably resilient. Nonetheless, roles within the family underwent some degree of alteration in the process of adjusting to an urbanized and industrialized city like Chicago.

Conditions in the United States altered the power dynamic between the Polish husband and wife. Because more single men than women immigrated to the United States prior to World War I, many marriages consisted of a first-generation husband and second-generation wife who was typically better educated and from an established household. As a result, some of the customs that had accompanied matrimony were reversed. For example, the wife was no longer expected to live in her husband's household as was the case in agrarian Poland, where it was necessary to stake a claim to one's share of the family land. Instead, the couple could immediately establish their own household. Although financial circumstances sometimes dictated that the newlyweds live with family initially, this temporary arrangement typically involved residence with the bride's more established family. Moreover, the traditional dowry fell to the wayside in the promising marriage market for prospective brides.[69] Indeed, the groom was expected to purchase the wedding dress and whatever else was needed to establish a household.[70] Although some contend that immigration to the United States encouraged more egalitarian marriages, others

---

67. Natalie Stefański Budzikowski, a Córy troop leader in the mid-1930s until the early 1940s, recalls that Stanisław Adamkiewicz, former president of the PRCU (1909–13), was adamant about choosing the name "daughters." Interview with Natalie Stefański Budzikowski, March 11, 2012.

68. Pula, *Polish Americans*, 24.

69. Radzilowski, "Family, Women, and Gender," 64.

70. Pula, *Polish Americans*, 62.

note that this process was not enough to completely destroy the image of a strong patriarch in Polonia's families.[71]

Despite the alteration of some marriage customs, Polonia nonetheless retained defined roles for men and women. A poignant reminder of the expectations for new brides was the *Kocia Muzyka*, a European practice that continued in the New World for some time. During this parade-like tradition in which well-wishers followed the wedding party through the neighborhood, the bride was often presented with a baby carriage.[72] Although the young bride may have been employed as a domestic servant or in a factory prior to marriage, she was expected to stop working outside of the home once she had a child. That mothers who worked outside of the home were considered to be in dire circumstances was apparent in a 1927 report of the Polish Welfare Association. In describing the recent completion of a new shelter for Polish girls, the article noted: "In a separate part of this building is a nursery for small children whose mothers are forced to go to work during the day."[73] Such women, one can infer, were certainly not helping, but more likely contributing to, the youth problem that was causing so much concern in Polonia. Indeed, women had assumed more responsibility for disciplining the children since husbands worked long hours—often six days a week—in factories some distance from their homes.[74] Socially, women were active members of a variety of religious and ethnic institutions, some of which were founded in response to the old fraternals' practice of limiting access to men only. Although they occasionally took on more public roles, even protesting in the streets, women's defense of the household and its members typically motivated such action. Thus, in fulfilling their roles as wives and mothers, Polonia's women assumed new responsibilities as they adapted to the complexities of urbanized living.

As the patriarch of the family, the Polish husband was expected to be the primary breadwinner outside of the home. In contrast to the autonomy associated with agrarian life, factory life stripped the Polish husband of control over his work. Pula notes that this loss resulted in lowered self-esteem, increased use of alcohol, and more authoritarian behaviors at home.[75] Besides a loss of autonomy, the meager wages earned by Polish husbands as unskilled laborers often meant that they had to

71. Helen J. Wojniusz, "Ethnicity and Other Variables in the Analysis of Polish American Women," *Polish American Studies* 34, no. 2 (Autumn 1977): 30. Wojniusz references the work of Helen Zand, Theresita Polzin, and Helen Znaniecki Lopata.

72. Pacyga, *Polish Immigrants and Industrial Chicago*, 140.

73. "Board Meeting of the Polish Welfare Assocation," *Dziennik Chicagoski*, January 7, 1928, in Chicago Foreign Language Press Survey: Polish Reel; available at http://www.archive.org/stream/5423968_7/5423968_7_djvu.txt (accessed February 2, 2012).

74. Radzilowski, "Family, Women, and Gender," 62.

75. Pula, *Polish Americans*, 25.

rely on income from other family members. Indeed, the Polish Americans' determination to achieve homeownership often necessitated such a consolidation of wages, a concept referred to as "penny capitalism."[76] For some families, this meant taking in boarders, which allowed the wives to contribute to the family purse without pursuing work outside of the home. In other instances, children in the family contributed their wages to help make the mortgage payments, an arrangement that limited the offspring's educational opportunities and social mobility. Regardless of the manner in which the family managed to pay the bills during temporary displacements in the labor market, Polish husbands typically retained their position as strong patriarchs.

The onset of the Great Depression in the early 1930s and its prolonged economic instability, however, wreaked havoc on Polish families. Indeed, the most important guarantees of the working-class Polish family's security—a steady job and a home—were severely undercut.[77] Lizabeth Cohen notes that although families had relied upon a "family economy" in the 1920s, the "delicate economic and psychological balance" that had characterized it was upset when fathers, especially those over forty, were no longer able to be the primary breadwinner in the family.[78] The income of the wife and children, who often had an easier time finding and maintaining a job during the Depression because of the lower wages they earned, frequently became the sole support of the family.[79] This change in the financial dynamic of the family altered authority patterns. In 1934, sociologist Ernest W. Burgess conducted a series of interviews in the Polish American community that reveal the extent to which the Depression altered family life. As Father Victor, principal of Holy Trinity High School in a Polish neighborhood of Chicago, observed:

> The autocratic domination and importance of the wage earner is profoundly shaken. You should remember that the Polish family is based on authority, not on love. . . . The prestige of the former wage earner is lowered by asking working children or women for spending money—for beer, for cigarettes, for carfare.[80]

Clara Odeski, a social worker in Chicago in the 1930s, also observed that the Depression had an emasculating effect on Polish husbands, a loss of status that led to much resentment.[81] Bernice Wozniak, a Polish wife who had been supporting her

76. Ibid. Pula attributes this expression to Ewa Morawska.

77. Radzilowski, "Family, Women, and Gender," 77.

78. Cohen, *Making a New Deal*, 246.

79. Ibid., 247.

80. As cited in ibid., 247–48. The original citation notes the location as: Interview with Father Victor, Panoff Project, "The Effect of Depression on Poles," 1934, Ernest W. Burgess Papers, University of Chicago Special Collections, Joseph Regenstein Library, Box 130, Folder 4.

81. As cited in Cohen, *Making a New Deal*, 248. The original citation notes the location as: Statement of Clara Odeski, Panoff Project, "The Effect of Depression on Poles."

family along with her oldest son during her husband's prolonged unemployment, confirmed this tendency. As she commented, "'I am the boss in the family. . . . You know, who make the money he is the boss.'"[82] The wife's new financial authority also changed her relationship with her children. Expressing a clear preference for her mother over her father, Wozniak's daughter stated, "I certainly like my mother lots more, for she buys me everything."[83] Polish fathers, already concerned about the loss of their daughters to the "flaperki" lifestyle of dance halls and American husbands, also had to worry about maintaining their daughters' respect within the home. Thus, the Depression caused cracks in the foundation of the traditional Polish family as it fundamentally called into question assumptions about prescribed gender roles.

• • •

The financial and psychological stress that accompanied the Depression perhaps provides insight into the aforementioned "spirited discourse" that occurred when the PRCU was deciding on a name for its girl troops. That "Daughters of the Union" was selected perhaps indicates an attempt to right a wrong that was developing in Polonia. As young Polish women increasingly interacted with a world outside of the *okolica* and as the Depression upset traditional gender roles, concern about the future of the Polish family emerged. Scouting for girls served as an antidote, both by providing an alternative to the temptations of mainstream American culture and by stressing the rich cultural heritage that the young women could someday share with their own children. Thus, daughters were recruited to save the Polish family.

Interestingly, one potential name not mentioned in the PRCU minutes was "Girl Scouts," one of the most popular scouting organizations in the United States for girls. The minutes from July 1934 note that the "program of American Organizations for Girls was not adaptable and therefore the committee recommends to adopt [our] own program for the girls."[84] Given its popularity at the time, it seems safe to assume that the Girl Scouts of America (GSA) was one of the "organizations" referenced. Although the PRCU rejected the wholesale adoption of the American scouting programs, the minutes later indicate that "the Extension Committee further recommend[ed] that a representative of the American Scout Organization be invited to attend the Union Convention."[85] While willing to enter into discussions with representatives of the American programs for girls in the future, the PRCU was clearly striving to create its own program for Polish girls. Their ambivalence

82. As cited in Cohen, *Making a New Deal*, 248. The original citation notes the location as: Interview with Bernice Wozniak, Panoff Project, "The Effect of Depression on Poles."

83. Ibid.

84. Minutes of the Executive Council, July 8–9, 1934, pp. 29–30, Polish Roman Catholic Union of America, Chicago.

85. Ibid.

toward the American models is particularly noteworthy because the boys' scouting program, organized a few years earlier, formally affiliated with the BSA. Why did the PRCU deem the GSA program inappropriate whereas the BSA program could be adapted to meet their needs? What does this imply about their perception of the GSA at the time? To what extent did it threaten the ideals that the PRCU program was hoping to foster?

The Girl Scouts of America: Pioneering Homemakers?

Founded in 1912 by a wealthy widow named Juliette Gordon Low, the GSA offered American girls a program of scouting modeled on the British Girl Guides. Low, groomed to be a proper southern belle, defied expectations for a woman of her time. Never finding fulfillment in her disastrous and childless marriage, she pursued artistic endeavors and travel to cope with her emotional insecurity.[86] In Great Britain, Low befriended Lord Baden-Powell, the founder of the British Boy Scouts and Girl Guides. This friendship intimately exposed her to scouting; organizing a comparable program for American girls would become her life's work.[87] In taking on this public role, Low reflects the shift from the traditional woman of the Victorian era to the "New Woman" of the turn of the century.[88] Since its inception, Girl Scouting had stressed two themes: traditional domestic tasks and "practical feminism" (survival skills, camping, citizenship training, and career preparation).[89] As the relative importance of these two themes fluctuated over time, the GSA both challenged and reinforced traditional assumptions about gender.

That Low's GSA defied expectations for girls at the time is apparent in its naming controversy that developed with the BSA. When Low first began her program in Savannah with two troops of eighteen girls, the group was initially referred to as "Girl Guides" after their British counterparts. During the first year of the program, however, the girls asked Low if they could change their name to "Girl Scouts." The girls contended that the use of the word "scout" in their name recalled the American pioneer spirit.[90] Low acquiesced, and the name has stood the test of time. Not everyone approved of this change, however, as evidenced by the most vocal objector: the chief Boy Scout executive, James E. West. Believing that the physical activities of scouting should be reserved for boys while girls' programs should focus

86. Rebekah E. Revzin, "American Girlhood in the Early Twentieth Century: The Ideology of Girl Scout Literature, 1913–1930," *Library Quarterly* 68, no. 3 (July 1998): 264.

87. Mary Aickin Rothschild, "To Scout or to Guide? The Girl Scout-Boy Scout Controversy, 1912–1941," *Frontiers: A Journal of Women Studies* 6, no. 3 (Autumn 1981): 115.

88. Revzin, "American Girlhood," 264.

89. Rothschild, "To Scout or to Guide?" 115.

90. Ibid., 116.

on domesticity, West repeatedly requested that Low remove the word "scout" from her group's name. According to West, the girls' use of the term "sissified" the name of "scout."[91] Therefore, Low's group should use the more appropriate term "guide" or consider merging with the Camp Fire Girl Guides, a group that stressed young girls' future roles as homemakers. For nearly two decades until his retirement in 1941, West attempted a variety of strategies to encourage the GSA to change its name, including a 1924 lawsuit (which never went to court) against the organization for supposed patent violations regarding the use of the word "scout" on camping equipment.[92] Moreover, West objected to the GSA's "mannish" khaki uniforms, the same color used by the BSA, instead of the dark blue worn by the British Girl Guides. The GSA's refusal to budge on both issues reinforced West's conviction that the girls' program was simply "aping" that of the boys. While the GSA rejected this claim, it nonetheless underscores their predicament.

The struggle to design a program that satisfied two constituencies with conflicting goals is evident in the revisions of the GSA handbooks during its first two decades. On the one hand, the GSA aimed to please adolescent girls who desired a novel program that offered them adventure on par with their brothers. On the other hand, the GSA formula had to respect the traditional assumptions about gender that had limited girls' opportunities in the past. As Mary Aickin Rothschild summarizes the dilemma: "[H]ow could Girl Scouts challenge the prevailing ideas of proper behavior and enlarge girls' spheres (especially in the area of physical fitness and outdoor survival) without weakening the ultimate goal of girls' growing up to be wives and mothers?"[93] The earliest handbook, *How Girls Can Help Their Country*, published in 1913, relied upon the oft-used rhetoric of Republican motherhood to resolve this dilemma:

> If character, training, and learning citizenship are necessary for boys, how much more important it is that these principles should be instilled into the minds of girls who are destined to be the mothers and guides of the next generation. . . . The Scout movement, so popular among the boys, is unfitted for the needs of girls, but on something the same lines has been devised the present system giving a more womanly training for both mind and body.[94]

Selecting the appropriate "spin" for the GSA program so as to achieve what Susan A. Miller refers to as a "benign middle ground" seems to have been key to the organization's early survival.[95]

---

91. Ibid., 118.
92. Ibid.
93. Ibid., 117.
94. As cited in Rothschild ibid.
95. Susan A. Miller, *Growing Girls: The Natural Origins of Girls' Organizations in America* (New Brunswick, NJ: Rutgers University Press, 2007), 33.

Scouting for Girls, the 1920 handbook and the first not to be simply adapted from Baden-Powell's Girl Guide handbook, continued to grapple with this paradox of tradition and innovation but with a "more modern and American sensibility."[96] This version included four proficiency areas: patriotism, outdoor living, domestic science (previously called "housewifery"), and community service.[97] Low devoted significant text to outdoor life including instruction in knots, mapmaking and orienteering, animal tracking, and camping, among other topics.[98] The section on domestic science stressed efficient housekeeping since, according to Low, "[w]e no longer believe that housekeeping should take up all a woman's time."[99] That women might need skills beyond the domestic sphere is apparent in the inclusion of a few career-oriented badges. Never wanting to push the boundaries of acceptable behavior too far, however, the GSA handbook mentions careers that were considered acceptable for women to pursue such as bookkeeper, interpreter, and photographer.[100] Of the forty-seven merit badges mentioned in the handbook, only two fall outside the realm of women's typical occupations: "Electrician" and "Telegrapher."[101] Interestingly, the text on community service encouraged the active participation of women in the public sphere as advocates for public health measures. These recently enfranchised "municipal housekeepers" were charged with monitoring the well-being of their homes *and* communities.[102] While not a radical departure from conventional roles for women, the 1920 edition nonetheless stressed a public role for woman while toning down its earlier emphasis on domesticity and morality.[103]

The revised 1933 handbook, published six years after Low's death, suggests that the GSA message continued to change in significant ways.[104] Elisabeth Israels Perry contends that the GSA shifted its focus from "achievement" to "happiness."[105]

---

96. Elisabeth Israels Perry, "From Achievement to Happiness: Girl Scouting in Middle Tennessee, 1910s–1960s," *Journal of Women's History* 5, no. 2 (Fall 1993): 79.

97. Ibid.

98. Ibid.

99. Ibid.

100. Ibid., 80.

101. *Scouting for Girls: Official Handbook of the Girl Scouts* (New York: Girl Scouts, 1920), 510, 530–31.

102. Laureen Tedesco, "Progressive Era Girl Scouts and the Immigrant: *Scouting for Girls* (1920) as a Handbook for American Girlhood," *Children's Literature Association Quarterly* 31, no. 4 (Winter 2006): 350–51. Tedesco attributes this term to Theda Skocpol in *Protecting Soldiers and Mothers: The Political Origins of Social Policy in the United States* (Cambridge, MA: Belknap Press of Harvard University Press, 1992).

103. Perry, "From Achievement to Happiness," 80.

104. The GSA issued a revision in the late 1920s as well, but its content did not change substantially from the 1920 edition.

105. Perry, "From Achievement to Happiness," 75–76.

For example, the 1933 edition's section on "homemaking," which was twenty pages longer than the 1920 edition, stressed the joy that resulted from domestic work (recall that the 1920 edition titled this section "domestic science" and encouraged efficiency so as make time for other activities). The 1933 edition also significantly altered the chapter on citizenship. Rather than the activist citizenship found in the earlier edition, the 1933 edition merely stresses knowledge of and obedience to the laws. As Perry sums it up, "Juliette Low's suffrage-movement rhetoric was gone."[106] Not surprisingly, this edition also eliminated all references to careers. Clearly, Low's vision of providing new opportunities for women had become somewhat diluted by the early 1930s. Indeed, the theme of the 1939 Girl Scout convention—"Girl Scouts: Half a Million Future Homemakers"—demonstrates the extent to which the GSA's new leadership crafted an image that more closely aligned with traditional gender roles.

At the same time the GSA was reconsidering its vision for young girls, so too was the PRCU designing its own program of scouting for girls. Even as the 1933 GSA handbook suggests increased emphasis on domesticity, the PRCU had reason to reject the wholesale adoption of the GSA program. Although the intensity of the debate with the BSA about the use of the word "scout" ebbed and flowed, the ongoing controversy may have been enough to sour the PRCU on the GSA's program.[107] While Low's vision was hardly radical, it may nonetheless have been viewed this way because it did provide opportunities not previously offered to young girls. As Rothschild explains in her comparison of Boy and Girl Scouts, "A commitment to new ideas about sex roles was not inherent in Boy Scouting as it was in Girl Scouting. Whereas Girl Scouting combined traditional roles with new roles for women, Boy Scouting stressed only traditional roles for men."[108] Given the stress that the Polish family was experiencing at this time, the PRCU likely was not interested in a program that had challenged, or had been perceived as challenging, traditional gender roles as was the case with the GSA.

Córy Zjednoczenia: Recruiting "Daughters" to Save the Polish Family

What were the guiding principles of Córy Zjednoczenia? To what extent was its program for Polish girls a departure from that described in the GSA handbook? While the two programs were similarly structured in their focus on outdoor life,

106. Ibid., 82.

107. Perhaps the Protestant roots of the GSA troubled PRCU leaders, but this seems an unlikely explanation because the BSA's Protestant background did not prevent the boys' troops from affiliating.

108. Rothschild, "To Scout or to Guide?" 120.

character building, and patriotism, resuscitating an interest in Polish culture was a central component of Córy. Indeed, the Córy program attempted to reverse the flow of cultural transmission that characterized earlier GSA programs targeting immigrant girls.

Although the GSA did not deviate from its initial focus on white middle-class girls in a numerically significant way until the 1960s, settlement troops and immigrant troops existed before and after World War I.[109] As part of the Americanization efforts in the first few decades of the twentieth century, the GSA along with the rival Camp Fire Girls attempted to teach immigrant girls English, patriotic rituals, and domestic skills.[110] Just as contemporary settlement and social workers sought to uplift the immigrant family via the daughter, so too did the American scouting organizations attempt to assuage the fears associated with "new immigrants" by "Americanizing" their daughters. As Leslie Hahner explains, "Education in English, domestic science, and hygiene redressed the failures of immigrant parents and ensured Americanized parents, children, and grandchildren."[111] To this end, the scouting organizations invited the girls to leave behind their former ethnic identities and embrace a new identity as an American. A 1918 edition of *The Rally*, a GSA magazine, featured a "Black Eyed Susan Troop" consisting of Italian girls whose experience in the GSA afforded them a new freedom in contrast to the "severe restraint" of their parents.[112] Not surprisingly, the uniforms played a significant role in this process of erasing ethnic identity and replacing it with a shared patriotic American identity.[113] A variety of factors, however, worked against the successful recruitment of working-class, immigrant girls: cost of dues, manuals, and uniforms; lack of leisure time among the working class; skepticism about the Protestant roots of the scouting programs among Catholic and Jewish immigrants.[114] Nonetheless, the model of assimilation espoused in these troops provides an interesting contrast to the Córy program. Although both programs attempted to use the daughters as vessels for reform, the GSA program attempted to "Americanize" the girls while the Córy program aimed to "Polonize" them.

The colors of the Córy uniform proudly announced these "Polonization" efforts. In addition to the special name given to the "Daughters," the PRCU chose uniforms that clearly marked the girls as Polish. Although it is difficult to decipher in the black-and-white photographs of the time, the girls wore white blouses with maroon skirts and scarves while the leaders wore one-piece maroon dresses with white

109. Tedesco, "Progressive Era Girl Scouts," 351.
110. Hahner, "Practical Patriotism," 114.
111. Ibid., 119.
112. As cited in ibid., 122.
113. Ibid., 126.
114. Tedesco, "Progressive Era Girl Scouts," 351.

scarves and maroon tams.[115] Selecting a shade of red and white as the uniform colors was a significant and deliberate choice, for the intent was to represent the colors of the Polish flag.[116] Moreover, these colors differed from the khaki used by the GSA; perhaps the PRCU was mindful of West and the BSA's objection to girls wearing such a "mannish" color. The Córy uniform also included a patch on the sleeve that identified the girls and leaders as members of the PRCU. Tammy M. Proctor has written extensively on the symbolism of scouting uniforms, particularly the extent to which they eradicated class distinctions, promoted gender roles, and solidified group identity.[117] That the uniform played a significant role in the Córy program is apparent in the inclusion of a page titled "My Uniform" in the Córy record booklet used by girls to record their progress.[118] On this page, a girl was asked to record the manner in which her uniform was obtained—whether it was purchased, made by the scout, or given to her—and the date and location of the first time she wore it. Natalie Stefański, a Córy troop leader in the 1930s, recalled the pride and satisfaction she felt when donning her uniform.[119] By designing such a distinctive uniform for the girls, the PRCU signaled that these daughters belonged to Polonia.

The Córy record booklet, in its cover design and initial pages, also clearly reflects the organization's embrace of Polish culture. The booklet, which is approximately the size of a 4 × 6 photograph, proudly announces its Polishness via a bright red-and-white cover, once again referencing the colors of the Polish flag. The title page includes an illustration of a young woman dressed in a Córy troop leader's uniform showing the way to a young girl dressed in a scout's uniform. In the background, the flags of both the United States and Poland are prominently displayed. The title page also lists the Scout's Promise in Polish (as is all the text in the booklet):

> I vow to try my best: 1. To fulfill my duties to God and to my country and to obey rules established by Córy and PRCUA.[120] 2. [To] help others always and everywhere. 3. [To] upkeep a healthy body, strong mind, and pure spirit.[121]

---

115. Interview with Natalie Stefański Budzikowski, January 28, 2012.

116. Ibid.

117. Tammy M. Proctor, "(Uni)forming Youth: Girl Guides and Boy Scouts in Britain, 1908–1939," *History Workshop Journal*, no. 45 (Spring 1998): 103–34.

118. Córy Zjednoczenia Record Booklet, PRCU (Chicago: Polish Museum of America, n.d.), 10. Although the booklet has no publication date listed, Natalie Stefański Budzikowski, a former troop leader and commissioner, recalls using this booklet for record keeping and promotions. She served in Córy from approximately 1934 to 1941, so the booklet was likely published in the mid- to late 1930s. Notes from conversation with Natalie on March 3, 2012. Anna Witowska translated this booklet for the author of this article.

119. Interview with Natalie Stefański Budzikowski, January 28, 2012.

120. PRCUA stands for Polish Roman Catholic Union of America (synonymous with PRCU).

121. Córy Zjednoczenia Record Booklet.

With the exception of the specific reference to the PRCU, this vow is similar to other scouting vows. The "Law[s] of Daughters of PRCUA" listed on the next page, however, suggest that this program specifically targets girls. The first law simply reads, "The daughter is pure."[122] Contrast this to the first law listed in the PRCU's 1934 handbook for boys which stresses the boy scout's confidence.[123] Interestingly, in the 1920 GSA handbook, a similar concern for purity was included in the laws—"A Girl Scout is Clean in Thought, Word, and Deed"—but it was listed as the tenth law.[124] Perhaps the reference to a daughter's purity as the first law indicates the degree to which the Polish leaders feared the influence of the dance halls and "flaperki." The other four laws mentioned in the Córy booklet—the daughter "never lies," "the daughter is ready to lend a hand," "the daughter is devout," and "the daughter is faithful"—reflect more generic scouting language, albeit with a significantly religious overtone.[125]

The remaining sections of the Córy record booklet offer clues as to the types of themes and activities stressed in the program. In the first portion of the booklet, the Córy member recorded autobiographical information including: the date she joined Córy and the PRCU; the date and place of her birth; her parents' names, dates and places of birth; her siblings; her school; her parish; and her hair and eye color. "The Candidate" page provided space for the member to record her mastery of the following required subjects: national anthem, flag history and protocol, Pledge of Allegiance, PRCUA hymn and three additional songs, how to make a bed, how to wash dishes, knots, outing, drill, and troop arrangement/policy.[126] It is unclear, however, whether the references to making a bed and washing dishes refer to skills associated with camping or general domesticity. Interestingly, few of these topics specifically reference Polish culture and history aside from the "PRCUA hymn and three songs" that, presumably, were sung in Polish. The majority of the topics listed suggest a focus on U.S. patriotism and scouting protocol. Thus, while the program aimed to "Polonize" young girls, this focus was not intended as a substitute for the inculcation of American patriotism. Unlike the early GSA formula, which aimed to completely replace ethnic identity with a new American one, Polonization, it seems, was meant to be merely additive. In the language of cultural pluralism, the Polish culture complemented the American mosaic.

Like the GSA, Córy members were encouraged to embark upon a program of personal achievement that included careful recording of various milestones. Indeed, the remainder of the booklet consists primarily of simple illustrations of

122. Ibid., 2.

123. *Scout Handbook for Polish Roman Catholic Union Troops in the United States* (Chicago: Polish Museum of Chicago, 1934), 15–22.

124. *Scouting for Girls: Official Handbook of the Girl Scouts*, 11.

125. Córy Zjednoczenia Record Booklet, 2.

126. Ibid., 11.

the various merit badges members could earn alongside blank spaces for recording the date of acquisition and the commissioner's signature. A comparison of the merit badges in the 1920 GSA handbook and the Córy record booklet suggests remarkably parallel programs.[127] The forty-seven possible merit badges listed in the GSA handbook have tremendous overlap with the thirty-six badges identified in the Córy record booklet. Many of the badges emphasize similar skills, albeit it with slightly altered names. The "Homemaker," "Child Nurse," and "Business Woman" badges in the GSA become the "Housewife," "Nanny," and "Shorthand Writer" badges in the Córy record booklet. Other categories listed in one are combined in the other: the "Camper, "Hiker," "Field Trip Expert" in the Córy record booklet all fall within the description of the "Pioneer" badge in the GSA handbook. Similarly, many of the very specific skills associated with the outdoors in the GSA handbook—beekeeper, zoologist, horsewoman, farmer, rock tapper, dairymaid—parallel skills incorporated into Córy's badges for the broad categories of "Nature Expert" and "Insect Expert." A few badges, however, are unique to each organization. For example, only the GSA lists the following badges: Electrician, Telegrapher, Crafts Woman, Handy Woman, Photographer, Sailor, Cyclist, Motorist, Hostess, and Milliner. The Córy record booklet's distinctive badges include: Housekeeper, Librarian, Outdoor Games Player, Student, Good Samaritan, and Poland Expert. Despite these exceptions, the rest of the badges are strikingly analogous, suggesting that the overall structure of the two programs was, in fact, not too divergent.[128]

The role of religion in the two organizations, however, reflects less convergence. As part of the "muscular Christianity" arm of the Progressive movement, the GSA aimed to build "strong bodies fit for service."[129] Although the promise listed in the 1920 GSA handbook opens with a commitment "to be true to God and my country," the program took on a nonsectarian character.[130] In contrast, the PRCU scouting program specifically promoted the Roman Catholic faith. The numerous Polish parishes provided an opportune organizational mechanism for the PRCU to recruit its "daughters." An attendance sheet for a "Patrol Leaders' Training Course" offered by the PRCU in 1935 indicates the participation of twenty-eight young women representing five Chicago parishes.[131] Troop meetings were conducted weekly at

---

127. The 1920 GSA handbook seems to be the most appropriate for comparison because the 1933 edition was just coming to publication at the time that the PRCU was organizing the Córy troops.

128. Indeed, Natalie Stefański Budzikowski, a Córy troop leader in the 1930s-1940s recalls attending GSA training courses.

129. Tedesco, "Progressive Era Girl Scouts," 347.

130. Proctor, *Scouting for Girls*, 60.

131. Attendance Sheet—Patrol Leaders' Training Course, Daughters of P.R.C.U., 1935, Chicago, PRCU Archives, *Hacertwo* Box, Polish Museum of America.

the parishes; a supervisor who visited one of the troop meetings in January of 1938 noted that the "session was cut short because of services in church."[132] From the perspective of PRCU scouting, an appropriate education in Polish culture specifically included religious study. One Córy leader who had accumulated enough points to advance to second rank was nonetheless advised to "study life story of [a] patron saint" along with "1 Polish and 2 American Scout Songs."[133] That religion played such an important role in the Córy program reflects the traditional devotional practices associated with Polonia's women and girls.[134] As the future mothers of Polonia, these "daughters" needed to be mindful of the role Catholicism played in their lives. Like the mother described in the preface of the PRCU Boy Scout handbook who tenderly sings Polish lullabies to her babies, these daughters would someday be expected to teach their children to recite their first Polish prayer. After all, it was Polonia's women who were charged with thinking "consciously about what it meant to be Polish and how to translate that into the rituals of daily life."[135] A vigorous religious life was clearly one of the most significant of these practices.

Even during camping excursions far from the parish, Córy members were able to participate in religious life. At Camp Gieryk, the camping site that the PRCU established outside of Chicago in the late 1930s, the open-air "chapel" was a significant structure. While a priest conducted mass from within this simple structure, a set of large doors allowed for the participation of the throng of faithful campers standing outside. Córy members also had the opportunity to say the rosary on a regular basis.[136] Father Boniface Slawik, a priest from Poland with a background in scouting, served as camp chaplain in residence in the late 1930s.[137] The presence of priests at the campsite underscored the significance of religion in the lives of Polish youth and likely reinforced implicit messages about traditional gender roles. The latter is significant, for many have noted the liberating effects of the camping experience, especially for girls. As Tammy M. Proctor explains, "[C]amp felt like an opportunity to move outside the bonds that society used to police gender roles. . . . The freedom of camp was intoxicating for girls."[138] Priests, the ultimate male authority in Polonia, perhaps reminded girls of the limits to that freedom.

132. "Argo," 1938, Chicago, PRCU Archives, *Harcerstwo* Box, Polish Museum of America.

133. Letter to Miss Helen Zawistanowicz, January 11, 1938, Chicago, PRCU Archives, *Harcerstwo* Box, Polish Museum of America.

134. Helen Stankiewicz Zand, "Polish American Leisureways," *Polish American Studies* 18, no. 1 (January–June 1961): 34.

135. Radzilowski, "Family, Women, and Gender," 71.

136. Interview with Natalie Stefański Budzikowski, March 11, 2012.

137. Ibid.

138. Proctor, *Scouting for Girls*, 55–56.

Figure 2: The Chapel at Camp Gieryk. The original caption on the reverse of the photo read "Kapliczka Św. Andrzeja Boboli." Courtesy of Natalie Stefański Budzikowski.

Besides camping excursions, the Córy troops participated in a variety of civic and social events in Chicago and elsewhere. They were regular attendees at parades commemorating both U.S. and Polish holidays. On May 30, 1938, the troop leaders gathered at the statue of General Kościuszko in Humboldt Park, the final destination of the annual Polish Constitution Day Parade.[139] Figure 4 shows troop members in their "Stars and Stripes" costumes, fresh from a tap dance performance at either a Flag Day or Fourth of July celebration.[140] Moreover, individual troops performed skits on either U.S. or Polish themes. Members of Troop 6, for example, decked in costumes from the colonial era, prepared for their show titled, "Colonial Daze."[141] The troop leaders, dressed in their maroon uniforms, supervised the performance and played piano in the background. A number of the activities allowed for Córy members to interact with their male counterparts.[142] Boys and girls, for example, often gathered together around the campfire. That the Córy members looked forward to

139. Natalie Stefański Budzikowski, personal correspondence, scrapbooks, and photo albums, 1930–45.

140. Ibid.

141. Ibid.

142. Interview with Natalie Stefański Budzikowski, March 11, 2012.

Figure 3: Córy leaders gather in Humboldt Park at the statue of Kosciuszko (May 1938). The troop name recorded on the back of the photo was "Druzyna Zrebów." Courtesy of Natalie Stefański Budzikowski.

these co-ed occasions is apparent in a 1937 letter written by Troop 6 leader, Genevieve Stefański, to her sister, another troop leader:

> I entered our girls in a folk dance contest at St. John Cantius [;] they were great. I had six couples and they danced the Polka Wegerka [sic]. . . . The girls all stayed till the end. You know why—dancing with [Polish] boy scouts. On the way home they wanted to know when the next parade was going to be.[143]

Presumably the girls were looking forward to the next parade because it would be an opportunity to mingle once again with the boy scouts. In contrast to the undesirable relationships found in American dance halls, the scouting organizations provided more wholesome opportunities for boy-girl interactions. Future research might investigate whether any marriages resulted from budding romances between scouts.

Like the GSA, the Córy program provided new opportunities for the young women who served as leaders. Many of these Chicago "Zreby" acquired significant skills that served them later in life. For example, Helen Kwiecen spent a year studying scouting in Poland, culminating in her participation in the Pan-Slavic Scouting

143. Letter from Genevieve Stefański to Natalie Stefański, May 26, 1937, in Budzikowski, personal correspondence, scrapbooks, and photo albums, 1930–45.

Figure 4: Córy members perform a "Stars and Stripes" tap dance. Standing, from left, are Evelyn Susmarski, Loretta Jaworski, and Sophie Depukat; kneeling are Jeanette Rak and Mildred Susmarski. Courtesy of Natalie Stefański Budzikowski.

Jamboree held in Warsaw in 1935 (see Figure 5).[144] She later served as a WAVE in the U.S. Navy and was stationed in the Intelligence Department as a Slavic-language translator during World War II.[145] Likewise, Dora Kuzmiński also served during World War II as a WAVE.[146] Natalie Stefański, a Córy leader from the mid-1930s until the early 1940s, spent a year in Poland studying its culture, literature, history, and scouting program on a scholarship from the Kosciuszko Foundation. In addition, she had the opportunity to finally meet relatives whom she had only known previously from her parents' stories. After resuming her scouting duties in the United States, Natalie was eventually promoted to "commissioner," overseeing Córy programs in

144. Photo courtesy PRCU Archives.

145. Memorial Service Program for Helen Kwiecen Kmiec, January 31, 2009.

146. Budzikowski, personal correspondence, scrapbooks, and photo albums, 1930–45; *Naród Polski*, September 8, 1994.

Figure 5: Córy Zjednoczenia participate in the 1935 Pan-Slavic Jamboree in Warsaw, Poland. From left: Lottie Wojciechowska Zawada, Clara Daniel, Helen Kwiecien Kmiec, Marie Chowaniec Solczyk, Marie Brzoza Zmuda, Dora Kuzminski Kalowski, and Bernice Troike Gorell. Courtesy of the Polish Roman Catholic Union Photo Archives.

twelve states. She also worked as the assistant to the director of the PRCU Youth Department. Besides the acquisition of skills, these young women formed lifelong friendships as evidenced by a luncheon held in 1994 to commemorate their sixtieth anniversary.[147] Many of those gathered had married Polish men, as indicated by their ethnic married names (listed along with their maiden names in the *Naród Polski* article). If asked about their lives' most significant work, most in this generation would probably comment on their accomplishments as wives and mothers.

Córy Zjednoczenia remained a vital force in Polonia through the postwar era. Indeed, the organization was particularly active during World War II. Whether participating in scrap metal and bond drives with fellow boy scouts or being trained by the Red Cross to roll bandages for soldiers, the daughters performed their patriotic duty.[148] For a short time after the war, the PRCU scouting program continued to thrive, but it ended in the mid-1950s when the PRCU decided to withdraw its

147. Ibid.

148. Radzilowksi, *The Eagle and the Cross*, 220.

support in favor of youth clubs.[149] Post–World War II émigrés, however, have kept the scouting spirit alive in Polonia by affiliating with the *Harcerstwo* Polish scouting movement. A 1999 *Chicago Tribune* article about this organization is aptly titled, "Polish Scouts Preserve a Culture: Harcerstwo Celebrates 50 Years of Honoring Ties, Teaching Values."[150] Future research might investigate the extent to which gender has played a role in this organization by comparing the programs offered to boys and girls.

Conclusion: "Scouting" for Identity

The concept of duty—to community, to nation, to God—lies at the heart of scouting. For the Polish American scouts of the interwar years, this concept also included a duty to respect their cultural heritage. Although the PRCU Boy Scouts were exposed to Polish culture in their scouting program, the special name and uniforms given to the PRCU "daughters" suggests that girls were charged with the duty of perpetuating this cultural legacy. As the future mothers of Polonia, they were recruited to save the Polish family from the deleterious effects of assimilation and the Depression.

The Córy program's formula—stressing the daughter's future role as the keeper of customs and religious faith—offered Polonia a way to cope with the uncertainty associated with the hyphenated identity it had assumed during the interwar years. As Polish Americans debated the merits and drawbacks of assimilation during this era, they expressed concern about Polonia's youth, especially the prevalence of juvenile delinquency and "flaperki." By locating the source of these problems in the family, the solution was simple: reinstatement of the traditional gender roles that had been the foundation of the family and, by extension, Polonia. As long as Polish girls could someday be counted on to raise strong Polish families, it would be less threatening to allow Polish boys to assimilate into mainstream America in order to advance their status. If Polish girls were sufficiently "Polonized," Polish boys would be free to "Americanize." As they scouted for an identity that respected the past yet prepared for the future, Polish Americans relied on prescribed gender roles to help them assume their proper place in the American cultural mosaic.

---

149. Ibid., 262–63.

150. "Polish Scouts Preserve a Culture: Harcerstwo Celebrates 50 Years of Honoring Ties, Teaching Values," *Chicago Tribune*, November 14, 1999

"The New Sportswoman"

Nationalism, Feminism and Women's Physical Culture In Interwar Poland

Nameeta Mathur

This article examines the interaction between the dual forces of nationalism and feminism in shaping women's physical culture in interwar Poland. The development of women's sports and physical education, as well as women's participation in mass cultural parades and military marches, all collectively termed "physical culture" in the Second Polish Republic, was more dynamic than the nascent apparatus of women's physical culture evident in the Polish Diaspora prior to the outbreak of the First World War. The male-dominated civil society of late partitioned Poland accommodated and used women's fledging interest in sports so as to build Polish national consciousness and patriotism, and recover the country's independence from the empires of Russia, Prussia, and Austria. After the Great War, the newly liberated Polish state similarly encouraged women's physical culture so as to foster sentiments of nationalism and patriotism, although its motives for doing so were more varied than the earlier single-minded objective of liberating Poland from foreign imperialism.

Women's physical culture in the interwar period also profited from the changing priorities of the "New Woman" that enabled women to play more sports and in larger numbers. While the first wave of Polish feminism in late partitioned Poland had provided the initial impetus for a discussion on the physical emancipation of women, the discourse on women's liberation in the interwar years provided both old and new stimuli for constructing the apparatus of women's physical culture. However, similar to the "woman question" in partitioned Poland that advocated for women's increased participation in public life without compromising their identities as good mothers and wives who resisted the imperial powers by keeping alive the spirit of "Polishness" at home, the interwar women's movement also conceded its subordinate status to the state's national interests. But even though sportswomen

From *The Polish Review*, vol. 48, no. 4 (2003), pp. 441–462.

closely followed the dictates of the political leadership, their energetic engagement in sports, within the enclosed spaces of female athleticism, positively influenced their personal and professional development in the direction of greater physical emancipation than during the earlier period of the partitions.[1]

Nationalism and Women's Physical Culture

Women's physical culture in the Second Polish Republic matured in response to the more structured ideological and institutional support from both the state and society. The motivations that articulated the need for women to participate in sports and the logistical details which defined the nature and governance of women's sports apparatus, though less committed and organized in the immediate years of independence, became more focused in the second decade of the interwar period.

The theoretical and practical accomplishments of women's sports must first be evaluated in the context of wartime devastation and acute shortages in material, financial, and infrastructural resources. Daunting political and economic problems faced the reborn Polish state. The overwhelming physical destruction, a war-ravaged economy marred by poverty and inflation, the multiplicity of parties and concomitant political instability, and the strain of military operations to secure the country's borders, all imposed immense misery upon Poland in the immediate aftermath of the war.[2] The organization of sport in the first decade of the interwar period, accordingly, was handicapped by the political contests that contained Poland's economic recovery. Because the government was preoccupied with more exigent issues, the revival of sports was achieved mainly through local and civil initiatives in the re-united territories.[3] It is important to note that while the Polish

1. For the development of Polish women's sports from the late nineteenth century until the outbreak of the First World War see Nameeta Mathur, "Women's Sports in Late Partitioned Poland," *Studies in Physical Culture and Tourism,* vol. 9 (2002): pp. 51–64.

2. Andrzej Korbonski, "Poland: 1918–1990," in *The Columbia History of Eastern Europe in the Twentieth Century,* ed. Joseph Held (New York: Columbia University Press, 1992), pp. 229–276; Richard M. Watt, *Bitter Glory: Poland and Its Fate, 1918 to 1939* (New York: Simon and Schuster, 1979), pp. 81, 197; Antony Polonsky, *Politics in Independent Poland 1921–1939: The Crisis of Constitutional Government* (Oxford: Clarendon Press, 1972), pp. 45, 52, 53, 60, 96, 100; and Joseph Rothschild, *East Central Europe Between the Two World Wars* (Seattle and London: University of Washington Press, 1974), pp. 28, 31, 33.

3. Zdzisław Grot, "Versuch eines Abrisses der Geschichte des Sports und der Körperkultur in Polen vom Mittelalter bis zum Zweiten Weltkriege," *Stadion,* 1, 2 (1975): pp. 284–315; Bernard Woltmann, "Gegensätze in der polnischen Sportbewegung, 1919–1939," in *Sport und Politik 1918–1939/40,* ed. A. Morgan Olsen (Oslo: Universitetsforlaget A. S, 1986), pp. 157–162; and Jerzy Gaj and Kajetan Hadzelek, *Dzieje kultury fizycznej w Polsce w xix i xx wieku. Koncepcje, uwarunkowania, i efekty instytucjonalnej działalności* (Poznań: Akademia Wychowania Fizycznego im. Eugeniusza Piaseckiego, 1991), pp. 88–90, 105–114, 133–135.

leadership, overwhelmed by the legacies of partition and the challenges of reunification, marginalized the construction of the sports apparatus, the Bolsheviks, by contrast, aggressively emphasized the utilitarian importance of formulating a sports policy to improve the society's health, win the civil war, facilitate the integration of the diverse peoples of the country, and project images of women's liberation under communist rule.[4] This is significant because the Polish women's sporting experiences would eventually begin to resemble the Soviet model.

Indeed, following Józef Piłsudski's military coup in 1926, the Polish physical culture, similar to its Soviet counterpart, came to be governed by state prerogatives. The political interests of the authoritarian state, with its increasingly militaristic underpinnings, undermined the initial social voluntarism and developed a more systematic and national sports apparatus. The organization of women's physical culture benefited to a surprising extent from this political coordination "from above."[5]

The Polish state endeavored to use women's sports for building nationalism within the country with a three-fold objective. First, the force of nationalism, through the medium of sports, was needed to integrate the various social classes and unite the society with its political leaders by creating a loyal citizenry. In this regard, women's physical culture was perceived by the state to have a positive impact on the development of the fledging Polish nation by creating families that were united in their efforts to remain physically healthy and well-disciplined in accordance with the needs of the state. Women, in other words, were to become fit themselves in order to strengthen the physicality and good morality of the young generation that was yet to be born. Interestingly, the state sought the help of both men and women to construct "happy and rational" lifestyles for their families. The strong emphasis on the need for both parents to serve as sports mentors to their children is significant for this can be considered as the first "domestic" task officially assigned to men who otherwise were rarely encouraged to share the burden of childcare within the household.

Second, "sports nationalism" helped to safeguard the country's infant nationhood and defend its territorial body from external aggression, now more so with the rise of Fascism and Nazism in Europe. The military impulses of the state apparatus

4. James Riordan, *Sport in Soviet Society: Development of Sport and Physical Education in Russia and the USSR* (Cambridge and New York: Cambridge University Press, 1977), pp. 65–118; and James Riordan, "The Rise, Fall, and Rebirth of Sporting Women in Russia and the USSR," *Journal of Sport History*, vol. 18, no. 1 (Spring, 1991): p. 191.

5. For the political coordination "from above" see *Poland Between the Wars: 1918–1939*, ed. Timothy Wiles (Bloomington: Indiana University, 1989); and Andrzej Chojnowski, "Polish National Character, the Sanacja Camp, and the National Democracy," in *National Character and National Ideology in Interwar Eastern Europe*, eds. Ivo Banac and Katherine Verdery (New Haven: Yale Center for International and Area Studies, 1995), pp. 23–38.

enthusiastically supported women's good health and physical fitness. Sports was considered beneficial not only for enhancing women's cognitive abilities and beauty, but also for collectively nurturing and building a "healthy and militarily strong Poland." Finally, in addition to the political rhetoric of national militarism, the interwar state used women's national and international accomplishments in sports to solidify sentiments of national pride and prestige. It identified its female athletes as celebrated national icons who simultaneously championed the cause of women's liberation and national patriotism.[6]

This stress on the mass character of Polish sport, which incorporated sentiments of nationalism, patriotism, and militarism, led to the construction of a number of sports facilities and a systematic apparatus of awards to honor both male and female athletes. Several women's sports associations, along with a host of political, civil, military, and medical institutions legitimized and promoted physical culture for women. The State Office for Physical Education and Military Training (PUWFiPW), staffed with representatives of the ruling *Sanacja* camp, along with the assistance of the Ministry for Military Affairs, the Ministry of National Education and Social Welfare, the Polish Olympic Committee, and the various branches of WFiPW in voivodeships and towns, regulated physical education and sports.[7] The PUWFiPW was bestowed with the principal responsibility of organizing sports for women, and one of its accomplishments was the creation of the Society for the Propagation of Physical Culture for Women (TKKFK) in March 1933 with the ambitious objective of promoting physical education for women as a healthy and rational engagement

6. For press reports on these national motivations see for examples, *Sport,* 10 (19 May, 1922): pp. 151, 152; *Bluszcz,* 6 (7 February, 1925): pp. 130, 131; *Kobieta w świecie i w domu* (hereafter, *KŚD),* 3, 12 (June, 1927): p. 12; *Start,* 2, 5 (1 March, 1928): p. 3; *Kobieta współczesna,* 3, 15 (14 April, 1929): pp. 5, 6; *Przegląd Sportowy* (hereafter, *PzS),* 10, 70, 559 (30 August, 1930): p. 4; *Moja przyjaciółka,* 3, 3 (10 February, 1936): pp. 35, 36; *Sport Polski,* 1, 3 (15 September, 1937): p. 11; and *Kobiety w pracy,* 1, 3 (April, 1938): pp. 10, 11, 15, 28. See also Dr. Władysław Hojnacki, *Higiena kobiety i kosmetyka* (Lwów and Warsaw: Nakładem Księgarni Polskiej B. Połonieckiego, 1925); *Uszkodzenia sportowe u kobiet,* eds. K. Muszałówna and E. Reicherówna (Warsaw: Główna Księgarnia Wojskowa, Państwowy Urząd W.FiP.W, 1935); and Kataryzna Sierakowska, "Macierzyństwo—wizje a rzeczywistość," in *Równe prawa i nierówne szanse: Kobiety w Polsce międzywojennej,* eds, Anna Zarnowska and Andrzej Szwarc (Warsaw: Wydawnictwo DiG 2000), pp. 209–219.

7. For the organization of [male] sports see Seweryn Warsicki, *Kultura fizyczna w Wielkopolsce w latach 1919–1927* (Poznań: Uniwersytet im. Adama Mickiewicza, 1966); Leonard Szymański, *Kultura fizyczna w polityce II Rzeczypospolitej* (Wrocław: Akademia Wychowania Fizycznego, 1995); Wiz. H. Olszewska, "Historyczna rola pierwszego Marszałka Polski Józefa Piłsudskiego na polu wychowania fizycznego w Polsce," *Wychowanie Fizyczne w Szkole,* 8–9 (1935–1936): pp. 223–228; and Jan Kęsik, *Wojsko Polskie wobec tężyzny fizycznej społeczeństwa, 1918–1939* (Wrocław: Akademia Wychowania Fizycznego, 1996).

with significant cultural and moral benefits for them personally, as well as for the development of the nation at large.[8]

With Piłsudski's state patronage that reflected his military predilections, Poland became one of Europe's foremost countries in athletics in a short period of time. Unfortunately, this achievement of Piłsudski's Poland in the realm of sports has been ignored in the secondary western literature. Sure, Piłsudski was an authoritarian ruler whose increasingly arbitrary actions alienated the society from the state and mitigated the construction of the much needed inter-class and inter-ethnic integrative bridges. Still, the organization and accomplishments of the male and female physical cultures provided some jubilance to a country overwhelmed by Piłsudski's dictatorial urges. For this reason, the Marshal's death in May 1935 was rightly mourned in the interwar Polish sports world.[9]

In the years that followed, the organization of sports and physical education benefited from the state's ambitious plans to resolve Poland's pressing economic problems and strengthen its precarious relationship with the society through industrialization, urbanization, and military mobilization. In this political climate of "advanced militarization," women's physical culture became even more militarized and was perceived as critical for nurturing a militarily fit citizenry capable of defending the increasingly vulnerable Polish state. The Camp of National Unity (OZN) sought to enlarge the sporting horizons of women to not only improve their physicality, but also defend the country from external threats and internal social unrest by fostering social solidarity in the developing nation and preserving gender harmony in the physically strong and healthy family. The OZN singled out mothers and children for "special care" and expressly stated that it was the civic duty of every Pole to raise "numerous and healthy offspring." The Polish government, henceforth, directed its efforts to encouraging the formation of "large healthy families" with the assistance of "sportive" parents and athletic children. In so doing, women's sports became more "obedient" to the state's "patriarchal and militaristic nationalism" at the family, regional, and national structures.[10]

More generally, the OZN continued to reaffirm the multiple agendas of the Polish sporting culture in improving the nation's health and hygiene, fostering national prestige and glory, facilitating social activism and mobility, indoctrinating a rational education in the youth, and building national patriotism for military preparedness.

---

8. The secondary literature on women's sports for this time period is very limited and the principal source is Maria Rotkiewicz, "Rozwój sportu kobiet w Polsce okresu międzywojennego," *Sport Wyczynowy,* 3–4/171–172 (1979): pp. 3–21.

9. *Start,* 9/10, (May 1935): pp. 2, 3.

10. *Bluszcz,* 9 (27 February, 1937): pp. 3/195–6/198. For the militarization of Poland see Edward D. Wynot, *Polish Politics in Transition: The Camp of National Unity and the Struggle for Power, 1935–1939* (Athens: University of Georgia Press, 1974), pp. 1–20.

Because of these multifaceted goals, Polish sport occupied an important position in the larger political and cultural contexts, and was reflected in the proliferation of sports in places such as Warsaw, Poznań, Lódź, Częstochowa, Upper Silesia, Kraków, Lwów, and Gdańsk.[11]

From a comparative perspective, it is ironic that the organization of a militarized, nationalist, and family-centered women's physical culture in interwar Poland resembled the pattern of women's sports in the Soviet Union. Given the fact that Imperial Russia had been one of the three colonial powers in partitioned Poland, one would have imagined the Poles distinguishing themselves more from a country with whom their bonds of friendship were not too strong. Still, the Polish female body was recruited by the state for purposes of military defense and strengthening the family institution. This was similar to the "physical strong and heroic" Soviet female physical culture that was, in addition, valued to a much greater extent for its contributions to enhancing economic production and fostering national unity in a large, multinational empire.[12]

By contrast, the Italian fascist state contained women's engagement in the male-dominated athletic culture. While Mussolini encouraged men to play, the fascist leadership, in conjunction with the Church, cautioned that women's sports would promote promiscuity and result in lower birth rates. Therefore, childbirth alone was perceived as the best physical exercise for Italian women![13] The German Third Reich, meanwhile, directed its male and female physical cultures for the sole purpose of racial eugenics. For men, sports helped to create the "courageous and physically strong human being."[14] But for women, the award of a Reich sports medal became the necessary proof of their health that allowed them to marry SS men. As one SS

11. H. Mlodzianowska, "Rozwój wychowania fizycznego i sportu w Polsce w latach 1914–1949," in *Z dziejów kultury fizycznej w Polsce: Materiały na plenum GKKFiT z okazji 100-Iecia sportu polskiego* (Warsaw: Komisja Historyczna Glównego Komitetu Kultury Fizycznej i Turystyki, 1967), pp. 63–140.

12. Richard Stites, *Russian Popular Culture: Entertainment and Society Since 1900* (Cambridge and New York: Cambridge University Press, 1992), p. 95; Robert Edelman, *Serious Fun: A History of Spectator Sports in the USSR* (New York: Oxford University Press, 1993), pp. 8, 9, 18, 23, 41, 58, 61, 64; Riordan, *Sport in Soviet Society*, pp. 124, 148, 150; S. L. Sobolev, *Soviet Youth at Work and Play* (Moscow: Foreign Languages Publishing Institute, 1939), pp. 6, 7, 29, 302; and Lynne Attwood, *Creating the New Soviet Woman: Women's Magazines as Engineers of Female Identity, 1922–1953* (New York: St. Martin's Press, 1999), pp. 71, 126–128.

13. John Hoberman, *Sport and Political Ideology* (London: Heinemann, 1984), p. 92; and Victoria De Grazia, *How Fascism Ruled Women: Italy, 1922–1945* (Berkeley and Los Angeles: University of California Press, 1992), pp. 162, 163, 218–221.

14. Arnd Kruger, "Breeding, Rearing and Preparing the Aryan Body: Creating Supermen the Nazi Way," in *Shaping The Superman: Fascist Body as Political Icon—Aryan Fascism,* ed. J.A. Mangan (London and Portland: Frank Cass 1999), p. 45.

official remarked, "the javelin and the springboard are more useful than lipstick in promoting health."[15]

While military and national considerations dictated the construction of women's physical culture in Poland and some of its neighbors, women's physical culture in interwar Great Britain, America, and Australia became popular only with the transformation in patterns of consumption and leisure opportunities.[16] Women's participation in sports in these societies increased not so much because of state intrusion as evident in the Polish sporting culture, but more due to an age of prosperity characterized by urban glamor and technological glitter. In this regard, Poland lacked an equally strong material culture. However, the emergence of the "New Woman" in interwar Poland made some amends and supported women's engagement in a host of sporting activities.

Feminism and Women's Physical Culture

The development of women's physical culture was intrinsically related to the emergence of the "New Woman" in the resurrected state. Women's participation in sports increased as a consequence of their greater access to higher education and material possessions, their increased visibility in social and cultural activities, and their demands for and achievement of voting rights. This heightened involvement of women in the public realm resulted in the efflorescence of a more sophisticated women's internal consciousness, the external expression of which came in the form of their projected images in intellectual activities, economic work, political interests, and cultural aspirations, all of which exhibited women's eagerness to once again create a modern national culture, but one that was now more professional, democratic, and "physical" in nature.[17]

The importance of women's physical culture was articulated in these public spaces of political organizations, schools and universities, and industries and

15. SS Chief Group Leader Jeckeln's remarks as they were reported in *Frankfurter Zeitung*, (June 1, 1937). Cited in George L. Mosse, *Nazi Culture: Intellectual, Cultural and Social Life in the Third Reich* (New York: Grosset and Dunlap, 1966), p. 43.

16. Susan Cahn, *Coming on Strong: Gender and Sexuality in Twentieth-Century Women's Sport* (New York: Free Press and Maxwell Macmillan International, 1994), pp. 33–47; Jennifer Hargreaves, *Sporting Females: Critical Issues in the History and Sociology of Women's Sports* (London and New York: Routledge, 1994), pp. 113, 137, 138; Derek Birley, *Playing the Game: Sport and British Society, 1910–1945* (Manchester: Manchester University Press, 1995), p. 137; and Marion K. Stell, *Half the Race: A History of Australian Women in Sport* (North Ryde: Angus and Robertson, 1991), pp. 39, 45, 49, 79, 100, 229.

17. Women's periodicals such as *Bluszcz, Kobieta w świecie i w domu, Kobieta współczesna, Moja przyjaciółka, Kobieta polska, Kobiety w pracy, Kobieta pracy,* and *Start* are significant sources for understanding women's identities in interwar Poland.

factories. For example, while women's visibility in the political arena remained sporadic, cautious, and confined to the lower levels of the political hierarchy, their involvement in "social politics" remained extraordinarily strong. Throughout the interwar period, and especially after 1926, a number of women's civil and paramilitary organizations were formed that eventually hosted many other smaller political, social, charitable, and cultural societies. Some of these included the *Rodzina Wojskowa* (The Military Family), the *Rodzina Policyjna* (The Police Family), the *Komitet Społeczny Przysposobienia* (The Social Committee for Training), *Komitet do Obrony Kraju* (The Committee for the Country's Defense), the *Zarząd Główny Komitetu d/sp. Przysposobienia Kobiet* (The Main Board of the Social Committee for the Training of Women), the *Związek Pracy Obywatelskiej Kobiet* (The Women's Union of Civic Works), the *Koło Polek* (The Circle of Polish Women) and the *Narodowa Organizacja Kobiet* (The National Women's Organization). The larger objective of all these women's military and non-military associations was to provide wide-ranging opportunities to their members to participate in sports and improve their health and physical fitness.[18]

The increased economic engagements of women also gave them a greater sense of independence and personal emancipation. Certainly, professional work was difficult, and female workers remained victimized under numerous economic, legal, and family burdens.[19] Still, the "new young woman" had more opportunities in the job market, and was more willing to indulge in exciting adventures, including and especially sports. Working women's sports received the patronage of the PUWFiPW, the Main Workers Inspectorate of the Ministry of Social Welfare, trade unions, youth and worker's sports clubs, and the individual supervision of Stefania Krygierowa, the director of the women's department of the Main Council of the Union of Workers Sports Societies. All of these institutions and individuals directed physical culture for female workers to improve their health, hygiene, and physique,

18. *Kobieta w Sejmie*, 1 (10 January, 1919): pp. 1, 2; *Przegląd Kobiecy*, 2, 1 (May 1920): p. 19; *Kobieta współczesna*, 2, 5 (29 January, 1928): pp. 5, 6, 16; *Kobieta Obywatelka*, (11 November, 1930): pp. 1, 3; *Bıuszcz*, 19 (13 May, 1933): pp. 10, 11; *Moja przyjaciółka*, 3, 23 (10 December, 1936): p. 488; *Kobieta polska*, 1, 1 (20 December, 1936): p. 7; *Kobiety w pracy*, 1, 3 (April 1938): p. 28; *KSD*, 14, 4 (15 February, 1938): p. 2; Marek Robert Jobda, *Działalność stowarzyszenia "Rodzina Wojskowa" w zakresie kultury fizycsntj kobiet* (praca magisterska, AWF Warsaw, 1980); Elżbieta Zawacka, *Czekając na rozkaz: Pogotowie społeczne organizacji Przysposobienia Wojskowego Kobiet w przededniu II wojny światowej* (Lublin: Redakcja Wyd. Katolickiego Uniwersytetu Lubelskiego, 1992), pp. 77–99; and Zofia Moraczewska, *Związek Pracy Obywatelskiej Kobiet* (Warsaw: Wydział Prasowy, 1932), pp. 21, 39.

19. *Bluszcz*, 13 (25 March, 1922): p. 99; *Kobieta pracy*, 1 (9 April, 1933): pp. 4, 6, 13; *Moja przyjaciółka*, 2, 3 (25 April, 1935): p. 114; *Kobieta polska*, 2, 3 (15 February, 1937): pp. 4, 5; *Kobiety w pracy*, 1 (3 April, 1938): p. 20; and Jan Jonczyk, *Ochrona pracy kobiet i młodocianych w polskim przemyśle w latach 1918–1939* (Warsaw: Książka i Wiedza, 1961), pp. 21, 31.

as well as to increase the quantity and quality of economic production. For these reasons, the state also recommended ten minutes' exercise breaks in factories. Łódź, an important industrial-textile center for women, was the first town to organize a sports movement for its working class. Here, women typically played basketball, volleyball, and track and field events.[20]

It must be emphasized that the working women's physical culture was part of the larger [male] workers' sports movement which matured greatly during the period of the Second Polish Republic. The workers' movement was heterogeneous, but sport served as an instrument of integrated cultural learning and social mobility. The *Sanacja* regime, fearful of the communist and social democratic currents of the workers movement, carefully supervised all sports activities of workers.[21] The Polish female workers' physical culture, though less dynamic than its counterparts in Germany, Finland, France, and Great Britain, where women workers typically organized their own sports federations, still benefited from the increased attention on the part of both the state and workers' communities to remain healthy, united, and physically strong.[22]

Women's interest in sports developed further as a consequence of the boom in women's higher education, especially between the years 1925–1936. Emboldened by the state's interest to conduct research in physiology, anatomy, and hygiene, the doctors, pedagogues, and psychologists reiterated the beneficial values of systematic physical education for women in enhancing qualities of attentiveness, solidarity, perseverance, and discipline. Dr. Eugenia Lewicka, a member of the Scientific Council of Physical Education, made significant contributions in sports medicine for women.[23] The Second Polish Sports Congress (April 1927) discussed ideas of promoting sport for women. The participants of the 1928 and 1934 sports conventions

20. *Kobiety w pracy,* 1, 5–6 (June–July 1938): pp. 14, 34, 35; Jolanta Kadziecka, *Działalność kobiet w robotniczym ruchu sportowym Łodzi do 1949* (praca magisterska, AWF Warsaw, 1980), pp. 4, 14, 19, 85; "Wychowanie fizyczne kobiet i dzieci," in *Wychowanie fizyczne,* 3–4 (1935): pp. 97–105; *10 minut gimnastyki pracownic fabrycznych,* eds. K. Muszalówna and E. Reicherówna (Warsaw: Główna Księgarnia Wojskowa, 1937), pp. 1, 23; and *Wychowanie fizyczne kobiet w przemyśle i handlu* (Poznań: Miejski Komitet W.F.iP.W., 1935).

21. The best books on the development of [male] workers' physical culture are Urszula Kowieska, *Kultura fizyczna w programach i działalności związków zawodowych w II Rzeczypospolitej* (Wrocław: AWF, 1997); and Henryk Laskiewicz, *Robotnicza kultura fizyczna w Polsce w latach 1918–1939* (Warsaw: Wydawnictwo Sport i Turystyka, 1971).

22. Allen Guttmann, *Women's Sports: A History* (New York: Columbia University Press, 1991), p. 162.

23. *Bluszcz,* 34 (1925): pp. 961–963; *Stadjon,* 25 (1931): p. 7; *Start,* 13 (1931): p. 2; and R. Wroczyński and K. Hadzelek, "Development of Sciences on Physical Education and Sport in the Academy of Physical Education," *Wychowania fizyczne i sport,* 22, 4 (1978): pp. 87–104.

presented papers on the positive impact of sports for women's physical, psychological, and physiological development.[24] Despite patriarchal resistance in academia, the increasing number of professional and trade schools for girls, and women's larger enrollments in universities for a wide range of subjects, including physical education, not only symbolized women's progressive liberation, but also marked a positive step toward the overall modernization of interwar Poland.[25]

The discussion on the physical emancipation of women in interwar Poland was closely related to the dialogue about women's sexuality. Polish women were now exposed to a myriad of emancipatory ideologies on topics ranging from sex and sexuality, motherhood and family planning, public morality, and fashionable esthetics and ethics, all of which questioned the traditional culture of religious conservatism. The intellectual and cultural ideas of several leading women reinforced the sentiments of the feminists in late partitioned Poland to create a far more liberating environment for women in the Second Polish Republic. For example, Irena Kosmowska, a famous personality of the interwar women's movement, supported freedom of individual conscience, and emphasized the need for a separation of the Church and state. Helena Radlińska also called for an "ethical" cultural transformation in the direction of greater democratic aspirations.[26] While the polemics of such debate weakened in the 1930s, the impact of these discussions on women's morality and sexuality was wide-ranging and visible even in the countryside where a rural women's physical culture developed in response to the urban tremors of modernity. Such gendered discourses permeated the peasant women's rural veneer to present them with new opportunities and realities in their economic, social, and cultural spaces. The "new peasant woman" became increasingly aware of the importance of good health and hygiene for her personal development and for the longevity of her

24. *Bluszcz*, 19 (12 May, 1934): p. 580; Rotkiewicz, "Rozwój sportu kobiet w Polsce," p. 20; and *Sprawozdanie z Drugiego Kongresu Kultury Fizycznej Kobiet odbytego w dn. 28 i 29 Kwietnia 1934 r. w Warszawie* (Nakładem Towarzystwa Krzewienia Kultury Fizycznej Kobiet), pp. 5–10, 21–30, 39–47.

25. *Bluszcz*, 20 (19 May, 1923): pp. 158, 159; *Świat kobiecy*, 21 (1 November, 1925): p. 489; *Kobieta współczesna*, 3, 6 (10 February, 1929): p. 3; and *Kobieta Polska*, 2, 3 (15 February, 1937): pp. 3, 4. For sports in educational institutions see also Ewa Kraskowska, *Piórem niewieścim: Z problemów prozy kobiecej dwudziestolecia międzywojennego* (Poznań: Uniwersytet im. Adama Mickiewicza, 1999), p. 13; Szymański, *Kultura fizyczna*, pp. 32, 51–54, 65, 115, 116, 125; Leonard Nowak, *Wychowanie fizyczne i sport w panstwowym szkolnictwie ogólnokształcacym w Polsce w latach, 1918–1939* (Poznań: Akademia Wychowania Fizycznego im. Eugeniusza Piaseckiego, 1996), pp. 35–40, 72, 73, 204–228; and Warsicki, *Kultura fizyczna*, pp. 42–47, 65–69, 74–96.

26. *Kobieta w Sejmie*, 3 (25 January, 1919): p. 3; *Kobieta współczesna*, 3, 15 (14 April, 1929): pp. 5, 6; *Kobieta pracy*, 1 (9 April, 1933): p. 6; *Kobieta polska*, 2, 4 (1–15 March, 1937): p. 21; and *Bluszcz*, 34 (20 August, 1938): p. 19/811.

family members. The various rural women's publications and organizations emphasized the importance of building a "rational" peasant society in which physically healthy rural women managed their home economies with greater independence and confidence.[27] However, the images of rural women in interwar Polish physical culture remained more passive than the newer images of Soviet peasant women who were displayed in the political posters of the 1930s with a far slimmer and youthful body.[28]

While the "new woman" sought to redefine her sexuality and physicality, it is important to recognize that she was not guilty of feminist insubordination to elite national politics. Women's greater independence, autonomy, and mobility, as exemplified by the term "feminism," did not devalue the importance of the role of the family as the pivotal social institution performing critical functions in safeguarding traditional public morality. The omnipresent societal and official vigilance underscored feminist attempts to radicalize the interwar women's movement. Women in interwar Poland, as in partitioned Poland, used their professionalism to further the interests of the state and not necessarily to pursue their personal goals of individual emancipation. This dichotomy between the political, economic, cultural, and sexual equality of women in theory, and the persistence of traditional social customs which in reality discouraged the dissolution of conventional family patterns, was well reflected in the apparatus of women's physical culture and in the projected images of female athletes as exemplars of Polish nationalism, patriotism, and moderated feminism.

The Interaction Between Polish Nationalism and Feminism in Women's Sports

Polish women participated in many amateur and high performance sports with dynamism, enthusiasm, and dedication, establishing several national and international records. Halina Konopacka's superlative performances in the discus throw enabled Poland to win its first Olympic gold medal in 1928. Thereafter, the

27. *Kobieta współczesna*, 4, 8 (23 February, 1930): p. 13; *Bluszcz*, 34 (20 August, 1938): p. 18/810; Zawacka, *Czekając na rozkaz*, pp. 84–86; Szymański, *Kultura fizyczna*, pp. 32, 82, 87; Jerzy Chelmecki, "*Problematyka wychowania fizycznego i sportu w działalności Związku Młodzieży Wiejskiej RP "Wici",*" *Kultura fizyczna*, 3 (1979): pp. 9–14; and Tadeusz Daszkiewicz, "Józef Piłsudski o wartościach nadrzędnych wychowania fizycznego," *Kultura fizyczna*, 3–4 (1999): pp. 1–3.

28. Victoria E. Bonnell, *Iconography of Power: Soviet Political Posters under Lenin and Stalin* (Berkeley: University of California Press, 1997), pp. 101, 105.

accomplishments of Stanisława Walasiewiczówna and Jadwiga Waysówna in track and field not only increased Poland's Olympic medal count, but placed this sport ahead of all others for women. In other sports, women's tennis, considered healthy and esthetic, celebrated the international successes of Jadwiga Jędrzejowska and Wiera Richterówna. Women's rowing, perceived as bold and democratic, burgeoned under the aegis of the Warsaw Oarswomen Club (WKW) and the oaring clubs of Bydgoszcz, Kalisz, and Poznań. WKW's membership increased from 268 in 1924, to 400 in 1929, and 692 in 1931. Meanwhile, the female fencers from Silesia performed extraordinarily well, and so did Janina Kurkowska-Spychajowa, the Polish "Mistress of Sports" and the world's best archer.[29]

In the 1930s women were encouraged to learn the art of rifleshooting to protect their families and defend the nation from external aggression. This sport, more widespread in the countryside and among urban workers, enabled women to overcome their presumed passivity and physical weakness. The Riflewomen's Union, along with women's scouting and Sokół groups, added sentiments of militarism and social integration to their traditional reservoir of patriotism. Meanwhile, women's gymnastics, volleyball, basketball, skating, and skiing were all considered enrapturing and character-building sports. The best female swimmers came from Warsaw and Kraków, and from the Jewish *Makkabi* Women in aviation (gliding and parachuting) were referred to as "queens of the air" who successfully undermined traditional biological conservatism according to which women possessed shortcomings and defects. Similar to their Soviet counterparts, Polish female aviators demonstrated abilities of rational reasoning, physical strength, and confidence. Finally, the Second

29. For a sample of the coverage on women's tennis, fencing, oaring, archery, and track and field during the interwar period see *Gazeta Kaliska*, (9 June, 1920); *PzS*, I, 18 (17 September, 1921): pp. 12, 13; *Sport*, 13 (9 June, 1922): p. 225; Świat *kobiecy*, 7 (5 April, 1925): p. 148; *Kobieta współczesna*, 3, 15 (14 April, 1929): pp. 5, 6; *Bluszcz*, 23 (9 June, 1934): pp. 711, 712; *Moja przyjaciółka*, 3, 16 (25 August, 1936): p. 321; *KSD*, 14, 21 (1 November, 1938): pp. 11, 12; *Kobiety w pracy*, 1, 3 (April 1938): pp. 10, 11; Anna Młoziankowska, *Początki i rozwój sportu szermierczego kobiet w Polsce do 1980* (praca magisterska, AWF Warsaw, 1982), p. 96; Tadeusz Karuga, "Rozwój sportu szermierczego kobiet na Górnym Śląsku do r. 1939," *Kultura Fizyczna*, 2, 31 (February 1977): pp. 79–82; *Statut Warszawskiego Klubu Wioślarek* (Warsaw, 1927); *Warszawski Klub Wioślarek, Regulamin Wioślarski* (Warsaw, 1933); *Warszawski Klub wioślarek swej prezesce członkini honorowej Dr. Zofii Zabawskiej-Domosławskiej w dowód wdzięczności i uznania dla jej pracy dla klubu w ciagu 10-letniej prezesury* (Warsaw, 15 December 1934), pp. 8, 14, 15; and Zdzisław Pawluczuk, "Miejsce sokolic w polskiej lekkoatletyce kobiecej w latach 1919–1939," in *Z najnowszej historii kultury fizycznej w Polsce*, ed. Bernard Woltmann (Gorzów: AWF w Gorzowie Wlkp., 1998), pp. 25–33.

Polish Republic also witnessed a developing interest in women's automobile racing and football.[30]

In regional variations, women's sports were best organized in Warsaw. In Poznań, women's basketball and handball made the town "sportive" and facilitated the city's integration with the rest of the country. In the Silesian towns, the Sokół nests and working-class sports clubs contributed to the development of women's sports. Events in track and field and gymnastics were popular among women in Toruń and Bydgoszcz. In Częstochowa, the Young Women's Christian Organization sponsored volleyball and "rational" courses in physical education. In Kalisz, women participated in track and field events and oaring, as well as in the not so recommended cycling and football. Kraków boasted of many talented sportswomen, while Bialystok took pride in its few accomplished female athletes, especially in track and field. In Kielce, the communist-sponsored *Sportówki* organized popular recreation, dance, and music for women. There is, however, scant reference to an emigrant Polish female physical culture, except for the fact that Polish women in Germany played volleyball.[31]

---

30. For some examples of women's participation in all of these sports see *PzS*, 2, 29, 62 (21 July, 1922): p. 5; *Bluszcz*, 39 (27 September, 1924): p. 691; *Świat kobiecy*, 8 (15 April, 1927): p. 160; *Start*, 2, 5 (March, 1928): p. 10; *Kobieta współczesna*, 3, 7 (17 February, 1929): pp. 15–17; *KSD*, 8, 10 (May, 1932): pp. 26, 27; *Kobieta polska*, 1, 1 (20 December, 1936): p. 17; *Moja przyjaciółka*, 4, 3 (10 February, 1937): pp. 54, 55; *Kobiety w pracy*, 1, 3 (April, 1938): p. 23; *Bluszcz*, 1, (1 January, 1939): p. 16; D. Rosenberg, *Teoretyczne podstawy ćwiczeń cielesnych dla kobiet ze szczególnym uwzględnieniem gimnastyki Bertram* (Warsaw, 1931); Maria Rotkiewicz and Alexandra Latek, "Maria Germanówna i początki koszykówki kobiet w Polsce (do 1939r.)," *Sport Wyczynowy*, 3–4/363–364 (1995): pp. 78–86; Eugeniusz Piasecki, *Dzieje wychowania fizycznego* (Lwów-Warsaw-Kraków: Wydawnictwo Zakładu Narodowego imienia Ossolinskich, 1925), p. 230; and *Regulaminy Organizacji Sokolic Związek Towarzystw Gimnastycznych "Sokół" w Polsce* (Warsaw, 1927), p. 3. For Soviet female aviators see Karen Petrone, "Gender and Heroes: The Exploits of Soviet Pilots and Arctic Explorers in the 1930s," in *Women and Political Change: Perspectives from East-Central Europe*, ed. Susan Bridger (New York: St. Martin's Press, 1999), pp. 7–26.

31. For regional variations in women's sports see Eligiusz Małolepszy, *Kultury fizyczna i przysposobienie wojskowe w Częstochowie i w powiecie częstochowskim w latach 1918–1939* (Częstochowa: Wyzsza Szkoła Pedagogiczna, 1996), pp. 96–104, 139; Elżbieta Fus, *Początki i rozwój sportu kobiecego w Kaliszu do 1939* (praca magisterska, AWF Warsaw, 1982), p. 105; Stanisława Trybowska, *Początki rozwoju sportu kobiecego w Krakowie do 1939 roku* (praca magisterska, AFW Warsaw, 1978), pp. 293–295; Wiktoria Niedbała, *Początki i rozwój kobiecego sportu w Białymstoku do 1939* (praca magisterska, AWF Warsaw, 1983), p. 59; Bolesław Makowski, *Krzewienie i popularyzacja kultury fizycznej na Pomorzu od czasów zaborczych do roku 1939 w świetle działalności organizacji gimnastycznej "Sokół"* (Ku czci 1000-lecia Państwa Polskiego na 100-lecie polskiej gimnastyki 1867–1967, July 1966), pp. 56–60; Edward D. Wynot, *Warsaw Between the World Wars: Profile of the Capital City in a Developing Land, 1918–1939* (Boulder: East European Monographs. Distributed by Columbia University Press, 1983),

The Polish press spoke highly of its accomplished athletes. They were well-received in popular opinion and glorified in the national and regional press coverage. While the literature on sportswomen may not have been as extensive as that concerning their male counterparts, the quality of this limited reportage was characterized by exceptional praise. Articles with titles such as "*Brawo nasze panie*" (Bravo Our Women) were common. The sports newspapers and women's periodicals remarked that Polish sportswomen had not only established themselves into an elite group of professionals and world record holders, but that they had also frequently taken the lead from men in sporting competitions. The women's sport periodical, *Start,* under the editorship of Kazimiera Muszałówna, also projected many such images of women's physical emancipation.

The press frequently displayed the professional images of Polish sportswomen alongside their domestic responsibilities. Female athletes were portrayed as good mothers and wives, and the newspapers and periodicals often showed pictures of sportswomen with their children. For example, Stanisława Walasiewiczówna was reported to be a good housewife and an excellent cook.[32] Many female athletes were married, and some were mothers of two or more children. Some sportswomen married their colleagues, in contrast to Nazi Germany which frowned upon marriages between its male and female elite athletes.[33] Moreover, female sports champions were not only projected to have successfully balanced their training regimen with family obligations, but also continued their professional service as pedagogues, trainers, and journalists in their post-athletic careers.

Polish sportswomen competed for the highest national and international honors in sports. For example, the prestigious *Państwowa Nagroda Sportowa* (State Sports Award) was awarded to Halina Konopacka in the years 1927 and 1928, to Stanisława

---

pp. 113, 153, 190, 213, 254, 258, 284–305; Zbigniew Dworecki, *Poznań i Poznaniacy w latach drugiej Rzeczypospolitej, 1918–1939* (Poznań: Media Rodzina, 1994), pp. 466–488; Bernard Woltmann, *Polska kultura fizyczna na wschodnim pograniczu niemieckim, 1919–1939* (Poznań: AWF, 1980), pp. 85, 96, 152, 237–270, 301; Antoni Steuer, *Sport na Górnym Śląsku, 1896–1996* (Katowice: Muzeum Historii Katowic, 1997), pp. 16–39, 66–74; Eleonora Sapia-Drewniak, *Aktywność kulturalna i oświatowa kobiet na Śląsku Opolskim w latach 1922–1939* (Opole: Związek Górnośląski, 1991), pp. 44, 45; Mirosław Ponczek, *Z przeszlości ruchu sportowego z Zaglębiu Dąbrowskim do 1939 roku* (Sosnowiec: Sosnowiecka Oficyna Wydawniczo-Autorska SOWA Press, 1992), pp. 22–54; and Regina Renz, "Kobiety i życie społeczno-polityczne kieleczczyzny, 1918–1939," in *Kobieta i świat polityki w niepodległej Polsce, 1918–1939*, eds. Anna Żarnowska and Andrzej Szwarc (Warsaw: Wydawnictwo Sejmowe, 1996), pp. 210, 212.

32. See *Bluszcz,* 32 (7 August, 1937): pp. 12/728, 13/729. For a picture of ice skater Zofia Nehringowa with her two children see *PzS,* 18, 1, 1361 (3 January, 1938): p. 1.

33. Graham McFee and Alan Tomlinson, "Riefenstahl's *Olympia:* Ideology and Aesthetics in the Shaping of the Aryan Athletic Body," *The International Journal of the History of Sport,* vol. 16, no. 2 (1999): p. 74.

Wałasiewiczówna in 1932 and 1933, to Jadwiga Waysówna in 1934 and 1936, and to Jadwiga Jędrzejowska in 1937.[34] The results of the popular annual plebiscites (see table) organized by the leading Polish sports magazine *Przegląd Sportowy* to vote for the top ten outstanding sportsmen or sportswomen of the year is suggestive of a popular social opinion that made no gender differentiation in awarding the nation's highest honors to female athletes. In eight of these fourteen years, a woman was voted as Poland's top athlete!

Results of Popular Plebiscites Conducted by *Przegląd Sportowz*[35]

Year	Name	Event	Position
1926	Halina Konopacka	Track and Field	2
1927	Halina Konopacka	Track and Field	1
	Janina Loleczkowa	Tennis, Skiing	7
1928	Halina Konopacka	Track and Field	1
	Halina Polańkowa	Skiing	9
1929	Stanisława Wałasiewiczówna	Track and Field	3
1930	Stanisława Wałasiewiczówna	Track and Field	1
	Halina Konopacka	Track and Field	5
	Jadwiga Jędrzejowska	Tennis	6
1931	Jadwiga Jędrzejowska	Tennis	3
	Jolanta Manteufflówna	Track and Field	6
	Halina Konopacka	Track and Field	7
1932	Stanisława Wałasiewiczówna	Track and Field	1
	Jadwiga Waysówna	Track and Field	3
	Jadwiga Jędrzejowska	Tennis	7
	Zofia Nehringowa	Skating	10
1933	Stanisława Wałasiewiczówna	Track and Field	1
	Jadwiga Waysówna	Track and Field	2
	Jadwiga Jędrzejowska	Tennis	5
1934	Stanisława Wałasiewiczówna	Track and Field	1

34. There was a good deal of celebratory coverage in the women's and sports press on the accomplishments of individual female athletes, such as Konopacka, Wałasiewiczówna, and Waysówna. For Stanisława Wałasiewiczówna's nomination as one of the best sportspersons in an American poll see *Bluszcz*, 9 (26 February, 1938): p. 13/205. For a good summary of Halina Konopacka's life and sporting accomplishments see *Halina Konopacka: Wznosiłam świat miłością* (Łomianki: Spółka Wydawnicza Heliodor, 1994).

35. The results of the plebiscite for each year were declared toward the beginning of the following new year in this sports newspaper.

Year	Name	Event	Position
	Jadwiga Waysówna	Track and Field	2
1935	Stanisława Wałasiewiczówna	Track and Field	3
	Jadwiga Jędrzejowska	Tennis	5
1936	Jadwiga Jędrzejowska	Tennis	1
	Jadwiga Waysówna	Track and Field	4
	Stanisława Wałasiewiczówna	Track and Field	6
	Maria Kwasniewska	Track and Field	9
1937	Jadwiga Jędrzejowska	Tennis	1
	Stanisława Wałasiewiczówna	Track and Field	3
1938	Stanisława Wałasiewiczówna	Track and Field	3
	Jadwiga Jędrzejowska	Tennis	4
1939	No Plebiscite		

The fact that Polish female athletes served as glorified models of nationalism and as powerful vanguards of feminism suggests a double victory for sportswomen. Unfortunately, this impressive growth in women's sports was ridden with problems and constrained by the economic and political weaknesses of the state, the persistence of social patriarchy, and the lack of women's solidarity. The continued scarcity of financial and infrastructural resources together with muddled bureaucratic interventions limited the popularization of most sports for women. There were voices of concern for the few women trainers, for the limited number of instructional courses in physical education, and for the need to construct more sports facilities for women.[36] The state's patronage of physical culture was contained by the widespread social and economic unrest that deprived the workers and peasants of the resources and leisure time required to engage in sports in a meaningful manner. Ethnic differences further weakened the institutional foundations of women's sports. For example, the Jews and Ukrainians formed their separate physical cultures. The Union of Jewish Women's Sports Societies, the largest Jewish organization for women's sport in Poland, even published its own sports periodical, *Kobieta Nowa* (New Woman). The organization of women's sports thus suffered from the state's political intractability, racial chauvinism, and persistent economic malaise. While the organization of sports in the Soviet Union was also impeded by a host of issues, the situation was more critical in Poland where the serious political factionalization undermined the

36. *Kobieta współczesna,* 1, 30 (23 October, 1927): p. 3; *Sport Polski,* I, 4 (22 September, 1937): pp. 12, 13; *Sport Polski,* 2, 30 (27 July, 1938): p. 6; *KŚD,* 4, 15 (August 1928): p. 18; *Bluszcz,* 48 (1 December, 1923): p. 477; *Bluszcz,* 13 (28 March, 1925): pp. 298, 299; *Bluszcz,* 51 (15 December, 1928): p. 11; *PzS,* 8, 13, 358 (31 March, 1928): p. 4; and *Pz.S,* 18, 91, 1451 (10 November, 1938): p. 2.

efforts to redress the socio-economic problems.[37] The forced militarization of Polish male and female physical cultures, on account of the urgent national considerations, forged an artificial semblance of social unity which the state naively hoped to use as a veritable force to defend the Second Republic against external aggressors. In this regard, the political leaders remained unsuccessful at using women's sports to fan the flames of nationalism.

Sports for women were still perceived as unethical, harmful, brutal, barbaric, manly, and wasteful.[38] The propagandists of women's physical culture were careful to place more weight on the esthetic femininity and attractiveness of female athletes amidst derisive images of strong and "crazy" sportswomen. Their cardinal aim was to project an image of "moderation" in women's sport, that is, on improving women's health and hygiene, and not necessarily on facilitating women's active engagement in sports.[39] Despite the rhetoric of women's equality, the state and the society remained conjoined in patriarchy, and lacked the motivation and determination to ease women's double burden. As a consequence, women were still expected to fulfill their domestic responsibilities in both the old and new patterns of household management.[40] For this reason also, the male-dominated host sports organizations, such as the Polish Olympic Committee and the PUWFiPW, often treated women as "subordinate" members or as "guests" without opportunities to participate in sports life.[41]

In response to the inharmonious juxtaposition of women's "athleticism" and "femininity" in popular consciousness, the press reports simultaneously celebrated the achievements of elite female champions and published the viewpoints of the opponents of women's sports who advocated stronger injunctions against building

37. *The History of Poland Since 1863*, ed. R. F. Leslie (Cambridge and New York: Cambridge University Press, 1980), pp. 148–184; Norman Davies, *God's Playground· A History of Poland, 1795 to the Present*, Vol. II (New York: Columbia University Press, 1982), pp. 411–419, 542, 544; Jan Kofman, *Economic Nationalism and Development: Central and Eastern Europe Between the Two World Wars* (Boulder: Westview Press, 1997), pp. 29–139; Andrzej Chojnowski, *Koncepcje polityki narodowościowej rządów polskich w latach 1921–1939* (Wroclaw: Zakład Narodowy im. Ossolinskich, 1979), p. 240; Laskiewicz, *Robotnicza kultura fizyczna*, pp. 19, 20, 28; and Szymański, *Kultura fizyczna w polityce*, pp. 22–72, 118–131. For problems in Soviet sports see Henry Morton, *Soviet Sport: Mirror of Soviet Society* (New York: Collier Books, 1963), pp. 142, 145, 196, 203.

38. *KŚD*, 3, 12 (June, 1927): p. 12; *Bluszcz*, 7 (14 February, 1925): pp. 154, 155; *Start*, 18, 2 (December, 1927): p. 4; and *Sport Polski*, 1, 8 (20 October, 1937): p. 3.

39. *Bluszcz*, 20 (15 May, 1937): p. 11/427.

40. *Pz.S*, 14, 22, 926 (17 March, 1934): p. 6.

41. *Bluszcz*, 12 (21 March, 1925): p. 274; and *Pz.S*, 10, 503 (15 February, 1930): p. 4.

women's physical culture.[42] Some of the harsher critics of women's sports, especially for women's cycling and football, targeted their caustic remarks toward French female athletes who increasingly made their presence visible in these sports. According to them, "since French sportswomen never forget to powder and put on rouge even in swimming, their mannish sporting interests were contradictory and utterly reprehensible."[43] The impact of such a discourse was evident in the numbers of women participating in sports. For example, in women's skiing, the majority of female athletes came from Kraków, mainly because women in Warsaw lacked the necessary support from their sports clubs to participate in far away Zakopane. The absence of women skiers from Lwów was criticized as "inexplicable."[44] Tennis remained elitist, and female tennis players were few and far between. Women's engagement in Sokół was also more circumscribed in comparison to male participation. Where numbers was not the issue, the sports attire became the question mark. Female fencers, for example, were required to demonstrate their "elegance" by being uniformed in a "suitable" outfit of white blouses and white trousers or black skirts up to the knee.[45]

The multiple weaknesses of the interwar Polish women's movement also limited the popularity of women's physical culture to a select few.[46] The emancipation of women in interwar Poland was in practice confined only to the privileged class that had access to both money and leisure time. Similarly, women's sports satisfied the sporting thrills of only a few predestined athletes. Women's physical culture remained enclosed in the larger cities, and the female athletes came mainly from the intelligentsia, less so from the working-class, and least from families of peasant background. This membership pattern was in contrast to the male athletes who mostly came from peasant and workers' communities, and least of all from the intelligentsia.[47] The inherent elitism of Polish sportswomen was characteristic of the entire Polish women's movement which remained quite exclusive in the interwar period. The Polish feminists also united under the banner of "Woman Citizen"

42. *Bluszcz*, 8 (24 February, 1934): p. 243.

43. *Bluszcz*, 50 (13 December, 1924): p. 929; and *Bluszcz*, 51–52 (23 December, 1924): p. 959.

44. *Bluszcz*, 42 (20 October, 1923): p. 405.

45. See Henryk Laskiewicz, "Rozwój organizacyjny ruchu sportowego województwa śląskiego w latach 1922–1939," in *Z dziejów kultury fizycznej na Śląsku i w Zagłębiu Dąbrowskim*. Ed. Henryk Rechowicz (Katowice: AWF w Katowice, 1989), pp. 117–191.

46. *Sport Polski*, 1, 8 (20 October, 1937): p. 3; *Bluszcz*, 7 (11 February, 1922): p. 53; *Bluszcz*, 12 (21 March, 1925): p. 274; and *Pz.S*, 10, 503 (15 February, 1930): p. 4.

47. The best book on this subject is Anna Pawlak, *Polskie olimpijki z lat 1924–1994: Miniatury czyli filigranowe portrety wielkich dam polskiego sportu* (Warsaw: Polskie Stowarzyszenie Sportu Kobiet, 1995).

(*Kobieta obywatelka*) that confined women to the mothering responsibilities of aiding their children's health as their only legitimate sporting duty. From this perspective, the expressions of class unity which resisted modernity, and class conflict which undermined the evolution of popular feminist consciousness, both mitigated the development of Polish women's physical culture in the interwar period.

Unlike the Bolsheviks, the interwar leaders of Poland never attempted to engineer a "withering away" of the family unit. In this context, the Polish state was less dubious in its understanding of the "woman question" and remained committed to strengthening the family institution at all times. The basic view of Polish women as good wives and mothers was not altered, and the fulfillment of these roles, consistently termed a woman's "mission," was understood and propagated as their obligatory duty to the nation. The association of women with domesticity did not wane throughout the interwar period, and the traditional image of the national and Catholic self-sacrificing *matka polka* remained the implicit ideal by which women's role in the nation was valued and judged.[48] In order to remain worthy citizens, the Polish women could become "sportive," but they were still to carefully nurture their families, preserve the Church-endorsed vision of "good" and "rational" public morality, and moderate their feminist predilections to accomplish the state designated task of social mobilization to defend the country's territorial integrity in an increasingly hostile international climate.[49] The weight of tradition remained heavy and kept Polish "sports feminism" submerged in the increasingly contested and diluted waters of interwar patriarchy.

Even in other countries, while sports and physical exercise were seen as essential activities by young women keen on being "modern," the patriarchal definitions of femininity were much slower to change.[50] In Canada, for example, strain, sweat, dirt, and improper clothing were simply incompatible with the traditional view of femininity.[51] Similarly, there was some confusion over what constituted an "appropriate" sports outfit for women in the Soviet Union.[52] Many sports remained marginalized

48. *Bluszcz*, 46 (12 November, 1938): p. 12/1116.

49. For a gendered discourse on the meanings of citizenship in interwar Poland see Dobróchna Kalwa, *Kobieta aktywna w Polsce międzywojennej:dylematy środowisk kobiecych* (Kraków, 2001).

50. Birgitte Søland, *Becoming Modern: Young Women and the Reconstruction of Womanhood in the 1920s* (Princeton: Princeton University Press, 2000), pp. 46–64.

51. Helen Lenskyj, "Physical Activity for Canadian Women 1890–1930: Media Views," in *From "Fair Sex" to Feminism: Sport and the Socialization of Women in the Industrial and Post-Industrial Eras*, eds. J. A. Mangan and Roberta J. Park (London and New York: Frank Cass, 1987), pp. 208–234.

52. Attwood, *Creating the New Soviet Woman*, p. 70.

for women in France, Britain, and New Zealand.[53] In America, the projected images of Mildred "Babe" Didrikson Zaharias as an amazon, tomboy, hustler and "mannish" athlete undermined her outstanding sporting accomplishments.[54]

Thus, Polish women were obliged to participate in sports but not seek strenuous competition and the quest for records. The "new athletic woman" did not transgress gender boundaries in sports and balanced her sporting interests with the national obligations. Still, the new style of "energetic and athletic femininity" provided some buoyancy to the socially constructed image of conservative womanhood as articulated in the period of the partitions. The newer cultural and professional identities of female athletes in different social surroundings awarded women with more opportunities to effect a transformation in patriarchal gender relations in the direction toward greater independence and emancipation. Their decision to identify themselves as defenders of the family institution and the Polish state, as well as to participate in those sports which conformed to public opinion, earned them national respect and social prestige, far more than the expressions of gratitude or heroism which may have been awarded to sportswomen of other interwar societies.

Conclusion

Polish women's participation in sports in the interwar period was required to conform to state-directed expectations of creating a healthy, rational, military-oriented, family-based, and nation-centered female physical culture. This Polish-style "national feminism" was designed by the state and accepted by the society to "nationalize" feminism and not "feminize" the Polish nation. For this reason, women's sports did not undermine the masculine construction of the country. Their sports interests adhered strictly to the prevalent social norms which regulated women's morality, sexuality, and physicality. While the female athletes presented images of professionalism, modernity, urbanity, and energetic femininity, their physical culture also was characterized by elitism, ethnic chauvinism, and conservative feminism. In this medley of images, one factor was constant: Polish female athletes were obedient players in their sporting culture refereed by the interwar political elites and custodians of social patriarchy.

---

53. Mary Lynn Stewart, *For Health and Beauty: Physical Culture for Frenchwomen, 1880s–1930s* (Baltimore: John Hopkins University Press, 2001), pp. 166, 167, 172; Richard Holt, *Sport and Society in Modern France* (London: Macmillan, 1981), pp. 8, 158, 163, 164, 177; Birley, *Playing the Game*, pp. 39, 40, 203–208; and Scott Crawford, "Pioneering Women: Recreational and Sporting Opportunities in a Remote Colonial Setting," in *From "Fair Sex,"* eds. Mangan and Park, pp. 161–181.

54. The best book on this subject is Susan Cayleff, *Babe: The Life and Legend of Babe Didrikson Zaharias* (Urbana: University of Illinois Press, 1995).

Unfortunately, this organization of Polish sports was destroyed in the Second World War. For all the interwar emphasis on national defense and military fitness, the Polish society and state succumbed to the occupation forces from both the east and west. The task of molding women's physical culture into a nationally enthusiastic defense mechanism to save the fatherland failed. But Polish women, similar to their male counterparts, continued to engage in the resistance efforts. Women's scouting troops were especially active in participating in the underground military resistance.[55] However, the onus would once again fall on the Polish nationalist and feminist ideologies to rebuild women's sports at the conclusion of the war. The motivations and logistics of restructuring the Polish women's physical culture would thereafter be governed by the competing forces of nationalism, socialism, and feminism, in both of their Polish and Soviet styles.

55. See *By nie odeszły w mrok zapomnienia: udział kobiet polskich w II wojnie światowej*, ed. Zofia Polubiec (Warsaw: Książca i Wiedza, 1976); Stanisław Broniewski, *Całym życiem: Szare szeregi w relacji naczelnika* (Warsaw: Państwowe Wyd. Nauk., 1983), pp. 196–199; and Katherine Jolluck, *Exile and Identity: Polish Women in the Soviet Union During World War II* (Pittsburgh: University of Pittsburgh Press, 2002).

Part Three

Image, Identities, and Consciousness: Gender, Class, and Ethnicity Entwined

Holy Mary, Other of God
Sacred and Profane Constructions of Polish-American Womanhood

John J. Bukowczyk

The study of Poles and Polish Americans within the conceptual framework of "Otherness" offers fresh perspectives on subjects like class formation; the development of civic, ethnic, and personal identities; interethnic relations; and nation-building.[1] Some scholars have contended that Polish women, meanwhile, have formed a special case of "Otherness," because they have been "the 'Other' of two cultures."[2] The point is well made that sex and gender bear heavily on articulations of "Otherness." Indeed, Polish women actually can be seen as the "Others" in multiple cultural contexts. In the context of Polish immigration to the United States, Polish women (and their daughters and granddaughters) became an "Other" for both American secular, or profane, culture and for Polish-American Roman

---

I would like to thank Anna Frajlich-Zajac and my fellow participants and audience members at the Kosciuszko Foundation's conference on "The Polish American Woman: The 'Other' of Both Cultures," for their helpful discussion and commentary. They, of course, bear no responsibility for the conclusions and interpretations presented in the essay, which are my own.

1. For examples of these, see *The Slavs in the Eyes of the Occident, the Occident in the Eyes of the Slavs,* ed. Maria Ciesla-Korytowska (Boulder, Colo.: Eastern European Monographs, 1992); Larry Wolff, *Inventing Eastern Europe: The Map of Civilization on the Mind of the Enlightenment* (Stanford, Calif.: Stanford University Press, 1994); John J. Bukowczyk, "Polish Americans, Ethnicity, and Otherness," *The Polish Review* vol. 43, no. 3 (1998): pp. 299–313; Izabela Kalinowska-Blackwood, "Between East and West: Polish and Russian Nineteenth-Century Travel to the Orient" (Ph.D. diss., Yale University, 1998); also see Ewa M. Thompson, *Imperial Knowledge: Russian Literature and Colonialism* (Westport, Conn.: Greenwood Press, 2000).

2. This was the title of the November 2002 Kosciuszko Foundation symposium on the subject organized by Anna Frajlich-Zajac.

From *The Polish Review,* vol. 48, no. 2 (2003), pp. 195–203.

Catholic culture.[3] In many respects, the latter has been the far more interesting and in some ways also the more significant cultural construction.

In both secular American mass culture and secular American popular culture constructions of Polish and Polish-American women have been collapsed together into a single, undifferentiated negative ethnic stereotype. In this genre, stereotyped secular representations of Polish and Polish-American womanhood have portrayed Polish and Polish-American women as, to varying degrees, bestial and subhuman. This stereotype has been as monotonously familiar as it has been painfully persistent. It has been embedded in and disseminated through popular culture forms and mass culture media as varied as literature, television sit-coms, film, the ubiquitous "Polish joke," and now, too, the internet. Three "jokes" listed on an internet website called "The Canonical List of Polish Jokes" present key themes in this offensive genre: The first—"How do you recognize the bride at a Polish wedding? She's the one with the braided armpits."—depicts the Polish woman as crude and uncouth.[4] The second—"What do you call a pool full of Polish beauty queens? Bay of Pigs,"—presumably means to show her as obese and ugly.[5] A third draws a crude connection between a hockey goalie and feminine hygiene in order to imply that Polish women are dirty and uncouth.[6] While Polish Americans do not recognize their mothers and sisters, their daughters and wives in this so-called humor, if they have lived in the United States for any extended period of time, they cannot have avoided encountering such representations. In one episode of the TV sitcom *Dharma & Greg*, one line, intended to evoke viewer guffaws, had character Greg and his father contriving a cover story, designed to deceive their wives, that they were traveling to Las Vegas in order to ogle "large Slavic women."[7] Meanwhile, perhaps the most visible fictionalized Polish-American female representation in contemporary American mass culture is "Mimi Bobek," the vulgar, clownish character on the *Drew Carey Show*. One could say that it only adds insult to injury that Carey's Polish nemesis is not even played by a Polish-American actress.

---

3. As historian Timothy Smith noted, historically ethnic cultures in America to a great extent have been ethno-religiously defined. See Timothy Smith, "Religion and Ethnicity in America," *American Historical Review* vol. 83, no. 5 (December 1978): pp. 1155–1185.

4. Joke no. 161, "The Canonical List of Polish Jokes," <http://www.lysator.liu.se/jokes/polish2.html>.

5. Joke no. 162, "The Canonical List of Polish Jokes," <http://www.lysator.liu.se/jokes/polish2.html>.

6. The actual joke ran: "How are a hockey goalie and a Polish woman alike? They both change their pads after 3 periods." See Joke no. 154, "The Canonical List of Polish Jokes," <http://www.lysator.liu.se/jokes/polish2.html>.

7. Broadcast in reruns on January 7, 2003, on the Fox network.

To date, no scholar has compiled a full inventory of such usages in the popular or mass culture, though no doubt it would be extensive were one to do so. To be sure, these secular stereotypes are connected to a subordinating patriarchal discourse on women that aims to impose upon girls and young women a subaltern femininity by prescribing standards for appearance, attitudes, and behavior. But the cultural constructions of this genre have involved gender less centrally than they have involved class and race. These representations of Polish and Polish-American women arguably have been largely the female analogues of the derogatory stereotypes of peasant and working-class male Polish Americans that depicted the latter—in racial and class terms—as stupid, dirty, oafish, brutish, and crude—a point several scholars have made elsewhere.[8]

The fact that the same stereotypes that have been applied to Polish-American woman also have been applied to the generic Slavic female—Russian women, Bulgarian women, etc.—as well, to the women of other subaltern groups—Arab-American women, African-American women, etc.—might suggest that such jokes and stereotypes have been a harmless trope—a figure of speech, so to say. Noted folklorist Alan Dundes even has argued that, to some extent, such jokes (and presumably also stereotypes) have become "part of ethnic identity" and that group members "may secretly take pleasure in the fact that their group is vital enough to stimulate such traditions."[9] Polish Americans themselves nonetheless might regard Dundes's speculation as both a reductive and withal preposterous proposition, whose ridiculousness might be revealed were one to propose that African-Americans in the 1950s "took pleasure in" the then widely prevalent, offensively anti-Black Sambo image. But if Dundes were correct, his observation would become a sorry, if inadvertent, commentary on the impact such stereotypes have had in distorting Polish-American psyches and self-identities. Recent research on "Otherness" and the postcolonial condition has ratified the trenchant assessment proffered by sociologist Bob Blauner, that such "[c]ultural domination is a major instrument of racial control, and [that] oppression has a negative, weakening effect on the cultures of

---

8. See Caroline Golab, "Stellaaaaaa......!!!!!!!!: The Slavic Stereotype in American Film," in *The Kaleidoscopic Lens: How Hollywood Views Ethnic Groups,* ed. Randall M. Miller (n.p.: Jerome S. Ozer, Publisher, 1980), p. 139; John J. Bukowczyk, "The Big Lebowski Goes to the Polish Wedding: Polish Americans—Hollywood Style," *The Polish Review* vol. 41, no. 2 (2002): p. 213; James S. Pula, "Image, Status, Mobility, and Integration in American Society: The Polish Experience," *Journal of American Ethnic History* vol. 16, no. 1 (Fall 1996): pp. 74–76. Historians Thaddeus Radzilowski and John Radzilowski also have discussed the anti-working-class content in derogatory anti-Polish stereotypes, as has folklorist Alan Dundes. See Alan Dundes, "A Study of Ethnic Slurs: The Jew and the Polack in the United States," *Journal of American Folklore* vol. 84 (April 1971): p. 202.

9. Dundes, "A Study of Ethnic Slurs," p. 202.

the dominated groups."[10] Interestingly, it was a Polish American, a self-described Yale computer science major, who compiled "The Canonical List of Polish Jokes" cited above.

One might speculate that young Polish-American women, embedded in a female youth culture that valorizes commodified good "looks" (as opposed to young Polish-American males, who partake of a male youth culture that, it seems, actually rewards vulgarity and crudity), might be less inclined than their male counterparts to normalize and embrace these demeaning stereotypes of themselves.[11] Even so, those same stereotypes unavoidably must inform their own self-image, and given the vulnerability of young women to prescriptive "feminine" cultural norms, perhaps the negative stereotypes do even greater harm to them. But American cultural practices also give them an escape hatch not as readily available to their male counterparts. For assimilated white ethnics, the principal ethnic marker is an identifiably "ethnic" surname. While both male and female Polish Americans can opt to obscure or deny their ethnic background by legally changing their surnames, ethnically exogamous Polish-American women, that is to say, those who have chosen ethnic intermarriage, merely have to acquiesce in the common American cultural practice of assuming their husband's surname upon marriage and, in the process, thereby discarding their socially stigmatized ethnic identity. But it must be recalled that negative Polish-American female stereotypes are not merely (nor perhaps even principally) gender formulations, but also and more basically racial and class constructions. In the case of intermarriage with partners of higher status ethnic groups, the practice of marital name-changing allows, indeed, encourages Polish-American women instantly to elevate their social standing and perhaps also enhance their own self-image by shedding Polish "maiden names" which are not only ethnic but also race and class markers.[12]

In an American mass culture which, as noted, valorizes a commodified form of sexual attractiveness and "beauty," perhaps it even might be suggested that a woman *cannot* be both "feminine" and "Polish" at the same time, when "Polish"

---

10. Bob Blauner, *Still the Big News: Racial Oppression in America* (1972; Philadelphia: Temple University Press, 2001), p. 82.

11. In the progressive vulgarization of mass culture, it seems that young women as well as young men now receive positive reinforcement for behaviors that in former times would have been considered rude and uncouth. Referencing such contemporary cultural productions as *The Jerry Springer Show* or *Extreme Dating*, female brawling, swearing, and belching seem to have become more acceptable elements of female discourse than they were thirty or so years ago.

12. To date, there seems to be no comparative studies that might establish whether Polish-American women have a greater or lesser tendency to adopt their husband's surnames upon exogamous marriage than the women of other ethnic groups.

has been associated with these assorted negative racial and class stereotypes—crudeness, uncouthness, etc.—that are considered "unfeminine." Meanwhile, an alternative form of religious or what I have term sacred "Othering" of Polish and Polish-American women, a form indigenous to Polish and Polish-American culture, has presented a powerful, prescriptive Polish female stereotype in its own right. Ironically, religiously inspired Polish-American female stereotypes have offered Polish-American women a way out of the conundrum over squaring Polishness with femininity, though one differently problematical.

Reminiscent of nineteenth-century America's so-called "cult of true womanhood" (which placed middle-class native-born women on a pedestal and ascribed "feminine" traits to them that essentialized their female identity), Polish Roman Catholic Marianism has provided a discursive framework for the construction of an alternative model of the Polish and Polish-American woman that is easier to reconcile, perhaps not with what might be called the *Playboy* (or *Cosmo*) image of woman as sexual siren, but certainly with what in American mass culture has been the dialectical alter—the flip side—of that *Playboy/Cosmo* image, namely, with what might be termed the Norman Rockwellian portrait of the wholesome, all-American "good girl." This articulation can be related, within American culture, to the much discussed binary "virgin/whore complex," but the Polish Roman Catholic ideal of Polish womanhood specifically derives from the image of Mary, the Mother of God.[13] Opportunities for inculcating Polish and Polish-American girls and young women in Marianism presented themselves in a variety of ways and settings: parochial education, catechism instruction, church liturgy, female socialization, Pre-Cana marital counseling, and Marian devotionalism.[14] As Polish and Polish-American girls and young women were taught to venerate and emulate the Blessed Virgin Mary, they were presented a template for thought, behavior, comportment, aspiration, demeanor, and feeling out of which they could construct—or be constructed into—the Ideal Polish Woman. It is not necessary to enumerate the Marian virtues ascribed to—and prescribed for—the Ideal Polish Woman in this Marian formulation—meekness, mildness, long-suffering, empathy, purity, chastity, devotion, self-denial, self-sacrifice. In doing so, however, one meets with a figure who, as in the Orientalist constructions of the non-European female Other,[15] has been, in a sense, exoticized, but unlike with the latter, exoticized by being etherealized. The Marian Polish woman thereby loses the corporeal female being that, in a sense,

13. On this general topic, see Marina Warner, *Alone of All Her Sex: The Myth and the Cult of the Virgin Mary* (New York: Alfred A. Knopf, 1976).

14. It remains for investigation how such education and socialization may have changed for different generations of Polish-American women, particularly in ethnically mixed families and suburban parishes and neighborhoods.

15. See Edward Said.

makes "her" physically or biologically a woman and, existentially, a gendered female person. One could argue that, in this loss, she also loses her Self.[16]

But it is from her role as intercessor and mediatrix between God and *Man* (and men) from which Mary (and, by extension, her Marian Polish-American lay sisters) derive their unique essence under Marian doctrine and hence also their essential power. From here, one could argue, arises a Polonized form of the nineteenth-century American social and cultural construction, "domestic feminism" and the "women's sphere." In its most heretical variant, this Marian construction might even render Mary, Mother Goddess, in some ways superior to both God the Son but especially God the Father in that, unlike them, she is fully tactile, available, accessible. By extension, it presents the Polish and Polish-American woman-*cum*-mother/virgin as in most ways superior to—or, at least, better than—the Polish and Polish-American man who, in contrast to God, does not have a divinity and sanctity that might tilt this comparison in his favor.[17] This, of course, contrasts sharply (and paradoxically and dialectically) with the variety of ways in which, in a patriarchal society, Polish-American men have enjoyed tangible advantages over Polish-American women by dint of their sex and gender.

Ironically, in this Marian exoticization-via-etherealization of Polish and Polish-American women one perhaps can locate a wellspring of Polish and Polish-American feminism or, at least, proto-feminism. This application, of course, was limited in the sense that it was not available to secularized Polish-American women who either never were steeped in or had departed from the Polish-Roman Catholic religious confession. Nonetheless, such women probably have not constituted a sizeable segment of the Polish-American female population until, at best, the past couple of decades. In more distant history, a range of scholars has found exactly such feminist or proto-feminist self-actualization and activism displayed by Polish-American women in a variety of domestic and public contexts—as strikers, as homemakers and wage-earners, as community organizers.[18] But perhaps the most perfect set-

16. Significantly, one of the personal traits prized by the Felician Sisters, one of the Poles' principal female religious congregations, was self-abnegation. The nuns, of course, also renounced their secular names upon dedicating their lives to the convent.

17. On subversive constructions of Marianism, see John J. Bukowczyk, "Mary the Messiah: Polish Immigrant heresy and the malleable Ideology of the Roman Catholic Church, 1880–1930," *Journal of American Ethnic History* vol. 4, no. 2 (Spring 1985): pp. 7–32.

18. See William J. Galush, "Purity and Power: Chicago Polonian Feminists, 1880–1914," *Polish American Studies* vol. 47 (Spring 1990): pp. 5–24; Joseph J. Parot, "The 'Serdeczna Matko' of the Sweatshops: Marital and Family Crises of Immigrant Working-Class Women in Late Nineteenth-Century Chicago," in *The Polish Presence in Canada and America,* ed. Frank Renkiewicz (Toronto: Multicultural History Society of Ontario, 1982), pp. 155–182"; Joseph A. Amato, David Nass, and T. C. Radzialowski, "The Women of Wilmar: Striking

ting in which scholars have seen Polish and Polish-American women engaged in feminist and proto-feminist projects has been in their lives as nuns—living and working in all-female social milieux; performing selfless labor on behalf of their female religious congregations and their ethnic communities; teaching children; preserving religion, ethnicity, and nationality "For God and Country"; leading largely anonymous heroic—or perhaps one should say "heroinic"—lives.[19]

In corrective scholarly works, these scholars laudably have recovered a forgotten side of Polish-American ethnic history by restoring historical agency to Polish-American women whom secular stereotypes objectified (and thereby denigrated) and sacred stereotypes etherealized (and, one could say, thereby evaporated). Nonetheless, these mostly male revisionist scholars themselves have fashioned another, romantic and filiopietistic stereotype in the process. In protecting her husband and sons, nursing her elderly parents and nurturing her children, maintaining and defending her parish, neighborhood, parochial school, societies, and communities, their Polish-American woman emerges from these studies as a kind of Super Woman who, in a sense, creates herself without reference to men and their world. In this broad range of secular activities, these romanticized Polish-American secular heroines, no less so than Polish-American nuns, incorporate and mobilize elements of the Marian stereotype that set them apart and above Polish-American men. The suggestion of this conclusion has met with a rather defensive and even hostile response from elements of the Polish-American community, as evidenced by reaction to the publication, in 1979, of anthropologist Paul Wrobel's *Our Way: Family, Parish, and Neighborhood in a Polish-American Community,* which broached these themes. Though Wrobel's book was a deft treatment of a complicated subject, some Polish Americans considered it damaging to the reputations of Polish-American

employes [*sic*] of a small-town bank attack a national pattern of sex discrimination," *The Progressive* (August 1978): pp. 25–27; John J. Bukowczyk, "In Search of Clara Cwieczkowska (1892–1986): Detroit Social Worker and Community Activist,' *Sarmatian Review* vol. 16, no. 2 (April 1996): pp. 385–92; Thaddeus C. Radzilowski, "Family, Women, and Gender," in *Polish Americans and Their History: Community, Culture, and Politics,* ed. John J. Bukowczyk (Pittsburgh: University of Pittsburgh Press, 1996), 58–79; Leslie Woodcock Tender, "Who Is the Church? Conflict in a Polish Immigrant Parish in Late Nineteenth-Century Detroit," *Comparative Studies in Society and History* vol. 25, no. 2 (April 1983): pp. 241–76.

19. See Thaddeus C. Radzialowski, "Reflections on the History of the Felicians in America," *Polish American Studies* vol. 32, no. 1 (Spring 1975): pp. 19–28. One also might note the various anniversary volumes and commemorative histories of various female religious congregations written by Polish-American nuns. For example, see Sr. Ellen Marie Kuznicki, *Journey in Faith: The History of the Immaculate Heart of Mary Province of the Felician Sisters, Buffalo, New York, 1900–1976* (Buffalo, N.Y.: Felician Sisters, Immaculate Heart of Mary Province, 1996); Rev. Henry M. Malak, *Theresa of Chicago,* tr. Ann K. Dudzik (Lemont, Ill.: League of the Servant of God, Mother Mary Theresa, 1975).

men.[20] In the realm of mass culture, the film *Polish Wedding* attempted a similar problematization of Polish-American male-female relations that provoked considerable kindred criticism from elements of the Polish-American community.[21]

Meanwhile, it is interesting that these secular Polish-American heroines (in contrast to the "Mary-like" women religious) in the process also invert or reverse the secular stereotypes of bestiality and subhumanity directed by American mass culture toward them. Those stereotypes, as well, their own active and assertive (that is to say, "unfeminine") behavior, in a sense "masculinize" Polish-American women which, in a male-dominated and oriented society, might offer them some political, social, and cultural advantages compared to more "feminine" women. A few feminist scholars in the United States and in Poland have developed this interpretive line in the context of filmic representations of strong, "masculinized" female characters.[22] It could be suggested that, to varying degrees, this also might involve a denial of "self" of a different sort and certainly a reconstruction of the latter. At best it might suggest the evolution of a "third way" that splits and collapses the dichotomous binary constructions of Polish-American womanhood. Lesbianism, it might be suggested, represents one logical destination for such "thirding," but it does not offer itself as a universal option for all—and perhaps not even many—Polish-American women. Moreover, while certainly referencing men (and patriarchy), it also does not encompass a full-range of female/male interfaces.

This discussion thus far may have unintentionally implied that these constructions of Polish and Polish-American female "Otherness," both the sacred and the profane, have been rather static or continual in content; but superficial examination of sketchy evidence suggests that this might not, in fact, be the case.[23] But this assertion should not pass without more thorough empirical investigation than I have been able to give it; and I know of no such other critical study that has attempted this task to date.

But another research agenda also is suggested by recent studies of Polish-American women or, rather, by what they leave out. What has been lacking in most of these corrective studies that have identified feminist or proto-feminist strands in the lives of Polish-American nuns, housewives, female factory workers, and mothers is any clear acknowledgement of the fact that these women operate within still largely

---

20. Paul Wrobel, *Our Way: Family, Parish, and Neighborhood in a Polish-American Community* (Notre Dame, Ind.: University of Notre Dame Press, 1979), especially pp. 155–72.

21. Bukowczyk, "The Big Lebowski Goes to the Polish Wedding."

22. See Elzbieta H. Oleksy, "American Feminism and Pedagogy: The Case of Poland," *American Studies International* vol. 38, no. 3 (October 2000): p. 44.

23. See John J. Bukowczyk, "Mary the Messiah: Polish immigrant Heresy and the malleable Ideology of the Roman Catholic Church, 1880–1930," *Journal of American Ethnic History* vol. 4, no. 2 (Spring 1985): pp. 5–32.

male-dominated families, churches, organizations, and ethnic communities. What I am describing, of course, is a lack of a critical apprehension and analysis of dynamics of patriarchy as they operate within the family, the workplace, the community, the parishes, and the Church. These instances of activism or self-actualization by Polish-American women must be understood and located within a social context, an ordered set of social relationships, most (though not all) of them hierarchical and unequal, with men: their husbands, fathers, male employers, male governmental officials, bishops and priests.[24]

Polish-American literature and scholarship only gradually is acquiring works that have begun to comprehend and unravel the entanglement of these both affective and coercive gender relationships. Recent and forthcoming works that have entered this thicket include *The Grasinski Girls: The Choices They Had and the Choices They Made* by sociologist Mary Patrice Erdmans, an examination of the lives of five Polish-American sisters,[25] and Karen Majewski's pathbreaking study of Polish immigrant literature, *Traitors and True Poles: Narrating a Polish-American Identity, 1880–1939*, which teases out feminist themes in this literary genre.[26] In this category also should be included the work of Polish-American novelist Suzanne Strempek Shea.

Nuanced, critical inquiries into patriarchy, household and family dynamics, and social life might allow us to place feminist and proto-feminist activity by Polish-American women in proper perspective and help lay to rest damaging sacred and profane stereotypes. Or maybe not. While the religious "Othering" of Polish-American women that produced "feminine" Polish-American female stereotypes is embedded in the discourse of patriarchy, the secular "Othering" of Polish and Polish-American women is located within the discourse of class and race. The scholarly dissection of those racial and class based forms of "Othering" and the political dismantling of the systems of power and privilege that sustain, use, and reproduce them are unfinished and vastly larger projects that will require much greater mobilization of Polish-American wills and resources than Polish Americans have accomplished to date, as well, a cultural sea change in American society that, while begun, is far from complete.

---

24. In the case of the Church, "patriarchal" discourse also extends to male members of the flock, arguably reducing male and female members of the flock to the status of obedient and compliant "children."

25. Mary Patrice Erdmans, *The Grasinski Girls: The Choices They Had and the Choices They Made* (Athens: Ohio University Press, forthcoming). Note that this is a working title.

26. Karen Majewski, *Traitors and True Poles: Narrating a Polish-American Identity, 1880–1939* (Athens: Ohio University Press, 2003).

It Knew Me for Its Own

Helen Bristol's Journey of Self Discovery

Rita Gladsky

Who is Helen Bristol? Her name, or the mention of her works, is rarely found in specialized reference works on American writers. Even the ethnic and women's literature movements, which have done so much to rediscover hundreds of neglected writers, have yet to discover her. Yet Helen Ogrodowska Bristol is important on both fronts: as an ethnic and as a woman whose contribution to documenting the ethnic female experience is as significant as that of many of her contemporaries. In fact, Helen Bristol's writing provides us with one of the earliest and dramatic examples of the immigrant struggle to unriddle the puzzle of ethnic identity and assimilation.

Bristol's background as an ethnic writer closely parallels on a superficial level those of other women writers of Polish descent, such as Monika Krawczyk and Victoria Janda, who had either arrived in America as young children, as had Bristol, or were first generation Polish-Americans born to immigrant parents. But, while these writers of Polish descent addressed themes of nationalism and Polish culture, Bristol struggled with the issue of denial and acceptance of her own cultural identity. She documented, through her own personal experience, the act of being caught between two worlds—her Polish childhood in Żyrardów and her adolescence and adulthood in Philadelphia.

Indeed, the question "Who is Helen Bristol?" posed an even greater dilemma for her than for her readers. Her two works, *Thirty Years After: Poland Revisited,* published in 1939, and *Let the Blackbird Sing* which appeared some sixteen years later, are characterized by examination and introspection as Bristol reexamines and questions her identity in an attempt to reconcile her dual cultural loyalties. Together, these two texts are vehicles through which Bristol articulates a journey

From *Polish American Studies,* vol. 52, no. 1 (Spring 1995), pp. 43–50.

of self-discovery from the confrontation of a Polish past in *Poland Revisited* to the sensitive and, at times, emotional chronicling of her immigrant parents' peasant origins in *Let the Blackbird Sing*.

Helen Bristol's own experience with transplantation, accommodation, and eventual assimilation to a new culture was not unique. In fact, the circumstances of her family's immigration from Poland to America in 1906 parallel those of many Poles immigrating at that time. As a nine year old arriving in Philadelphia, Bristol would, like so many others, undergo the universal crises associated with transplantation and the resultant dilemma of shifting ethnic identities. Danuta Mostwin, in her study *The Transplanted Family*, clearly documents the now familiar patterns of reorganization and identity shift which were to characterize Bristol's response to her new world environment. As Mostwin's study suggests, Bristol gradually moved from a Polish to an ethnic identity where she no longer perceived herself as Polish among Polish nationals but still felt perceived as Polish by Americans. Ultimately, she would assume a two-directional identity, both Polish and American. In the context of Mostwin's study, Bristol's comments, including her ambivalence, follow a predictable immigrant pattern.[1]

Nowhere is this ambivalence more apparent than in the Prologue to *Poland Revisited* in which Bristol explains her reasons for returning to visit Poland: "Spiritually I was a Pole, and I was going back to fulfill my national heritage—to quaff from a brimming vessel a deluge of that Beauty which for thirty years I had been able to enjoy only fitfully in Polish music and poetry."[2] However, a few paragraphs later, Bristol states that "The influences which shaped my intellect and spirit in the next 30 years were necessarily different from what they could have been had I remained in Poland. I acquired, with the English language, a love and a reverence for its beauty and for its literature and, although I spoke Polish, I no longer felt myself a Pole among the Poles in America."[3] Yet, at another point in the Prologue, she describes herself socially as "a strangely mongrelled being—politically impartial to either Poland or America."[4]

Her conflicting allegiances are apparent in other of her writings as well. In a 1939 letter to the *New York Times* in which she tries to pay tribute to Poland in its darkest hour, Bristol would say, "Sometimes . . . I try to forget that I am by heritage a Pole and for short periods of time I succeed indifferently."[5] Even as recently as 1976,

1. Danuta Mostwin, *A Transplanted Family* (New York: Arno Press, 1980), p. 45.
2. Helen Bristol, *Thirty Years After: Poland Revisited* (Rutland, VT: The House of Tuttle, 1939), p. 20.
3. *Ibid.*, p. 17.
4. *Ibid.*
5. Helen Bristol, letter to *New York Times*, 1939, Bristol Papers. Polish American Collection, Immigration History Research Center, Minneapolis, Minnesota.

almost fifty years after her arrival in the United States, she explains in an interview in the *Kosciuszko Foundation Newsletter* that she always had a sense of herself as an outsider and that despite the fact that an Anglo-Saxon name helped, she would always remain a "gauche foreigner."[6]

This acute sense of "otherness" which she felt throughout her life among Americans, Polish-Americans, and Poles notwithstanding, Helen Bristol's accommodation and assimilation to a new culture follows a linear pattern of upward mobility. Already an apt student in Poland, on her arrival in America she quickly learned English, became an outstanding student, completed degrees in both music and in English, and eventually became a respected teacher of literature at the prestigious Girl's High School in Philadelphia. Despite her intellectual and professional accomplishments, Helen Bristol's writing reveals her internal struggle with her dual identities and her continuing efforts to place her Polish and American identities in perspective. Her return to Poland in 1936 after a thirty year absence would lead her, however, toward a partial resolution of the conflict and toward the next stage in the restructuring of her ethnic identity.

Needless to say, *After Thirty Years: Poland Revisited* is a unique immigrant document providing valuable insight into the study of ethnicity and the invention of the ethnic self. Moreover, Helen Bristol in this work does what other immigrant writers of her time had not done; she makes public to an English speaking audience her search for an understanding of her ethnicity. Yet, this dimension of *Poland Revisited* was ignored even by her reviewers. For example, the *Saturday Review of Literature* relegated the book to the travel section and dismissed it as "a homely tale of Polish life and culture," a "familiar travelogue."[7]

However, *Poland Revisited* is much more than a tourist's account of a visit to Poland. While Bristol carefully describes her journey from Warsaw through Żyrardów, Kraków, and Zakopane, providing ample historical and geographical background, the major theme of *Poland Revisited* emerges as the discovery of her ethnic identity through which Bristol gives shape and form to the experience of confronting her Polish past. In the Foreword, she confesses that "I did not go to study economic or political conditions. I had no pedantic axe to grind or even a clear idea of perpetuating my experiences in writing. But when I returned, something of my past and present experiences crystallized and became articulate. So I wrote because it was a pleasure to relive an emotional experience."[8]

6. "Recollections of an American from Poland," an interview with Helen Bristol, *Kosciuszko Foundation Newsletter,* Vol. 31, No. 1 (1976), p. 15.

7. *Saturday Review of Literature,* Vol. 20 (October 14, 1939), p. 39.

8. *Poland Revisited,* p. 7.

But Bristol does much more. She lays bare the imprints of both Poland and America on her psyche and soul and takes a spiritual and emotional journey to that dimension of memory where, as Stuart Dybek says, home is most truly located—childhood.[9] In her own words, she explains that she was to "return to Poland to claim what as a child, I was too young to make my own"[10] and that "In spite of my fears, my desire was ever to return, before it was too late to feel the thrill of recognition."[11] Bristol's journey back in time begins with her mother's departing words to "go back and be a child again."[12] *The Saturday Review of Literature* criticized Bristol, however, for the "artificial emotionalism" which pervaded the entire chronicle of her return to Poland.[13] Indeed, Bristol candidly communicates her sensations, her disappointments, and her confusion in confronting her ethnic past. But her emotions must be viewed in the context of an American ethnic returning for the first time to the land of her birth. Given the limited understanding in 1939 of either the psychology or sociology of immigration, it is not surprising that the reviewer would misjudge Bristol's intent to candidly relate even the most seemingly insignificant of her responses to Poles and Poland after a thirty year absence.

It is, in fact, precisely this dimension of *Poland Revisited* which renders it almost a casebook study of the two directional nature of ethnic identity: the emotional pull and tug of feeling through her Polish soul yet seeing through American eyes. The inevitable resulting clash of cultures emerges in a variety of contexts, in her personal interaction with Poles, as well as non-Poles and in her responses to Polish culture, history, and language. It is a confrontation alternating between recognition and identification and alienation and estrangement by which Bristol ultimately reaches a higher plateau of reconciliation and understanding.

In the Prologue, Bristol's remarks foreshadow the feelings of "otherness" she would experience in confronting her past in Poland. Anticipating the reunion with her only relative remaining in Poland, she describes her godmother as a "phantom," a "gracious memory who had remained Polish, with all her national prejudices ingrown and atrophied." Bristol declares, moreover, that "I could not look forward to seeing her, without a fear that she would be shocked by my transformation, which she could never understand. I would have to hide it as best I could. . . ."[14] Bristol's sense of estrangement and even alienation extends beyond her aunt to those whom she designates "Poles of my social class whom I knew would find me more strange

9. Stuart Dybek, "You Can't Step Into the Same Street Twice," in Michael Martone, ed., *Townships* (Iowa City: University of Iowa Press, 1992), pp. 43–47.

10. *Poland Revisited,* p. 200.

11. *Ibid.,* p. 19.

12. *Ibid.,* p. 21.

13. *Saturday Review,* p. 39.

14. *Poland Revisited,* p. 18.

than I should find them, so I did not want to be one of them, but rather to observe them dispassionately as might a stranger."[15] The realization that she is culturally different from this class of Poles emerges when they reproach her for her love of the English language which in their eyes is tantamount to disloyalty to Poland. Unable to respond to their question, "And you can say that, you who are a Pole?"[16] Bristol later observes that "I had fallen into the very trap I had resolved so hard to avoid, to betray myself as different from them." Offended by their intense nationalism, she concludes that "I felt at the time I had no place among them, that we had grown too far apart."[17]

She is alternately distanced by a deep sense of estrangement and yet delighted by a sense of recognition of her godmother's use of a former childhood name of endearment, Helushka, and the familiar objects in her godmother's apartment which as a child she frequently played with. Her godmother is, in fact, a repository of Bristol's Polish childhood over which she presides, an unchanging touchstone with a Polish past which is non-retrievable, yet not disappeared, guarded and preserved over time despite her godchild's transformation from a Polish child to an American woman of Polish descent.

Yet it is Bristol's growing awareness of and tendency to separate that which makes her a stranger to her past and that which touches her Polish soul which eventually leads her to a clearer understanding of her identity. Significantly, despite the fact that the Polish language serves as a strong cultural tie to Bristol's Polish origins, it is her adoption of the English language and the cultural values of the English-speaking world that sets her apart from contemporary Poles and Poland and distances her at the same time from her heritage. This symbolic relationship between language and kinship ties occurs soon after Bristol arrives in Warsaw when she hears Polish "as one who has heard it before, but never listened to it before—as it might sound to a stranger."[18] Throughout her visit, she delights at being told that "you speak like one of us"[19] by waiters, chambermaids, and guides. And even though she is at times hesitant to speak Polish with the peasants because she had not spoken with them for a number of years, she remarks that "Their dialect fell gratefully on my ears, and whatever I had of peasant ancestry awoke to it."[20] Bristol further describes the language of a peasant woman, Franceszka Regulska, "like a bird song; warm and liquid, purged of harsh sounds and flowing."[21] Significantly,

15. *Ibid.*, p. 19.
16. *Ibid.*, p. 55.
17. *Ibid.*, p. 57.
18. *Ibid.*, p. 40.
19. *Ibid.*, p. 46.
20. *Ibid.*, p. 146.
21. *Ibid.*, p. 147.

however, Bristol relinquishes the duty of negotiating in Polish with droszka drivers, waiters, and railroad employees to her non-Polish speaking husband because the unfamiliar and offensive task of bargaining is "foreign" to her. Linguistically, she, chameleon-like, shifts back and forth, assuming that identity which makes her feel most culturally comfortable and which represents the least challenge to her adopted American values and loyalties.

Her movement back and forth between identities is not, however, limited to language. In interacting with educated Poles, peasants, and other non-Polish tourists, she moves from alienation to recognition to criticism. While she is offended and consequently estranged by the nationalism of educated Poles, she feels a keen sense of kinship and a sense of the familiar with peasants, and with peasant life, "remnants of the past which knew me."[22] For Helen Bristol, clearly the Polish peasant, who represents the unchanging Polish past, is the strongest link to her Polish cultural identity. She criticizes the urban Pole who "too often feels inferior to his Western neighbors, and in his foolish notion of civilizing himself, superimposes upon his own natural beauty, the borrowed and ill-fitting garments of western culture."[23] But she praises the peasants "who knew no better than to be themselves" and who have "unwittingly preserved the Polish spirit in its primitive purity."[24]

Bristol's comments take on a feminist perspective at this point. In particular she identifies with the peasant women who are hard-working, loyal, deeply committed to preserving and respecting the past, who live in harmony with and demonstrate a primitive but deep union with nature. Conversely, her judgement of peasant male behavior, as seen through her American eyes, is far less enthusiastic. The subservience of the peasant female juxtaposed against the aggressiveness of the peasant male offends her. Watching a folk dance group perform at a tourist hotel, she is embarrassed by the arrogant and aggressive, ill-smelling male performer who invites her to join in the dancing, declines his offer and flees the room. Bristol's differentiation between male and female peasant behavior suggests that her own sense of self is at least in part gender based.

Cultural distancing and reevaluation are also apparent in Bristol's contacts with other English-speaking tourists. In response to an American's criticism of Polish inefficiency, she silently and bitterly laments the tendency of Westerners to measure and label inferior the values and customs of less developed nations. But she is even less tolerant of the Englishwoman who dresses inappropriately by Polish standards in hiking shorts and who therefore, in Bristol's eyes, demonstrates a disrespect for Polish values. Bristol is equally critical of the American students at Wawel Castle

22. *Ibid.*, p. 40.
23. *Ibid.*, p. 20.
24. *Ibid.*, p. 20.

who in her estimation make only a pretence at learning about Polish culture. She asks herself, "But what would they know of Polish culture—in three quarters of an hour they were out and gone—with several pages of notes—only a Pole is capable of recapturing the spirit of Wawel."[25]

Bristol's Polish inheritance, what she calls her Polish spirituality awakens to those unchanging vestiges of the past embodied in such shrines as Wawel Castle. Of Kraków, she says, "Nowhere before had I felt the inherent Pole within me so quickened," and she adds that "the city bespeaks the basic verities and essential elements of Polish life and temperament."[26]

Like many second and third generation Polish-Americans, Bristol has reduced cultural complexities to a set of understandable cultural icons. For Bristol, Wilanów and Jan Sobieski, Piłsudski, the music of Chopin, the art of Mehoffer and Matejko, and the poetry of Adam Mickiewicz all define Poland and Polish culture. It is in these cultural icons that she finds the essence of what she calls "native tradition." "Wawel," she says, "made me understand the best traits of Polish nature—it reflects a dignity which does not estrange—a rich ornamentation which in some curious way had joined to itself an austere simplicity."[27] The passage of time and the changes wrought by time have distanced her from contemporary Poles and Poland. But Wawel, Chopin, Mickiewicz, Wilanów remain suspended in time unchanged and it is within these cultural icons that her spiritual inheritance resides.

In *Poland Revisited* Bristol has given valuable insights into the dynamics of cultural identity. Her journey to Poland, motivated by a desire to search out that which she had left behind as a child, yields a Sesame of unexpected treasures for her as well as for those who seek to understand the process of transplantation and assimilation. Bristol discovers that a shared language and a shared national origin cannot in themselves form a strong basis for cultural identity. Unable to arouse sympathy toward the intense nationalism of contemporary Poles and Poland, she reaches an understanding that she has become an American by consent and by conviction and that in her own words, she could "no longer see things through colored glasses merely because they were Polish."[28]

Clearly, the question of her ethnic identity was one which preoccupied Helen Bristol most of her adult life. For her, the answer resides in her Polish spirituality and in the unchanging, timeless cultural icons of the past. Yet, Helen Bristol's preoccupation with her cultural past and her cultural identity would not cease with the writing of *Poland Revisited*. Some fifteen years later, she would again return to

---

25. *Ibid.*, p. 135.
26. *Ibid.*, p. 120.
27. *Ibid.*, p. 140.
28. *Ibid.*, p. 17.

the themes of cultural assimilation in *Let the Blackbird Sing,* a book length narrative poem. Dedicated to the memory of her Polish parents, this work, described by Sculley Bradley as a "narrative poem of heroic proportions," chronicles her parents' peasant origins in Poland, their eventual uprooting, and final transplant to American soil. But *Let the Blackbird Sing* is as much a celebration of her own continuing struggles as it is a celebration of her parents who, of course, represent all Polish immigrants.

This work is different, however, in substantial ways. Bristol is more relaxed, more at ease with the complexities of dual ancestry, and the status of the ethnic woman at mid-century. More importantly, *Let the Blackbird Sing* is the realization and full expression of the ethnic self which Bristol had earlier flushed out in *Poland Revisited.* In fact, the whole of *Poland Revisited* serves as an extended prologue to this narrative poem in which Bristol has reduced cultural complexities to an idealized representation of ethnicity expressed through her immigrant parents. In this work, Bristol's ambivalence is transformed into romanticism; the reality of Poland gives way to an idealized past; and Bristol's cultural selves appear to be at rest. This transformation comes as no surprise, however. Near the end of *Poland Revisited,* Bristol perfectly captures her changing attitudes: "Poland had ceased to exist for me, in terms of territory, or institutions, or even human beings. It was larger and more beautiful, purged of all that hurt and estranged of all its ways. It knew me for its own yet was not surprised by my adopted loyalties."[29]

---

29. *Ibid.*, p. 200.

"The Silent One"

The (Absent) Voiceless Mother in Recent Narratives by Leslie Pietrzyk and Ellen Slezak

Grazyna J. Kozaczka

Reading "The Silent One," a poem by Linda Nemec Foster, one is struck by the aptness of its poetic framing of the mother-daughter discourse to much of the current Polish American fiction authored by women. In "The Silent One," the speaker, a daughter, ostensibly sets out to create a portrait of her mother and to lend a voice to the older woman. However, the first line of Foster's poem—"My mother never told me fairy tales"—poses an interesting question. Why is it that this mother refuses to introduce her daughter to common ethnic traditions embedded in such stories? Could it be the mother's own unease with these texts? After all, the traditional stories often perpetuate women's narratives acceptable in a patriarchal culture. Perhaps, the mother's experience has taught her that passive acceptance of one's lot in life might be preferable to imagining a change which could easily lead to dissatisfaction with her present condition:

> She remembered the stories her grandmother
> told but tried to forget them, always wondering
> if she wasn't someone else—an untamed
> firebird covered in jewels, a princess
> bewitched into marrying the wrong man.[1]

But after all it does not matter how much we speculate about the mother's curious behavior, about her strong belief in the power of language that paralyzes her and takes away her ability for self-expression. We will never have the answers to our questions. In "The Silent One," the mother has no voice and she never tells

1. Linda Nemec Foster, "The Silent One," in *The Amber Necklace from Gdansk: Poems* (Baton Rouge: Louisiana State University Press, 2001), 13 (lines 8–12).

From *Polish American Studies,* vol. 66, no. 1 (Spring 2009), pp. 43–54.

her story. And no matter how well intentioned the daughter-speaker might be, she inadvertently silences and possibly marginalizes her mother by creating a maternal narrative. In this daughter-dominated discourse, the younger woman constructs her mother out of the mother's silences or perceived fears as she situates herself within this mother-daughter dyad. Even though she acknowledges their kinship, she clearly brands her mother as the silent other and asserts her separateness from the mother.

> My mother refused to speak the words
> Of myth, of the small hidden heart
> Waiting to be discovered. I tried
> to discover it myself . . .
> . . . My eyes
> the same colors as hers, the silent one.[2]

In contrast to the silent mother, the daughter's voice is strong; she is the storyteller who searches and discovers. So while the overt subject of "The Silent One" is the mother, it is really the daughter's creation that we see; the mother has no voice, since she is seen only through her daughter's eyes and heard through her daughter's voice. The mother becomes a creation of her own creation.

The premise of this article is that in the context of many recent texts by Polish American women, mothers do not own their stories, but become characters in their daughters' narratives. Often, the discourse owned by the daughter assigns the position of "Other" to the mother while the child constructs a mother image from facts, memories, fantasies, and omissions as a substitute for a physically or emotionally absent mother. This, then, may lead to a tension among several mother constructs revealed by the narratives.

This article will focus mainly on texts by Ellen Slezak and Leslie Pietrzyk, although Suzanne Strempek Shea's novels could also provide interesting material for analysis. Both Pietrzyk and Slezak share their Midwestern and working class roots with the poet Linda Nemec Foster whose poem opened this article. They also follow in the footsteps of a Minnesotan, Monika Krawczyk, who, during the 1930s and 1940s, published numerous short stories in popular women's magazines. Her depiction of womanhood, if not the artistic quality of writing, can be compared to the work of Willa Cather. Krawczyk places her Polish immigrant women firmly in the domestic sphere where they realize their calling to nurture the family as they simultaneously acculturate their daughters to the traditional female narrative of wifehood and motherhood while struggling to become Americans. Thomas S. Gladsky and Rita H. Gladsky praise Krawczyk for her efforts to "capture the evolution of ethnicity and the particular identity of the ethnic woman . . . her stories illustrate

2. Foster, "The Silent One," lines 22–31.

the ways in which women decide which parts of Polish culture would remain and which would be discarded."[3]

Leslie Pietrzyk and Ellen Slezak represent the generation of Krawczyk's granddaughters or even great granddaughters for whom ethnic discourse hinges less on descent which suggests heredity and bloodlines, but more on consent with its emphasis on conscious choices made in creating one's identity.[4] Most of their characters are fully ethnic women of the third and the fourth generation for whom ethnic identity has been constructed so many times that as Mary Patrice Erdmans suggests in *The Grasinski Girls,* that it "at most bears only a shadow of a semblance to something from Poland."[5] Both Pietrzyk and Slezak, with the exception of Pietrzyk's first novel, *Pears on a Willow Tree,* seem to be more interested in gender identity and its construction and reconstruction through female relationships, especially mother-daughter relationships.

Much of the critical interest in the depiction of mother-daughter or mother-child relationships in literature was initiated in the mid to late 1970s by the publication of two seminal works on the subject, namely Adrienne Rich's *Of Woman Born: Motherhood as Experience and Institution* and Nancy Chodorow's *The Reproduction of Mothering: Psychoanalysis and the Sociology of Gender.*[6] Chodorow, a psychoanalyst and a professor of sociology, sets out to "investigate the mother-daughter relationship and how women create and recreate this relationship internally,"[7] while Rich, looking at her own experiences as a mother, considers the importance of the idea of daughterhood and motherhood in defining women's identity. In Britain, Ann Dally outlines a comprehensive history of motherhood in a book bearing a suggestively postmodern title, *Inventing Motherhood: The Consequences of an Ideal.*[8] Crucial to my discussion of the narratives by Slezak and Pietrzyk are the findings of Marianne Hirsch, who building upon ideas of Chodorow and Rich, analyzes mother-daughter relationships in women's fiction, starting with the eighteenth century and carrying it through postmodernism. However, she limits her analysis to selected women authors representing the Western literary traditions, especially English and

3. Thomas S. Gladsky and Rita H. Gladsky, *Something of My Very Own to Say: American Women Writers of Polish Descent* (New York: Columbia University Press, 1997), 105.

4. Werner Sollors, *Beyond Ethnicity: Consent and Descent in American Culture* (New York: Oxford University Press, 1986), 5–6.

5. Mary Patrice Erdmans, *The Grasinski Girls* (Athens, OH: Ohio University Press, 2004), 62.

6. Adrienne C. Rich, *Of Woman Born: Motherhood as Experience and Institution* (New York: Norton, 1976); Nancy Chodorow, *The Reproduction of Mothering: Psychoanalysis and the Sociology of Gender* (Berkeley: University of California Press, 1999).

7. Chodorow, *Reproduction of Mothering,* vii.

8. Ann Dally, *Inventing Motherhood: The Consequences of an Ideal* (New York: Schocken Books, 1983).

French, with the addition of two African American texts. In her book, *The Mother/Daughter Plot: Narrative, Psychoanalysis, Feminism,* Hirsch suggests that much of the fiction of the latter part of the twentieth century "is centered almost entirely on the experience of daughters, with mothers no more than objects supporting and underlying their daughters' process of individuation. . . . It is the woman as *daughter* who occupies the center of the global reconstruction of subjectivity and subject-object relation."[9] The only departure Hirsch sees from this pattern in ethnic fiction occurs specifically in African-American fiction where writers such as Toni Morrison or Alice Walker move away from the strictly daughter discourse into mother discourse. Thus, a question to be asked is whether Polish-American fiction corroborates Marianne Hirsch's vision of women's narratives. Reviewing the literature, it quickly becomes obvious that, with some exceptions, most of the Polish American texts silence maternal voices, privileging daughter discourse while at the same time eliminating most of the male presence.

Paradoxically the most striking illustration of Hirsch's claim comes from the polyphonic narrative by Leslie Pietrzyk. It would seem that her novel, *Pears on a Willow Tree,* resounds with a multitude of women's voices, both mothers and daughters, as each section is narrated by a different female member of the large Marchewka clan, a device not uncommon in ethnic narratives with Amy Tan's *The Joy Luck Club,* Tanya Maria Barrientos' *Frontera Street,* or Julia Alvarez's *How the Garcia Girls Lost Their Accents* coming immediately to mind. Yet, already in the novel's second epistolary chapter, Pietrzyk's narrator, Rose, tells her immigrant story of the first year in America through a series of letters written to her illiterate mother who remained in Poland. So not only is the reader's access limited to the daughter's words, since the mother cannot respond herself, but also the reader is not allowed even a glimpse of the letters that the mother presumably dictated to one of the sons and later, after the son's departure for America, to a parish priest. The reader is only privy to Rose's references to the letters received from Poland. Rose separates herself both from her mother and symbolically from her mother tongue. She writes, "Dearest *Matka,* you will not understand this easily, so best I tell you quickly. Now my name is Rose," and she continues not by addressing her mother directly but by using a brother as an intermediary, "Stanislaus, reading this letter to *Matka,* ask her to say my name. She should feel for one moment what it means to be in America, where everything is new and different, even something so little and so grand as a name."[10] The silent mother from Foster's poem would surely understand the power of words evoked here by Rose who has just separated herself from her

9. Marianne Hirsch, *The Mother/Daughter Plot: Narrative, Psychoanalysis, Feminism* (Bloomington and Indianapolis: Indiana University Press, 1989), 135–36.

10. Leslie Pietrzyk, *Pears on a Willow Tree* (New York: Avon Books, 1998), 9.

mother by accepting a name that was not the one with which her mother called her to life, with which her mother named her as her own. Rose engages in "othering" of her mother who now has no access or understanding of her daughter's situation as she is physically removed by distance, while at the same time she is even more distant due to cultural and linguistic differences.

It is interesting that in her subsequent letters, Rose proceeds to describe to her silent parent how she constructs a mother to fulfill her needs as she herself faces motherhood. This mother construct is cobbled together from memories and dreams, "Nights have always been for dreaming, so that is when I dream of you *Matka,* and everything behind me."[11] Pietrzyk's Rose augments her dreams with the memories, but even in these visions from the past, the mother remains silent. Rose recalls their last meeting,

> When I went to say good-bye, you were surrounded by chickens, you were tossing out their feed. Neither of us spoke. Only the chickens squawked, as handfuls of food rained down upon them when it was supposed to be just one. These months later, I want to hear your voice, but it's chickens I remember.[12]

In her review of *Pears on a Willow Tree,* Mary Patrice Erdmans stresses the fact that Rose "left her mother and reinvented herself" in America.[13] And of course she did that, but at the same time she also reinvented her mother in a continuous process of storytelling to herself, later to her daughters and granddaughters, and even, through letter writing, to her own mother back in Poland. Rose's mother-creation is completed out of prayers, recipes and fairy tales remembered from childhood and now retold to interpret the strange, American reality. Sensory images, especially visual, olfactory, and gustatory, enliven the portrait. This is how Rose describes "a special dinner" for which she chose to roast a duck:

> It was supposed to be *your* duck, *Matka,* with the sauerkraut and onions in butter. To write the words is to have the taste overwhelm my mouth, my mind, to see you standing in front of the fire on Sunday dinner, to be there next to you wrapped tight in the smells of your cooking.[14]

Yet Rose does not follow this cherished recipe, but creates something new, more appropriate for her changed situation since after all she does not identify herself anymore with her mother or the mother's reality. She clearly asserts this opposition between the two of them by reminding her mother of the different rhythm of life

---

11. Pietrzyk, *Pears on a Willow Tree,* 11.
12. Pietrzyk, *Pears on a Willow Tree,* 11.
13. Mary Patrice Erdmans, book review of *Pears on the Willow Tree* (from a typescript sent to the author in October 2001), 1.
14. Pietrzyk, *Pears on a Willow Tree,* 14.

"back in your village, *Matka*."[15] So even though loved and imagined, the mother takes on the role of the "other" for Rose. The story of Rose's mother exists only in her daughter's plot which centers on subject creation through the process of separation from her mother. The mother, coming to terms with the loss (to immigration) of her daughter, remains silent in the suffering we can only imagine.

Pietrzyk continues to focus on the daughter narrative in her second novel, *A Year and a Day*. Here also the mother's physical presence is removed, not by immigration as before, but by a suicidal death which prompts her daughter to embark on a seemingly impossible journey in two opposite directions: into the past to penetrate her mother's silences and secrets and into the future, to construct her womanhood by answering her own question "So who am I supposed to be?"[16] And so unfolds the story of Alice, a fifteen-year-old, who over a period of a year comes to terms with her mother's suicide through reinventing both the mother and herself. Alice struggles with the realization that she has not known nor has understood her mother as she remembers that whenever she and her brother asked serious questions, especially about their absent father, they never received answers. "We wanted to know, but asking made Mama turn silent and sad and empty, like a lamp that's been clicked off. And she never answered anyway, not even a tiny hint."[17] The same silence has followed the mother's tragic death on the railroad tracks. There has been no suicide note, no explanation, no apology, no reassurance of love.

To penetrate the silence, Alice becomes convinced that not only can she hear her mother's voice, but also that occasionally she can carry on a conversation with the dead parent such as in the first line of the narrative reminiscent of the Resurrection story—"Mama came back three days after her funeral."[18] It is clear from the beginning that this mother returned-from-the-dead is not a ghostly manifestation, but rather a construct put together by a grieving child searching for love and understanding; it also illustrates the tension between the mother remembered and the mother reconstructed. During their first conversation, three days after the funeral, Alice notices that "Her words floated like dandelion seeds, breathy, shadowy whispers—nothing the way she had talked when she was alive, loud and too fast, so I always felt a sentence behind, my ears straining to catch up, not wanting to miss a word she said."[19] So there is a different quality to this mother presence. At first, the mother's voice provides Alice with practical, but rather impersonal, guidance about fashion or makeup which could be easily gleaned from women's magazines. The mother's responses are often independent of and unconnected to the daughter's

15. Pietrzyk, *Pears on a Willow Tree*, 17.
16. Leslie Pietrzyk, *A Year and a Day* (New York: Harper Collins, 2004), 12.
17. Pietrzyk, *A Year and a Day*, 11.
18. Pietrzyk, *A Year and a Day*, 1.
19. Pietrzyk, *A Year and a Day*, 2.

questions. When Alice pleads for advice about her boyfriend, the mother gives her suggestions about hair care. But soon her own reasoning process becomes framed in these mother and daughter dialogues; thus the mother becomes an expression of Alice's internalized values or repeats statements made by other older women and overheard by Alice, "'No,' Mama said. 'You are not having sex. I forbid it'—the sort of thing Becky's mom would say to Becky."[20] Gradually as the daughter gathers more information about her mother's past from people who knew her, these conversations get more personal, and the mother's voice begins to express the daughter's interpretations of the mother's actions. However, creating a mother's voice does not seem enough to Alice, as her need to understand is so strong that it translates into a desire to become her mother by wearing her mother's favorite dress, using her perfume, and putting on her lipstick while marveling about the fit of her own lips into the lipstick groove worn by her mother's lips. So at this point, Alice becomes conflated with her mother construct as if reverting to an earlier stage of development, a stage which Nancy Chodorow would call "pre-oedipal oneness" with her parent. Alice's identification with her imagined mother continues with the unrelenting logic of her reality into her attempted suicide in the same spot where her mother killed herself. And only then when faced with death in front of a speeding train, is Alice able to comprehend the separateness of her own self. "I could say that not hearing Mama's voice when I needed it most was worse than what any train could do to me."[21] This is the final moment of individuation for Alice; she is not her mother, and she would not behave like her mother. She finally grasps the meaning of her experiences in a conversation with her friend, Joe, who explains in a true postmodern fashion, "The future's the future, only what we think will happen. But hardly anything happens the way we think. And the past—we make it up afterward."[22] Is that not what she has been doing all along? It her grief as an abandoned child, she invented a mother for herself.

So in Pietrzyk's novel the absent and silent mother is given a voice by her daughter, but of course this voice expresses the daughter's issues, not the mother's issues. Alice's mother is the silent other throughout the narrative, and she only exists in her daughter's story. Alice constructs a mother-character, through the tension between what she perceived as facts about her dead mother and her wishes for a perfect supportive mother. Yet to create her own womanhood, she has to reject not only the real mother but also the mother construct built so painstakingly during her year of mourning. The mother's own narrative exists on the peripheries, and it will never be told. Just like Rose's mother's sorrow has no voice, Alice's mother's

20. Pietrzyk, *A Year and a Day,* 85.
21. Pietrzyk, *A Year and a Day,* 167.
22. Pietrzyk, *A Year and a Day,* 316.

despair, which led to her suicide, also remains unexplained because the maternal plot is suppressed. She will forever be the unnatural mother who abandons her children and who forces them to question their own worth.

It is quite significant that in Ellen Slezak's novel, *All These Girls* (2004), the tragic death of a mother also provides an occasion for the narrative's origin. The novel begins with Melissa Golden's funeral which brings together three women representing three generations: Candy, Melissa's teenage daughter; Elizabeth Branningan, Melissa's half-sister; and Gloria Derlinski, their aunt. Melissa, a recovering alcoholic, has died tragically in a car accident caused by a speeding driver. The complicated plot of this novel leads the three women brought together by death to a journey not only of self-creation, but also of re-imagining of the silent Melissa. Each of the women constructs her own story through a version of Melissa's story. Consequently, Elizabeth considers the influence of her own (and Melissa's) alcoholic and absent mother, as well as her involvement in Melissa's pregnancy and very difficult delivery, on her own fear of commitment and motherhood, while Gloria confronts her conflicted understanding of the place of sexuality within her strong religious devotion and her role in committing Melissa to a rehab. Not surprisingly, Candy, the character most affected by her mother's death, assumes the crucial role in re-creation of Melissa; thus again a daughter discourse focuses on the story of an absent and voiceless mother. And as Slezak's novel develops the daughter's plot, the mother will never break her silence.

Candy's grief at the loss of her mother manifests itself in anger at Elizabeth who, she feels, has betrayed both her and her mother by leaving them after twelve years of struggle with Melissa's alcoholism. She resents Elizabeth for never acknowledging the fact of Melissa's recovery and her five years of sobriety. Quite conscious that her mother never blamed Elizabeth nor Gloria for giving up on her, Candy is not afraid to assign blame: "They were her only family, but they hadn't helped her mom the way they should have. Elizabeth hadn't helped her at all. Her mom hadn't seen it in that way, but Candy wasn't afraid to say it was so. Moving in with Glo or Elizabeth would be a betrayal of her mom."[23] It seems that Candy almost consciously changes her mother's story to create a person she needs at that particular moment. To counteract her knowledge that for the first twelve years of her life, her mother chose drinking instead of her daughter, she desperately needs to believe that she was a wanted and loved child. She rejects the possibility that her mother might have opted for an abortion were it not for Elizabeth's convictions and support. Like Alice in Pietrzyk's *A Year and a Day,* Candy realizes that there is very little she really knows about her mother. "She looked at her T-shirt, imagining her mom as one of the skeleton heads in the stands watching her play [basketball]. She should know

23. Ellen Slezak, *All These Girls* (New York: Hyperion, 2004), 8.

if her mother liked the dead. What other simple stuff didn't she know about her mom?"[24] As a result of this realization, she begins to re-construct her mother for the first time as someone separate from herself, "Since her mom died, she'd had these moments when she felt as if she were separate from her own breath and bones."[25]

Slezak appears to be preoccupied with the concept of an absent or silent mother since in her short story collection, *Last Year's Jesus*, in seven out of ten texts, a child, most often a daughter, has to come to terms with a mother absent either physically due to death or abandonment or absent emotionally because of total involvement with another child who is sick or dying. The most comprehensive treatment of the latter plot variation can be seen in the novella "Head, Heart, Legs or Arms." The narrative, set in 1967 during the bloody race riots in Detroit, chronicles about eighty days of the life of an eleven-year-old, Mona Palazolla, a middle child whose older sibling, Rose, prepares for college while her younger sister, DeeDee, lays in the hospital, slowly dying of cancer. As Mona witnesses the world around her disintegrate, she longs for reassurance through physical connection to her mother, "she felt desperate to cuddle next to her mother, to hold on to her so tightly she'd feel her bone-to-bone, to feel her mother's lips at her ear, and to hear her mother say, 'You're right, Mona. Everything will be fine. It really will.'"[26] Mona, just like Alice and Candy, still longs for what Nancy Chodorow calls "the sense of oneness"[27] with her mother, a very physical oneness, which she tries to achieve in a rare moment when her mother is actually in the house and not in the hospital staying with sick DeeDee. "Mona stood next to her [mother] and dried the dishes, purposely bumping into her every now and then just to feel her, until finally her mother wrung out her dishrag and bent down to look at Mona closely. 'Are you feeling okay, Mona? You're awfully wobbly this morning.'"[28]

But Mona's mother, even though ever present in the girl's consciousness, only has guest appearances in her daughter's discourse. The framework of the story forces the mother to be mostly silent, recognized by Mona only in a fleeting expression on her sister's face, or as an impersonal type if not to say, stereotype, of a mother caring for a terminally ill child. It becomes clearly evident when Mona searches for her mother at a party organized by the hospital staff for the families of their small patients. As Mona looks at the crowd, "Most women reminded her of the things she noticed about her mother whenever she saw her at the beginning or end of the day—shoulders drooping, scuffed up shoes with worn-down heels, lipstick bitten

---

24. Slezak, *All These Girls*, 277.
25. Slezak, *All These Girls*, 333–34.
26. Ellen Slezak, *Last Year's Jesus* (New York: Hyperion, 2002), 225.
27. Slezak, *Last Year's Jesus*, 109.
28. Slezak, *Last Year's Jesus*, 211.

off, hair dry with gray roots showing."[29] Thus the mother in her suffering loses her identity; she is not an individual anymore but almost a stock character to Mona. In the process of subject-formation through the loss of innocence and a separation from her mother, Mona casts her mother in the role of the silent other. Slezak's novella does not foreground maternal discourse where the mother could voice the tragedy of caring for a dying child. She is silent about her suffering while her second daughter, Mona, identifies the mother's inadequacies in failing to respond to the needs of her other two children. Mona is still too close to the discovery of her mother's otherness to be able to construct for herself a supportive mother figure, so she continues to imagine her mother from before DeeDee's illness.

"Head, Heart, Legs and Arms" is not the only text by Slezak that materializes Marianne Hirsch's idea that "the stories of mothers are the plots of sons and daughters."[30] For example, in the short story "By Heart," the plot of the silent, because absent, mother is created by her thirteen-year old son, Joey. Even though Slezak, as in most of her fiction, uses a third person narrator, there is no doubt that she creates Joey's plot. His mother's abandonment of the boy has been precipitated by the death of her younger daughter. The mother disappears four days after the daughter's funeral and only a day after she and Joey clear away little Allison's belongings. After several days of waiting for his mother in an empty Detroit apartment, the boy finally reaches for help to his father who lives in Chicago with his new wife. As the story progresses, so does the conflict between Joey and his cold, sterile, and rule-driven stepmother who desperately wants to control every aspect of life around her. As a means of survival, the boy continuously recreates his mother, hoping for her return as a savior; but as the time progresses, he begins to understand that he "would relinquish another bit of his true story."[31] Joey sees his mother as a spunky, courageous woman whom life dealt some lousy cards. After a divorce from Joey's father, she drifts from job to job, has another child out of wedlock, and barely survives on child support and factory job earnings. This is a precarious existence, and while Joey admires her beauty and determination, he fails to understand her act of desperation when she abandons him and disappears after her daughter's death.

As a young adolescent male, he situates himself in a paradoxical situation of simultaneously searching for his mother's protection and also framing himself as his mother's protector. He warns her about the dangers of their neighborhood at night; and after his sister's death, he is desperate to find a way to help alleviate his mother's suffering. "He thought maybe fresh air would help him think of what to do, of how

---

29. Slezak, *Last Year's Jesus*, 231.
30. Hirsch, *The Mother/Daughter Plot*, 4.
31. Slezak, *Last Year's Jesus*, 139.

to somehow save his mother from this grief that had downed her."[32] And of course he fails to come up with any viable ideas. The mother leaves. Was it despair over the fact that she could not save her daughter from death that drives her to abandon the living child or was it something else? The reader does not know and Joey does not know; his mother is silent, absent. Is she even his mother anymore, or has she become a stranger, an "other." After a three months stay with his father "he hadn't lost hope that his mother would return, but he was no longer certain he'd run into her arms when she did."[33]

It would be unfair to say that Slezak and Pietrzyk completely discount maternal plots. Pietrzyk certainly engages in maternal discourse in her complex narrative, *Pears in a Willow Tree,* which centers on an interaction between the maternal and the daughterly while Slezak explores maternal narratives in a couple of short stories such as "Patch" or "Here in the Car City," both from her collection *Last Year's Jesus.* The second of the two stories mentioned above is particularly interesting because of an innovative application of the "mother-construct" concept. It appears that for Slezak, children are not the only ones engaged in creating a mother-construct. In "Here in the Car City," she offers an important variation on invention of motherhood. Lodzia Szczotka, a character in this story, is a Polish immigrant living in one of Detroit's dilapidated neighborhoods. She ekes out a precarious existence, hustling and covering up her alcoholism. Although she has lost custody of her two small daughters who have been placed in foster care, she creates an elaborate story to fulfill her need for acceptance and approval. In this self-narrative, she becomes a loving and caring mother who provides for the welfare of her children by surrendering her own aspirations. She casts herself in a role, which in her perception corresponds with the society's ideal of a self-sacrificing mother. Lodzia retells her story when she shares the photographs of her daughters with CeAnn, the owner of the rooming house where she lives. In this narrative told in broken English, her daughters have stayed "[i]n Poland, with my mother. I came here to make money to bring them over. It's better here. Too hard in Poland. I was a doctor there, but my license is no good here, they say. Here I have to take classes at the university to get licensed. So I do that and I work and soon I'll send for them all."[34] "I had to leave them to help them."[35] Lodzia denies abandoning her daughters by reinventing herself into what she considers to be an ideal, self-sacrificing mother and enhances her self-esteem by presenting herself as a professional woman thus conforming to the societal pressures and perceptions of status which probably contributed to her

32. Slezak, *Last Year's Jesus,* 136.
33. Slezak, *Last Year's Jesus,* 137.
34. Slezak, *Last Year's Jesus,* 83.
35. Slezak, *Last Year's Jesus,* 91.

alcoholism in the first place. In "Here in the Car City," the mother's voice is not silenced, not marginalized although the woman herself is marginalized by the social system. Lodzia tells her story in the way she wants to believe it.

It seems fair to conclude that in the texts by both Pietrzyk and Slezak, maternal discourse is for the most part suppressed in favor of daughter-discourse and, on rare occasions, son-discourse. The children are entrusted with the creation of the mother-narratives, which of course seem to be more representative of the children themselves than the mothers. Mothers, cast as "other," remain voiceless and are often absent, their stories marginalized. We might consider why it is so. One possible and simple answer could be that the experience of "daughterhood" or "son-hood" is universal while the opportunity to parent is not; thus writing from the point of view of a child seems more natural. Likewise, a child writing her mother's story encounters numerous difficulties identified by Adrienne Rich in *Of Woman Born*, "It is hard to write about my own mother. Whatever I do write, it is my own story I am telling, my version of the past. If she were to write her own story other landscapes would be revealed."[36] It is also possible that both Pietrzyk and Slezak identify the creation of self, the movement from being an object to asserting the position of a subject, as an important theme to explore. And in the process of individuation, they understand that the child must turn away from a parent and possibly even turn against the parent. Othering of the mother might be an integral part of a rite of passage.

When considering specifically recent Polish American fiction authored by Ellen Slezak and Leslie Pietrzyk, the material suggests that the maternal narratives which often illustrate women's plots created within the confines of a patriarchal society have to be suppressed or rewritten so that a new ethnic woman can emerge—a woman less tied to the working class family model with its dependence on a male. It seems that Polish American fiction provides examples of yet another layer of "othering," this time from within the family unit itself, and specifically from within the mother-daughter dyad. It is possible that this is a stage necessary in the development of a particular ethnic literary discourse, yet it is sad that we are missing so many stories—so many maternal narratives.

---

36. Rich, *Of Woman Born*, 221.

Exile in Postwar Polish Women's Prose

Bożena Karwowska

The article deals with the lives of postwar Polish emigration as portrayed in literary works by Polish émigré women writers. It begins with the "domestic" theme whose prominence in the works in question can be at least partly explained by the fact that in Poland, for historical and political reasons, the public and private spheres had acquired a different character than in the West. The blurring of the line separating the two spaces and the image of Matka Polka *(a patriotic mother) are then used as points of departure for the description and analysis of the role of women of the first generation of postwar émigrés as wives and mothers. This is followed by a discussion of women authors as observers of their new countries (Great Britain, France, Argentina, and the United States) and their inhabitants (including other émigré diasporas and visible minorities). Their view of social change and the beginnings of the feminist movement is largely shaped by the "domestic" patriotic perspective typical of Polish women of their generation. Finally, the article discusses the problems that the mothers encounter in raising the next generation (and generation one-and-a-half) in the context of the cultures and mores of their new countries.*

In his canonical essay "Reflections on Exile," Edward Said indicates that a crucial difference between the immemorial myth of being "an exile" and exile as a phenomenon of the twentieth century is its vast scale.[1] In our times exile not only affects individuals such as writers, artists, and intellectuals but also has become the fate of

---

The author dedicates this article to her daughters.

1. Edward W. Said, "Reflections on Exile," *Reflections on Exile and Other Essays* (Cambridge, MA: Harvard University Press, 2002), 173–86.

From *The Polish Review*, vol. 59, no. 1 (2014), pp. 69–86.

large social groups, often deprived of both a place of their own and a "tellable history." But there is another important feature: the United Nations High Commission for Refugees estimates that between 75 percent and 80 percent of the world's population of "migrants" are women and children—and these are indeed people deprived of "tellable history." Many of them—before settling in the country of exile—had gone through tragic experiences of war, loss of family members, humiliation, personal or witnessed violence, torture, or rape.[2] No one would deny that there is a considerable difference between the exilic narratives of men and those of women. The theme of exile, still strongly present in culture and literature, derives principally from the image shaped by men's narratives and concerns mainly the social and intellectual sphere, which is symbolically male. And while the category of exile underlies various discussions concerning constructed and flexible identities—and thus mirrors the contemporary, postcolonial vision of humanity—researchers emphasize that women's experiences of exile and migration are still largely marginalized or passed over in silence.[3]

The picture projected by postwar[4] Polish women exiles is certainly different from the intellectual image of exile created by male émigré writers such as Czesław Miłosz and Witold Gombrowicz,[5] although it is not only the differences that are worth considering. Of interest is the range of themes and the "feminine" presentation of the problems that confronted all Poles after the war dispersed them over the globe. Our focus here will not be on exceptionally creative individuals seeking their own identity in the cosmopolitan tradition of "the exile"[6]—that is, writers who "concentrate

2. See Jennifer Langer, "Introduction," *Crossing the Border: Voices of Refugee and Exiled Women* (Nottingham: Five Leaves, 2002), 1–19.

3. See Halleh Ghorashi, "When the Boundaries Are Blurred," *European Journal of Women's Studies* 12, no. 3 (August 2005): 363–75, here, 363; and Diana Kay, "The Politics of Gender in Exile," *Sociology* 22, No. 1 (February 1988): 1–21. The relatively recent interest in women is focused mainly on women exiles and refugees from the so-called Third World in the last three decades of the twentieth century.

4. My article deals with women writers who wrote in exile in the wake of World War II. I call this a postwar generation of émigrés to emphasize the importance of the wartime experiences in the formation of their identities.

5. The evolution of the concept of exile is treated in Bożena Karwowska, "Kategoria wygnania w anglojęzycznych dyskursach krytycznoliterackich," in *Pisarz na emigracji. Mitologie, Style, Strategie Przetrwania*, ed. Hanna Gosk and Andrzej Stanisław Kowalczyk (Warsaw: Dom Wydawniczy Elipsa, 2005), 79–95, and in "Introduction," Bożena Karwowska, *Druga płeć na wygnaniu. Doświadczenie migracyjne w opowieści powojennych pisarek polskich* (Kraków: Universitas, 2013).

6. On the formation of post-émigré identity, see Bożena Karwowska, "Tożsamość postemigracyjna—przypadek (między innymi) Czesława Miłosza," *Przegląd Humanistyczny* 4 (2005): 1–12.

primarily on themselves, since they value above all their own development,"[7] and who are unique by their very nature, capricious, and presumably, as exiles, are denied natural successors. Our attention will be on women whose gender constructs are shaped by motherhood, thus ensuring continuity through birth and raising children.

Many problems in applying traditional "exilic" categories to women's writings are perhaps due to the delimitation, traditional in Western culture, between men's "public" and women's "domestic" spheres, which are governed by different rules. Much of the critical interest in the subject has been focused on the exilic narratives of men,[8] and many categories related to exile simply do not fit the domestic, private perspective, nor are they helpful in the depiction of the processes taking place in an émigré/immigrant family, thus confining them to critical limbo. Even in exilic texts written by women writers,[9] the domestic perspective—being "private"—has often been treated as less important, with the authors presenting themselves primarily as writers/intellectuals, that is, in the public space defined by men. In the case of the works that will be discussed here the characters/narrators are not outstanding, creative individuals, active on the public stage; they are so-called ordinary people shown primarily in their private, domestic space. However, for Polish women abroad, "home" meant a space that combined both private and social spheres,[10] and

---

7. Langer, "Introduction," 15.

8. See Marc Robinson, "Introduction," *Altogether Elsewhere: Writers on Exile* (Boston: Faber and Faber, 1994), i–xii.

9. Robinson's anthology—comprising canonical texts—also includes pieces by women authors, such as Mary McCarthy, Mary Antin, Marina Tsvetaeva, Hannah Arendt, Madame de Staël, Hilde Domin, and Eva Hoffman.

10. See Małgorzata Fidelis, "'Participation in the Creative Work of the Nation': Polish Women Intellectuals in the Cultural Construction of Female Gender Roles, 1864–1890," *Journal of Women's History* 13, no. 1 (2001): 108–25. Fidelis argues, that "[p]atriotic goals significantly shaped private and public spheres in nineteenth-century Poland. Independent statehood was identified with family life, and political activity often was conducted at home and included women. In Western Europe, the spheres were distinct but mutually supportive: state protection of the private sphere served to maintain bourgeois social and economic order. In contrast, in Poland, the public realm, controlled by a hostile state, was perceived as alien, while the private sphere was a source of freedom and independence in need of defence against state-imposed laws. When Konopnicka [a popular woman poet] wrote 'our homes will be our fortresses,' she expressed the widespread perception that a Polish household was a state unto itself, a bastion of resistance against political and cultural domination by the partitioning powers. Elevation of the roles of women as mothers and ladies of the house had implications beyond literary meanings; although Poland was not an independent state, women presided over the spiritual Poland at home," 111. See also Pamela Chester and Sibelan Forrester, eds., *Engendering Slavic Literatures* (Bloomington: Indiana University Press, 1996); and Helena Goscilo and Beth Holmgren, eds., *Poles Apart: Women in Modern Polish Culture*, special issue of *Indiana Slavic Studies* 15 (2005).

this fact had a huge influence on the ways in which women were coming to terms with their exilic lives.

Quite typically, intellectuals first deal with the reasons for their exile, justify their own decisions that thrust them into the exilic fate. Many literary texts and critical reflections have been devoted to this preliminary stage in forming the identity of "an exile."[11] But women's decisions to stay abroad seem almost nonreflective, and even if they occur in literary texts, they are principally as issues belonging to the sphere of men's thinking and decision making. Instead, critics who have written about women's literary testimonies of exile emphasize that emigration/immigration is usually preceded by traumatic events that have a significant effect on the situation of women (including their families).[12] And although in Polish literature there is an apparent differentiation between the theme of war and occupation on the one hand, and of emigration on the other, women's fiction often recalls earlier experiences as having had an influence on women protagonists. Teresa, the narrator of the cycle of novels, *Gringa*, by Janina Surynowa-Wyczółkowska, experienced mass rape;[13] the husband of Mrs. Dubiel—one of the women protagonists of Janina Kowalska's novel *Pogranicze* (Borderland)—"disappeared somewhere in the Soviet Union"[14]—to mention only the most typical situations.

Traumatic experiences, however, for the postwar generation of émigrés seem the norm. It is rather the absence of such experiences that is viewed as significant. Teresa, the narrator of *Gringa*, equates the lack of traumatic experiences with "immaturity" when she writes about her fiancé: "It always seemed to me that he was younger than me: Younger because he did not live through the years of war and bitter experiences. He has never suffered. Dear God, he certainly was never hungry."[15] In Maria Kuncewiczowa's *Tristan 46*, the eponymous hero, whose mother spent the years of the war and occupation in England, while he was accumulating

---

11. According to Robinson, the exile goes through a process that can be defined as the transformation of an "émigré" into an "immigrant." The first phase of this process is the establishment of the type of exile that is being experienced and the formation of an émigré identity. See Robinson, "Introduction," i–xii.

12. Langer, "Introduction," 6.

13. See Janina Surynowa-Wyczółkowska, *Gringa* (London: Polska Fundacja Kulturalna, 1968).

14. Janina Kowalska (Alina Świderska), *Pogranicze* (Paris: Instytut Literacki, 1980), 43.

15. "Miałam zawsze wrażenie, że jest ode mnie młodszy. Młodszy o całą wojnę i ciężkie przeżycia. On nigdy nie cierpiał. Na pewno, Mój Boże, nigdy nie był głodny." Surynowa-Wyczółkowska, *Gringa*, 95. All quotations from Polish literary works have been translated by Bogdan Czaykowski.

bitter memories in occupied Warsaw, notes: "What does it mean: mother and son, how those years were different in her and in my case."[16] And a little further on:

> [I]t never occurred to me that I had such a young mother. . . . This spawned all kinds of difficulties. If only she were old, is she had breasts like a mattress, perhaps I would shed tears, open up, quarrel, and then settle near her like an ordinary son.[17]

Experiences of war and occupation made the women mature and age faster than their coevals who lived in relative security. I have quoted the opinions of a young girl about her fiancé and of a young man about his mother because the family sphere is the most frequent and best-treated theme in émigré women's writings. In their exilic situation the protagonists of these writings attempt first and foremost to reconstruct their domestic (safe) space and assume the traditional roles of wife and mother, and this irrespective of where they find themselves after the war.

The émigré locations most commonly depicted are England, South America (Argentina), and the United States, though other countries also appear (France and Canada). England represents the period right after the war, later called by the Polish émigrés the "pioneering" stage. Reminiscing years later, Janina Kowalska compares the attitude of local people toward Poles at that time to their later resentments toward other national (in fact, racial) minorities:

> Our former place at the bottom of the social ladder has been for quite a while now taken by the immigrants of color and the above-mentioned [Anglo-Saxon] xenophobic fellow, remembering the olden days, but now muzzled by the law on the harmonious coexistence of races, would not dare to advise the black and dark-skinned newcomers to go home. If reminded that once upon a time he called upon us to go home, though at first sight we were hardly different from the indigenous people, he would only sigh sadly.[18]

A similar attitude to the Poles as a "lower" ethnic group is also evident in works whose action takes place in the United States. However, the presence of Polish diasporas in North America, established by earlier waves of uneducated peasants

---

16. "Cóż to znaczy matka i syn, jak te lata u niej były inne i u mnie inne." Maria Kuncewiczowa, *Tristan 46*, 2nd ed. (Warsaw: Czytelnik, 1968) , 67.

17. "Żebym ja naprawdę miał taką młodą matkę, to sobie nie wyobrażałem. . . . Powstała kupa trudności. Gdyby ona była stara, gdyby miała biust jak materac, może bym się popłakał, wygadał, wykłócił i bym osiadł przy niej jak zwyczajny syn. A tak to sie tylko napuszyłem i albo eleganta odstawiam, albo uciekam od niej." Ibid., 73.

18. "Nasze ówczesne miejsce u dołu drabiny społecznej od dawna zajęli kolorowi i onże ksenofob, pamiętający dawne lata, a teraz zakneblowany ustawą o harmonijnym współżyciu ras, nie odważy się zalecać czarnym i brunatnym przybyszom, aby sobie poszli precz. Przypomnijmy mu, że ongiś wzywał do tego nas, bądź co bądź na oko mało różniących się od tubylców, a westchnie smętnie." Kowalska, *Pogranicze*, 7.

emigrating for economic reasons, complicated the situation and put an interesting twist on the issue of the national identity of Polish exiles.

Commenting on the fates of contemporary Polish writers living in North America, Halina Stephan writes that Polish émigrés often emphasized their politically defined image, stressing—especially in the United States—the absence of any bond with the uneducated prewar (late nineteenth- and early twentieth-century) economic emigration from Poland.[19] Putting the emphasis on the political aspect enabled the new émigrés to seek their roots in the "immemorial myth of an exile" and to present themselves as a group that, though it continued to be viewed as "the others," nevertheless had an appreciably higher status in the West than did the older immigrant ethnic diasporas. The women's narratives, however, do not treat the earlier Polish economic émigrés as disparate, instead viewing them as "pioneers," that is, as an earlier émigré generation struggling to overcome basic handicaps. As Danuta Mostwin has described it, the older, "peasant" émigrés collided with the already settled Irish immigrants, who looked down on the Poles. This allows Mostwin to present the "otherness" of the new Polish émigrés as regarded in relation not only to the Americans but also to "other" immigrant diasporas (mainly Irish), and previous waves of Polish emigrants. In her story "Stryjcio z Ameryki"[20] (The uncle from the United States), even finding accommodation proves a far from easy task:

> They only entered houses that looked modest and had a piece of paper in the window or nailed to the door: "Room for rent." Women usually opened the doors. The number of such elderly women was a wonder, all tall, rough, with a penetrating-examining gaze. "Where are you from?" the women would ask. "Polacks? No, no" and they would retreat shutting the door. "Blast it" Kramarz's companion would swear—"Blast it, an old Irish hag."[21]

The "new," postwar wave of Polish immigrants who came to America was also hardly welcomed with open arms. The reality that awaited them on the new continent was far from what they had expected. This disappointment may contribute to the fact that, although the United States—contrary to Britain—was a country they chose, they did not feel that the choice they were making was really theirs,

19. See Halina Stephan, "Introduction: The Last Exiles," in *Living in Translation: Polish Writers in America* (Amsterdam: Rodopi, 2003), 7–28.

20. Danuta Mostwin, "Stryjcio z Ameryki," *Kultura*, no. 5 (1959): 61–88.

21. "Zachodzili tylko do domów wyglądających skromnie i kierując się wystawioną w oknie lub przybitą na drzwiach kartka: "Room for rent." Otwierały zwykle kobiety. Aż dziw ile było tych starszawych kobiet, wysokich, kanciastych o spojrzeniu świdrująco-badawczym.—Where are you from?—pytały. Polaks? No, no,—cofały się zamykając drzwi. Cholera—przeklinał towarzysz Kramarza—cholera, stara wiedźma Ajriszka!" Mostwin, "Stryjcio z Ameryki," 69.

but rather that they were compelled to migrate. Mr. Wiśniewski, the protagonist of Danuta Mostwin's story "Córki" (Daughters)[22] thinks of his decision thus:

> Mrs. Wiśniewska [his wife] sighed: to the United States! Indeed, could they go back? To Poland? To its ruins? He himself saw the house go up in flames, the walls crumbling. They stood side by side watching their perishing home. . . . He lacked the courage to go back. Fate had decided everything, pushed him forward: First on foot in a crowd of defeated Underground fighters, then on trains going westward. . . . Was he to go back to a country from which people were running away? . . . What to do? . . . Longing or fear? Indecisiveness? . . . I do not want my children to go through similar horrors. Two laughing girlies milled around him. He fed and clothed them. He tried to insulate them from the past and at the same time to tie them to it. "Let's emigrate to the United States" Mrs. Wiśniewska was urging him.[23]

The work that the new immigrants could obtain, did not always match their ambitions, plans, and European education (more precisely: the education that they obtained in prewar Poland or in England). This is depicted in many stories by Mostwin, a writer who was particularly sensitive to the question of the education of American Poles (the so-called Polonia).[24] Though women authors focus on the fates of female characters, she presents the problem of professional and social declassing also using non-gender specific examples. Similarly, though the issue of getting a higher education occurred frequently in women's writings, it is not presented as a problem related specifically to female immigrants. University education translates into the possibility of social advancement by means of professional work (although in the postwar period even educated American women usually did not work professionally after marriage) and is a value to which in cultural terms women have access equal that of men. In the reality of émigré life, however, this is not easy to achieve, and to have a family (especially children) is an obstacle in obtaining American education not only for women but also for men—as is the case of Andrzej, Boga's husband.

The place of émigrés in the American society, however, was determined not only by their education but also by the physical space, the location of their homes, and the quality of the neighborhoods they lived in. Irrespective of their education

22. Danuta Mostwin, "Córki," *Kultura*, no. 7–8 (1962): 57–78.

23. "Wiśniewska wzdychała: Do Ameryki! Gdzie mieli wracać? Do Polski? Do gruzów? Widział sam przecież jak dom się palił,waliły ściany. Stali oboje, patrzyli na ginące mieszkanie. . . . Nie miał odwagi wrócić. To już los decydował o wszystkim, pchał go naprzód. Najpierw pieszo w tłumie rozbitków powstańczych, potem pociągami na zachód . . . Miał wracać, gdy stamtąd uciekali ludzie? . . . Co robić? . . . Tęsknota czy obawa? Niezdecydowanie? . . . nie chcę aby moje dzieci miały przechodzić przez podobne okropności. Kręciły się koło niego dwie roześmiane frygi. Karmił je i odziewał. Odgradzał od dawnego i z dawnym związywał.—Emigrujmy do Ameryki—zachęcała Wiśniewska." Mostwin, "Córki," 64.

24. See Danuta Mostwin, *Trzecia wartość* (Lublin: Katolicki Uniwersytet Lubelski, 1985).

and ambitions, uninformed Polish newcomers often found a place to live in poorer districts of American cities, neighborhoods inhabited by "people of color," from which it was difficult to move out—as is the case with the characters in Mostwin's "'Lanczeneta' przy Alei Północnej" (Luncheonette on Northern Alley):

> They were simply thrown in here. Żuławski initially got a job as a night cashier. Money that he had saved in England was running out and had to be invested right away. They wanted to make their savings safe and at least to have a small return. They were totally inexperienced, the city seemed alien, the world hostile, people unapproachable. Żuławska knew how to cook, so they bought a restaurant near the Northern Alley. . . . And got stuck.[25]

It is worth noting that the decision to open a restaurant is based on a woman's domestic skills, once again pointing to the blurred boundaries between private and public spaces.

The American world surrounding Polish immigrants baffled them with its ethnic-racial mix, which they did not always understand. To many Poles emigration meant the first direct encounter with "people of color," and an opportunity to reflect on the question of the "other." The woman narrator of "Pierwszy krok" (The first step) describes it thus:

> Walking along the street I observe the passing Negroes. I know nothing about them. Is their suffering different? . . . But perhaps they hate me because I am white? What kind of a human being is this man with shiny skin, thick lips, and eyes that are moist and protruding?[26]

In fact the African Americans are, in the eyes of the Polish newcomers, what the entire "colored" world of North America amounts to. Polish women writers refer to "Negroes" primarily to illustrate the absence of racism of Poles (especially in contrast to other "white" Americans); however, those reflections on the racial minority only make the contemporary reader aware of the naiveté of the new immigrants and of their colonial mentality.[27]

---

25. "Wrzuciło ich tu po prostu. Żuławski dostał najpierw pracę jako nocny kasjer. Pieniądze oszczędzone w Anglii topniały i trzeba było natychmiast je ulokować. Myśleli o zabezpiecze niu kapitału i o skromnym chociażby dochodzie. Nie znali się na niczym, miasto wydawało się obce, świat wrogi, ludzie nieprzystępni. Żuławska umiała gotować, kupili więc restaurację przy Alei Północnej i już . . . ugrzęźli." Mostwin, "'Lanczeneta' przy Alei Północnej," 37.

26. "Idąc ulicą przyglądałam się mijającym mnie Murzynom. Nie znam ich. Czy cierpienie ich jest inne. . . . A może oni mnie nienawidzą za to, że jestem biała? Jakim na prawdę jest ten człowiek o błyszczącej skórze, grubych wargach i oczach wilgotnych i wypukłych." Mostwin, "Pierwszy krok," 150.

27. See Edward W. Said, *Orientalism* (New York: Vintage, 1979).

Interestingly, a different image of the Pole (as himself an "other" of color) can be found only in Janina Surynowa-Wyczółkowska's *Gringa*, set in Argentina. This no doubt has something to do with—once again using Janina Kowalska's expression—"differing visually from the locals." More precisely, with having a whiter skin color because—as is typical of a colonial society—"all those who belong to the elite want to whiten their progeny and marry a white woman."[28] The protagonist of *Gringa* is a young, unmarried daughter of a quite well-to-do father. The otherness of her body is, however, amplified by her cultural otherness, which involves behavior that differs from the norm set for women in Latino culture. This cannot but lead to conflict with the indigenous women in a country where—as Teresa puts it years later—"widows never remarry." Even her closest friend, the self-reliant maker of artistic rugs, is unable to understand cultural otherness, and as a result accuses Teresa of deliberate attempts to seduce men.

> Here one dances only with one's own husband and one walks arm in arm only with one's own husband. What's inside you? What motivates you, what drives you when you thus flirt and lead men on? I often curse watching you, your charm and grace, your cleverness, wit, your elegance, with which you wear this cheap fur and those slacks on long legs.[29]

These words, put in the mouth of an Argentinean woman, constitute a description of Polish femininity, so different not only from the Argentinean but also from the Anglo-American model (at least of half a century ago), and that, too, was the source of numerous misunderstandings. Let us note here, however, that at that time, irrespective of the country where Polish émigrés arrived, the model of femininity was conditioned by the (local) rules of patriarchy and connected to the role of a wife (and mother).

Getting married was thus of special importance for women of the generation of postwar émigrés. It was a way of trying to overcome the postwar trauma and to re-create a safe, stable, and familiar place offering women the traditional identity of a wife. Describing Crowley (and in fact English hostels and camps for Poles),[30]

---

28. "Każdy należący do elity chce wybielić swoje potomstwo i żeni się z kobietą o białej skórze." Surynowa-Wyczółkowska, *Gringa*, 66.

29. "U nas tańczy się tylko z własnym mężem i chodzi się pod rękę tylko z własnym mężem. Co w tobie siedzi? Co tobą kieruje, kiedy tak kokietujesz i uwodzisz? Przeklinam nieraz patrząc na ciebie, ten twój czar i wdzięk, ten spryt, dowcip, tę elegancję, z którą nosisz to swoje tanie futerko i te spodnie na tych długich nogach." Janina Surynowa-Wyczółkowska, *Jesień Gringi* (London: Polska Fundacja Kulturalna, 1976), 157.

30. Crowley was one of around 500 camps and hostels built on the British Isles for members of the demobilized Polish Army after World War II.

Kowalska defines women according to their marital status: there are married women (and mothers), four eligible misses, and an old maid. Being a wife also meant patriotic obligations toward future generations (it was the leading role of *Matka Polka* [the Polish Mother]), thus a relationship between a Pole and an English woman is regarded negatively by the "Crowleyan" Polish women. Polish men were attractive to Englishwomen, but foreigners were not what a "wife" should be. Although this is not the main theme of émigré women writers, it is worth quoting the observations of Janina Kowalska, according to whom young Poles from the military camps for foreign troops were also trying to (re)establish their masculinities and become husbands and fathers. They

> were raring to get married and quickly seized whatever came in hand, while it is well known that a good product seldom pushes itself on you on its own. They clicked their heels and kissed hands, which was a novelty and enchanted the women. . . . No wonder that local girls fell for them. . . . But after a general reckoning, which the end of the war brought about, among the newlywed men there was no lack of those, who said of each other, where the hell did he dig her out like a dog with its paws. Everybody knows that a woman should know how to make beet-root soup and pierogi, how to laundry and house-clean and raise children.[31]

Polish women decidedly seem to put a very high value on the patriarchal traditions of domestic roles, which the English women are just beginning to shed, entering a more public space. In Kowalska's narrative this "public" space is far from being understood in the feminist sense and embraces—almost in an ironic way—mainly shops, pubs, and streets. Similar in tone are comments on the "Scottish wife" in Mostwin's "Luncheonette on Northern Alley." While there is no doubt that cultural differences (and more precisely—differences in the gender constructions of womanhood) stood in the way of Polish women's acceptance of "foreign" women as wives of Polish men, one cannot exclude rivalry or jealousy since they deprived Polish émigré women of men whom they would rather have had as "their" potential husbands.

In the writings of the postwar émigré women the role of wife is directly related to the role of mother, who is responsible for making a home and maintaining the Polishness of the next generation. Raising children "in exile"—which meant also

31. "Palili się do żeniaczki i szybko łapali co im lazło w łapy, a wiadomo, że dobry towar sam pcha się raczej rzadko. Trzaskali kopytami i całowali rączki, co było nowe i zachwycające. . . . Nic dziwnego, że dziewczęta leciały na nich. . . . Ale po generalnym rachunku sumienia, który przyniósł koniec wojny,wśród nowożeńców nie zabrakło i takich, co wzajemnie mówili jeden o drugim, że gdzie on takie coś wygrzebał jak pies łapą. Każdy wie, że kobieta ma się znać na barszczach i pierożkach, praniu, sprzątaniu i dzieciach." Kowalska, *Pogranicze*, 98.

fulfilling society's "expectations"—is perhaps the most interesting émigré theme in women's fiction, and as far as one can see it is present in women's narratives only. The pressure of the patriotic tradition was so strong that it led to the defining of home as the "space of Polishness," irrespective of the nationality of the spouse. Non-Polish wives naturally could not fulfill the hopes placed in a mother who was Polish.

Women writers realize that Polishness is not a matter of language alone, but mainly the problem of language that they describe in relation to children. This may be the result of identifying nationality with language as a distinguishing feature and as a "sign" that clearly differentiates Poles from other nationalities. Many of the observations concerning linguistically conditioned changes in national consciousness (and identity) made by Polish-born Eva Hoffman in her best-selling *Lost in Translation*,[32] were already made years earlier in Polish émigré women's fiction. Interestingly, before the protagonists of the literary texts face the language issue in relation to their children, they note it in themselves (or in other adults). Teresa, the narrator of *Gringa*, as an unmarried young woman already realizes that she unconsciously intermixes Spanish words when speaking Polish:

> And suddenly I realized that I am attached to that city near the Cordillera Mountains and that I call in my thoughts its scent perfume, and its freshness frescura. For these words come handily and easily (and not Polish words).
>
> You are losing your Polish identity, Teresa—I think to myself on my way to the bus.[33]

The problem of language is neither new nor exclusively émigré, which Teresa, the daughter of a Czech father and Polish mother, realizes when talking to her father:

> So I begin shouting that you cannot take into account in this case any negocio, asunto, or comercio, because I am muy feliz. Dichosa.
>
> "You say szczęśliwa [happy]"—he corrected me. "Teresa, make up your mind in which language do you want us to talk. I used to get flogged as a boy when I mixed German and Czech."
>
> To which I respond: "For two years now I have been speaking only in castellano, and sometimes in English, and I am not even aware that I am forgetting Polish words".

---

32. Eva Hoffman, *Lost in Translation: Life in a New Language* (London: William Heinemann, 1979).

33. "I naraz uświadomiłam sobie że jestem przywiązana do tamtego miasta pod Kordy-lierami i że zapach jego w myśli nazywam 'perfume,' a świeżość 'frescura.' Bo tak właśnie jest mi pomyśleć poręczniej i łatwiej (nie po polsku).
"Wynaradawiasz się, Tereso"—myślę idąc do autokaru." Surynowa-Wyczółkowska, *Gringa*, 137.

He interrupted me: "Yes," he said. "One loses one's nationality surreptitiously, gradually."[34]

The author points here to the general issue of language and its importance for maintaining national identity, but she also hints on the differences between the situation of Gringa and that of her father. The purity of speech required of children in one's own country (e.g., during the Partitions, or by national minorities) meant maintaining one's national identity, independence, and cultural continuity. Teresa in Buenos Aires (the capital of the country she lived in) thinks of this city, however, as "the future capital of my Argentinean children,"[35] and is aware of the inevitability of the process of assimilation, of the difference in nationality between herself and her prospective children.

The children who appear in émigré women's writings are usually raised to be Poles—they attend a Polish kindergarten, are taught Polish songs and nursery rhymes, and are dressed in national costume. But above everything else they are taught the language, and this is usually their parents' conscious decision. The process is excellently described in Zofia Romanowiczowa's novel *Baśka i Barbara*, which deals with raising a daughter in a French-language milieu. The writer also provides a rationale for using Polish at home:

> It's an alien world around us. Our house is like a tiny boat on an ocean. Are we ourselves to hollow the bottom of the boat so that it would sink, so that there would be no home? So that, when coming back in a few years from school, or an excursion, our daughter would slow her steps at the thought that there, behind the doors, she is awaited by a pair of strangers?[36]

Baśka i Barbara is devoted to the first years of a girl's childhood and her parents' decisions are not yet subjected to the test of the influence that the culture of "her"

---

34. ". . . ja w krzyk, że nie może tu wchodzićw rachubę żadne "negocio," "asunto" czy "comercio," bo jestem "muy feliz." "Dichoza."

—Mówi się "szczęśliwa"—poprawił. Zdecyduj się, Tereniu, w jakim języku mamy mówic? Za takie mieszanie słów czeskich z niemieckimi dostawałem w dzieciństwie baty.

A ja:—Od dwóch lat mówię tylko po "castellano," czasem po angielsku i nie zdaję sobie z tego sprawy że zapominam słów polskich.

Przerwał mi:—Tak—powiedział. Wynarodowienie przychodzi chyłkiem, nieznacznie." Ibid., 141.

35. "Przyszła stolica moich argentyńskich dzieci." Ibid., 137.

36. "Dookoła obcy świat. Dom nasz jak łupina na oceanie. Mamy sami w tej łupinie drążyć dno, żeby pogrążyła się, żeby nie było domu? Żeby, wracając kiedyś, za parę lat, z jakiejś szkoły, z jakiejś wycieczki, nasza córka Barbara zwalniała kroku na schodach na myśl, że za drzwiami czeka na nią para cudzoziemców?" Zofia Romanowiczowa, *Baśka i Barbara* (Paris: Libella, 1956), 51.

country will start exerting on Baśka through her peers and in school. Romanowiczowa just hints about future problems by referring to her daughter by two names: Polish—Baśka, and French—Barbara, with the stress falling, differently than in Polish, on the last syllable. Discussing with his already grown-up children about which language children should be raised in, Jose Maria, Gringa's husband, says:

> In that respect the parents cannot have any certainty, there is no guarantee. Children do what they want. First they wanted a colorful ball. Then a plastic swan in the swimming pool. At some point you have to open a bank account for them, buy a car. They demand. They require. They ask . . . They refuse to be persuaded about anything, to have anything imposed on them. So if they speak one or another language, then it won't be because we teach them that language, but because Bibi graciously consents to speak Spanish, Antek to speak English, and Barbarita Polish.[37]

None of the literary works under discussion gives a clear and consistent explanation in regard to why preserving Polish would have been important to émigré children. Was it because they were to return to Poland, or because that would make their relations with their parents closer, or make them able to share in the culture of their parents? Perhaps teaching children to speak/be Polish enabled their mothers to inscribe themselves in the tradition of the Polish Mother engaged in patriotic tasks, even despite the many doubts they had. One of the characters in "Luncheonette on Northern Alley," Żuławska, is hardly an exception, when she thinks to herself:

> Oh, that desperate struggle to preserve the language! That struggle, tragic, going down to defeat like the tenacious flame of a resistance detachment melting away. What instruments, what tools to use? Who will help? She reflects: Mother taught him: "good morning, sausage, lick my a. . . . Oh, I have it all you know where."[38]

Without demonstrating the advantages of teaching the native tongue, émigré women writers show the conflicts resulting from this struggle, arising especially at the age when children form their personalities—often in opposition to their parents. These conflicts are described principally in the case of the daughters. The protagonists and narrators are as yet unaware that the problems they are having with

---

37. "Rodzice pod tym względem nie mają żadnej pewności, ani gwarancji. Bo dzieci robią co chcą. Najpierw chodzi im o kolorową piłkę. Potem o plastykowego łabędzia na basenie. Z kolei trzeba imdać konto bankowe, samochód. Żadają. Wymagają.Proszą. . . . Nie pozwalają sobie nic wypersfadować ani narzucać. Jeśli więc będą mówić takim czy innym językiem, to nie dlatego że my ich tego języka nauczymy, ale dlatego że Bibi łaskawie zechce mówić po hiszpańsku, Antek po angielsku a Barbarita po polsku." Surynowa-Wyczółkowska, *Jesień Gringi*, 193.

38. "Ach ta walka rozpaczliwa o zachowanie języka! Ta walka,tragiczna, przegrana niby nieustępliwy ogienek topniejącej partyzantki. Z czym się na to porywać? Kto pomoże? Żuławska myśli: Nauczyła go matka:dzień dobry, kiełbasa, mam cie w d. . . . Och, mam to wszystko w de." Mostwin, "'Lanczeneta' przy Alei Północnej," 48.

their children are also the result of broader issues, which feminist criticism later labeled "the mother–daughter relationship." The women writers are convinced that the source of the conflicts lies in the struggle to maintain Polishness, since often for the children Polishness becomes an obstacle to finding their place in their "own" country (the country in which they live), in which they feel at least partly "foreign." In the women's version, exile means a rift not only between "themselves" and the country of origin—as Edward Said called it—but also between their own cultural identity and the culture of their children. This rift may be—as in the case of Gringa and her daughter—quite complicated.

> "Oh!" shouts Barbarita. "Gringa, you are awful!"
> We are now facing each other, so much alike. We both have light hair and wear dresses in gay, colorful stripes. We both move the tips of our noses the same way.
> "You too are Gringa," I say harshly, "because you are my daughter."
> I get a nasty look from under her disheveled bangs. And she shouts: "I am ashamed to be the daughter of Gringa. The daughter of una Polaca."
> I look horrified at my child, the way my mother must have once looked at me. "It's your own children that wrong you most," passes through my mind. "You suffer at the hands of bitten nails and dirty fingers." "I would prefer," Baśka shouts, "to be an Argentinian like my father. Una pura cepa (a pure offspring)."[39]

Conflicts between daughters and mothers do not always involve (at least on the surface) the question of Polishness, but may involve the need to be independent, which often resulted in the daughters marrying Americans. Such marriages—according to the parents—had to lead to the loss of Polish identity, both in terms of "language" and of the gender construction of femininity, though the language aspect was easier to describe. In her "Córki" (Daughters) Mostwin writes:

> Our daughter left us first. She married a pal from college, an American. It's not that she simply walked out on us, no, it was rather a departure through a series of gateways, doors, gates. Not a farewell, not a parting, not at one stroke, one turning of the key in the lock—but a constant distancing, a continuous grating of the key. With every meeting she seemed more remote, her Polish acquiring an American

39. "—Oh!—Krzyczy Barbarita.—Jesteś wstrętna Gringa!
Stoimy teraz na wprost siebie. Podobne jedna do drugiej. Obie mamy jasne włosy i suknie w wesołe, kolorowe paski. Obie poruszamy czubkiem nosa.
—I ty jesteś Gringa—mówię twardo—bo jesteś moją córką.
Złe spojrzenie spod roztargaanej grzywki i krzyk:—Wstydzę się, że jestem córką Gringi. Córką de una Polaca (córką Polki).
Z przerażeniem patrzę na moje dziecko, tak jak kiedyś mama musiała patrzeć na mnie. "Największych krzywd w życiu doznajemy od własnych dzieci—pomyślałam. Z rąk o poobgryzanych paznokciach i o poplamionych palcach."—Wolałabym—krzyczy Baśka—być Argentynką jak ojciec. Una pura cepa (czystą latoroślą)." Surynowa-Wyczółkowska, *Gringa*, 215.

accent. With increasing frequency she would stop in the middle of a sentence looking for the appropriate word.[40]

In the same story the troubles the parents are having with their maturing daughters concern mainly how to make them marry Poles. First the family had to leave Germany. "Oleńka graduated from high school, she started being interested in boys. What if she marries some German guy?" Subsequently, in the United States they worry because "Grażynka says she will marry an American, a Jew, a Protestant, she'll just leave."[41]

The two daughters mentioned here—Oleńka and Grażyna—belong to a group that Rubén G. Rumbaut called "generation one-and-a-half,"[42] comprising children of émigrés, who in moving to a new country are old enough to remember their native culture and to enter (more or less) consciously the culture of their new country. At the same time, they are young enough to become part of the peer groups in the country of arrival and associate with them their whole social identity. Rumbaut believed that as a result they could easily move between two cultures.[43] However, the émigré women writers also depict them as having problems with finding a place in either.

In the situations described in the Polish narratives, children born and/or raised outside Poland share a number of features with "generation one-and-a-half." But instead of actual memories of Poland they have a remembered/imagined notion of Polishness (related above all to their childhood and home) constructed by the patriotic émigré narrative. For this generation the Polishness of the public sphere is only the émigré, Polonian diasporas often governed by their own rules and having their own dynamics. Moreover, the image of these diasporas in the women's prose is not very flattering—to mention only Kowalska's *Pogranicze* or Mostwin's "Córki."

---

40. "Córka odeszła pierwsza, wyszła za mąż za kolegę z college'u, Amerykanina. Było to odejście nie jednorazowe, odejście, jakby przez szereg następujących po sobie bram, drzwi, furtek. Nie pożegnanie, nie rozłąka, jeden cios, jedno przekręcenie klucza w zamku—ale nieustanne oddalanie się, nieustanny zgrzyt klucza. Za każdym spotkaniem córka wydawała się jej coraz bardziej odległa, jej język polski nabrał amerykańskiego akcentu. Coraz częściej zatrzymywała sie w połowie zdania szukając odpowiedniego słowa. Generałowa z wysiłkiem wsłuchiwała się w angielski szczebiot wnuków." Mostwin, "Córki," 67.

41. "Oleńka zrobiła maturę, oglądała się za chłopcami. Jeszcze im za jakiego Niemca wyjdzie?" "Grażynka mówi, że wyjdzie za Amerykanina, za Żyda, za protestanta, pójdzie sobie." Ibid., 65.

42. Rubén D. Rumbaut and Rubén G. Rumbaut, "Self and Circumstance: Journeys and Visions of Exile," in *The Dispossessed: An Anatomy of Exile*, ed. Peter I. Rose (Amherst: University of Massachusetts Press, 2005), 331–57.

43. Differently from the "first generation," immigrants who belong to the "one-and-a-half" group, according to Rumbaut, are free "of the impulse of self-justification," which motivates the exilic outlook of their parents. Ibid., 332.

Literary protagonists may occasionally question forcing children to learn Polish, and they understand that the assimilation processes start earlier than in the second generation, but maintaining national identity is such an obvious need for them that they never consider questioning the motivation and sense of imposing Polishness on children. They do not understand that the "Polishness" of the postwar emigration undergoes closure at the particular historical moment of exile, and hence it differs from the national identity that evolves in the homeland. Not realizing this, émigré families can at best transmit to their children the Polish version of their émigré identity. The only motivation explicitly formulated is the possibility of finding a common language with the grandchildren. But this depends also on the nationality of sons-in-law and daughters-in-law.

Interestingly enough, the marriage of the daughter to a Pole—which theoretically should guarantee the preservation of the Polishness both of the parents and their children and is often the goal of the émigré family—does not guarantee a happy-end scenario. The subsequent "generations" of émigrés from Poland differ from the postwar wave; their history is different from the history of those who did not experience daily life in the Polish People's Republic. Consecutive generations of émigrés are different, and many of the works (especially the "American" narratives of Mostwin) testify to this, and also to the lack of understanding between Polish émigrés and Poles in Poland. One is immediately reminded of Marc Robinson's observation of how it is impossible for exiles to return to their country.[44] Women authors present an analogous, though as yet unnamed, problem of immigrant identity, which differs from the identity created back home or by émigrés of other generations and makes the émigré lonely and homeless.

Yet women, it seems, accept the immigrants' reality more easily than men. The latter are often unable—at least in the pages of the women's writings—to give up their titles and ranks of "presidents," "colonels," "generals," and "majors," and the functions of soldiers, insurrectionists, or patriots, none of which have anything to do with their new country. They can perform these roles only in the "domestic" sphere or in the various émigré associations and groupings. They cocoon themselves in diasporas that let them preserve their pre-exilic male identities (as patriots conducting a struggle for independent Poland). Émigré life is characterized by the narrowing down of the public sphere, and groupings based on direct bonds. In the temporal sense the "social" life of émigrés is characterized by living in local time (similarly to traditional societies), and more precisely, by living in the identity-forming history of their own (though, at the same time, collective) experiences of war and occupation. In terms of the new country, members of Polish exilic diasporas found

44. According to Robinson, exile becomes a second nature and makes a return very difficult, if at all possible. See Robinson, "Introduction," i–xii.

themselves on the margins of the social sphere. No wonder then that such a model was not attractive to the next generation, which tended to adopt the culture of the new country as its own. Niato, Gringa's son, in his conversation with his "uncle" (a veteran of the Battle of Monte Cassino) says to him:

> You would want, uncle, to imprison me in a Polish ghetto, but I cannot be a foreigner in the country of my father. Do understand. I am proud of the origin of my mother . . . but I cannot listen over and over again to how Aunt Fafa was beaten by the Gestapo . . . or how you fought at Monte Cassino. Do try to understand, Dios mio, that I have responsibilities toward the country in which I was born.[45]

The young generation rejects the social role imposed on them. In both of the above cases it occurs in a conversation with a male who finds his own identity in this social sphere. And although women characters are almost exclusively shown in their domestic sphere and in the functions related to it of wife and mother, it is precisely the women who more easily accept what Josef Skvorecky has aptly called "the double landscape."[46] Recalling once again Robinson's observations, one can say that women more easily feel loyalties toward both cultures—their own (the culture at the point of exit) and their children's (the country of arrival).[47] One should add, however, that gendered subordination of private and public spheres becomes somewhat altered in the world of the émigré. Men can "enact" their "social" identity only in the private sphere while women are linked with the social sphere of the new country through their children.

It is loneliness that women—the characters of the émigré narratives—experience most painfully. Postcolonial studies not only envisage exile as the ethos of a writer but also pay attention to the human tragedies in the background. Exile—according to Said—is above everything else loneliness, lack of belonging, alienation; rather than the lack of identity or cosmopolitan identity, it is a constant sense of one's own otherness, of not being quite congruent with the surrounding culture and mores. Emigration deprives people of the dignity that comes with the sense of belonging, of the kind of assurance that derives from being rooted in a place and a

45. "Ty byś mnie, wujciu, chciał zamknąć w polskim getcie, a ja nie mogę być obcym w kraju mojego ojca! Zrozum! Ja jestem dumny z pochodzenia mojej mamy . . . ale nie mogę w kółko słuchać, jak ciotkę Fafę bili w gestapo . . . , jak tyś walczył pod Monte Casino. Zrozum, Dios mio, ja mam obowiązki w stosunku do kraju, w którym się urodziłem." Surynowa-Wyczółkowska, *Jesień Gringi*, 193.

46. Orm Overland, "Visions of Home: Exiles and Immigrants," in Rose, *The Dispossessed*, 7–26, here, 7.

47. Robinson sees the second phase of the process that he calls the transformation of an émigré into an immigrant a formation of divided loyalty towards both the culture of origin and the new culture. See Robinson, "Introduction," i–xii.

time.[48] Robinson, too, says that all émigré writers go through a period of doubt and loneliness and although with time they become accustomed to the new reality, the feeling of alienation never leaves them.[49] For women, exilic loneliness is loneliness within the family. It is strongly felt even by protagonists such as Teresa (Gringa) or Boga ("Luncheonette"), though both are surrounded by large, multigenerational families. Because of the cultural differences between the parents and the children domestic space ceases to be a place in which women, mothers who with time become grandmothers, can fulfill themselves by enacting the role created for them by the patriotically oriented Polish patriarchal tradition. In émigré conditions, for women, home is often their only space just as the roles of wife and mother are their only identity. Hence, after almost twenty-five years of marriage (and with four grown-up children) Teresa, the heroine of Surynowa-Wyczółkowska's novel, regrets her erstwhile and long ago buried scientific ambitions:

> [T]hey . . . all had "intellectual hopes" for me. And I myself used to devour scholarly books, went to conferences to the Sorbonne, and wanted to study art history.
>
> It almost defies belief that I ended up with cosmetics, pots and pans, cradles and English lessons.
>
> I began uncovering in myself long-buried grievances. On life's balance sheet I am on the side of the vanquished. . . . I consoled myself only with this, that if I went off the rails, then it was not of my own fault. . . . It was the war that had derailed thousands of émigrés. But what kind of a consolation was that? None whatsoever. It was just difficult to accept reality.[50]

Thwarted plans, unfulfilled aspirations, disturbed spaces, domestic and social, and "outdated" identity, but above all else acute loneliness—such is the balance sheet of postwar émigré women's narration. Circumscribed by the consciousness of a prefeminist generation, the writings of Polish émigré women writers reveal the multilayered character of the otherness with which the postwar émigrés/immigrants

48. Edward W. Said, *Culture and Imperialism* (New York: Knopf, 1994), 326–36.

49. Robinson believes that the third phase involves a period of doubt and solitude, and the everydayness distant from familiar places is heavy to bear and hopeless. See Robinson, "Introduction," i–xii.

50. "[W]szyscy . . . pokładali we mnie tak zwane 'intelektualne nadzieje.' I ja sama zaczyty-wałam się w naukowych książkach, latałam na konferencje do Sorbony i chciałam studiować historię sztuki.

To po prostu nie do wiary, że skończyło się na kosmetyce, garnkach, kołyskach i lekacjach angielskiego.

Odkrywałam w sobie zadawnione żale. W saldo życiowym znajduję się po stronie zwyciężonych. . . . Pocieszałam się tylko tym, że jeżeli wykoleiłam się, to nie zmojej winy. . . . To właśnie wojna wykoleiła tysiące emigrantów. Ale czy mogło to być pocieszeniem? Oczywiście, że nie. Było tylko—trudną do pogodzenia się rzeczywistością." Surynowa-Wyczółkowska, *Jesień Gringi*, 152.

had to cope. Different from "Polish" (though not only Polish) men, different from the women but also men of the new culture, different from other immigrants, and different from the Poles (and Polish women) in their native land, different from blacks, Indians, Métis, different from their own parents but also different from their own children, still unaware that many of the problems with which they had to cope on a daily basis link them with women of other races and nationalities, and not even interested in seeking an understanding with them, the émigré women writers provide in their work a history of those, who have traditionally lacked a "tellable history." Subsequent chapters have been written by subsequent generations of émigrés—the exilic falling apart of homes, professional problems, addiction to alcohol and drugs. But that is a topic deserving a separate treatment.

"Am I That Name?"
Feminism, Feminist Criticism, and Gender Studies

Halina Filipowicz

This article takes up three overlapping sets of issues. The first set brings into sharper relief current debates about work–family balance and persistent gender inequality. The second set traces the emergence of women's studies as a scholarly discipline, examines a shift from women's studies to gender studies, and considers the reception of Western feminist discourse in Poland. The final set builds on the first two by addressing assumptions about the history of Polish women and their supposedly benighted sisters in the West, by questioning the presupposition that archives are passive depositories, and by exploring prospects for future work.

In 1988, the British poet-philosopher Denise Riley published a brilliant, groundbreaking, but now forgotten book, *"Am I That Name?" Feminism and the Category of "Women" in History*.[1] In it, she draws on the existentialist understanding of what a human being is to offer an alternative to contemporary theories that make a clear-cut distinction between biological sex and a social construction known as gender.[2] The sex/gender distinction was enormously useful in the 1970s and 1980s as a bulwark

1. The quotation embedded in the title of Riley's book comes from Shakespeare's *Othello*, 4.2.1622. It is a question that Desdemona asks in a scene with Iago.

2. In the words of Joan W. Scott, gender is "a social category imposed on a sexed body." Scott, *Gender and the Politics of History*, rev. ed. (New York: Columbia University Press, 1999), 32.

From *The Polish Review*, vol. 59, no. 1 (2014), pp. 3–15.

against biological determinism, but has developed a life of its own and generated pseudo-problems.[3] So how do we extricate ourselves?

Riley's argument is as follows:

> [The category] "women" is historically, discursively constructed, and always relatively to other categories which themselves change; "women" is a volatile collectivity in which female persons can be very differently positioned, so that the apparent continuity of the subject of "women" isn't to be relied on; "women" is both synchronically and diachronically erratic as a collectivity, while for the individual, "being a woman" is also inconstant, and can't provide an ontological foundation. . . . That "women" is indeterminate and impossible is no cause for lament. It is what makes feminism. . . . On such shifting sands feminism must stand and sway.[4]

To put these points somewhat differently, history and contingency count. "Being female" is not a fixed category, constant across time and space, but a process, subject to both natural laws and the human production of meaning in concrete historical situations. Accordingly, Riley's discussion is based on a flexible but rigorously argued concept of identity as relational. From her perspective, therefore, it is vital to acknowledge women's diversity, rather than define the category "women" by referring to the biological characteristics of sex. Riley does not press the point, but the conclusion seems inescapable that a conception of women as a community or "sisterhood" of like-minded individuals exaggerates the degree to which women are united by common interests, whereas in fact they have been divided by class, racial, ethnic, religious, and ideological barriers.

In invoking Riley's book, my purpose is twofold. Now overshadowed by theorists like Judith Butler, Riley's work merits closer attention. Here, within the brief compass of this introductory essay on cross-cultural approaches to debates about gender and feminism in Polish culture, I want to restore to view Riley's ideas that have received scant acknowledgment in scholarship even after feminist discourse began to move away from the notion that women speak "in a different voice" (to quote the title of Carol Gilligan's study) or the voice of care and compassion, that they are practitioners of tenderness in an otherwise heartless world, and that their communitarian ethos offers a badly needed alternative to competitive individualism,

---

3. The distinction between sex and gender is at times attributed to Judith Butler. In fact, it was first formulated by Robert Stoller in the 1960s and developed for feminist theory by Gayle Rubin in the 1970s. For a history of the sex/gender distinction, see Toril Moi, "What Is a Woman? Sex, Gender, and the Body in Feminist Theory," in *What Is a Woman? And Other Essays* (Oxford: Oxford University Press, 1999), 3–120. For a reprint of Rubin's pathbreaking essays written in the 1970s, see Gayle S. Rubin, *Deviations* (Durham, NC: Duke University Press, 2011).

4. Denise Riley, *"Am I That Name?" Feminism and the Category of "Women" in History* (Basingstoke: Macmillan, 1988), 1–2, 113–14.

cutthroat rivalry, militarism, and environmentally destructive technologies.[5] My primary interest, however, is in situating this special issue of *The Polish Review* within a broader discursive framework, which Riley's ideas help to illuminate.

One of my aims in what follows is also to contextualize the special issue for scholars outside the field of gender and women's studies, as well as to address issues of concern to specialists. This introductory essay, then, is a story about stories, about versions of evidence and fragments of information that circle around the categories "women" and "men," "East" and "West." The essay begins with a recent American debate about working mothers and work-family balance, takes a look at the concept of "having it all," attempts to hack its way through the thickets of feminist theory, spills over into the reception of Western feminist discourse in Poland, detours through the realm of Polish misapprehensions about the history of women in the West, and ventures into an area cautiously tiptoed around by many commentators. Along the way, it reveals disagreements over the meaning of feminist criticism and gender studies, exposes a variety of doubts and anxieties, and raises questions of evidence and verification, credulity and credibility, national myth-making, and the elusiveness of historical narratives.

In 2012, the *Atlantic* published a cover story that broke readership records for the magazine. Titled "Why Women Still Can't Have It All," it was written by Anne-Marie Slaughter, the first female director of policy planning at the State Department.[6] In the article, she describes her experience as a working mother during her two years in Washington and explains why she has chosen to leave her high-powered position at the State Department and return to her former life as a professor at Princeton University. At the same time, however, she addresses a larger problem in hopes of launching a public debate about it. This problem—persistence of inequality between men and women—is exemplified by "an empirical fact: having a family is a career barrier for women in a way that is not for men."[7] Slaughter acknowledges the success of the women who have made it to the top, but points out that "the success of the few cannot be the answer to the problems of the many."[8] Although women have made "tremendous progress . . . thanks to generations of feminist women and men, we need another round of deep social, economic, political, and cultural change to achieve real equality and to be able

5. See Carol Gilligan, *In a Different Voice: Psychological Theory and Women's Development* (Cambridge, MA: Harvard University Press, 1982).

6. See Anne-Marie Slaughter, "Why Women Still Can't Have It All," *Atlantic* 310, no. 1 (July–August 2012): 85–102.

7. Anne-Marie Slaughter, "Anne-Marie Slaughter Replies," *Atlantic* 310, no. 2 (September 2012): 21.

8. Ibid.

to draw on the full talents of both halves of our society."[9] Slaughter explicitly identifies what has to change in American society if Americans truly believe in equal opportunity for all women.

In Poland, the media have reported on Slaughter's article, but commentaries about it have been replete with heavy-handed moralizing on both sides of the political divide. For example, a leading feminist journalist has disregarded a complex of social and political proposals put forth in the article and instead reduced Slaughter's multilayered argument to a mix of self-reproach and self-sacrifice: "[A]n important female director in the State Department of the United States moved from her prestigious and well-paid position to academic lecturing in order to have more time to raise her children."[10]

In the United States, Slaughter's article unleashed a flood of controversy. Thousands of readers responded online and via more traditional media with comments on issues such as work–family practices and policies, the lack of support for women's lifecycle choices, the vast wage gap between men and women, gendered division of domestic labor, privilege, role models, and feminism. Many of the readers shared Slaughter's concern about the social realities that still block women's paths and make gender equality elusive. They argued that the United States needs a workplace culture that would not "treat all employees as if they were 'men' in a historic sense, with wives at home taking care of their lives."[11] At the same time, however, even sympathetic readers were quick to throw vitriol at Slaughter for using the phrase "having it all." The dispute over this phrase has revealed how little many Americans know about feminism. In feminist discourse, the idea of "having it all" refers to a scenario in which women have the same choices as men do when it comes to balancing professional and family duties. But most of Slaughter's readers understood the phrase "having it all" literally, as a synonym of "having everything you want."

This misunderstanding suggests that it has become standard practice to equate feminism with the narcissistic pursuit of individual self-fulfillment. As the feminist activist Ruth Rosen argues in her commentary on Slaughter's article, the media, along with self-help publications, have played a major role in distorting the goals of feminism.[12] The feminist movement sought to create gender equality at home and at the workplace and thus to improve the lives of all women. In the 1970s, however,

9. Ibid.

10. Aleksandra Klich, "Nim nadejdzie matriarchat," *Tygodnik Powszechny*, no. 26 (June 30, 2013): 11.

11. Rebecca Traister, "Can Modern Women 'Have It All'?" *Salon*, June 21, 2012, http://www.salon.com/2012/06/21/can_modern_women_have_it_all/ (accessed September 9, 2012).

12. See Ruth Rosen, "We Never Said 'We Wanted It All': How the Media Distorts the Goals of Feminism." *Alternet*, August 5, 2012, http://www.alternet.org/we-never-said-we-wanted-it-all-how-media-distorts-goals-feminism (accessed September 9, 2012).

the media began to misrepresent feminism by recasting it into a training program for superwomen. This misrepresentation was reinforced by self-help publications such as Helen Gurley Brown's best-selling *Having It All* (1982) that

> tried to teach every woman how to achieve everything she wanted in life. . . . Millions of women first heard of the [feminist] movement when they read about the different clothes they needed to buy in order to look like a superwoman and the therapy they needed to become a confident and competent superwoman. Self-help books and magazines ignored the economic and social conditions women faced and instead emphasized the way in which each individual woman, if only she thought positively about herself, could achieve self-realization and emancipation.[13]

This kind of advice, as Rebecca Traister points out in her response to Slaughter's article, is a "booby trap" because it "sets an impossible bar for female success and then ensures that when women fail to clear it, it's feminism—as opposed to persistent gender inequality—that's to blame."[14]

Notwithstanding the reductive view of the goals of feminism, propagated by the media and self-help publications, the 1970s marked an era in feminist thought. The feminist movement that reemerged in the West in the late 1960s galvanized scholars in several disciplines to question widely established disciplinary assumptions about gender-neutral methodologies and to develop methodological approaches and analytical procedures that incorporate feminist concerns. Their research concentrated on uncovering women's activities and experiences, examining discriminatory discourses and practices, and investigating how and to what ends societies conceptualized the signs of sexual difference. For scholars who studied and taught literature, the feminist project involved "exposing the sexual stereotyping of women" in both literature and literary criticism, "demonstrating the inadequacy of established critical schools and methods to deal fairly or sensitively with works written by women," subjecting works by male writers to a feminist scrutiny, recovering "previously lost or otherwise ignored works by women writers," and reconsidering established canons.[15] For example, in her 1981 study of a narrative by an eighteenth century American author who used the pseudonym Abraham Panther, Annette Kolodny detailed two areas that are of particular interest to the feminist scholar working on literary and cultural history: "(1) How do contemporary women's lives, women's concerns, or concerns about women constitute part of the historical context

13. Ibid.

14. Traister, "Can Modern Women 'Have It All?'"

15. Annette Kolodny, "Dancing Through the Minefield: Some Observations on the Theory, Practice, and Politics of a Feminist Literary Criticism," in *Feminisms: An Anthology of Literary Theory and Criticism*, 2nd ed., ed. Robyn R. Warhol and Diane Price Herndl (New Brunswick, NJ: Rutgers University Press, 1997), 171–90, here, 171–72. Kolodny's article was originally published in 1980.

for this work? and (2) What is the symbolic significance of gender in this text?"[16] The pioneering work of scholars such as Kolodny, Sandra M. Gilbert, Susan Gubar, and Elaine Showalter laid the foundations for a new academic discipline, women's studies, that won, however grudgingly, institutional recognition and support in the 1970s and 1980s.

Using a wide array of material, feminist scholars have documented women's lives and achievements that seemed to have vanished from the culture's radar. They have also revealed how representations of women have been infused and informed by contemporary assumptions about the proper relations between men and women and about the (allegedly) intrinsic nature of women or their (supposedly) typical female traits; the representations have thus served as metaphors for the inequitable social and political order they have meant to justify. But the discipline of women's studies does not stand still; its boundaries are continually in debate and flux. Some of the most dramatic changes occurred during the late 1980s and early 1990s, when African American scholars and poststructuralist theorists burst onto the feminist stage. The former demonstrated how inextricably interwoven questions of race and gender are; the latter performed revisionist interventions into the conceptual framework of feminist discourse. Judith Butler's theory of gender performativity has proved to be particularly influential; her books now function for many feminist scholars as both a philosophical buttress and a formal model. Butler's argument is "that there need not be a 'doer behind the deed,' but that the 'doer' is variably constructed in and through the deed."[17] It follows from this that "what is called gender identity is a performative accomplishment"; that is, the so-called gender identity is created through a series of sustained social performances "compelled by social sanction and taboo."[18] Playing on the double sense of the word *performance*, she concludes that instead of being understood as a role being acted out, gender must be understood as an act that constructs the reality of gender entirely through its performances, as in a performative speech act. Butler's primary target, however, is the dependence of feminist identity politics on the idea of "normative" binary heterosexuality, which she deconstructs by deploying her concept of performativity. She argues that "normative" binary heterosexuality is not innate but an illusion, a fiction, a "phantasmic construction."[19] She thus suggests that sexual identity itself is a kind of performance in its own right.

---

16. Annette Kolodny, "Turning the Lens on 'The Panther Captivity': A Feminist Exercise in Practical Criticism," *Critical Inquiry* 8, no. 2 (Winter 1981): 329–45, here, 345.

17. Judith Butler, *Gender Trouble: Feminism and the Subversion of Identity*, 2nd ed. (New York: Routledge, 1999), 181.

18. Judith Butler, "Performative Acts and Gender Constitution: An Essay in Phenomenology and Feminist Theory," in *Performing Feminisms: Feminist Critical Theory and Theatre*, ed. Sue-Ellen Case (Baltimore, MD: Johns Hopkins University Press, 1990), 270–82, here, 271.

19. Butler, *Gender Trouble*, 186.

Butler's performativity theory has sparked vigorous polemics and wide-ranging discussions among feminist scholars. For example, Nancy Fraser argues that Butler overestimates the emancipatory potential of gender-bending performative possibilities in everyday life and underestimates the ease with which the concept of gender performativity can be depoliticized.[20] In other words, if gender identity is just a self-invention or a form of performance, why is it so difficult to overcome gender discrimination and inequality in societies? Toril Moi points out that Butler's analysis brilliantly obscures the fact "that a sexed human being (man or woman) is more than sex and gender, and that race, age, class, sexual orientation, nationality, and idiosyncratic personal experience are other categories that always shape the experience of being of one sex or another."[21] And J. Hillis Miller, in a Derridean critique of the philosophical underpinnings of Butler's theory, exposes its cavalier misapprehensions and conceptual slippages, although he acknowledges that her book, *Gender Trouble*, "has done much good in the world" by "making a space for gay and lesbian sexuality and gender."[22]

The early 1990s, moreover, saw the emergence of gender studies as an academic discipline. Many scholars have welcomed it as an opportune expansion of the field of inquiry. From their standpoint, merely reading for representations of women is a necessary, but not sufficient, condition for practicing feminist criticism in ways that would challenge entrenched collective presumptions about the sexes. Because gender studies recognizes that men have historically held themselves to ideas of masculinity as unrealistic and coercive as anything they have imposed on women, this discipline, its supporters have argued, is indispensable to the efforts to understand more completely how and why gender continues to be constructed in ways that perpetuate patriarchy and homophobia. Other scholars have been skeptical about "the lure" of gender studies.[23] Despite major strides forward, as they point out, the deck is still stacked against women outside the "charmed world" of the academy, hence it is crucial to preserve the discipline of women's studies that maintains a focus on women's experiences and concerns.[24] Still others find that the discourse of gender studies is "less critical" than feminist scholarship in addressing persistent

---

20. Nancy Fraser, "Pragmatism, Feminism, and the Linguistic Turn," in *Feminist Contentions: A Philosophical Exchange*, ed. Seyla Benhabib et al. (New York: Routledge, 1995), 157–71, here, 162–63.

21. Moi, *What Is a Woman?* 35.

22. J. Hillis Miller, "Derrida's Special Theory of Performativity," in *For Derrida* (New York: Fordham University Press, 2009), 133–73, here, 138.

23. Mary Evans, "The Problem of Gender for Women's Studies," in *Out of the Margins: Women's Studies in the Nineties*, ed. Jane Aaron and Sylvia Walby (London: Falmer Press, 1991), 67–74, here, 73.

24. Ibid.

inequality between men and women.[25] To compound the problem, the current realities of the American academic marketplace are such that graduate students and junior faculty rarely profess feminist sympathies, if they want to survive in the profession and perhaps even to attain academic prestige. While critical studies that contain words such as "gender," "body," and "sexuality" in their titles are welcome, the term "feminism" is not.

In postwar Poland, feminist discourse and activism met with little interest until the early 1990s. Although Gabriela Mycielska and Maria Leśniewska's Polish translation of Simone de Beauvoir's feminist classic, *Le Deuxième sexe* (The Second Sex, 1949) had been published in 1972 and Teresa Hołówka's cutting-edge anthology of Western feminist scholarship, *Nikt nie rodzi się kobietą* (One Is Not Born a Woman), in 1982, both publications fell on the deafest of deaf ears. In the 1990s, by contrast, the pace of feminist inquiry became fast and furious. The intensity of this inquiry can be gauged by the fact that the scholarly journal *Teksty Drugie* (The Other Texts) published a triple issue on feminist literary criticism in 1993 and a double issue on the same topic in 1995; both issues were edited by Anna Nasiłowska. Urszula Chowaniec, among others, attributes the explosion of interest in feminist theory and activism in post-1989 Poland, on the one hand, to the "disappointment with the new Polish democracy," haunted and hampered by patriarchal habits, and, on the other, to certain freedoms, notably of expression, assembly, and association, made possible by the fall of communism.[26] At the same time, she makes an intriguing point that when Polish academics and activists turned to Western feminist theory in the early 1990s, they were initially "somewhat intimidated by the long western feminist tradition."[27] One would have thought that the last thing one would find in the Polish reception of Western feminism would be a sense of insecurity, but that was not the case.

Over the past twenty years, programs in women's and gender studies have sprung up at a number of Polish universities, and the vigorous scholarly activity in these disciplines has been decisive in recovering neglected or forgotten writers, works, and aesthetics, as well as opening established classics to more complex analysis and richer appreciation. Admittedly, nonbelievers in feminism—as well as

25. Urszula Chowaniec, "Feminism Today: Reflections on Politics and Literature," in *Women's Voices and Feminism in Polish Cultural Memory*, ed. Urszula Chowaniec and Ursula Phillips (Newcastle upon Tyne: Cambridge Scholars, 2012), 1–23, here, 19. For related observations that the term *gender* has become "a handy label" whose application is reassuring because it suggests orthodoxy and that "some feminists seem now to have retreated" from a position of critique and acquiesced to "the imposition of orthodoxy in formerly troublesome fields such as women's studies," see Joan W. Scott, "History-writing as Critique," in *Manifestos for History*, ed. Keith Jenkins et al. (London: Routledge, 2007), 19–38, here 20–21, 33.

26. Chowaniec, "Feminism Today," 5, 11.

27. Ibid., 13.

many agnostics, fence-straddlers, and soft-core dabblers—have been quick to brand this body of scholarship as (among other things) reductive, essentialist, superficial, positivistic, deterministic, caught in the trap of dogma, and insulting. Judging by the flood of scholarly books, journal articles, research projects, and conferences devoted to questions of gender and sexuality, however, the rich gamut of hostile responses has not been particularly effective. In Polish literary studies, gender and sexuality are now among the hottest topics. Some sixty years ago, a typical scholarly article might be titled "Class Struggle in Zygmunt Krasiński's *Nie-Boska komedia* (The Un-Divine Comedy)." Thirty years later, "Window Imagery in the Later Stefan Żeromski" was a more predictable topic. By the turn of the century, articles with titles like "Engendering Henryk Sienkiewicz" and "Queering Maria Dąbrowska" arrived on the scene. Passions once invested in the images of the urban poor in Bolesław Prus or the question of line-endings in Adam Mickiewicz have been gradually transferred to women's and gender studies.[28]

In the early 1990s, I joined the Polish project in feminist literary criticism by contributing articles to the special issues of *Teksty Drugie* and other publications.[29] Then and now, my transnational perspective has involved a good deal of questioning and reenvisioning of "our established canons, our aesthetic criteria, our interpretive strategies, our reading habits, and, most of all, ourselves as critics and as teachers."[30] This is an appropriate point, then, to consider the prospects for future work and to suggest at least some areas that call for sensitive and open-minded debate.

As might be expected, a great deal of cross-cultural work still needs to be done, but this enterprise seems to have reached an impasse. For almost two decades, Polish gender and women's studies was characterized by a strong pro-Western orientation, as scholars in Poland were eager to catch up with Western scholarship. The reception of Western feminist traditions was enthusiastic but indifferent to the political, social, and cultural contexts in which they arose and uninterested in the disagreements, polemics,

28. For an overview of scholarship on women and gender in global Polish studies (i.e., both in Poland and outside it), see Urszula Chowaniec, Ursula Phillips, and Marja Rytkönen, eds., *Masquerade and Femininity: Essays on Russian and Polish Women Writers* (Newcastle upon Tyne: Cambridge Scholars, 2008), 16–27.

29. See Halina Filipowicz, "Przeciw 'literaturze kobiecej,'" *Teksty Drugie*, no. 4–6 (1993): 245–58; Halina Filipowicz, "*Białe małżeństwo* i *Wierna rzeka* (rekonesans feministyczny)," *Teksty Drugie*, no. 3–4 (1995): 248–56. For a longer version of the 1993 article, see Halina Filipowicz, "Przeciw 'literaturze kobiecej,'" in *Ciało i tekst: Feminizm w literaturoznawstwie--antologia szkiców*, ed. Anna Nasiłowska (Warsaw: Wydawnictwo Instytutu Badań Literackich PAN, 2001), 222–34.

30. Kolodny, "Dancing Through the Minefield," 172.

and debates that have been part and parcel of women's and gender studies in the West.[31] Instead, the diversity of conceptual and analytical frameworks in Western feminist criticism was buried under the deceptively attractive notion of women's and gender studies as either a coherent system or a unified set of methodologies. Recently, the tide has turned, and it has become fashionable to raise one's voice against the hegemony of Western, and particularly American, feminist discourse.

The call to resist this alleged hegemony is motivated by the imperative to respect local specificity and to study gender, or the social understandings and conventions surrounding sexual difference, within particular historical and cultural contexts. Undeniably, gender does not exist as an isolated category, but must be considered in relation to the strains and stresses of local time and circumstance. However, the project of countering universalism with local difference often reflects a lack of familiarity with local specificity elsewhere. For example, for many feminists outside the United States it comes as a surprise to find that the American women's movement was born out of resistance to racism, war, and male chauvinism, in that order. It was antislavery activism that was crucial to the rise of the women's movement in the United States. For Lucretia Mott (1793–1880), a Quaker and the foremost white female abolitionist in nineteenth-century America, the two reforms—abolitionism and feminism—were inextricably related, part of the same impulse to liberate the individual from the bonds of tradition, custom, and organized religion. Both her abolitionism and her feminism grew out of her conception of liberty, in which women's rights were part of a larger struggle for human rights.[32]

The call to resist the hegemony of American feminism also raises the question: which American feminism? In other words, this call collapses the broad diversity of feminist discourse in the United States into one convenient monolith, even though the imperative of respecting group specificity has been central to American feminism since the 1960s. Some groups within American feminism have sought to resist liberal universalism by asserting their group's specificity and exposing the universal ideal as fragmented and fluid, an assemblage of particulars. These groups have struggled

31. For example, American controversies over Butler's theory of gender performativity have gone unremarked in Poland even after Karolina Krasuska's translation of *Gender Trouble* was published in 2008. For accounts of disagreements in Western feminist discourse, see especially Michèle Barrett and Anne Phillips, eds., *Destabilizing Theory: Contemporary Feminist Debates* (Stanford: Stanford University Press, 1992); Betsy Draine, "Refusing the Wisdom of Solomon: Some Recent Feminist Literary Theory," *Signs: Journal of Women in Culture and Society* 15, no. 1 (Autumn 1989): 144–70; Sandra Harding, ed., *The Feminist Standpoint Theory Reader: Intellectual and Political Controversies* (New York: Routledge, 2004); Marianne Hirsch and Evelyn Fox Keller, eds., *Conflicts in Feminism* (New York: Routledge, 1990).

32. For an excellent account of Mott's dual struggle for racial and sexual equality, see Carol Faulkner, *Lucretia Mott's Heresy: Abolition and Women's Rights in Nineteenth-Century America* (Philadelphia: University of Pennsylvania Press, 2011).

no longer simply to incorporate the marginalized, but to alter the terms of inclusion itself. Other groups have struggled to balance separatist and integrationist modalities.

Something else, more fundamental, is also at issue. The East-versus-West claim is based on a perception that history has made us acutely conscious of what divides us rather than what we share in common in feminism. It should not be particularly surprising, then, that some essentializing assumptions have crept into Polish gender and women studies. Admittedly, it would be merely an error to fail to notice that Polish women did far more than wait and weep while their men fought unjust regimes in the past. Although expected to be docile and submissive, they not only kept things running on the home front, but also assumed many responsibilities in the struggle for national liberation—as fundraisers, nurses, couriers, gunrunners, and soldiers. However, it is a myth to claim that the fight against foreign oppression broke down the barrier between separate "spheres"—a public sphere for men and a private one for women—in Poland, or to suggest that patriarchy fell apart after the 1863 uprising because with equal danger came equal opportunity.[33] In truth, women in Poland, as elsewhere, lived in a society where the concept of gender difference was firmly established and gender inequality was the norm. Yet the fantasy that Polish men and women were equal partners at a time when other societies continued to maintain the public/private divide and to shield women from the hurly-burly of public life has taken deep root in Polish gender and women's studies because it conveniently casts Polish women as foil to their (supposedly) benighted sisters in the West.[34] The seductive appeal of this fantasy has not been lost on Polish women. Recalling her coming of age in communist Poland during the 1970s, Eva Stachniak

33. Among the many examples of this claim, perhaps the most notable are: Małgorzata Fidelis, "'Participation in the Creative Work of the Nation': Polish Women Intellectuals in the Cultural Construction of Female Gender Roles, 1864–1890," *Journal of Women's History* 13, no. 1 (Spring 2001): 108–31, here, 111; Maria Janion, "Szalona," *Twórczość* 44, no. 10 (October 1988): 72–85, here, 73; Elżbieta Ostrowska, "Filmic Representations of the 'Polish Mother' in Post-Second World War Polish Cinema," *European Journal of Women's Studies* 5, no. 3–4 (November 1998): 419–35, here, 420; Krzysztof Tomasik, *Homobiografie: Pisarki i pisarze polscy XIX i XX wieku* (Warsaw: Wydawnictwo Krytyki Politycznej, 2008), 37; Sławomira Walczewska, *Damy, rycerze i feministki: Kobiecy dyskurs emancypacyjny w Polsce* (Kraków: Wydawnictwo eFKa, 1999), 41.

34. For an overview of the debate about the separate spheres, see Robert B. Shoemaker, *Gender in English Society, 1650–1850: The Emergence of Separate Spheres?* (London: Longman, 1998), 6–10. For overviews of the historiography on the idea of separate spheres and for reassessments of the split between the public/political and private/domestic realms, see especially Dena Goodman, "Public Sphere and Private Life: Toward a Synthesis of Current Historiographical Approaches to the Old Regime," *History and Theory* 31, no. 1 (1992): 1–10; Joan B. Landes, ed., *Feminism, the Public and the Private* (Oxford: Oxford University Press, 1998); Johanna Meehan, ed., *Feminists Read Habermas* (London: Routledge, 1995); Amanda Vickery, "Golden Age to Separate Spheres? A Review of the Categories and Chronology of English Women's History," *Historical Journal* 36, no. 2 (June 1993): 383–414.

remarks, "Our mothers kept reminding us that Polish women were always heroic, reliable partners of their men. . . . Our role was sacred. . . . We felt powerful, worshiped, and we never looked behind the myths."[35]

Another area that merits careful and open-minded discussion is the massive investment of Polish gender and women's studies in explorations of the modern period. As a result, the gender dynamics of Polish literature and culture prior to the nineteenth century remains largely uncharted territory in scholarship, apart from publications documenting either misogynist attitudes or the gender-bending achievements of elite women who attained affluence and power. At a time when the Enlightenment continues to be "one of the most debated themes of contemporary intellectual discourse,"[36] a reductive and misleading dichotomy—a conventional opposition of an Enlightenment of unoriginality, emotional restraint, and decorum versus a Romanticism of aesthetic daring, sublime emotionality, heroic individualism, and edgy, threshold-crossing subjects—dominates the thinking about Polish culture of the eighteenth and nineteenth centuries. Nowadays the meaning of the Polish Enlightenment has shrunk and narrowed so much that its cultural history appears uncontroversial, unproblematic, even boring. It is not particularly surprising, then, that the Enlightenment has become one of the most neglected periods in Polish gender and women's studies. This neglect is unfortunate. For example, the fixation with the rationality of the Enlightenment misrepresents trends in eighteenth-century moral philosophy that resorted to the sway of the passions, the language of sentiment and feelings, and the heightened appreciation of sensibility. Moreover, although masculinity and femininity were key categories of Enlightenment thought, we know surprisingly little about the Polish Enlightenment's debate about gender.

It is time to return to Riley's book with which I began this essay. One way of summarizing her argument would be to say that restoring the visibility of women throughout history is not enough because the very category "women" ought to be historicized, that is, treated as an object of historical study. Riley's approach has not always been welcome because it refuses to regard the category "being female" as static and monolithic. Instead, her argument is that this category is precarious and porous rather than self-contained and stable, that there is no singular or essential identity, and that supposedly fixed identities are in fact always in flux. This argument opens in turn a series of questions for which I have no ready answers. How do we talk

35. Eva Stachniak, "Why Did We Not Become Feminists? Women in Poland," *NWSA Journal* 7 no. 3 (Autumn 1995): 69–80, here, 78. I am grateful to Elwira Grossman for sharing this article with me.

36. Robin May Schott, "The Gender of Enlightenment," in *What Is Enlightenment? Eighteenth-Century Answers and Twentieth-Century Questions*, ed. James Schmidt (Berkeley: University of California Press, 1996), 471–87, here, 471. See also Anthony Pagden, *The Enlightenment and Why It Still Matters* (New York: Random House, 2013).

about identity without either resorting to the biological determinism of essentialist paradigms or sidelining the experiences of those who continue to feel the social effects of identity through gender-based discriminatory practices? Does all discovery of women's achievements need to be linked to biology and anatomy or predicated on sexual difference? Has the celebratory focus on a few exceptional women not occluded discriminatory practices in societies, while feeding into nationalist myths and self-congratulatory fictions? How do we resist the temptation of linear readings between the biological sex and/or the sexual orientation of the author and his or her work? Is the misappropriation or superficial acceptance of the vocabulary of feminist theory not in fact a strategy, however unintentional, in the service of its domestication aimed at canceling out the potentially disruptive effects of feminist critique?

Feminist and queer theories have, if nothing else, taught us to be suspicious of the deterministic connections between the author's biological sex or sexual orientation and the constructions of gender in texts. A case in point is Coleridge's poem, "Christabel" (left unfinished and first published in 1816), long one of the most celebrated English Romantic poems. The poem's central incident is the seduction of its eponymous heroine by a lamia-like older woman—a slithery sorceress called Geraldine. And yet the lesbian element in this poem by a male author has remained invisible for almost two hundred years. As Terry Castle has asked, "How could one *not* talk about such a poem as a sapphic fantasy, and an ultra-bizarre one at that? Yet only very recently has it ever been examined as such, as if for two centuries nobody took note of, thought worthy of comment, or even saw, what now seems to be (in the ubiquitous phrase) that large pachydermous entity staring us in the face, the elephant in the room."[37]

In Polish literature, such elephants staring us in the face in works by straight writers are legion, yet they continue to be overlooked. One can only hope that a later generation of readers, born into some critically altered social and perceptual world, will be ready to see those elephants, to recover them from an unconscious collective limbo, and, as it were, to "catch up" with the secret life of literature itself.

Meanwhile, I hope that this special issue of the journal will help to aid, abet, and document the growing interest within Polish studies in gender issues in general, and feminist concerns in particular. The articles that follow do not progress forward to tell a sequential story. They offer, rather, a series of perspectives on the heterogeneity of critical perspectives in gender and women's studies. Perhaps it is not too much to hope that the special issue will inaugurate a new stage in the debate about gender and feminism in Polish culture.

---

37. Terry Castle, "You Better Not Tell Me You Forgot," *London Review of Books* 34, no. 18 (September 27, 2012): 3–11, here, 11.

For Further Reading

Erdmans, Mary Patrice. *The Grasinski Girls: The Choices They Had and the Choices They Made.* Athens: Ohio University Press, 2004.

Gladsky, Thomas S. "I Now Have Something of My Very Own to Say: Monica Krawczyk, Victoria Janda and the Voices of the Ethnic Woman Writer." *Polish American Studies* 52, no. 1 (Spring 1995): 31–41.

Gladsky, Thomas S., and Rita Holmes Gladsky, eds. *Something of My Very Own to Say: American Women Writers of Polish Descent.* n.p.: Eastern European Monographs, 1997.

Kozaczka, Grażyna J. "The Invention of Ethnicity and Gender in Suzanne Stempek Shea's Fiction." *The Polish Review* 48, no. 3 (2003): 327–45.

———. *Writing the Polish American Woman in Postwar Ethnic Fiction.* Athens: Ohio University Press, 2019.

Łobodzińska, Barbara. "Domestic and External Perception of Family and Women's Issues in Poland and Other Post-Socialist Countries." *The Polish Review* 45, no 3 (2000): 258–303.

Mishtal, Joanna. *The Politics of Morality: The Church, the State, and Reproductive Rights in Postsocialist Poland.* Athens: Ohio University Press, 2015.

Napierkowski, Harriet. "Fathers, Daughters, and the Polka: Accordion Crimes and Misdemeanors in *Hoopi Shoopi Donna*." *Polish American Studies* 61, no. 2 (Autumn 2004): 25–34.

Napierkowski, Thomas J. "Anne Pellowski: A Voice for Polonia." *Polish American Studies* 42, no. 2 (Autumn 1985): 89–97.

Radzilowski, Thaddeus C. "Family, Women, and Gender: The Polish Experience." In *Polish Americans and Their History: Community, Culture, and Politics*, edited by John J. Bukowczyk, 58–79. Pittsburgh, PA: University of Pittsburgh Press, 1996.

———. *Immigrant Women and Their Daughters.* Fiedorczyk Lecture in Polish Studies. New Britain: Central Connecticut State University, 1990.

John J. Bukowczyk is a professor of history at Wayne State University and the author of *A History of the Polish-Americans*.

The University of Illinois Press
is a founding member of the
Association of University Presses.

University of Illinois Press
1325 South Oak Street
Champaign, IL 61820-6903
www.press.uillinois.edu

Printed by Printforce, United Kingdom